Also by Virginie F. and George A. Elbert
Dolci—The Fabulous Desserts of Italy

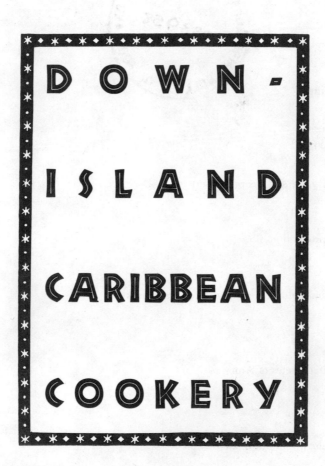

DOWN-ISLAND CARIBBEAN COOKERY

◆ Virginie F. and George A. Elbert ◆

Simon & Schuster
New York, London, Toronto, Sydney, Tokyo, Singapore

Simon & Schuster
Simon & Schuster Building
Rockefeller Center
1230 Avenue of the Americas
New York, New York 10020

SIMON & SCHUSTER and colophon are registered trademarks
of Simon & Schuster

Designed by Bonni Leon
Manufactured in the United States of America

10 9 8 7 6 5 4 3 2 1

Library of Congress Cataloging in Publication Data

Fowler, Virginie, date.
   Down-island Caribbean cookery / Virginie F. and George A. Elbert.
      p.   cm.
   Includes index.
   1. Cookery, Caribbean.   I. Elbert, George, date.   II. Title.
TX716.A1F69   1991
641.59729—dc20   90-48091
                                                         CIP

ISBN 0-671-67203-7

To all those down-island

stalwarts who maintain

the standards of

creole cookery

despite the new invasions.

CONTENTS

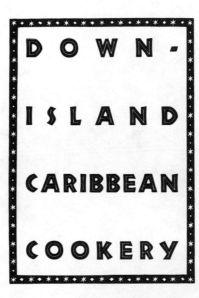

DOWN-
ISLAND
CARIBBEAN
COOKERY

✦ One ✦

TROPICAL

GLAMOUR

There are about thirty large islands in the Caribbean chain and hundreds of smaller ones, extending from the Bahamas, off the coast of Florida, in a great curve down to and west along the north coast of South America. Their diversity is inexhaustibly interesting. The scenery is just as fine as the fabled islands of the western Pacific, and much more accessible to Americans and Europeans.

The islands are all either coral or volcanic formations. The former are low-lying and possess endless beaches of the finest sand surrounded by coral reefs for underwater adventuring. The latter are rocky, mountainous—often spectacularly so—and rich in tropical vegetation (where the land has not been burned over for farming). There are fewer beaches than on coral-formed islands, but these are beautifully situated. Places like the limestone karst country of Puerto Rico, Soufrière in St. Lucia with its glorious pitons, Dominica's great mountain spine of virgin rain forest, and the incomparable Man-O-War Bay of Tobago embody all that we expect from the color and languor of the tropics.

As frequent visitors, we also find the islands' inhabitants among the most attractive to be seen anywhere. The Creole people are famous for their beauty and are as great an aesthetic show as the scenery. The beaux and belles on islands such as Martinique and St. Lucia are difficult to match anywhere.

Without heavy industry of importance the islands are free of pollution and the climate is ideal most of the year. Temperatures rarely fall below sixty-five degrees Fahrenheit but always stay refreshingly cool in the shade and never reach the higher summer levels of our mainland states. The waters are clean and sparkling. In short, the Caribbean is a superb vacation spot for the weary workers of our northern hemisphere.

To top off all the advantages, the local Creole cuisine is spectacular and has been famous for a very long time. Originally, the cooking was a mating of cultures, enriched by both exotic local products and foreign ingredients introduced to give even greater variety. It is now beginning to fade under the weight of imports from abroad. The numbers of tourists have increased so that the island products no longer suffice to supply the hotels and other resorts being implanted throughout the area.

Inevitably, the down-island, real cookery of the people will become more and more difficult to find as the waters become fished out and the islanders themselves turn from the raising of crops to the business of caring for the needs of the hordes of visitors from abroad.

Our book is intended to record the real quality of Caribbean genius in the kitchen.

◆ The Invasions ◆

Columbus made his landfall smack in the middle of the great curve of islands and established his capital settlement in Cuba, the largest of all. Soon the Spaniards colonized it, wiping out the primitive Arawak who lived there and scattered throughout the other islands. A few descendants of these people are said still to live in Dominica. Early immigrants on all the islands may have learned from them about cassava and the island "bush" herbs, much like the Pilgrims learned about corn and other indigenous foodstuffs from our New England native Americans. ← UP TO ON TASK 2.

The Spaniards also gained control of Puerto Rico and the western end of Santo Domingo, to better protect their shipments of silver and gold from the mainland of South America. To launch and support their conquests they needed well-provisioned bases on these islands. Thus, it came about that they were the only European people to settle in the islands in large numbers. More than any other immigrants, the Spanish established their language and culture permanently as an extension of their homeland.

After the Spanish seized the largest prizes, little time passed before the English, Dutch, and French descended upon the islands. Like competing vultures, they struggled to establish bases of their own from which to attack treasure ships forced to sail between gaps in the island chain on their way to Europe. When that game became unprofitable, strenuous attempts were made to create wealth from the agriculture. But to grow cane and turn it into molasses, sugar, and rum, and to cultivate the islands' natural spice trees and bushes to meet the demand at home, required a host of laborers. As Europeans proved averse to heavy manual labor in the tropics, Africans were forcibly collected and transported to the New World.

Soon, everywhere except in the Spanish islands, West Africans were present in far greater numbers than the European landowners and seamen. Today they are the dominant population of the islands, and it is they who have set up independent governments. As part of their culture the West Africans have contributed their inherited cookery to the island world.

We often use the word Creole to describe Caribbean cuisine, because the island populations have become more and more an inextricable mix of peoples from many countries, though especially from Africa and Spain. It is only in those islands with a greater percentage of Spanish people that the dishes almost duplicate the European originals. The differences in the island versions are mainly in the use of some local products not available in the home country.

◆ The African Influences and Creole Cookery ◆

The African influences are everywhere but very difficult to trace in detail. The use of coalpots came from Africa (see page 23), and along with them the special skills for grilling meats and seafood. The knowledge of yams, beans of various kinds, and gourds also indicates an African connection. But probably overriding everything else is the tradition of and instinct for sound, simple cooking and a joy in lively flavors. Not all world cultures have an intense interest and pleasure in cooking, as any experienced traveler can attest. The Africans generally do, however, and feasting is enjoyed as a kind of heaven on earth. The sight of Jules in Tortola reigning over his big grill is at least as impressive as any three-star chef in his French kitchen. Mother/cooks, turned superb restaurateurs, are a prominent feature of the island culture. Among the down-islanders we sense a true love of cooking as one of the major arts of living.

Throughout the islands the culinary skills of the Creoles have been tested by years of very difficult economics. All equipment for cooking was minimal. Coalpots were the stoves. Even today in remote places bread is baked in crude ovens built of local clay brick. They are odd, ramshackle affairs, hardly visible behind some house in the village. But they work very well and the bread is infinitely better than what is delivered to the local grocery. Firewood hasn't been plentiful lately, since the forests were cut down. The better wood was exported for furniture and building, and the remainder was fed to the molasses caldrons. Today one sees big bean pods and seed used as fuel for outdoor grilling.

The most plentiful sources of food have been the sea and local vegetation. Dasheen grows wild; heavy-bearing fruit trees and the breadfruit tree were brought in from the east and established early on. But meats have always been scarce. In early days the tenderer parts of the animals were reserved for the wealthy. Creole cooks learned to get along with heads, hoofs, chitterlings, tails, and jowls, as did our own cooks from the South. Goats, though tough, have always been appreciated because they survive and multiply in this difficult climate for domestic animals. Spices were seasonal and some islands still have a poor supply. Creoles learned to use the flavors of "bush"—the leaves from local shrubs and wild herbs.

There are any number of countries so lacking in variety of foodstuffs that their cooking is confined to a very few dishes. Creole cooking might have suffered that same fate had the islands not experienced a history one may legitimately describe as odd. The island territories were such a bone of contention between the great European powers that, either by conquest or by means of treaties designed to settle affairs in Europe not remotely connected to the Caribbean, the islands were continually bandied about from one government to another. The consequent interchanges of populations caused automatic interchanges of information—recipes—and foodstuffs—ingredients.

In between these transactions, the European governments were busy exploiting the agricultural potential of their lands and ended up with populations too big to be fed from island products suitable for daily consumption. Hence strenuous efforts were made to introduce all kinds of plants. Some of these found their new home congenial and increased the resources of Creole cuisine immeasurably. The surprising diversity of this cookery is the result.

◆ English, Dutch, and French Influences ◆

English, Dutch, and French influences are less overwhelming than the Spanish and, for that reason, real down-island cookery is more purely Creole, or mixed. The English introduced their rather primitive cookery at the time of colonization and persist in the attempt to preserve its purity. But it has been the Africans who have created whatever is original and more sophisticated in the cookery of the British islands. There we have found "good food" in the real sense almost exclusively confined to the homes and restaurants of the Creole people. And even those who have been most assiduous in their efforts to imitate English recipes achieve the most pathetic results.

Trinidad changed hands between Spain, France, and England, and ended up with the latter. The English judged rightly that the land and climate would suit many Indians. Today the number of Trinidadians from the Asiatic subcontinent almost equals those descended from Africans. Although there are roti stands on many street corners, there is only one Indian restaurant of quality in Port of Spain. To savor the excellent cooking of the island there is no choice but to accept an invitation from a local family. On the other hand, Indians came earlier to Martinique and from their cookery a mild curry mix called Colombo has been adopted as almost a national dish.

The Dutch story is complicated by the introduction of workers from Indonesia and other former possessions in the western Pacific. Now adapted to local ingredients, the cookery of these peoples has reduced the incidence of true Dutch recipes on Sint Maarten, Curaçao, and Aruba to a mere handful of curious relics. The cuisine here is Indonesian-Creole, of which the Asiatic half includes repetitive use of sweeteners, vinegar, chili, and soy. More recently it has been enlivened with additional spices, herbs, and fruits of the islands. The Indonesian Rijstafel (Rice Table) is popular with tourists. It is a collection of dishes similar to a buffet but served at table with plenty of rice, and the chili spicing carefully toned down for northern palates.

The French arrived with a very high culture in cooking, achieved by applying the same meticulous care to the preparation of food that they devoted to the other arts. The cuisine is less well known in the States because the French islands attract many more tourists from Europe than from our shores. Nevertheless, few disagree that the food of Martinique, Guadeloupe, and St. Barts is tops. Haiti, where we have never visited, seems to be more under African than French cultural influence, at least in regard to cooking.

French Creole in the islands is independent of, but related to, our own Louisiana cuisine. It is amusing to note that blackened fish, the Cajun dish so favored by New Yorkers recently, has been a normal way of grilling down-island. French discipline and discrimination are mated to Creole talent with, at times, breathtaking results.

We have not mentioned the influence of the Danes who were in possession of the current U.S. islands of St. Croix, St. Thomas, and St. John during the eighteenth and half of the nineteenth centuries. They have left their names on towns and streets, and some charming colonial architecture still exists, especially on St. Croix (if all was not blasted away by the hurricane of 1989), but there hardly remain any vestiges of Danish cooking. In those islands one can describe the situation as down-island Creole cookery with a new overlay of American and international commercial adaptations to local conditions.

◆ How to Find Island Cooking ◆

Tourists in the islands from Germany, France, and elsewhere are no different from Americans in that they prefer either their own home-style cooking or that wonderful invention, "International Cuisine." The Creole dish on the menu, presented as a novelty, is often merely a variation of the national cookery of the guests. Hotels have learned to play it safe, as it can be difficult for tourists to adjust immediately to the cultural shock of very different foods whose effect on the digestive system is suspect, especially at a time when it is something of a disgrace not to be on a diet. It is also more by necessity than by choice that resorts import most of their food. The islands are not able to supply the quantity of provisions that must be on hand all through the year at centers of tourism. In short, the culinary tourist must look about a bit in order to have the opportunity to sample real Creole cookery.

Should you be curious about the down-island way, the easiest places to sample the local cookery are the public beaches. These are normal gathering places for local island people and for tourists who break away from the resorts looking for a change of ambience—and better lunches.

At Luquillo on Puerto Rico, in huts with a few tables that line the road close by, you can have deep-fried *empanadas* with a variety of stuffings, skewered meats, grilled chicken, and grilled fish. At Ste. Anne on Guadeloupe the beach is circled by panel trucks, rather permanent looking huts with outdoor counters and tables and small restaurants from which you can also take out your choices. Crepes with fillings are available in bewildering variety and so many other goodies are listed that they would rival the biggest restaurant menus. On Tortola, lobsters are at Stanley's at one end of Cane Garden Bay beach and fabulous rotis at the other. At Grand Case on St. Martin the ladies line up in front of the little pier, appetizing smoke from their grills billowing in the air, and load you down with grilled meats, and fish with johnny cakes and other baked goods to take to the tables in the shed behind. In Martinique, a magnificent Creole lady arrives with a brand-new panel truck at Salines Beach. The side opens to reveal storage and a counter. She sets up her grill under the trees, and soon after the smell of marinated meats, chicken, and fish is wafted down to the magnificent beach. Nowhere in Europe can one find anything comparable to these midday island feasts.

For a Creole lunch or dinner—"in town" or along the main roads—consult, to start with, the publications of the island tourist offices. There will be numerous advertisements for restaurants. Look for those that have unpretentious names and specify Creole or island cooking. Avoid names like the Venetian Gondola or the Jolly Roger, listing food with names that you know too well. The same sources list restaurants by alphabet or area and give short descriptions of each. Look for menu items that relate to local products.

When you arrive at a place, do not expect modern architecture outside and luxurious decor and seating inside. There will be no soft music and there shouldn't be any loud enough to deafen you and prevent conversation . . . unless the restaurant has been "discovered" and the soul of island ambience has fled along with its food. More likely it will have four posts for corners, a palm-thatch roof, one wall on the kitchen side, wooden plank tables, and hard benches.

They don't get worse than that; but note that the food is often better, the simpler the setting. Service is carefree and easy and everybody is equal. You may have trouble with the local dialect—there being no menu and all the items being more or less yelled at you—but everybody ultimately pitches in and works it out.

The above description is the safe average to look for but does not deny the existence of very good cooking at restaurants more like the ones you may be used to at home. Successful island cooks with managerial skills have succeeded in a few cases in preserving identity while upping the comfort and service. We have the feeling, though, that once the local people no longer patronize a place it is a pretty good indication that the proprietors have decided that real down-island cooking is not as profitable a business as catering to the food prejudices of vacationers. That is bound to happen anywhere in the world when the business of cooking is no longer carried on for "our people" but for "them people," the visitors.

The final stage of familiarity with the real art of island cuisine begins when one is invited to a home-cooked meal. "Home-cooked" is the heart of Caribbean cookery. But do not be misled by hosts who, with sacrificial hospitality, treat you to a feast, graced not with the food they love but with what they hope will be most appreciated by the foreign guest.

Our book offers you the means to make a fair reproduction of down-island cuisine in your home. Have ten cooks make the same recipe and you will have ten different dishes—not extremely different, but noticeably so. Attempting to match exactly the cooking of a different region *must* fail because the ingredients are never exactly the same. That might change in the future if all the necessary foodstuffs could be canned or otherwise preserved precisely alike. But for the present we must be satisfied with approximations. To achieve even that requires temporarily stocking your cupboard and fridge as much as possible with special island products.

The above does not mean that our recipes will not produce delicious results. As any instinctive cook knows, the art is very flexible. Avail yourself of whatever island products are available and fill out the rest with imagination and good judgment. It is reasonable to believe that, in many instances, island cuisine can actually be improved upon once you get the hang of it. Caribbean cookery can be matched beautifully if you have grasped the essence of its character. And that can launch you on a gastronomic adventure that is endlessly fascinating.

· *·* *·* *·* *·* *·* *·*

· Two ·

THE

CARIBBEAN

CUPBOARD

· *·* *·* *·* *·* *·* *·*

Be of good cheer when starting to cook in the Caribbean-island way, even though your cupboard may not always contain the necessary ingredients. Just lay in a supply of a few essential herbs, spices, and prepared sauces, most of which will be found with a little searching at local food stores. You will discover that they are wonderful flavorants to have handy for any kind of cooking. Visit nearby Hispanic, Asian, island, or gourmet stores and make yourself familiar with the contents of their shelves so that you can shop quickly if you want to make Caribbean dishes. Cooking magazines frequently carry advertisements for mail order firms that supply basics for tropical cookery. Many of the fruits and vegetables are seasonal. When you see them in the market look up recipes that employ them. Cornmeal, cassava flour, corn starch, and different kinds of dried tropical beans are always available.

The packagings of flavorants are small and the prices modest. Many items are now stocked by grocery chains, especially those situated amid Hispanic or island populations. Herbs that formerly could not be bought anywhere on the mainland are beginning to drift into our markets. Keep a lookout for them and buy them when you can, for stores may not stock them permanently.

The following list is far from complete because each island has a somewhat different cuisine and all are influenced by each other. Hence an extraordinary number of flavorants is in constant use. Even the transient sailing population carries recipes from one island to another and, not infrequently, seeds or small plants in the bargain. Such exchanges of foodstuffs have been going on ever since the first settlements.

We indicate synonyms for the names of ingredients along with descriptions of those that are relatively unfamiliar to the mainland reader. This device is useful because of the large number of local island dialects and the confusing mix of culinary ingredients, some indigenous to the islands, some introduced from distant tropical lands. We cannot begin to cover them all but we have tried to deal with the names of products that are the most widespread in the islands.

We place all of this up front with frequently used utensils and groceries, to make this information more accessible. The page reference refers either to a recipe or to some other part of the list.

◆ Drinks ◆

Assorted Fruit Nectars   Sold in cans or bottles: banana, guava, lemon, lime, pineapple, mango, orange, passion fruit, soursop, tamarind.

Ginger Beer   Not a beer. A dilution of gingerroot syrup. The islands also produce a bottled concentrate very useful in mixed drinks. Diluted, with lime or lemon and rum added, it makes a superior summer drink.

Ginger Wine   A currant wine strongly flavored with gingerroot.

Mauby   A popular drink in the islands. Made from the bark of a small, local tree.

Orange Squash   A superior orange concentrate bottled in Jamaica.

Roselle   See *Sorrel.*

Shrob   French island liqueur. Rum and orange peel.

Sorrel   Roselle *Hibiscus sabdariffa.*   Jamaica sorrel. Indian sorrel. A shrub with smallish yellow mallow flowers. The fleshy calyxes of the flowers are brilliant red, large, and long lasting. These are collected, dried, and boiled to extract flavor and coloring. When sweetened and fortified with herbs and spices they make a refreshing and popular drink.

◆ Equipment ◆

Most of the utensils we recommend here are those we find to be necessities in kitchens where cooking is a daily activity of some consequence. They have nothing to do with Caribbean cooking per se (except the coalpot and swizzle stick as curiosities). A few of our suggestions may offer helpful antidotes to current fads we find impractical.

Beaters, Electric and Hand   In Creole cooking most jobs require beating only by hand. None require electric stationary beaters that waste time and energy to take down, clean, and set up again. We find hand-held electric beaters clumsy and also in need of separating for cleaning. Nevertheless, they are standard household equipment these days, and you may find them helpful for some recipes.

Formerly, there were only light metal beaters that were always snagging. But some years ago we discovered a heavy hand beater made of metal, possibly aluminum, bearing the brand name Rival. What a beater! The action is as smooth as silk and a long period of active use has not affected it in the least. We love it for light work—eggs, cream, thin doughs, and more. We have seen similar, less-well-constructed beaters recently. If you come across this type of perfect beater, we recommend acquiring it. Even small electric beaters will seem inferior for effortless and rapid efficiency.

Coalpot   Despite well-meant efforts to demonstrate its existence, a real Caribbean handicraft culture is hard to find. Weavings of the leaflets of coconut fronds, shell jewelry, local macramé, elegant carvings on large gourds (especially by an elderly gentleman in Ocho Ríos), and a certain amount of very crude sun-dried or straw-fired pottery . . . are just about all the handicrafts available today. However, among the few pottery objects still in existence are the impressive coalpots used on St. Lucia and other islands for the family cooking.

Large pots are up to eighteen inches high and ten to twelve inches in diameter, made of hand-raised-and-molded brown clay. Each consists of a wide and rather deep bowl with holes bored in the bottom, which forms the top of a broad, hollow column, partly open on one side near the base and broadened at the bottom to provide stability.

The fire is started in the bowl and the cooking takes place inside it, on pans big enough to be supported by the sides, or on a grill. The hole in the side creates the draft which makes the fire very hot, and is also used for the removal of excess ashes. The larger coalpots are beautiful objects and, at the same time, such excellent cookers that the design has never changed except to be duplicated in iron.

During a visit to Portugal we noticed in the National Museum in Lisbon a sixteenth-century painting of Portuguese gathered around an iron coalpot. As the Portuguese were the first to explore the west coast of Africa, they probably brought coalpots home with them. So we guess that Africans brought them along to the islands.

We always wanted to take one of these attractive monsters home with us but were discouraged by their weight and fragility when new. After being used for a while they become tougher. Small imitations are sold as souvenirs to vacationers in some of the island markets.

Casseroles and Saucepans   There are many new kinds of heavyweight and acid-resistant pots and pans. We still prefer the French-Belgian enamel-on-metal type which are ideal for long-cooking stews and for clean tasting, evenly heated sauces.

Cleavers   The heavy butcher-type cleaver for bone as well as meat is just too heavy and unwieldy for domestic cooks. We recommend a lighter weight and smaller size made of a superior carbon steel. They are a great convenience if properly handled. As a starter, do not attempt to cut anything, even bones, by applying a lot of force, like a woodchopper. Blows should be short and directed over and over again to the same spot. Chinese cleavers are thinner, sometimes with larger blades but lighter in weight. They are used exclusively for vegetables and meat without bone. They should be held close to the blade and rocked or directed by short blows. With practice it is possible to gain considerable cutting speed.

Fryers, Deep-Fat   If you can't get a fryer with thermostatic controls you are better off using a pan, a clip-on thermometer, and a metal basket.

Garlic Press   This is always useful, especially in Caribbean cooking.

Graters   Graters have numerous uses and we recommend four kinds. First, there is the old-fashioned four-sided, more-or-less-pyramidal grater with one side devoted to a slicer blade or two. Two of the other three sides have useful different size gratings and then there's the one side we never seem to use that just chews away at things.

The Mouli grater, the little hand one with the rotating grater and the two-part holder, is the best for small quantities of cheese and some nuts.

There is a much bigger grater that attaches to a table by a pressure screw and has a horizontal drum that grates larger quantities of anything. It is especially valuable for grating nuts for baking and other purposes.

The nutmeg grater is a small version of a stationary grater just for grating the large, woody nuts. It is about three inches long. Always have one handy, as nutmeg is an important spice, especially in Caribbean cookery.

Mallet   A light but large-surfaced wooden or rubber mallet is invaluable for flattening halves of poultry, spreading and thinning sheets of poultry meat or veal, and other chores of the same general type.

Mill, Pepper   A pepper mill should have adjustments for different sizes of gratings: fine, medium, and coarse. Black pepper should always be grated fresh.

Pans   Other than saucepans, which should be of enamel on metal, or other nonreactive materials, pans should be of good weight, preferably stainless steel. Nonstick finishes can be labor savers and reduce the amount of oil or fat required. Be sure that the pan is heavier than the handle. Why some manufacturers turn out pans that tip over because of heavy handles is incomprehensible.

Pestle and Mortar   So many households lack these little items that are so useful for crushing spice seeds and any other small, hard pieces of flavoring material. The mortars are no more than three to three and a half inches across and the pestles are made in proportion to that. They should be made of extremely hard white ceramic. The French make excellent culinary ones, and one can also buy similar equipment from pharmaceutical supply houses.

Extremely hard items such as mineral crystals must be broken up by pounding, but most of the culinary whole seeds and spices require less effort. Press down on the pile of material with the pestle using your shoulder weight, and twist. Lift slightly, bring the pestle down, and twist. You will be surprised at how quickly the material becomes a very fine powder.

Potato Masher and Ricer   Don't try mashing potatoes in a food processor. Some ricers are a bother, as they have to be attached to a table, but they guarantee a much more delectable texture. Hand-held ricers are good for smaller quantities. A heavy wire masher doesn't do as good a job but is useful for mashing other vegetables.

Pressure Cooker   A most helpful and time saving piece of equipment. It is the answer to the tenderizing of conch and is great for root vegetables. We do not recommend it for stews, only because in our personal experience the result has proved, for some unknown reason, thoroughly tender but indigestible. Try it yourself; if it works out, so much the better.

Processors and Blenders   We admit we have not used a blender for many years, so we are not up to date in our knowledge of their advantages and disadvantages. We leave the choice to the cook. We do have a processor and use it constantly. In our own cooking we use the regular metal blade almost exclusively and find it altogether adequate for our needs. We have an inexpensive model with a very powerful engine and it does the trick.

The principal difficulty is encountered in handling large amounts of material; for instance, processing raw spinach leaves. The blades are set low and are soon clogged with ground material while the rest of the load floats above. The secret is to open the bowl with appropriate precautions and spoon down the upper material. Even easier is to angle and bump the machine a bit, with care, during the time it is processing. That shakes things down enough most of the time to complete the job. That's how you can make the wonderful, dry Belgian spinach without pain. Formerly the milling was done patiently by hand!

Sieves   Down-islanders often use plastic sieves that are sold in the States in the cheaper variety stores. Their reasons probably have to do with the fact that plastic does not rust in the sea air. We use regular metal sieves and colanders but have also become attached to the plastic utensil, which we often use while baking instead of a regular metal flour sieve. No hot materials in plastic!

Spoons, Wooden   For all stewing and sauce-making we like the feel of a wooden spoon. It should be the right length for your hand and the right weight. Olive wood is beautiful for the purpose. One becomes quite attached to such a spoon with time. It is good for stirring and for light scraping when necessary.

Swizzle Stick   We use the word for a plastic stick used to stir drinks. In the islands it started out as a thin trunk with a number of short woody roots attached. Rubbed between the hands it was a means of stirring foods. Now it has developed into a dowel which bears at one end two or three rows of coiled wire nailed or stapled on. It isn't an ideal beater but usage skills are developed through practice, and down-islanders can do wonders spinning them between their palms.

Whisks, Wire   Americans tend to avoid whisks in favor of beaters. What we can say about whisks is that they are fun to use and the technique, once mastered, is very effective and very fast. We always make our pancake doughs with them as well as our eggs for omelets. Potatoes are also whipped up with whisks once enough liquid has been added.

◆ Flour and Meal ◆

Cassava Flour   The root (see page 46) must be grated. This is hard work by primitive means but quite simple in a processor. The meal is then squeezed through cloth to remove the juice which can be converted into casareep. The dry residue is then sun- or oven-dried. Use the flour for making bread and for sprinkling on hot foods. The brittle grains offer a pleasant contrast in texture. The flour is now offered by many health food stores in the States.

Cornmeal   Islanders use a very finely ground cornmeal—called *masa harina* in the Spanish islands—to thicken sauces and make baked goods and the fungi of the English islands.

Plantain Flour   Plantain flour is very common in the islands because excess plantains can be preserved and used in this way. Suitable for baking, it is more frequently used as a thickener for sauces. It can replace cornmeal in coo-coo or fungi. Two cups of the flour are about equivalent to the same amount of cornmeal. It can replace wheat flour in sauces but does not brown.

Some health food stores are now selling the flour. To make it yourself, peel green plantains, slice them on the slicer blade of your processor, and place on a baking sheet in the oven to dry out slowly and completely without browning. When quite crisp, put in the blender or processor bowl and reduce to a floury consistency. Sift through a fine sieve and store in a screw-top jar.

◆ Fruits ◆

We list below some Caribbean fruits we have not described in the introductions to our recipes. Most are readily available in the States, with time they are beginning to appear in our shops more frequently. They are essential contributions to the local diet, either as desserts or as ingredients of main course dishes. Visitors to the islands should not fail to try these fruits as well as any others that they may notice in the markets. Not all of them will appeal to everyone because tastes vary, but the assiduous sampler would be most unlucky not to find one or another enjoyable.

Acerola   Barbados Cherry.

Bananas   The bananas we buy in our markets are uniform and of good quality. But when picked off the plants in the islands there is a notable difference. They are even more aromatic and flavorful than anything we normally experience with imported fruit. Most of our bananas come from Central America. In England we noticed that Mr. Geest—a major shipper of the Caribbean fruit—imported island bananas that were superior to those we are used to.

Lately we are seeing more of the very small bananas that the French call *Ti-Figues* (*Figues* are bananas in Martinique and Guadeloupe). They are used a great deal in all kinds of cooking. Small reds, less mealy, but very sweet, are less common.

Banane flambée, the tourists' delight, is nothing more than ripe bananas baked in the oven and, when soft, placed under the broiler to color, then doused with rum to be lit at the table.

In true down-island restaurants bananas are used to flavor soufflés, omelets, flans, puddings, tarts, and tortes. When green, bananas are cooked as a vegetable like the plantain, although they are not as popular.

Carambola   Star Fruit   *Averrhoa carambola*   These grow on small trees native to Southeast Asia but were introduced to the islands like so many other foreign tropical fruits. When ripe they are yellow, longer than they are broad, sharply angled, and star-shaped in cross-section. The skin is very thin, the flesh is mild and sweet, and the seeds are concentrated along the central axis. Caribbean fruit is four to five inches long, but we have seen Star Fruit in Europe that was one and a half times as large and very imposing with its beautiful shape. They appear occasionally in our markets, and are to be eaten fresh.

Cashew Apple   *Anacardium occidentale*   In the States we are most conscious of the cashew nut which is very popular. The Cashew Apple, the fruit, is unexpectedly pretty, rather like a russet red pear. Equally surprising is the green, curved shell of the nut sticking out of the bottom, the bud end. The nuts are dried, shelled, and roasted, and the fruits, though tart, are very aromatic and full of flavor and have many uses. They are made into jams, jellies, conserves; canned whole in sugar syrup; blended into cool, refreshing drinks; and used as fillings for tarts. Grocers importing from South America may carry canned Cashew Apples.

Cherimoya   Custard Apple   *Annona cherimola*   What an amazing and delicious fruit! You may have heard of Custard Apples. Other Annonas go by the name, but this is the real thing. We saw the fruit for the first time on a visit to a coffee plantation in Puerto Rico. On a medium-size tree hung what appeared to be inverted, large artichokes. When picked, the "leaves" turned out merely to be a very pretty design of the skin. Since they were ripe we immediately cut the thin skin and went off to find spoons, for the interior was entirely a creamy custard interspersed with smooth black seeds. And what flavor: a blending of all the most delicious fruits one has known, pre-pureed for one's enjoyment. Later, on another adventure, we enjoyed quantities of the fruit in Spain where they grow in the hills south of Granada and move to market in great piles when fall comes, selling at prices no higher than the most common and ordinary of fruits. They grow only in higher altitudes in the islands and are not common. Don't miss the opportunity to savor them.

Citron   French for lemon.

Citron vert   French for lime.

Custard Apple   *See Cherimoya.*

Figues   French island word for bananas. *Ti-Figues* are the little bananas.

Fruta Bomba   Papaya.

Genipa   *Genipa americana*   Genipas turn up in our markets in the fall and are easily recognized. They look like large green grapes with much thicker skins and woodier stems. They are eaten as juicy, pleasantly sour pseudograpes. We like them in hot weather for a change. They grow on large trees.

Guanabana   Soursop   A large, heart-shaped fruit covered with soft spines (*Corossol* or *Cachiman épineux* in French), close relative of the Cherimoya, but more tolerant of warm temperatures and low altitudes. Widely grown in the islands for its refreshing juice. The skin is thin and the flesh white and watery with numerous dark seeds. It makes an excellent sorbet, which we freeze at home in the States when the fruit comes to market.

Guava   Guayava   *Psidium guajava*   Source of delicately flavored jellies that are especially popular in Cuba and other Hispanic islands. They are small fruits, round, about the size of small lemons, thin skinned, and pulpy with many tiny seeds. Extraordinarily aromatic. We remember the time we first collected wild guavas on Sanibel in south Florida. We put them in the fridge overnight and the next morning were astonished by the concentrated, very sensuous perfume that belched forth from the cold interior. Florida guava jellies are generally insipid but those from the Hispanic islands labeled Guava Paste (*pasta de*

Guayaba) are intensely flavored and a treat served with cream cheese and spread on cassava or other crisp breads or crackers. Guava nectar is a popular canned fruit juice in our stores.

Lechosa   Hispanic island word for papaya.

Lemon Citron   (French. Not the true citron). The lemons of most of the islands are quite different from those of Florida or California, being smaller, completely round, light yellow, and thin skinned. However, they are anything but inferior. The juice content for size is usually greater and the taste is intensely citrus-acid with a strong aroma. They are wonderful for drinks, for flavoring sauces, and for sorbets. When using American lemons in Creole cookery it is often advisable to add the gratings of the skins to provide zest and make up for the shortage of flavor in the juice itself. Be careful to avoid the bitter pith just under the skin.

Lime Citron vert   The limes of the islands are close to our Key Limes, whose flavor is so consistently absent from most Key Lime pies. They are small and round like the lemons, and supertart. Their principal uses are in mixed drinks and fish dishes. We cannot imagine Caribbean cuisine without them. They freshen the fish and form the base of the true Creole flavor of court bouillon, Blaff, au Nage, Escabeche, etc., that are at the heart of this cookery.

Mammey *Mammea americana*   The tree is very magnificently ornamental and widely used for the purpose. The fruits are up to six inches in diameter with a matte-brown surface. Most people will find the flesh too firm and tough in texture and will prefer to stew it. But many Puerto Ricans have expressed their joy as children in pulling down these large, sweet fruits and working away at them.

Mango Mange *Mangifera indica*   Products of very large, beautiful trees native to southern Asia. They have been introduced not only to the Caribbean islands but to Central America, Florida, and California. Breeding has produced fruit weighing as much as a pound, with firm, juicy, sweet flesh, not stringy and without the least astringency. They are available in our markets during the warm months. Many of the older trees survive in the islands where they produce small fruit, no larger than big lemons, but still delicious when ripe. Local children love them.

The sweet, ripe fruit is a common dessert and makes the most delectable ice cream and sorbet, the latter finding its way to the Ile St. Louis in Paris and to our own home in summer. Green mangos are a main constituent of the best chutneys and are used in down-island stews as a vegetable and extender.

Naseberry   See *Sapodilla*.

Papaya Pawpaw *Carica papaya*   Not to be confused with the paw-paw of our southern states. We see five- to six-inch papayas in our markets from late spring to fall. The tree is really nonwoody—in short not a true tree, grows very rapidly, and is relatively short lived. The single trunk without branches is topped by handsome, deeply cut leaves. The fruits hang close to the trunk.

Piña   Spanish for pineapple.

Plantains   Plantains can be distinguished in appearance from large bananas by a consistently greater bulk and their wider, sharper-angled shape. The skins are thicker and tougher, the flesh as sweet and mealy as the banana. They are not eaten raw by choice, but cooked as a vegetable are very popular both in the green state when they are rather tasteless, and when yellow-ripe. Then they acquire a sweetness that is offset by an attractive winey undertaste. We discuss them further when we talk about vegetables. See page 47.

Pomelo   Shaddock.

Sapodilla Naseberry *Achras zapota* **or** *sapota*   Source of chicle for chewing gum. It is the white sap that the Indians discovered could be boiled down into a pleasant way of exercising their jaws. A rounded, applelike fruit and brown in color, it is generally eaten raw, turned into juice and jam, fermented into vinegar, and more. Commonly grown in the islands and available in the island markets from May to August. Occasionally beginning to be found in mainland stores at the same time of year.

Shaddock   Very large citrus fruit shaped like an ill-formed grapefruit. Very tart.

Soursop   *See Guanabana.*

Star Fruit   *See Carambola.*

Surinam Cherry   Pitanga.

◆ Herbs, Spices, and Condiments ◆

Way back in time, islanders learned to flavor their food with local herbs, which they call simply "bush": small plants, roots, leaves of shrubs and trees, even barks. These have never become commercial and, indeed, herbs of any kind, fresh or packaged, are difficult to find in stores on the islands. It is an almost impossible task to find out from down-islanders just what plants they mean by their local names. And it is equally difficult for them to find the real plants for you. Often the indications are misleading, not from malice, but either from honest ignorance of which they are ashamed or a desire to please their visitor.

The majority of cooks get their supplies from the village herb specialists who, like citizens of Italian villages, pursue the modest profession of gathering all kinds of natural products known only to them. The knowledge has been handed down from their ancestors; culinary herbs, medicinal herbs, and love potions.

Nevertheless, because of the many immigrants among us with friends and relatives in the islands, there has grown up a small trade in some of the herbs. Among them are items that are quite essential to Creole cookery, such as Spanish thyme, small-leaved thyme (not European but island and quite different), lemon bay leaves, sorrel (for drinks), and coriander. The chives or cives of down-island recipes really refer to the local wild onions. Our scallions are similar but not as strongly flavored. Some of the herbs come from introduced shrubs and trees, for example, Neem leaves (*Melia azederach*) which are quite sharp and spicy and Curry (Carupida) leaves, *Murraya koenigii*, which smell like a curry mix. We grow the graceful plant in our apartment.

We list in the following pages herbs and spices commonly used in the islands for making condiments, sauces, and marinades. These are many of the items that the cook interested in Creole cuisine should try to find in the markets and store in the cupboard.

The first impression is very likely to be that these are more or less the essentials for mixing homemade curries. This is true to the extent that island families, immigrant from India in the past, do continue to compound traditional curries. But the list has also other uses.

As those who made the islands their permanent homes experimented in new combinations with the products they found locally—such as "bush" herbs (see page 33), ripe and unripe fruits, imported or naturalized from many parts of the tropics—a gamut of new recipes developed that belong under the general term of Creole. The new uses contributed new meanings to Creole and hence Caribbean cuisine.

All the items in the list are sold either in grocery chains and Hispanic or other island stores. They are becoming more familiar on the mainland every year as people discover how much they enhance cookery.

The following list of herbs and spices is meant to serve only as a shopping list. It includes items that are not specifically discussed in this section because they are standard in American kitchens. But they are used in Caribbean cookery and this will serve as a reminder. In the following pages we discuss more fully the less familiar products or ones about which we attempt to provide some useful bits of information.

◆ Dried Herbs and Spices ◆

Allspice, whole and ground

Anise, ground

Asafoetida or masala containing same

Bay leaves, laurel

Bay rum leaves

Cardamom, seed and ground

Cassia, ground

Cayenne pepper, ground

Chilis, powdered and whole, dried

Cinnamon, stick and ground

Clove, whole and ground

Laos powder

Lemon grass, dry and powdered

Mace, ground

Malagueta, whole seed

Marjoram leaves

Mustard, dry powder

Neem leaves

Nutmeg, whole and ground

Onion powder

Paprika

Parsley leaves

Colombo powder	Pea flour
Coriander, ground	Pepper, black, whole and ground
Curry leaves	Peppermint leaves
Curry mix, Madras and/or other	Star anise, whole
Fenugreek leaves	Tandoori Masala
Galanga, dry slices or powder (related to ginger)	Thyme, European
	Thyme, small-leaved Trinidadian
Garlic powder	Thyme, Spanish
Ginger, ground	Turmeric, ground

Allspice and Bay Rum Trees   These two trees, closely related botanically, grow in the same regions of the Caribbean and northern South America and are so frequently confused that it is best to discuss them together. *Pimenta*, the Latin name of both is confusing because, while the French word *piment* means not only spice but red or chili pepper, in English we use the word pimiento, to describe canned, bottled, boiled, or roasted red bell peppers. Seeds and leaves of both trees are among the most typical flavorings of the islands.

Allspice is *Pimenta dioica*, which is widely grown on Jamaica and Grenada. It is a big tree with shiny, leathery leaves that have much the same aroma as the seeds, which are the most widely used in Caribbean recipes.

The dried seed pods are brown, perfectly round, and up to a quarter inch in diameter. The pods are easily crushed, releasing several blackish irregular seeds that impart a mixed flavor of cinnamon, pepper, anise, and coriander to dishes in which they are cooked. The seed is available in powder form but with some loss of flavor and aroma. We have become very attached to the use of this spice since becoming familiar with island cooking. It is readily available in northern grocery stores.

The bay rum tree is *Pimenta racemosa* with more roundish, prominently veined leaves. It is mainly cultivated on St. John in the U.S. Virgin Islands. The leaves are distilled to produce bay rum perfume. Local recipes do not mention the leaves in cooking but, in practice, they find their way into the pot. The flavor is deliciously lemony. Though not sold commercially, you may have friends who can bring back a bag of these leaves that impart a wonderful flavor in chicken, veal, and fish sauces. The leaves themselves are then discarded before serving.

The whole seed, called malagueta, turns up in Creole recipes, principally Spanish ones. We have had no experience with the seed, which is difficult to come by. Our Trinidadian grocery man tells us that the flavor is very similar to allspice.

Achiote or Annatto Bija Bixa *Bixa orellana*   There are three natural food colorants used in the Caribbean: turmeric, saffron, and achiote (annatto). Of these only achiote is a Caribbean product. It is one of the most intriguing elements of Creole cookery. The cultivation of the middle-sized tree, *Bixa orellana*, is widespread in the American tropics. It bears pendant white-to-pink, two-inch flowers that produce short spires of large, red, spiky pods that last a long time and are so attractive that the tree is often planted as an ornamental. Within the pods, which dry and split, are numerous irregularly shaped seeds. These are packaged as is or turned into powder and sold in Hispanic sections of groceries in many parts of the States.

The brilliant yellow color extracted from the seed was used by the American Indians of the tropics as body paint. Settlers in the islands no doubt learned from them how to use the coloring in food. The seeds can be ground in a standard pepper mill and sprinkled on or mixed into eggs, soups, vegetables, and meat dishes. It supplies egg yolk coloring to pastry doughs. It is widely used to color rice but lacks the sharp, unique flavor of saffron.

The color is also extracted from the seed by cooking in oil. See page 110 for our recipe for homemade Achiote oil. Has achiote a flavor? Not an obvious flavor, but it certainly imparts a sense of warmth and sumptuousness to the ingredients with which it is mixed, much like monosodium glutamate (MSG), but without the unpleasant side effects.

Amchur Powder   Dried raw mango powder imported in small cans from India. It is very useful in all kinds of sauces to counteract any trace of insipidity. Use much like tamarind concentrate.

Anise   A flavoring related to licorice but much more delicate. The aroma is shared by a number of related plants. Anise seed and powder is made from *Pimpinella anisum*, a European plant. The beautiful star anise is from the tree *Illicium verum* of Asia. The unripe fruit with its seed is dried, but one must boil it to extract the flavor and then discard the woody husk. This is one of the very mild spices.

Bay, Laurel   Sweet Bay   *Laurus nobilis*   Do not confuse this with bay rum, bay rum leaves, and other plants called bay. It is the classical European bush and the leaves most used in cookery, with a spicy, aromatic odor that is not far distant from allspice. It can be used in Creole dishes as a substitute for allspice and bay rum leaves because it is altogether compatible with the island cookery.

Bay Rum   An old-fashioned perfume and hair conditioner, mainly for men. Not a liquor. The seeds and leaves of the bay rum tree, which is grown on St. John and elsewhere in the islands, are used in Creole cooking. See *Allspice* and *Bay Laurel*.

Bush   Bush is the most-used word in the islands for herbs and spices that are gathered locally. They are the leaves and seeds that grow in the scrub on hillsides and are sometimes brought into cultivation in backyards. True knowledge of bush appears to belong almost entirely to the poorer island people, whose ancient links to nature remain intact because they have not been able to spend for commercial flavorants. Real knowledge of these cookery resources is, as we have found out, extremely difficult to come by and requires a systematic and lengthy study.

The possession of this lore permits the local cook to wander in the scrub and collect any necessary flavoring ingredients. A Trinidadian told me his father would harvest the leaves and seeds in season and put them all into cans or jars, mix them up, and add water, oil, alcohol, or whatever would make up concentrated stock that was used in the daily cookery. Many of the shrubs and herbs are not natives to the islands. As we have pointed out, throughout history immigrants from all over the tropics have scattered seed which has settled in places and gone native. Two examples are the Neem Plant (*Melia azedarach*) and the Curry Leaf (*Murraya koenigii*). The former is interestingly bitter, and the latter imparts a currylike taste to sauces.

In our recipes, more familiar herbs and spices must take the place of these island specialties, except when they have become reasonably common in our markets. Not as much of the true Creole flavor is lost or compromised as one might expect. Herbs and spices have certain family relationships in flavor that are very similar and usually quite easily replaceable with the ones on our grocers' shelves. The real differences between the results of mainland Caribbean cooking and the island originals are more often than not due to kitchen methods, the basic vegetables, fish, and meat used, and the types of various common flavorants. But the result, in our opinion, can be, for those very reasons, as frequently superior to the originals as the opposite. Essentially, Creole cooking combines the same flavors we know from the past in different and interesting combinations.

Cardamom   *Elettaria cardamomum*   Indian and Southeast Asian spice seeds with a very mild flavor suitable to delicate foods, desserts, and pastry. Usually employed in its powder form.

Casareep   A very thick, very dark, very sweet syrup of the southern Caribbean islands, widely used in the cooking of traditional meat and vegetable dishes. Cassava is grated, squeezed, and pressed to release its juice. When the liquid is boiled it turns brown; salt, molasses or brown sugar, cloves, and cinnamon are then added. Further boiling reduces it to a thick syrup. It appears on the shelves of island stores. A mixture of Barbados molasses and concentrated tamarind ends up tasting pretty much like casareep.

The syrup has been a constituent of Pepperpot since time immemorial (see page 202). This ragout, one is told, can be stored even in the hot climate without refrigeration as long as sufficient casareep has been included. A container devoted to Pepperpot is constantly replenished with specially prepared or leftover meats, somewhat like the fabled Scotch Haggis. If you can't find casareep, we doubt you will go through the process of making it. Substitute molasses and tamarind along with the cloves and cinnamon as suggested.

Cassia   Chinese Cinnamon   *Cinnamomum cassis*   It is a less-refined and cheaper substitute for bark cinnamon and widely used for that purpose. True cinnamon bark is made from *Cinnamomum zeylanicum* which is Sri Lankan, while cassia originally came from Burma.

Chili Peppers   Chili peppers, whether sweet or hot, should not be confused with black pepper seeds or with white or green pepper seeds which are just forms of the same. Black pepper is *Piper nigrum* and grows on a western Pacific vine. Sweet bell peppers and hot chili peppers are native to the New World and grow on bushes. Of the *Capsicum* genus, they belong to the same family of plants, the Solanaceae, as potatoes, nicotine, and tomatoes.

The chili peppers have become popular in most tropical countries and are staple fla-vorants of Caribbean cuisine. Many varieties grow wild in the Americas or have been cultivated, ranging in size from that of a pea to the three or four inches of a sweet pepper.

Wilbur L. Scoville is to be thanked for an advance warning system. In 1912 he developed the Scoville Heat Units, which rate the violence of the peppers. The range is huge, from the moderation of Anaheim chilis at one thousand units to the seventy and eighty thousand units respectively of tabasco and *habañero* chilis. The most widely grown pepper of the islands is the Scotch bonnet (called bonney in Jamaica), a lovely melon-shaped pepper, an inch to an inch and a half in diameter, turning as it ripens from green to yellow to orange-red. Very pretty and among the hottest of all.

Chili addicts gradually acquire near immunity to the fires of these little vegetables. But those who have not been properly trained can come in for a spectacular shock, as happened to us once on Martinique. We ordered *crabes farcies*, which is usually quite a mild bread crumb and crabmeat stuffing. The first bite offered the sensation of sweetness, which left us totally unprepared for what followed, and which we can only describe as an almost total blackout. The tops of our heads seemed to lift off while we suffered from the most intense sense of brain refrigeration. It was frightening, and all we could do to relieve it was to drink water and endure. After about five minutes we slowly began to recover. We have since been told that a mauby drink is the antidote but, of course, it has to be handy at the right time. Chili connoisseurs will probably laugh at our sensitivity. We have seen a friend take a whole, large, fresh Scotch bonnet, pop it into his mouth, and munch it with obvious pleasure and no apparent bad effects.

We recommend that the reader remember that not everybody has a high tolerance and that, for those who don't, too much chili is no joke. Go easy on the chili and place a bottle of the island yellow sauce on the table with a verbal warning. Then everyone can load up with chili according to preference. Note that even tiny amounts of the stronger chilis can have an explosive effect and that there is no rule requiring the exclusive use of Scotch bonnets. Milder chilis, such as *jalapeños*, are equally suitable.

The following are some of the popular varieties of chili peppers: Anaheim, *ancho*, *de arbol*, bonnet, *cacabel*, cayenne (from which much of the powdered chili is made), *chalupa*, *chimichanga*, *chipotle*, *flauta*, *habañero*, *jalapeño*, *mulato*, *pasilla*, *pequín*, *poblano*, *serrano*, and tabasco. It will be noticed that a majority of these names are Mexican.

Handle with care. This warning is for those who have never before used hot peppers in the kitchen. If you have tender skin, wear plastic gloves when handling chilis. Whether using your bare hands or wearing gloves do not touch eyes or other tender parts of the body. After handling wash hands very thoroughly in hot, soapy water.

Scotch bonnet peppers, favorites in the islands, appear in the markets in the late summer and fall. At other times of year islanders depend on dried fruits or bottled sauces. A number of the chili peppers are now available in the markets dried and packed in plastic bags, but not Scotch bonnets. However, the yellow sauce frequently seen in our chain stores and sometimes called Bonney Pepper Sauce is made from them. There are plenty of other liquid chili sauces including Tabasco and Pickapeppa, and both bottled and canned *jalapeños*. There is no shortage of material to add fire to our recipes.

Chives Cives Ciboulette　　These are the island breed and are much bigger and stronger flavored than our delicate herb. The larger and tastier scallions we now find in our vegetable markets are a good substitute.

Cinnamon　　The wonderful spice that comes in bark form or is used powdered in so many candies and sweet dishes. The true cinnamon, *Cinnamomum zeylanicum*, from Sri Lanka, is very delicate. There are considerable differences in the quality of the product. We are accustomed to associating it exclusively with sweets, but like peppermint and chocolate, cinnamon is a quite different spice when used in ragouts and combined with other spices to make savory sauces. It should always be considered for these purposes.

Cloves *Syzygium aromaticum*　　Originally from the Moluccas islands of the western Pacific, the up-to-thirty-foot-tall trees are now grown in the Caribbean, especially on Grenada. The spice is the dried bud of the flower, which becomes woody and dark brown. It is very aromatic—sweet in odor. Also available as a powder, it is a standard island spice.

Colombo　　Colombo is the name for the curry powder of the French Antilles, and the dishes made with it are called Colombo of this or that, which includes just about any meat or seafood. Until we actually bought it in local shops packed in plastic bags, we assumed it was no different from true Indian curries or than those of France itself, which are pleasant and aromatic but a rather pale imitation of the lively originals. Its flavor was much the same, but the texture was decidedly gritty and we soon realized that it was not a powder but cassava flour with a very modest addition of mustard seed, turmeric, clove, cumin, coriander, and anise, all in powdered form.

After experimenting in the kitchen we have come to the conclusion that the mainland cook will find it much easier and just as good to use a Madras curry powder, such as Sun Brand, which is widely distributed, or any of the other excellent *milder* curry powders sold in Indian and gourmet shops.

A Colombo recipe calls for less Indian curry but more of other vegetable, herb, or spice flavorings commonly grown on the islands themselves. See page 112 for homemade Colombo powder.

Coriander, Ground　　Coriander is the name of both the parsleylike herb and the powder made from its seeds. The latter is light brown in color and tastes vaguely of nutmeg with a little bitterness added. Like other Asian spices this very mild flavor blends with and enhances others and is invaluable in all kinds of vegetable, meat, and seafood cookery.

Cumin, Ground *Cuminum cyminum*　　A powder that tastes remarkably like cedar cigar boxes smell (if you can still find them), but is a necessity in meat cookery, in curries, and all kinds of sauces.

Curry　　Name of mixtures of Indian spices. A Madras curry powder, the most renowned, contains turmeric, chilies, salt, cumin seeds, fennel seeds, black pepper, garlic, ginger, fenugreek, cinnamon, cloves, anise, and mustard. Curries may be mild (less chili) or hot (more chili). Another word for curry is "masala." There are any number of trademarked curries on the market.

Essence A liquid flavorant, bottled in Trinidad, consisting mainly of vanilla, almond, and anise extract. The vanilla is sometimes replaced with *coumarin* from tonka beans, which is a vanilla substitute. To be used in desserts and pastries to which the combination imparts an enticing flavor. You can make the mix by combining the extracts yourself.

Fenugreek A bean plant grown in Europe and Asia; Latin name: *Trigonella foenum-graecum.* The seeds are occasionally used in curry mixes and as bases for dyes and medicines. In cookery the leaves are an interesting and important addition to the repertory of flavoring ingredients. They possess an odor which is instantly recognizable as that of maple syrup or its sugar, but, not being sweet, the effect on sauces and stews is quite different; in fact, it enriches meaty flavors and imparts a pseudoroasted flavor. Available from Asian food shops in cardboard and plastic packaging. It can be used freely, as the flavor is mild.

Galanga A grassy, tuberous plant related to ginger. The roots are bigger and woodier and the flavor milder. The roots are sliced and dried to be sold loose or packaged. When cooked up with ragouts, the pieces must be fished out at the end before serving. The spice is very popular in Southeast Asia and Indonesia. Conimex Laos Powder is made from galanga.

Ginger Gingerroots are readily available year-round in American vegetable stores. The pieces are sold by weight. The fresher they are the better the flavor and the easier they are to handle. When even the slightest bit shrivelled, they are spoiled or woody and tasteless. The color should be light tan, the surface smooth, the skin thin. When sliced fine ginger is very aromatic. It can be grated with a Mouli grater. There is no comparison between the flavor of fresh root and the powder sold in our grocery stores. Recipes often reverse the quantities needed, specifying less powder to more fresh ginger, although the fresh is actually much stronger. Also, quantities listed are usually too small to make a difference. A tablespoon is a better measure than a teaspoon. Gingerroots survive and grow very well in pots indoors.

Girofle Clove.

Jalapeño Three- to four-inch green chili peppers; very popular in Mexico. See *Chili Peppers.*

Laos See *Galanga.*

Lemon Grass *Cymbopogon citratus* A tall grass from southern India widely used for cooking in southern Asia and the Caribbean. The grass is cut into short lengths and cooked in the pot with other ingredients of ragouts. The grass can be grown in pots and propagated by division. It is also sold in plastic bags and as a powder. The flavor is very delicate and we, ourselves, do not feel we have ever mastered its use in the sense that we succeed in deriving a distinct flavor from it. So we substitute lemon zest. Nevertheless, millions of southern Asians and Caribbean Creoles can't be wrong, and the grass is repeatedly included in tropical recipes. *Cymbopogon nardus* is the source of citronella oil.

Mace   The outer coating of nutmeg seeds. As the thin, fleshy integument dries it shrinks and forms a brittle, coarse network, orange in color. The flavor is soapy by itself but it is very useful in combination with other spices.

Malagueta   Fresh or dry seeds of the bay rum tree. See *Allspice and Bay Rum Trees*.

Masala   General name for curry powders of various kinds.

Mustard Seed   Yellow and black; the latter very tiny. The seed is commonly used in ragouts.

Nutmeg *Myristica fragrans*   A woody nut from Indonesia intensively grown on Grenada. A favorite spice of the great island chefs. It is sold in powder form, but the nuts are available everywhere and one uses small graters to sprinkle the spice over food. Sweetly aromatic and subtle, it is useful for all types of cookery. The outer skin of the shell is made into mace by drying.

Papain   Extract of papaya which acts as a tenderizer on meats. Down-islanders slice the green papaya fruits and interlayer with meat for a shorter or longer time depending on the suspected toughness. The fruit can also be cooked right in with the meat.

Pepper, Chili   See *Chili Peppers*.

Pepper, White, Black, and Green   All the seed peppers are *Piper nigrum*, a vine that grows on the islands in the South Seas. (All the fruit peppers—including sweet bell peppers—and the chili peppers are various forms of the shrubby *Capsicum*.)

The ground black pepper in small containers, sold under spice merchants' labels, is generally of inferior quality. The spice should be bought only as seed so that it can be ground at the time of use. Of the bulk seed types, the finest is Tellicherry. Sniff this pepper and you will appreciate the difference. This richness imparted to dishes easily compensates for a slightly higher price. Other good peppers are labeled Malabar or Lampong. However, caveat emptor. Some well-known gourmet shops and mail-order catalogs sell pepper under these names of such poor quality that they suggest ignorance on the part of the seller.

White, or decorticated pepper, is fancied by some chefs because it is milder and doesn't discolor their precious sauces. Beyond that it has little merit.

Green pepper, lately so faddish, is much less peppery and not particularly aromatic but it is very pleasant. Don't try to grind. Pound it with mortar and pestle, which is easy because it is rather soft. Green pepper is especially good on eggs.

Islanders use either inferior pepper or stick to their chilis. But the addition of a good pepper can only improve a dish.

Piment   French for chili pepper. Not to be confused with pimiento, which is Spanish and English for roasted or stewed red bell peppers.

Rougail   Condiment of vegetable or shellfish.

Shrub   Island generic word for wild herbs. See *Bush*.

Spanish Thyme *Coleus amboinicus*   From the South Seas. An aromatic herb with large, hairy leaves which are very pungent. On St. Lucia they prescribe six leaves to a turkey stuffing. Makes a pretty houseplant. As a substitute use marjoram or northern thyme.

Tamarind *Tamarindus indica*   Another valuable tree brought from India that has been a success in the islands. These south Asian trees are widespread in the Caribbean. They are big, beautiful trees, almost as spectacular as the breadfruits. In season they bear quantities of fat, velvety-gray bean pods that are filled with brown, gooey pulp surrounding a large, shiny brown seed. Plastic packs containing the seeds still in their pulp appear in our markets in the fall.

Soak and boil the mass in water and the seeds will float free or can be strained out. What remains is an extremely tart liquid. Add plenty of sugar, dilute it with water to taste, and cool it in the fridge, and you'll have one of the most refreshing of hot weather drinks. It can be mixed with other island juices to make a whole repertory of thirst quenchers which can be spiked with rum according to your pleasure.

The sweet concentrate is bottled in Jamaica and other islands. From India come eight-ounce plastic jars filled with the concentrate reduced to a paste. It is this last product which is most useful in cookery. To arrive at that indefinable flavor of perky sourness desirable in many meat sauces, tamarind is a boon and a trademark of Caribbean cooking. The little jars should be in every cupboard. If you cannot find the concentrate look for amchur powder (Taj Mahal brand), which is green mango powder, or the preserved fruit itself. Both can be used in much the same way as tamarind in cooking, if not in sweet drinks.

Thyme, European, Spanish, and Small-Leaved   European thyme, the standard herb of bouquet garni and an indispensable flavorant, is a small woody shrub with the tiniest of leaves and dependably hardy. Our tropical thymes, Spanish and small-leaved, are both larger leaved and strictly for warmer climes. In appearance, these latter are as different from each other as they well can be and their flavors are equally unalike. Nor are they related to European thyme, which is *Thymus vulgaris*. Spanish thyme is *Coleus amboinicus*, relative of the colorful-leaved pot ornamental. As for the island small-leaved thyme, we have seen and used it fresh, but we do not know its proper name. It resembles the neem leaf but almost certainly isn't the same. In cooking both the tropical herbs are quite the equal of the more famous member of the trio.

Spanish thyme, which is actually from southern Asia, is a very hairy, thick-leaved sprawler, usually green, although there is a pretty variety we grow whose leaves are edged with white. The odor is much more intense than European thyme; you either love it or hate it. Like rosemary, it must be used sparingly or it will usurp the territory of other flavors. Some herb nurseries in the States grow the plants, and grocery stores owned by down-islanders are beginning to import it fresh in plastic packaging. A good substitute is half and half oregano and marjoram.

The uses of small-leaved thyme are similar but the flavor much more mild and subtle. Half and half tarragon and sage is an approximation. Excellent for salad dressings.

Both these herbs can be kept fresh by freezing in a plastic bag. When needed, take out and bring to room temperature. Cut fine and use immediately.

Turmeric *Curcuma domestica*   Relative of ginger, usually sold as a powder and essential in most curries. Pleasantly bitter. It is a strong yellow colorant for rice and other dishes. Figure a tablespoon to a cup of boiling rice. Beware of spotting cloth that can't be treated with chlorine, for the dye is very tenacious.

Vanilla   The greatest of flavorants for desserts and pastries. The extract is derived from the long beans of a vine of the orchid family that are incredibly fragrant. The beans are dried and sold in island markets and exported. In this country we buy the single beans in glass vials or the extract in bottles. The extract has been so debased in recent years that the amount used must be three to four times more than the recipes recommend. Pieces of freshly dried vanilla beans make a great difference.

◆ Milk, Cream, and Cheese ◆

Coconut Milk and Cream   It is convenient to buy canned coconut milk, formerly sold in health food stores but now found on the shelves of grocery stores everywhere. The same applies to coconut cream. The milk should be sugar free, as it is one of the flavor bases of Caribbean cooking. The sweet cream is used in desserts and drinks.

Notice that the milk contains a considerable amount of coconut oil, as does the cream to an even greater degree. High in stearin, it is taboo in the diet of many people. An alternative is to use half-and-half flavored with coconut extract.

For homemade coconut milk you will need a husked fresh nut. Knock out a couple of the eyes with a screwdriver or ice pick and hammer. Drain out the coconut water, which is rather tasteless, but a thirst quencher in an emergency. Break up the coconut with the hammer and remove the meat from the shell with a sharp knife. Remove the thin brown skin from the meat. Grate the meat in a hand-held nut grater or in a processor with a grater attachment. Measure the coconut into a large bowl. Add half the quantity of boiling water and let steep for twenty minutes. Pour the mixture into a second bowl through a double-thickness of cheesecloth. Squeeze hard on the solids by twisting the cloth.

This process will produce a fairly rich milk. For a thinner milk, add one-half to one cup more boiling water to the milk. For a thicker "cream," steep the grated coconut in less boiling water or in hot milk or cream.

Fresh Milk and Cream   Neither milk nor cream has been an ingredient of island cooking because of the shortage of cattle and the difficulty of maintaining freshness. Coconut milk has had to do for a long time. Since the introduction of refrigeration to the islands, the use of fresh milk has become nearly universal.

Milk, Sweetened Condensed   As a canned product not needing refrigeration, this sweetened milk became an ingredient in tarts, cakes, and puddings, as well as a sweetener in coffee.

Milk, Evaporated   Evaporated milk has been the island substitute for milk until recently. It is not ideal, however, and many island dishes will be improved by using fresh milk, half-and-half, or cream. On the other hand, there are a few recipes for which evaporated milk has just the right flavor and consistency to match the other ingredients. A substitute whipped cream can be made with evaporated milk and we give the recipe on page 285.

Queso Blanco   A white cheese of the Hispanic islands and stores in the States. Virtually the only cheese used in Caribbean cookery, it is sold by weight in large rectangular blocks. Excellent when cubed in salads and stews or sliced and fried in oil, and more. It is rather like the consistency of tofu but firmer and saltier.

◆ Nuts ◆

Almonds   Almonds came over with the Spaniards and have always been used in their island cookery. But the "almonds" used by the African population have been mostly from the common sea almond tree, *Terminalia catappa*, which was brought from the Malay Peninsula and now grows everywhere along the shores of Caribbean islands and well north to Florida.

It is a big tree, with massive limbs and large, blunt, oval leaves, and is surprisingly similar to the sea grape tree (*Coccoloba uvifera*). The almond tree produces clusters of two-inch green fruits that are woody but soft when dried. Once, on a trip to St. Lucia's Pigeon Island* with a young islander friend, we came to a grove of these trees and the ground was literally covered with the dried husks of the seeds. He promptly set to work gathering as many as he could in bags to take home to his mother.

We do not know how the seeds should be husked to harvest enough nuts to make their use worthwhile in cooking. Apparently local people know the trick. We managed to beat a

---

* Pigeon Island, now connected to the mainland by a short causeway, was the home of the redoubtable Mrs. Snowball. The lady was in her eighties when we knew her, and she was the leaseholder of the whole island. For a long time she owned a tiny restaurant, to which famous people were rowed out from the mainland to consume her seafood and rum. She was Scottish by birth and had enjoyed a brilliant career as the leading soubrette of the D'Oyly Carte (Gilbert & Sullivan) company. When England's Queen Mother visited the Caribbean she never failed to have herself carried ashore from the yacht to share a picnic with her old friend on the beach.

couple of husks long enough to extract the seed, which was half an inch long and seemingly tasteless. Their inclusion in recipes seems to be more for a matter of texture and nutrition than flavor. Almost any mild-flavored crushed nuts will do as substitutes.

Cashew Nut   The cashew is the most common nut of the islands, coming, in fact, from a New World tree, though now grown in greater numbers in India. The fruit and nut, borne of a medium-size tree, are a curious sight. The hanging fruit (see page 27) is reddish and rather like a hard-surfaced pear. Growing out of the bottom of the fruit is the half moon of the nut in its shell. The shell is dried and the nuts removed and roasted.

Peanuts   We recommend using fresh peanuts in your Caribbean cooking. There are two reasons for grinding and roasting your own rather than simply using chunky peanut butter. The first is to prevent the peanuts from being ground to a smooth peanut butter consistency. The peanuts should retain separate, crisp grains, which impart an entirely different texture. The second is that you are better off buying raw African or Spanish peanuts, which are short and roundish. When roasted they possess a flavor that is much less intrusive and dominating than the American peanut.

To cook a small quantity of raw peanuts—up to a cupful—simply heat one-half tablespoon oil in a small pan and toss in the whole nuts or the full amount of processed or grated raw nuts. Reduce heat to medium and keep the nuts moving in the pan. The raw odor is very noticeable. When it disappears and is replaced by the familiar smell of roasted peanuts, the nuts are cooked. For a crispier nut and a sharper flavor, cook a little longer until the nuts are a deeper brown in color. Lighter-colored cooked peanuts are preferable for soups and gravies. Store in a screw-top jar.

It is also not difficult to roast a pound and store it. You will find the procedure worthwhile, for the flavor is quite delightful and different from anything to which we are accustomed. In cooking, ground peanuts have many uses, which explains their popularity in various cuisines. See page 116 for our recipe.

◆ Oils and Fats ◆

In early times coconut oil and lard were the only fats used on the islands. As they possess their objectionable features they are being rapidly superseded by various imported vegetable oils and by butter and margarine. The butter is imported from the EEC (European Economic Community) and New Zealand, both of which have surpluses so that the price remains reasonable and some of it is of superior quality.

Coconut oil and for that matter lard in the form of fat pork parts rendered in the pan remain the leading cooking fats of the islands. The oil, usually unrefined, has simply been pressed from the dried nut and is still sold in reused bottles of all sorts. If kept on shelves too long, it becomes rancid. We cooked with it on St. Lucia for a month and found it far from ideal, being very heavy with stearin and distinctly flavored. It tended to form a sticky film on a hot pan surface. We find that corn and peanut are two of several oils that are superior.

We are not concerned so much with what Caribbean cooks are obliged to use as we are concerned with the fats and oils employed in our recipes. Certainly, we find corn or peanut oil superior to coconut oil. As for the solid fats, we have frequently specified butter *or* margarine. Quite aside from the cholesterol controversy, we recommend a vegetable oil margarine, especially that made from corn oil, over butter because we find that our butter from chain grocery shelves has no flavor whatsoever. A fresh, superior butter makes a big difference in cooking. But without taste we reckon margarine mechanically superior and not in the least inferior to butter in other respects.

◆ Sweeteners ◆

Sugar and Molasses   Although the islands import more and more and produce less and less, sugar seems to be a partial exception. To protect local growers, the sugar in the stores is often local sugar, which is not fully refined, and closely resembles our light-brown granulated sugar. When we come from the stores down-islanders will ask us, "How's the color of the sugar today?" If it is darker the sweetness is less and they will wait a few days in the hope that the next lot will be lighter, and sweeter. Imported refined white sugar is slowly becoming standard in island grocery stores. Dark-brown sugar sold in northern stores is not granulated.

Island unsulphured molasses is sold in our stores and is a very superior product, with a rich, caramel flavor we have found nowhere else. It is wonderful for making cakes and as a pancake or waffle syrup. Several islands have their own. We particularly recommend that of Barbados.

◆ Vegetables, Rice, and Legumes ◆

Avocado *Persea americana*   The avocado is now sold throughout the year in our markets and has become a favorite salad vegetable that blends well with tomatoes and cucumbers as well as cold seafood and shellfish. The very big seeds are sprouted in water to produce ornamental indoor trees. The fruit grows on all the islands. On Tobago it is almost round, two to three times as large as those in our markets, and of superb quality. It is shipped into the States from different regions of the tropics. One soon discovers that there are many varieties, varying in appearance and difficult to tell apart as to quality. One should shop for fruit that is ripe and without blemishes, the flesh rich and somewhat fatty, and the flavor nutty. Inferior varieties are watery and can be disagreeable in taste.

It is our experience that round, rough-skinned, pear-shaped fruits are usually the best. The flesh is ripe when the surface yields even slightly to finger pressure. Once the surface is soft the fruit is overripe. Beware also of fruits with very dry, brittle skin; they have taken too long ripening on the way to market.

Cutting and peeling: Using a sharp, broad-bladed knife, cut vertically down and around the fruit starting from the stem end. Then insert the blade as far as possible in the stem end and waggle it so that the two halves come loose from the seed at the same time. This will result in the halves being neat, and each provided with a clean depression that can be used for filling.

Peel each half by holding it gently in one hand and lightly cutting the skin vertically into four or five strips. Lift the upper tip of each one and pull downward to free it.

Beans and Peas, Canned and Dried   The varieties of dried and canned beans and peas sold from the shelves of the Hispanic sections of American groceries are very close to the same sold throughout the Caribbean islands.

Canned beans and peas

Black-eyed peas
Black (turtle) beans. *Frijoles negros.*
Chick peas. Garbanzos.
Cooked dry peas. *Chicharos.*
Field peas with snaps. *Frijoles verdes.*
Green pigeon peas. *Gandules verdes.*
Pink beans. *Habichuelas rosadas.*
Pinto beans. *Habichuelas pintas.*
Red kidney beans. *Habichuelas coloradas.*
Small red beans. *Habichuelas coloradas pequeñas.*
Small white peas. *Habichuelas blancas.*

Dried beans and peas
Pinto, black-eyed peas, green or yellow split peas, chick peas, lentils, great northern beans, large limas, small limas, California small white, roman beans, red kidney beans, small red beans. Indian stores carry red, yellow, and green lentils.

One cup dried yields about four cups cooked.

All the dried beans except the lentils require soaking, sometimes overnight, and long, slow cooking. (See page 232 for our cooking instructions and recipes.)

Islanders cook the beans with onion and spices as staple vegetables, either whole or reduced to a puree in soups, or mashed as extenders of meat or seafood to be eaten with folded pancakes of different kinds. Soups made with the beans, especially those that are pureed, are suave and delicate besides being extremely nourishing. A most popular dish is Rice and Beans (page 233). Beans are more prevalent in the diet of the Spanish-speaking islands than the others.

Black (Turtle) Beans   The meat of the bean is really black, somewhat grainy when diluted, and not as starchy as some other beans. It has a slight bitterness which is very pleasant with meaty flavors and tart juices. Both in Europe and the islands it is the bean that makes the richest of soups (page 86). Add spices, spicy sausage, beef or lamb, onion, and a dose of chili pepper. Serve with slices of lemon floating on top and sprinkled with chopped egg. Also sold cooked in cans.

Chick Peas   Garbanzos   These are almost round beans, off-white in color, crisp, and the closest to a nut of any. They do not expand much in cooking. They are usually served separately. In stews they stand out, because of their shape and color, rather prominently. They can be marinated as salad beans with onion, oil, garlic, and herbs. They are not usually mashed or pureed. Sold cooked in cans and dried in plastic bags.

Gandules   Pigeon Peas   They are similar to those labeled split or dry peas and are used for thickening and for pureed soups. They blend well with green vegetables and herbs.

Lentils   See page 89.

Red Kidney Beans and Small Red Beans   Two sizes of the same type of bean. They are rather mealy and meaty. They are commonly preferred for "Rice and Beans" dishes. Sold also in cans.

White Beans and Black-Eyed Peas   These are standard vegetable beans, very starchy and nearly neutral in flavor. Thus, they are very good when flavored with tomato, garlic, onion, or spices. They are favorites for marinated salads. The black-eyed pea is simply a smaller white bean with a black spot, but is used less in salads and more in stews or as a separate vegetable.

Breadfruit   A tree, *Artocarpus altilis*, and its fruit, brought to the Caribbean islands from the South Seas by Captain Bligh and others. The fruit is a starchy vegetable. See page 239.

Breadfruit Nuts   Breadnuts   Châtaigne   Pana de Pepita   Large, edible seeds of the smaller variety of a breadfruit which itself is not used for food.

Calabaza   Giraumon   Pumpkin   Calabazas are squashes of considerable size, whose vines ramble around homes in the Caribbean, climbing over porches and startling visitors with the big, two- to five-pound fruits dangling above their heads. They are not round, like pumpkins, but rather flattened and broad, colored green with yellow splotches that grow larger as they ripen. The flesh is yellow to reddish. It is an excellent vegetable, now common in American markets where they are often quartered and sold by weight.

The flesh should be firm when ripe; if soft it has passed its prime. Though called pumpkin in the English-speaking islands, the flavor is mild, slightly sweet, and not at all like that of the American pumpkin. Island recipes often recommend hubbard squash as an adequate substitute, but butternut squash, in our opinion, is closer. However, we consider calabaza far better than either. If there is one squash that could make as regular an appearance at our mainland meals as carrots or string beans, this is it.

Callaloo Calalou   Rich ingredient of the soup made with leaves of dasheen (taro). See page 91.

Cassava Manihot Manioc   Known also as yuca (but not to be confused with the American yucca, *Agavaceae*). It is a New World tuberous root plant of the Euphorbia family. *Manihot esculenta*, despite its name, contains poisonous milky sap containing prussic acid. If the tuber is boiled or the juice pressed out and the flesh fried or roasted, the poison disappears. However, the cassava of our markets is *Manihot dulcis*, the sweet cassava, which is free of prussic acid and the only species whose importation is permitted into the States.

It is a somewhat spindle-shaped root, either rough or rather shiny brown when waxed, about ten inches long. The flesh is very white, crisp, and hard. Cut into chunks it is boiled until soft and used like potato.

Chayote Christophine Cho-cho   Popular pear-shaped vegetables of the gourd family. Yellow when ripe. See page 248.

Cilantro Coriander *Coriandrum sativum*   Known also as Mexican or Chinese parsley. It is a coarse looking kind of parsley with a rank odor and strong flavor. But, when used judiciously, it does wonderful things to salads, dressings, sauces, stews, egg dishes, seafood, and just about anything. Much of Caribbean cooking is inconceivable without this herb. Just don't use to excess as it can easily drown out and blanket other flavors. When storing the fresh cilantro, do not remove the roots.

Dasheen Coco Eddo Callaloo Taro   Names for both the leaves and the tuberous roots of *Colocassia esculenta*. The arrow-shaped leaves are used in the famous callaloo soup. The tubers are a rather coarse potato substitute, less agreeable than yam, for example, but varying from island to island. See page 254.

Dion-dion Djon-djon   Tiny, spindly Haitian black mushrooms used for flavoring and coloring rice dishes. See page . . . . The dion-dion is boiled to color the water, strained, and the mushrooms discarded. The rice is then cooked, frequently along with beans, in the black liquid. Very similar mushrooms grow on Jamaica.

Eddo   See *Dasheen*.

Giraumon   See *Calabaza*.

Gumbo Gombo Okra   See *Okra*.

Habichuelas.   See *Red Kidney Beans*.

Igname Name   See *Yam*.

Malanga Tannia Yautia   Starchy root. See page 254.

Melondrone   Dominican Republic word for okra.

Okra Gombo Gumbo   Asiatic relatives of the Hibiscus whose upstanding green seed pods have become a standard vegetable in the States. We find it fresh, frozen, and canned in the markets. It is the thickening constituent of Louisiana Creole gumbos. Grown in the islands and used in soups and ragouts when in season.

Onion   The wild onions of the islands are extremely strong flavored and, for those allergic to them, they can be almost poisonous. The so-called chives or cives are much larger than ours and hardly to be differentiated from the onions. The new type of large scallions in our markets are ideal for Creole cooking, as are yellow onions.

Pana de Pepita   See *Breadfruit Nuts.*

Plantains   Plantains are hardly distinguishable from bananas. They are merely larger and heavier. One distinction is that they usually come into market quite green but soon turn yellow. The flesh however is somewhat firmer than that of the banana and considerably less sweet when raw, which is why it is always cooked and served as a vegetable.

Green plantains are used for chips that, when carefully made, are at least as good as potato chips. They are cubed and cooked in ragouts and similar dishes where they serve both as a vegetable and a thickener of the sauce. They are also made into excellent soups.

The yellow or ripe plantains are more often gently fried and served as a separate vegetable.

Especially when green, the skins of plantains do not come off with anything like the ease of banana skins. Cut off both ends; draw the tip of a small, sharp knife lengthwise between each angle of the fruit. Work one of the strips free at an end and ease it off by hand or with the aid of the knife. The other strips will be easier, as the knife can be inserted under the skin to aid the process.

When cutting green or yellow plantains we generally slice as much as possible on the bevel so as to make longer and larger slices.

Rice   The favorite of the islands is a southern Asian long-grain rice, called Basmati, which is excellent for all purposes. We recommend Basmati rice because it is almost impossible to turn into mush. The Spanish and Italians prefer their rice mushy which we consider something of an abomination. We can use the excuse that the Trinidadian Indian cooks prefer it as a justification for recommending Basmati in general. Asian food shops in this country usually carry it.

We boil it in the normal way until just soft, drain it, and suspend it over boiling water in the sieve or colander to keep hot until used. It is invariably light and fluffy, just what we most admire in a rice.

Shallots   Some shallots are grown in the islands but the quantities are not large. Our vegetable stores offer the brown bulbs in plastic bags year-round, and they do make a pleasant change from onions. But anyone who has had the real thing, freshly dug out of a French garden, and three times as big, knows that the resemblance is faint indeed. The true shallot is enormously aromatic in its own particular way with a special sweetness, almost all of which is, seemingly, lost in the drying process—or maybe our American varieties are less tasty.

If you can get fresh shallots they are ideal replacements for scallions in most of our recipes, with the exception of salads. One can, of course, never duplicate exactly a vegetable grown in a different region and climate.

Tomatillo   Mexican Ground Cherry, *Physalis ixocarpa*, is a close relative of the tomato. It is an annual, and widely grown in the Spanish-speaking Caribbean islands. They are sold fresh in Hispanic grocery stores in the States and are also available in cans.

The appearance is that of a small, green tomato encased in a brown, thin, dry, papery balloon. The flavor is sour, which makes it an excellent additive to many foods that are too bland. Remove the balloon and cut the fruit into chunks or slices. The fruit cooks very quickly either boiled or fried. They are a distinctive feature of Caribbean cooking, with which northern lovers of good food should become acquainted. We have become accustomed to using them frequently in all kinds of hot dishes and even raw in salads.

Tomatoes Tomato Paste   The local tomatoes are better than most of ours have become, though smaller in size. Tomato paste is used in island recipes. We recommend the canned product imported from Italy.

Yam Name Igname Batata Yampi   Tuberous roots that are both the most widespread and the most popular in the tropics. See page 255.

Yautia   See *Malanga*.

Yuca   See *Cassava*.

• *Three* •

D O W N -

I S L A N D

APPETIZERS

As so many of our popular appetizers, dips, salads, and their dressings are made with tropical ingredients, it comes as no surprise that they are even more common and varied in the islands. In addition to the recipes in this chapter you will find excellent appetizers and dips from the Rijstafel in chapter eight.

◆ Cold Sauces ◆

AVOCADO MAYONNAISE 1

◆

1 ripe avocado, peeled, pitted, and cut into chunks
Juice of ½ lime or lemon
3 tablespoons olive or other vegetable oil
Salt
Freshly ground green or black pepper

MAKES 1½ CUPS

This is not really a mayonnaise because it lacks egg yolks; dressing might be a better term. However, it has much the texture of a mayonnaise and is used in the same ways, as dressing for all kinds of cold foods.

Choosing avocados can be tricky; the quality of fruit is uncertain as well as the correct ripeness. Do not look for fruit that is soft to the touch, for by the time it has reached that state it is past its prime. Choose, rather, avocados that are very slightly less than hard for they are usually quite ripe. Or pick rock hard ones and ripen them in a warm place. It usually takes no more than a day or two. The moment the pressure of a finger makes a bit of a dent, the fruit is ready to eat.

1 Combine all but the salt and pepper in the blender or processor bowl. Process for 6 seconds.
2 Decant into a bowl and stir in salt and pepper to taste.

Variation

Thin the mayonnaise by adding heavy cream a little at a time. The cream can also be whipped to firm peaks and folded into the dressing.

AVOCADO MAYONNAISE 2

◆

1 ripe avocado, peeled, pitted, and cut into chunks
6 parsley or cilantro sprigs, snipped
1 garlic clove, through the press
2 scallions, roughly chopped

1 Place the avocado, parsley, garlic, and scallions in the processor bowl.
2 Blend or process for 4 seconds. Add the lemon juice and oil to the bowl and process for 10 seconds.
3 Decant into another bowl and add the salt, black pepper, and chili pepper to taste. If the sauce is not sufficiently tart, add more lemon juice.

Variations

A Add ½ cup drained capers to the sauce after processing and before adjusting the seasoning. When adding the seasoning you will need very little extra salt because of the capers.

B When the sauce has been seasoned with salt and pepper, add 1 tablespoon of a good Madras curry powder, then stir in the chili pepper.

Juice of ½ lemon
½ cup vegetable oil
Salt and freshly ground
  black pepper
Scotch bonnet (chili) pepper, seeded and forced through a garlic press, to taste

MAKES 1½ CUPS

Homemade mayonnaise is so easy to make and so superior to bottled products that it is incomprehensible that so few cooks go to the trouble. The instructions often turn people off, although no special skill is required. Readers are always warned that the oil, egg, and liquid may separate unless one is very careful. That is not our experience and we have never made a mayonnaise that didn't turn out well. Moreover, the sauce is made—without haste—in three or four minutes at most. There's nothing to it.

Creole mayonnaise is different only because lemon or lime juice is used instead of vinegar. By adding "bush" and other herbs and spices a great variety of interesting sauces can be whipped up for any occasion, special or ordinary.

1 In a small bowl stir the lemon or lime juice with the egg yolk.

2 Add the parsley, scallion, and coriander and stir well.

3 With a small balloon whip stir the mixture very well and pour in the oil, using 1 teaspoon (approximately) at first, then doubling the amount and continuing to increase while stirring vigorously. All you have to watch for is that each addition of oil is homogenized thoroughly before more is added. After three or four small amounts you can venture substantial gobs on the same principle. Very soon the sauce will thicken noticeably. When the last of the cup of oil is thoroughly absorbed give the mayonnaise a very short rest before finishing.

4 Now start whipping again very rapidly and add more oil until you have a cup or more of thick-textured mayonnaise.

5 Taste and add the salt, black pepper, and chili powder. Stir to blend well. If the mayonnaise is too bland, add a teaspoon or more of additional lemon or lime juice.

CREOLE MAYONNAISE

◆

Juice of ½ lemon or lime
1 egg yolk, at room temperature
1 teaspoon dried parsley leaves or snipped fresh Spanish thyme leaves
3 fresh scallion leaves, very finely snipped
¼ teaspoon ground coriander
1 cup vegetable oil, plus additional if needed
Salt and freshly ground black pepper to taste
Chili powder or chili sauce to taste

MAKES 1 CUP

Guadeloupe

CURRIED MAYONNAISE

◆

1 egg yolk, at room temperature

3 tablespoons white vinegar

1 cup vegetable oil as needed

1½ tablespoons Colombo powder *or* 1 tablespoon Madras curry powder

Salt and freshly ground black pepper to taste

MAKES 1 CUP

On Guadeloupe the mayonnaise is made with Colombo curry flavoring. The cassava content of the Colombo also thickens the sauce. It is absolutely first rate on cold seafood, cold meat, eggs, avocados, and asparagus.

1 Combine the egg yolk and vinegar in a bowl.

2 With a small balloon whip (which frees one hand) stir together the egg and vinegar and add the oil a little at a time while beating constantly. As the mixture starts to thicken, the oil may be added in larger amounts; continue to add oil only after the last lot has been thoroughly absorbed.

3 When the mixture has thickened, beat in the curry powder, adding more oil and beating vigorously until you have at least 1 cup of mayonnaise.

4 Add the salt and pepper.

Variations

A Add ½ garlic clove, through the press, to the mix.

B Although certainly not a Creole recipe, we have found that folding ¼ pint sour cream into the finished mayonnaise makes a superb coating for cold cooked or raw vegetables, such as cauliflower, broccoli, and mushrooms, or for eggs. Mix the sauce with finely sliced kielbasa sausage and minced sour pickles to make a superb salad. You may add considerable quantities of curry to taste, a little at a time.

SALAD DRESSING OF OIL AND LEMON OR LIME

◆

It stands to reason that in countries where citrus fruits grow the population prefers picking fruit from the backyard tree to buying vinegar in the store. As noted on page 29, island lemons and limes are small and round but ever so much more juicy and sharp than our citrus from Florida or California. It is equally obvious that islanders would use their homegrown coconut oil rather than imports, especially the more expensive olive oil, despite its excellence. They also flavor with the local "bush" leaves and spices with the result that the typical island taste of salad dressings is quite different from that of a typical "French" dressing.

To produce the likes of Caribbean dressings, mainlanders are obliged to use the lighter store-bought oils and the available citrus juices, plus any comparable herbs, such as thyme, oregano, marjoram, curry leaf, parsley, and others. Add to that a bit of garlic, a touch of dry mustard, and a *soupçon* of chili. The traditional proportion of oil to lemon or lime, three parts oil to one part juice, must be modified to taste. Herbs and spices should be mixed into the fruit juices before adding the oil. Allow the herbs to soak well so that the flavor is absorbed.

Whatever the quantity of dressing, pour into a tightly covered screw-top jar for storage. The jar is also a great help in mixing the dressing. Just before serving, shake thoroughly until the liquid and oil are temporarily emulsified. Then mix the required quantity with the salad.

We are not addicted to very sharp flavors, but this sauce—very French Creole, though widespread in the islands—is a jewel that should be on everyone's list of good things for party snacks and cold appetizers. The best concoction we've ever had was not in the Caribbean at all but at a Thai restaurant in New York, proving that good ideas travel and that quality in cookery is the product more of talent than tradition. Place the sauce in a little dish at the center of snack plates or with appetizers at dinner in separate dishes for each guest. It is a major treat with accras, all cold seafood, cold meats, and raw vegetables. Though the mixture is very hot, each person can adjust it to their own taste by simply dipping tentatively or greedily.

1 Process or blend the scallions, sweet peppers, chili pepper, and cilantro to a finely chopped consistency.
2 Decant to a bowl and add the vinegar, lime juice, and sugar.
3 Let stand covered for at least 2 hours, and preferably overnight in the fridge.
4 Add the salt and serve in very small dishes.

SAUCE CHIEN

◆

4 scallions, bulbs only, *or* 1 small onion
1 small sweet green or red bell pepper
½ to 1 whole Scotch bonnet or similar chili pepper
6 cilantro leaves, finely minced
½ to 1 cup white vinegar or rice vinegar
2 tablespoons lime or lemon juice
½ teaspoon sugar
Salt to taste

MAKES 1 CUP

Trinidad

CUCUMBER SAUCE

◆

2 large, ripe cucumbers, peeled, cored, seeds discarded, and cut into chunks

1 medium yellow onion, peeled and sliced

1 green bell pepper, seeded and cut into chunks

4 tablespoons lime juice

Salt and freshly ground black pepper to taste

Chili pepper to taste

MAKES 1 TO 1 1/2 CUPS

Like a number of others the following recipe is both a dip and a sauce for cold dishes. This doesn't surprise us since the uniform high temperatures (which are not as high as some fierce days on the mainland in July and August) make these cool sauces very welcome. Why being in the tropics induces a liking and tolerance for quantities of chili still lacks a credible explanation, but so it is.

1 Put the cucumber, onion, sweet pepper, and lime juice in the blender or processor bowl and reduce to a puree. Decant and strain out part of the excess watery liquid (if any). The sauce should be semiliquid.

2 Add the salt, black pepper, and chili pepper and stir well.

3 Refrigerate for at least 1 hour before serving. Serve with accras, fried fish and other seafoods, or cold meats.

This excellent sauce concentrate has many uses. Mix it with butter, with other sauces, in dressings, and in dips. It is bottled in Trinidad and can be purchased on the mainland in some island stores. Make it at home in one of two ways, depending on the length of time it will be stored. Fresh or raw, it can go off in only a few days, even when refrigerated. Simmered for a few minutes, bottled, and placed in the fridge, it usually lasts for several weeks in winter and a shorter time in summer. We especially recommend mixing this sauce with plain homemade mayonnaise (see page 51) or sour cream.

1 Process all the ingredients except the cornstarch, salt, black pepper, and chili pepper for 10 seconds. The consistency should be about the same as ketchup. If too thick, add a little water. If too watery, allow to stand for a few minutes and spoon or pour off the excess liquid.

If you intend to use up the sauce within 1 or 2 days it may be stored in the fridge in a covered bowl overnight.

2 A longer-lasting sauce can be made by pouring the puree into a saucepan and simmering for twenty minutes. If too thin, add cornstarch to thicken.

3 Store in a glass container with a tight cover in the fridge. The heated sauce should keep rather well for 2 to 3 weeks, but watch for any sign of mold after about 1 week. If that happens, immediately discard.

4 For both methods, add the salt, black pepper, and chili pepper *before* serving.

Trinidad

GREEN SAUCE

◆

5 or 6 scallions (1 bunch), leaves sliced in pieces
1 garlic clove, through the press
1 medium yellow or red onion, peeled and cut into chunks
1 large celery stalk, cut into chunks
1 tablespoon fresh or dried thyme leaves
¼ cup snipped Spanish thyme leaves (optional)
1 tablespoon fresh or dry-crushed curry leaves *or* 1 teaspoon mild Madras curry powder
2 tablespoons white vinegar
Cornstarch (optional)
Salt and freshly ground black pepper to taste
Chili pepper or sauce to taste

MAKES 1 CUP

◆ Accras and Fritters ◆

Various accras and fritters are made with similar doughs. Accras are lumps of dough mixed with fish, shellfish, and, less often, vegetables. Fritters are flattened disks of dough mixed with mashed fruits. Our northern fritters, in contrast, are made with sliced fruit dipped in batter. Accras and fritters are usually deep fried, but fritters are also frequently fried in a pan.

Of the two, accras are by far the more popular. As appetizers or snacks they have no competition in the islands. The size is small, for essentially they are beignets and should be light, crisp, and very tasty. The quality of a restaurant can often be judged by whether the accras are piping hot and rich in salt cod, conch, or shrimp. If they're sodden and tasteless, head for the door.

Accras (acras, achras, akkras, achrats, acrats)   Accras, however spelled, are the most popular down-island appetizers. They are small, deep-fried lumps of dough enriched with a variety of ingredients. Most common are salt cod accras (accras *de morue*), hot, crispy, and especially seductive when loaded with plenty of the fish. Other versions of these enticing pastries employ conch, shrimp, almost any fish, breadfruit, yam, banana, spiced beef, goat, or chicken. They appear piping hot piled on your plate while you linger over your drinks. They should become immensely popular in the north as cocktail snacks or for buffet lunches or dinner hors d'oeuvres, for once the dough is made, one can turn out large numbers of them very fast. They gain piquancy from being dipped in a side dish of Sauce Chien (page 53). Make the sauce very hot-hot and leave the amount of dipping to the guests with suitable warnings.

These recipes are not rigid. We find the secret of success is not to skimp on the additional ingredients. Restaurant formulas are almost invariably anemic. The more meat or fish, the more liquid you may be obliged to add in order to have a light but firm dollop to drop into the hot fat. Our recipes usually produce fifteen to eighteen accras.

Keep in mind that all the accras recipes employing root starches or breadfruit are basically interchangeable.

ACCRAS DOUGH

◆

1 Stir the baking powder into the flour. Add the water in a steady stream while stirring with a soup spoon or a whisk. Add the oil and stir. The mix can also be made in a processor.

2 Allow to stand for 1 hour or more. The dough should be just firm enough to shape into lumps or fritters. If too firm, the accras will not be sufficiently light. If necessary, add a little extra water or milk and stir. But be careful. A very little additional moisture can change the texture to flowing. If that happens add a little more flour and be on guard the next time.

Note

Do not add salt or spices to the basic dough. The egg in Dough 2 replaces the baking powder in Dough 1

DOUGH 1

1 teaspoon baking powder
1 cup all-purpose flour
½ cup water or milk
1 tablespoon vegetable oil

DOUGH 2

1 egg
1 cup all-purpose flour
½ cup water or milk
1 tablespoon vegetable oil

MAKES 15 TO 18 ACCRAS

Martinique

SALT COD ACCRAS

◆

1 recipe Accras Dough 1
  or 2 (page 57)
½ pound prepared salt cod
  (see page 129)
1 whole scallion, finely
  chopped
1 garlic clove, through the
  press
2 tablespoons dried pars-
  ley leaves
½ teaspoon freshly grated
  nutmeg
½ teaspoon ground corian-
  der
½ medium green bell pep-
  per, seeded and finely
  chopped
Salt and freshly ground
  black pepper
Scotch bonnet chili pep-
  per, seeded and forced
  through a garlic press, or
  chili sauce to taste
Vegetable oil for frying

**MAKES 15 TO 18
ACCRAS**

Why salt cod rather than fresh fish? Though salt cod is now sold in chain groceries as well as fish stores, it is usually Mediterranean, Hispanic, and island people who buy it. For other mainlanders even cod fish cakes, which are made with this salt-cured product, are no longer popular. Yet this preserved fish possesses a very distinct and delicious individuality, stores much better than fresh fish, and is easy to prepare.

The cod is caught, salted, and put out to dry on racks in the clean, cool air and bright sun of Newfoundland and Nova Scotia, acquiring a unique, pleasant flavor that is far more enjoyable in accras than any other fish.

Why is our recipe from Martinique? Because the Matador at *Trois-Ilets* prepared the best accras, as it did of many other island dishes. The substantial house at the crossroads to Point du Bout, where the marina and the major hotels are located, embodies this spacious, attractive restaurant. M., the chef, and Mme., the manageress, Crico are the extraordinarily able owners. Every season their tables are occupied by vacationers who appreciate Creole cookery at its best.

1 Set aside the prepared dough for 1 to 2 hours. It should be just firm enough to shape with a spoon. If more liquid is needed, add milk, ½ teaspoon at a time, and stir.

2 Thoroughly shred the prepared cod or pound it in a mortar. Then mix with the flavorants, adding the salt, pepper, and chili pepper last, very cautiously, to taste.

3 Add the fish mixture to the dough and stir vigorously until evenly distributed. The dough should be soft but not flowing. If it is too firm, add a little liquid; if it is too soft, add a bit of flour, by sprinkling a little at a time, and stir.

4 Heat the vegetable oil to 370 degrees. Drop heaping tablespoons of the mix into the fat and cook until crisp and brown. Drain on paper towels in a hot oven and serve promptly. (The accras can be frozen and reheated in a 400-degree oven.)

Variation

Mix the prepared and cooked cod with the flavorants, except the salt, pepper, and chili pepper, and process for about 3 seconds. Do not reduce the mix to a mush. Then add the salt, pepper, and chili pepper, cautiously, to taste.

Although they know perfectly well how to make them, chefs of island restaurants turn out Conch Accras that are rarely as good as they should be. For one thing, the conch is often as undetectable as clams are in some northern chowders. Pounding and tenderizing is neglected. Accras loaded with small but thick bits of very tough gristle is not our idea of bliss. The waters around St. Thomas must still be rich in these shellfish, for conch appears more frequently on the menus than elsewhere and the quality is usually satisfactory. Beat the conch gently but patiently and cook in your pressure cooker or a long time with a minimum of water in a pot (as we describe on page 139), and the conch will prove both tender and sweet, making this dish a memorable gourmet experience.

1   Prepare the dough and set aside for 1 to 2 hours.

2   For a coarse texture, chop the prepared conch very fine and mix with other ingredients.

For a smooth consistency, cut the prepared conch into small cubes, mix with other ingredients, and process for 4 seconds.

3   Add the conch mixture to the dough and stir thoroughly.

4   Drop heaping tablespoons of the mixture into oil heated to 370 degrees and cook until golden. Drain on paper towels in a hot oven. Serve promptly.

Note

Conch accras should not be fried as dark in color as some others.

St. Thomas

CONCH ACCRAS

◆

1 recipe Accras Dough 2
  (page 57)
Meat of 3 prepared conchs
  (see page 139)
½ teaspoon ground ginger
1 teaspoon mild Madras
  curry powder
2 scallions, leaves snipped
  and bulbs chopped
1 green bell pepper,
  seeded and finely
  chopped
1 tablespoon grated lemon
  zest
Salt to taste
Fresh chili pepper or chili
  sauce to taste
Vegetable oil for frying

**MAKES 15 TO 18
ACCRAS**

St. Martin

SHRIMP
ACCRAS

◆

MAKES 28 SMALL
ACCRAS

This recipe is basically the same as for Conch Accras. But the flavor of shrimps is far less distinct, disappearing very quickly after the extremely short cooking time. Hence the shrimp should be coarsely chopped, and the accras should be no more than one inch across and fried just to the point of light yellow coloring.

In general follow the recipe for Conch Accras (page 59). The exceptions are:

1 Replace the prepared conch meat with ½ pound shelled, deveined shrimp. Drop them into boiling water and cook for no more than 3 minutes.

2 Drain the shrimp and chop to a crumbly consistency.

3 Mix with the other seasoning ingredients of Conch Accras (including the prepared dough). Madras curry *or* Colombo powder is optional.

4 Drop rounded teaspoons into oil heated to 365 degrees and remove when they have turned light yellow. Drain on paper towels in a hot oven. Serve promptly.

Various nonfatty fish, such as boned smelts, fresh cod, sea bass, flounder, whiting, the nonoily parts of tuna, and canned lump tuna make excellent accras and fritters. Adventurous cooks will find that the addition of small quantities of Indian spices are also appetizing.

1 Prepare the dough and set aside for 1 to 2 hours.
2 Boil the fish, drain and discard the liquid, and remove any bones and skin. Mash the flesh.
3 Mix all ingredients except the salt, pepper, and chili sauce in the processor bowl and process to a somewhat coarse puree. Add the salt, pepper, and chili sauce.
4 Combine the fish mixture with the dough so that it is soft but not flowing. For fritters, the dough should be more spreadable.
5 For accras, drop heaping tablespoons of the mix into deep fat heated to 370 degrees. Cook till brown and crisp. Drain on paper towels in a hot oven. Serve hot.

For fritters, drop by the tablespoon onto a hot skillet with a small amount of heated oil and fry till the outsides of the fritters are crisp. Drain on paper towels in a hot oven.

Serve promptly with a hot, spicy sauce.

FISH ACCRAS OR FRITTERS

◆

1 recipe Accras Dough 1 or 2 (page 57)
½ pound nonfatty fish
Juice of ½ lemon or lime
1 clove garlic, through the press
1 medium yellow onion, coarsely chopped
½ large celery stalk, cut into short lengths
½ medium green bell pepper, seeded and coarsely chopped
½ teaspoon dried thyme leaves
6 cilantro sprigs, shredded (optional)
Salt and freshly ground black pepper to taste
Chili sauce to taste
Vegetable oil for frying

MAKES 15 TO 18 ACCRAS *OR* 15 FRITTERS

Tortola

BANANA ACCRAS OR FRITTERS

◆

½ cup all-purpose flour
1½ teaspoons baking pow-
  der
¼ to ½ cup milk or half-
  and-half
1 egg
3 ripe, medium bananas
Salt to taste
Vegetable oil for frying

**MAKES 12 TO 15
ACCRAS**

On Tortola, at the end of a day of sun and beach, we would stretch out on the paved terrace at Sebastian's, viewing the water through a fringe of palm trees, for a long, cool predinner drink. Part of the relaxing joy was the basket of small, round banana accras brought out hot from the frying pan. Brown and crisp on the outside, puffy and savory on the inside—not sweet, but redolent of banana flavor. This is luxury and contentment combined. Down-islanders also make these accras without eggs, but the result is less puffy and flavorful.

1 In a bowl stir the flour and baking powder together.
2 Whisk in the milk, stirring rapidly and making a soft, nonflowing dough. Add the egg and stir well.
3 Mash the bananas with a fork or a potato ricer and stir thoroughly with the dough. One may also process the banana, but we find that the flavor comes through much better when the fruit is a bit lumpy in the cooked accras.
4 Add the salt. If the dough is too thick, a little extra milk may be necessary.
5 Drop heaping teaspoons of the mix into oil heated to 365 degrees, or fry in a heated pan in a little hot oil. Cook until crispy brown all over. Drain on paper towels in a hot oven. Serve promptly.

Variation

1½ teaspoons vanilla extract or essence (page 37) reinforces the banana flavor.

Note

The cooked accras can also be stored in the freezer until needed. Heat the frozen accras in a 400-degree oven until crisp.

Because there was a huge, gorgeous-leaved breadfruit tree near our cottage on St. Lucia, we picked our own ripe fruit to make accras. How much better these were, fished directly out of the hot fat, aromatic and crackling crisp! The vegetable accras here are not made with a flour dough. Essentially they are puffs, similar to deep-fried potato puffs. These less-familiar starches, however, make quite a difference. They are yummy garnishes for meat and seafood dishes of all sorts.

1 With an electric beater or processor mix all the ingredients except the milk and oil. Add a little of the milk *only* if the mix is very firm.

2 Drop heaping tablespoons of the mix into hot oil at 370 degrees.

3 Fry till light brown and the edges are crisp.

4 Serve immediately or hold in a hot oven on paper towels for no more than 10 minutes. (The accras can also be frozen until needed. Reheat in a 400-degree oven.)

Variation

Use a pound of fresh, boiled dasheen tuber, malanga, yam, or breadfruit. Adjust the liquid for texture.

St. Lucia

BREADFRUIT ACCRAS

◆

1 pound canned bread-
fruit, drained, skinned,
and processed for 10 sec-
onds
4 tablespoons softened
butter or margarine
2 to 3 eggs
2 tablespoons parsley
leaves
½ teaspoon ground mace
Salt and freshly ground
black pepper to taste
Chili pepper or chili sauce
to taste
¼ cup milk
Vegetable oil for frying

MAKES 24 ACCRAS

Trinidad

BREADFRUIT NUT ACCRAS OR CHATAIGNE BEIGNETS

◆

½ cup all-purpose flour
1½ cups canned breadfruit
 nuts, drained, skinned,
 processed, grated, or
 passed through a potato
 ricer
2 eggs
½ cup grated sharp cheese
½ cup milk *or* half-and-
 half
2 tablespoons vegetable
 oil, plus additional oil for
 frying
1 scallion, finely chopped
¼ cup minced fresh pars-
 ley
Freshly ground black pep-
per
Chili pepper to taste

MAKES 24 ACCRAS

The French island name for breadfruit nuts, *chataigne*, has traveled around. Accras are really a form of French *beignets*, specially adapted to the produce of the islands. This recipe is different from the others because the processed or grated breadfruit nuts, though not roasted crisp or milled, do take the place of flour. These are very unusual pastries that are splendid as appetizers but can also be served as a vegetable with meat and gravy. They are popular in Trinidad, which had a period of French occupation.

1 Stir the flour thoroughly with the breadfruit nuts.
2 Add the eggs and stir well. Follow with the grated cheese.
3 Add the milk gradually to produce a soft, nonflowing texture.
4 Add the 2 tablespoons of oil, the scallions, parsley, pepper, and chili pepper. (Caution on the last.)
5 Heat the oil in a pot to 365 degrees and drop heaping teaspoons of the mix into it. Brown well and remove with a slotted spoon. Drain on paper towels in a hot oven. Serve promptly.

Malangas, also called *yautias* and *tannias*, and yams, also called *batata* and *igname*, are now being shipped in regularly from Central and South America (see page 227) to our vegetable markets. Always buy hard, crisp-fleshed tubers. The yams are often much bigger than potatoes so that one or even one-half will be all you'll need. The purchase of halves is usually permitted. Cooking is no different than for potatoes. These accras are often served with meats or seafood. They can be dipped in Sauce Chien (page 53) or some other sauce served separately.

Jamaica

MALANGA OR YAM ACCRAS

◆

1   Peel the malanga, cut into chunks, and process with the lemon juice just long enough to reduce to a fine-grated texture. Or, peel and grate the vegetable by hand and stir in a bowl with the lemon juice.

2   Process with the other ingredients for 5 seconds or mix thoroughly by hand.

3   Drop heaping tablespoons of the mix into oil heated to 365 degrees. Cook until browned. These will take a little longer than the other accras because the ingredients are uncooked. Drain on paper towels.

4   Place the accras in a single layer in a pan in a 300-degree oven for up to 30 minutes. (The fried accras may also be stored in the freezer until needed, then heated in a 400-degree oven.)

1 pound malanga or yam
Juice of 1 lemon
1 medium yellow onion,
   cut into chunks
1 small garlic clove,
   through the press
1 tablespoon ground
   cumin
1 tablespoon dried marjo-
   ram or parsley leaves
2 teaspoons baking powder
1 egg (2 eggs optional)
Salt and freshly ground
   black pepper to taste
Vegetable oil for frying

MAKES 20 ACCRAS

◆ Appetizers, Salads, and Dips ◆

In the islands the difference between appetizers and salads is usually no more than a matter of quantity and of chili pepper. The salads are courses or side dishes; the appetizers or snacks are dips and spreads with much the same ingredients but usually more delicately textured and very much hotter. These latter are served alongside or spread on top of crackers, toast, cassava bread, and the like.

Dutch Islands

CHEESE BALLS

◆

1 Mix together the cheeses, eggs, and cornstarch.
2 Shape the mix into small balls and drop into oil heated to 370 degrees. Cook until golden. Serve hot or cold. They make good snacks, speared with toothpicks and can be kept for several days in the fridge until needed.

1 pound sharp yellow cheese, grated
1 pound white cheese (*queso blanco*, ricotta, feta, or other), pass through a potato ricer or crushed
6 eggs, well beaten
3 tablespoons cornstarch
Vegetable oil for frying

MAKES 36 BALLS

Plantain Chips are being sold packaged at grocery stores and health food stores as an alternative to potato chips. The slices are smaller and somewhat firmer than potato chips. Homemade chips possess a flavor lacking in the packaged product.

PLANTAIN CHIPS

◆

1 Peel the plantains (see page 47).
2 Slice crosswise into very, very thin rounds.
3 Pour the vegetable oil into a large saucepan to a depth of 3 inches. Heat to 375 degrees.
4 Drop the plantain slices into the oil a few at a time to avoid crowding, cook until golden, and remove to paper towels to drain.
5 Salt liberally or spice them up by shaking the powdered chili pepper lightly over the slices before serving.

Store in a cookie can or tightly closed plastic bag until serving.

4 large green plantains *or* 6 small ones
Vegetable oil for frying
Salt
Chili powder (optional)

SERVES 8

Guadeloupe

AVOCADO AND COD APPETIZER

◆

¼ pound prepared salt cod
  (see page 129)
1 ripe avocado, pitted,
  peeled, and cubed
½ cup vegetable oil
Juice of 1 lime or lemon
1 small yellow onion,
  chopped fine
1 small garlic clove,
  through the press
½ cup chopped fresh pars-
  ley *or* 1 tablespoon dried
  parsley leaves
½ cup cassava meal or
  finely grated cashews or
  breadfruit nuts
½ cup coconut milk or
  half-and-half with ¼ teaspoon coconut extract
Salt and freshly ground
  black pepper to taste
Chili pepper to taste

SERVES 8

The statement by some that this recipe was brought from Africa is hardly tenable. Called interchangeably *féroce d'avocat* or *féroce de morue*, the recipe is always made with avocado, which is an American fruit.

1   Shred the prepared salt cod and mix with the avocado.
2   Stir together with the oil, lime juice, onion, garlic, parsley, cassava, and coconut milk. Add the salt, pepper, and chili pepper and refrigerate for at least 1 hour.
3   Serve in scallop shells or small dishes, with crisp crackers.

Variation

Add 1 tablespoon tomato paste to the mix.

ESCABECHE

Escabeche, also known as scabechi and escovitch, is an hors d'oeuvre consisting of fried fish marinated in a tart and spicy sauce and served cold. In some island recipes called seviche or ceviche, raw fish is marinated. In the tropics this has risks, so, in general, we recommend cooking seafood. The marinade is in line with other typical seafood preparations of the islands—tart, sour, spicy, and hot. The use of lime and/or vinegar is very much a Caribbean discovery. A rather free use of chili pepper, especially of the Scotch bonnet type, which is quite sweet before the fires take effect, blends perfectly.

One afternoon, from our cottage porch, we heard a long, deep sound like a demanding car horn, coming from the beach toward Charlotteville village on Tobago. We left the porch on the second note, quickly starting down the beach to where a group of men were gathered around their fishnet, which they had just pulled out of the water. Standing at the edge of the group was a large man with the noble head of a tribal chieftain, blowing into the pointed end of a large Trumpet Triton shell.

The call was a signal to the villagers to come buy the small fish in the net. We paid happily for our share, as we were a little bored by the fishermen's co-op's unvarying kingfish. Our purchase later became escabeche, the main course for the next day's meal.

For this dish we prefer to use white fishes, but many down-islanders make do with mackerel or kingfish and other smaller, local fish.

2 pounds filleted fish
2 tablespoons vegetable oil
6 scallions, minced
½ cup white wine vinegar or lime juice (not lemon)
¾ cup very finely sliced carrots
2 garlic cloves, through the press
6 whole allspice, crushed
Pinch of freshly grated nutmeg
1 tablespoon freshly grated ginger *or* ¾ teaspoon ground ginger
1 medium bell pepper, seeded and finely chopped
½ Scotch bonnet pepper, seeded and forced through a garlic press
2 cups water
Salt and freshly ground black pepper to taste

SERVES 8 AS AN APPETIZER

1 Fry the fish gently in the oil until it is tender, turning over once.

2 Simmer the remaining ingredients in a saucepan for 20 minutes.

3 Cut the cooked fish into convenient serving squares or cubes.

4 Pour the marinade over the fish. Allow to cool to room temperature, then store in the fridge overnight. Serve cold on individual hors d'oeuvres plates or on salad plates with lettuce and French bread, croutons, toast, or non-sweet crackers on the side.

Variation

A common practice in the islands is first to dredge the fish in a mix of half flour and half bread crumbs, and then to fry in very hot oil. If doing so, follow the recipe from step 2 on.

ESCABECHE OF SCALLOPS OR SHRIMP

◆

3 garlic cloves, unpeeled and crushed

2 medium yellow onions, finely sliced

10 tablespoons olive or vegetable oil

1½ pounds bay or sea scallops (see Note) *or* 1½ to 2 pounds shrimp, peeled and deveined

10 whole allspice, crushed in a mortar and pestle, *or* 1 teaspoon ground allspice

½ teaspoon freshly grated nutmeg

½ teaspoon freshly ground black pepper, plus additional pepper to taste

Chili pepper or chili sauce to taste

½ cup white vinegar or white wine vinegar

Salt to taste

SERVES 6 AS AN HORS D'OEUVRE

The following recipe may be served hot or cold, as an appetizer on individual plates at table, or as an hors d'oeuvres or snack for everyone to help themselves. Hot, it should be brought directly from stove to table; cold, it must be prepared long enough before serving to have time to chill in the fridge. We prefer to make it a day ahead and to serve it cold.

When serving the dish hot, it is important to time its completion so that the scallops or shrimp will cook the minimum time necessary. As hors d'oeuvres or snacks both temperatures can be served: hot in a small casserole, the scallops or shrimp in their sauce, transfixed with toothpicks; cold in a suitably decorative serving dish, also with toothpicks. This dish is very easy and distinctly different.

1 In a pan gently simmer the garlic and onion in the oil until the onion is softened.

2 Meanwhile, in a bowl, stir the scallops or shrimp together with the allspice, nutmeg, the ½ teaspoon of pepper, and the chili pepper to distribute the spices evenly.

3 With a slotted spoon remove the garlic cloves from the pan. Pour in the vinegar. Bring the mix to a simmer.

4 Pour the scallops or shrimp into the pan, raise the heat, and bring the mixture quickly to a boil. Lower the heat and simmer for 3 minutes. Add the salt and the additional pepper. If serving hot, have your guests seated so that you can serve immediately. If serving cold, the preparation should be done a day ahead and stored in a covered bowl in the fridge overnight.

Note

Sea scallops, cut into pieces the size of bay scallops, may be substituted.

This recipe can be used as an appetizer or as a condiment with various meats and seafoods. Quantities are quite flexible. Different cooked and cold fish can be substituted for the salt cod. Fans of hot-hot dishes can go to town with this one while others should just go easy on the chili.

1 Shred the prepared salt cold.
2 Mix very thoroughly with the remaining ingredients.
3 Store, covered, in the fridge at least overnight.
4 Serve as an appetizer snack with verbal warnings or just keep the amount of chili sauce low.

St. Martin

CHIQUETAILLE DE MORUE

◆

½ pound prepared salt cod (see page 129)
2 tablespoons white wine vinegar
½ teaspoon tamarind concentrate *or* 1 tablespoon amchur powder
1 medium yellow onion, very finely sliced and chopped
¼ cup cilantro leaves, snipped (optional)
1 tablespoon fresh Spanish thyme leaves, snipped, or dried marjoram leaves
1 teaspoon ground ginger
¼ teaspoon finely ground black pepper
Salt to taste
Yellow island chili sauce (Matouk's or other) to taste

SERVES 12 AS AN APPETIZER

Martinique

ROUGAIL OF SALT COD (DE MORUE)

◆

½ pound boned and soaked salt cod, (see page 129)

4 tablespoons vegetable oil

2 yellow onions, finely chopped, *or* 4 scallions, sliced

3 very ripe medium tomatoes, peeled and chopped

2 fresh tomatillos, cooked and mashed, or 2 canned tomatillos, mashed (optional)

½ teaspoon tamarind concentrate

1½ tablespoons chopped and pounded fresh ginger *or* 1 tablespoon ground ginger

1 teaspoon dried Spanish thyme leaves or dried marjoram leaves

1 teaspoon dried parsley leaves

½ teaspoon ground allspice

Salt and freshly ground black pepper to taste

Scotch bonnet or other fresh chili pepper, or chili sauce, to taste

A *rougail* is a traditional Creole, homemade, very spicy condiment, commonly served with rice, seafood, cold or hot meats, and to accompany other appetizers. We have even used small quantities to enliven various sauces. Recipes are flexible as to quantities and types of ingredients, changing according to seasons. Eggplant or green tropical fruits are frequently the basic constituents. A *rougail* should be so spicy that it can be used only in very small quantities on cassava bread and crackers as cocktail snacks. Here we give three examples.

1 Drain and dry the prepared salt cod, cut it into small pieces, and shred it. Fry gently in 2 tablespoons of oil until golden. Lift out with a slotted spoon and set aside.

2 In the same pan, using the remaining oil, if needed, fry the onion until nearly cooked. Then add the tomatoes, tomatillos, tamarind, ginger, thyme, parsley, and allspice. Simmer for at least 8 minutes.

3 Stir the cod into the tomato mixture. Add the salt, pepper, and chili pepper. Simmer for 40 minutes over very low heat, covering the pan when the sauce begins to thicken. Add a little water if the mix becomes oily.

4 Leave the cover on while the mixture cools, then store in the fridge until needed. (It can also be frozen and thawed to serving temperature.)

SERVES 6 AS AN HORS D'OEUVRE AND 10 AS A COCKTAIL SNACK

St. Barts

ROUGAIL DE MANGUES VERTES

◆

1 Peel the mangoes and cut the flesh into chunks. Discard the seeds.

2 In a sauce pot with water to cover, simmer the mangoes for 15 minutes.

3 Combine the mangoes with the scallions, onion, thyme, and oil. Reduce to a paste in the blender or processor.

4 Store in the fridge in a covered bowl. Add the salt, pepper, and chili pepper before serving as a dip or spread on canapés, crackers, toast, or cassava bread.

3 green mangoes
4 scallions, cut into pieces
1 small yellow onion, sliced
⅛ cup snipped Spanish thyme leaves *or* 1½ teaspoons dried marjoram leaves
1 tablespoon vegetable oil
Salt and freshly ground black pepper to taste
Chili pepper to taste

MAKES 1½ CUPS

St. Lucia

ROUGAIL OF SHRIMP

◆

½ pound fresh shrimp, head and shell on
2 tablespoons vegetable oil
1 yellow onion, sliced and chopped
1 fresh or canned toma-tillo, chopped (optional)
1 tomato, peeled and quartered
1 teaspoon dry mustard
Juice of 1 lemon or lime
Salt and freshly ground black pepper to taste
Chili pepper, seeded and forced through a garlic press, or chili sauce

SERVES 10 AS AN APPETIZER

1 Fry the shrimp in the oil until just pink. Remove with a slotted spoon and set aside.

2 Fry the onion until golden in the same pan. Add the tomatillo and fry until soft (or add a canned tomatillo after the tomato). Add the tomato, mustard, lemon juice, salt, and black pepper. Fry gently until the tomato is soft.

3 Set the pan and its contents aside to cool.

4 Remove the heads and shells of the shrimp and discard. Add the shrimp to the mixture in the pan and stir well. Empty into a blender or processor bowl and reduce to a paste.

5 Decant the paste into a storage bowl and stir in the chili pepper to taste. The mix should be very hot to be authentic, but go easy on the chili pepper, if necessary, to suit your taste.

6 Store, covered, in the fridge for several hours before serving as a snack or appetizer with canapés, crackers, cassava bread, or toast.

Buljol might be called escabeche or something similar on other islands, for it is also a salt cod dish that is served cold as an appetizer or salad. This is the Tobagan variation. There, the little, yellowish limes are all juice and intense flavor. With chili added this is something to make you sit up and take notice no matter how jaded you feel.

1   Mix all the ingredients and store in the fridge for at least 2 hours. Serve on lettuce leaves as a salad or on crackers or toast as an appetizer.

Tobago

BULJOL

◆

½ pound prepared and
  thoroughly shredded salt
  cod (see page 129)
1 garlic clove, through the
  press
1 scallion, tops only,
  minced
2 small tomatoes, peeled
  and chopped
1 small green bell pepper,
  chopped
Juice of 2 limes
4 sprigs of cilantro,
  snipped (optional)
Salt and freshly ground
  black pepper to taste
Fresh chili pepper,
  minced or forced through
  a garlic press, to taste
3 tablespoons vegetable oil
Lettuce leaves (optional)

**SERVES 4 AS A
SALAD OR 8 AS AN
APPETIZER**

Tobago

AVOCADO SALAD

◆

1 firm, large head of Boston or similar lettuce *or* 3 to 4 Belgian endives
1 large, ripe avocado
½ cup salad dressing (page 52)

SERVES 4 TO 6

A simple, easy salad with a difference. Mixing the avocado directly with lettuce and dressing results in a suave richness. Remembered from Tobago where we picked superb avocados from the trees, it has become our favorite salad in summer for special occasions.

1 Cut off and discard the hard core of the lettuce and any outer damaged or tired leaves. Then slice into ½-inch-wide strips. Or cut the endives into 1-inch chunks and separate the overlapping leaves. Wash in a colander, drain well, and store, uncovered, for at least 1 hour in the fridge.
2 When nearly ready to serve, halve the avocado, remove the seed, and peel the skin. Cut into small cubes.
3 Place the chilled lettuce in a mixing bowl, stir in the avocado chunks, and mix thoroughly.
4 Slowly pour on the prepared salad dressing and stir thoroughly. Use no more than is needed to coat the lettuce and avocado well. Store in the fridge for at least 10 minutes before serving.

Variations
A At step 1, add ½ teaspoon ground allspice to the salad dressing.
B At step 4, add ½ teaspoon Tandoori masala powder or Madras curry powder to the salad dressing.
C Make a basic mayonnaise of oil, egg yolk, salt, and pepper (follow instructions for Avocado Mayonnaise 1, page 50) and add either lemon or lime juice, 1 teaspoon dry mustard, ½ teaspoon ground cumin, and ½ teaspoon ground coriander.

A mix of sliced, thoroughly ripe avocado and crisp lettuce or endive in a French dressing has always been one of the more satisfying salads available. The recipe here adds the refreshment of cucumbers; raw or cooked, they are more popular in the islands than among us. Moreover, they are picked large and ripe, then peeled and cored, so that only the broad white, outer ring is used. It makes the dish less watery, milder in flavor, and easier to digest.

1 Peel the cucumbers, cut them in half lengthwise, and core with a melon cutter or long, narrow knife, discarding the pulp and seeds. Slice the flesh moderately thin. Salt the slices in a bowl and refrigerate for at least 1 hour. Drain and dry with a cloth or paper towels.

2 Cut the avocados in half along the narrow side (see page 44) and remove the seed. Use a melon scoop to separate the flesh from the skin or peel the halves and cut the flesh into cubes. Combine with the cucumber slices.

3 Mix the oil with the lemon, garlic, pepper, and additional salt to taste. Stir together with the avocado and cucumber and store in the fridge for at least 1 hour. Serve cold on the lettuce leaves.

Sint Maarten

AVOCADO AND CUCUMBER SALAD

◆

2 large cucumbers
Salt
2 avocados
¼ cup vegetable oil or
  olive oil
1 lemon
1 small garlic clove,
  through the press
Freshly ground black pep-
  per to taste
Large lettuce leaves

SERVES 6

Puerto Rico

BEAN SALAD (MARINATED BEANS)

◆

1 cup of any of the following uncooked dried
beans: pigeon peas,
chick peas, small white
beans, black-eyed peas,
small red beans, or other
1 red onion, finely
chopped
3 tablespoons white vine-
gar or white wine vinegar
½ garlic clove, through
the press
10 tablespoons vegetable
or olive oil
1 canned tomatillo,
mashed, or 1 fresh toma-
tillo, boiled until tender
and mashed
Salt and freshly ground
black pepper to taste
Scotch bonnet or other
chili pepper, seeded and
forced through a garlic
press, to taste

SERVES 5

Southern Europeans have always cooked and marinated beans to serve cold in salads. Our mainland restaurant hors d'oeuvres cart usually displays a container of chick peas (garbanzos) or white beans. The following recipe uses various kinds of beans and is sharpened by adding tomatillos and chili pepper.

1 Soak the beans overnight (see page 232).
2 Drain the beans, then simmer in lightly salted water to cover until tender.
3 Meanwhile, mix the other ingredients to make the marinade.
4 Drain the beans and cool, covered, in the fridge.
5 Mix the marinade and beans in a bowl. Cover and leave for 1 or 2 days in the fridge before serving.
6 Serve as part of an hors d'oeuvre selection or as a salad with lettuce.

Note
Excess marinade can be used as part of the salad dressing.

This basic salad recipe can be varied in many ways, some of which we suggest. It is similar to salads in the north but with a richer combination of flavorants. The enticing changes should become popular on the mainland now that many of the extra ingredients are more available in our markets. Vegetable-lettuce salads are always usable, of course, as surroundings for more substantial cold preparations of seafood and meat. The dressing for the latter should be the same as that of the vegetable salad or compatible with it.

1 Cut off the base of the lettuce and discard damaged and limp leaves. Slice the rest into ½-inch ribbons. Wash and drain very well. Store, uncovered, in the fridge for at least 1 hour.

2 Peel the cucumber and slice in half lengthwise. Core with a melon cutter or long, narrow knife, discarding the pulp and seeds. Slice the white flesh very thin.

3 Chop the bell peppers as finely as possible. Mince the scallions and cilantro.

4 Place the cucumber, bell peppers, scallions, and cilantro in a bowl and stir in sufficient salad dressing to coat it well. Cover and store in the fridge for 1 hour.

5 When close to serving time peel and cut each tomato into 6 or 8 wedges.

6 Blend the remaining dressing with the lettuce and divide among the salad plates.

7 Stir the vegetable mixture and heap on the beds of lettuce. Distribute 3 or 4 tomato wedges as decoration.

Variation

You may choose to use other vegetables in the mix, including finely sliced raw celery, eggplant (cooked, cooled, and then marinated in the salad dressing), sliced fresh or parboiled mushrooms, canned artichoke hearts cut into quarters, sliced boiled green bananas or plantains (in moderation), small amounts of marinated beans, cubed or sliced boiled cassava, yam, dasheen, or malanga, boiled and cubed chayote, and more. The additional vegetables will increase the number of servings.

St. Thomas

BASIC ISLAND VEGETABLE SALAD

◆

1 head Boston or other fresh, crisp lettuce
1 large, ripe cucumber
2 medium green or red bell peppers
4 whole scallions, chopped
12 sprigs of cilantro or parsley, snipped (optional)
½ cup salad dressing (page 52)
2 ripe tomatoes

SERVES 4

Dominican Republic

Here is a rich and lusty salad that can be served as a separate luncheon course. It is a combination of our Basic Island Vegetable Salad and Bean Salad. Simply mix the two salads together.

BASIC ISLAND VEGETABLE SALAD WITH MARINATED BEANS

◆

SERVES 5

1   Make ½ recipe Basic Island Vegetable Salad (page 79).
2   Make ½ recipe Bean Salad (page 78).
3   Stir the salads together and serve. (For 10 servings make the full recipes and stir together.)

Barbados

BASIC ISLAND VEGETABLE SALAD WITH RICE

◆

SERVES 8

As this is a cold dish we recommend cooking long-grain or Basmati rice until just tender, dry, and fluffy. Avoid the Hispanic and Italian methods of overcooking until soft.

This salad consists of the Basic Island Vegetable Salad (page 79), with the addition of ½ cup dry rice cooked, drained, and cooled in the fridge. Mix the rice and the vegetable salad together and chill to blend the flavors. (The rice can also be cooled faster by putting it in a sieve and passing very cold running water through it.)

Variation

Try adding *queso blanco* to the above recipe before chilling. Because of the increase in quantity to the full recipe you may need ½ head more of lettuce and more salad dressing.

Queso blanco is a white cheese made in rectangular loaves like our sandwich cheeses. It is the Hispanic equivalent of cottage cheese but is molded and fine grained. We buy it in slabs by the pound, slice it, and then cut it into cubes. It has many uses with both hot and cold dishes. One can even fry it and use it as a garnish or as an added texture to sauces. With a barely noticeable flavor of its own, the taste of sauces and dressings is enhanced. The texture is most agreeable—crisp even when cold—adding variety to a dish.

Follow the instructions for Basic Island Vegetable Salad (page 79), adding the *queso blanco* at step 4.

Puerto Rico

BASIC ISLAND VEGETABLE SALAD WITH QUESO BLANCO

◆

6 to 8 ounces *queso blanco*, sliced ½ inch thick and cut into small cubes

SERVES 5

AVOCADO DIP, SALAD DRESSING, OR SAUCE

◆

1 ripe avocado, peeled,
  pitted, and cut into
  chunks
1 ripe medium tomato,
  peeled and chopped
½ cup finely chopped yel-
  low onion or scallion
Juice of 1 lemon or lime
3 cilantro sprigs, finely
  snipped
1 canned or cooked fresh
  tomatillo
Salt and freshly ground
  black pepper to taste
Chili sauce to taste

SERVES 6 AS A DIP

This dip is similar to guacamole, which is normally used only as a dip, served with chips or crackers. The following versatile recipe can be used as a dressing for all kinds of salads (except fruity ones) and as a cold sauce for meats and seafood. Considering that cold dressings and sauces are almost exclusively liquids with a high proportion of oil, this rich vegetable puree should be a welcome change and become very popular.

1   Put all ingredients except the salt, pepper, and chili sauce together in a bowl and blend thoroughly or process for 10 seconds.
2   Decant to a serving bowl and add the salt, pepper, and chili sauce. Serve with cassava bread, Indian breads, or crackers.

Variations
To make dip a dressing, stir into the mix a little white wine or water and vegetable oil in order to thin for a preferred consistency.

To serve as a cold sauce, thin with a little white wine and do one of the following: A)   Add a quarter cup finely chopped gherkins (sour pickles); B)   Mix in 2 tablespoons of an old-fashioned brand of tartar sauce (one sharper than Hellmann's); C)   Add 2 teaspoons best Madras curry powder; D)   Add 1 tablespoon French-style mustard.

The dip is made with the same ingredients as the appetizer (page 82). The only difference is that the mixture is processed for 8 seconds, refrigerated, and spread on crackers or toast rectangles as canapés. It may also be served in a bowl with crackers on the side.

Note

While making the mixture withhold part of the oil before processing so that the dip will not be too liquid. If it turns out too thick, the remaining oil can be mixed in with a spoon or a whisk. One tablespoon of tomato paste may be added to the dip later as well as a half dozen sour pickles (gherkins), finely chopped.

St. Martin

AVOCADO AND COD DIP

◆

SERVES 15 TO 18

This is a refreshing dip, when used with caution, for mussels, shrimps, conch, clams, oysters, squid, octopus, and fish, as well as plantain chips, chops, and chicken.

1 Put all ingredients except the chili pepper in the processor and reduce to a finely chopped consistency. Sauce should be quite liquid with pieces of the solids swimming in it. If too mushy add more vinegar.

2 Mix in the crushed Scotch bonnet pepper very cautiously, allowing the mix to stand for 15 minutes between tastes. The dip is best when it is quite hot.

Variation

Add 1 chopped, ripe medium tomato *or* 2 plum tomatoes.

TOMATILLO DIP

◆

½ pound husked and quartered tomatillos *or* 1 11-ounce can tomatillas
½ cup cilantro leaves, snipped
½ small red bell pepper, chopped
½ cup white vinegar
Salt to taste
Scotch bonnet pepper, forced through a garlic press, or yellow island chili sauce

MAKES 1½ TO 2 CUPS

* · * · * · * · * · *

· _Four_ ·

S O U P S

* · * · * · * · * · *

S oups are a much more important feature in the island diet than in our own. Meat of good quality has been scarce in the past, and expensive. Fish and other seafood are no longer cheap, either, and the best pieces end up on the tables of the tourists. Nevertheless, there is enough range-fed beef, goat, pork, and free-ranging, hard-working chicken to supply strongly flavored stocks when simmered long enough. As for fish, the smaller, delicate ones and the coarser groupers, and the like, are perfect in broths. There is also no lack of starchy roots and dried beans for nourishment and thickening. "Bush herbs" are like some of ours but they cannot be exactly duplicated, which is not a necessity in any event. Chili peppers are invariably added—sometimes too many for our taste but easily reduced in quantity to tolerable intensities. The soup pot is often left to simmer until every molecule of flavor and food value has been drained from the meats and bones. The results are some pretty fine soups that will be appreciated as much in our cold winters as they are in the islanders' hot ones.

Puerto Rico

BLACK BEAN SOUP

◆

1 cup dried black beans
1 or 2 meaty, strongly
  smoked ham hocks
4 scallions *or* 1 3-inch
  onion, coarsely chopped
2 garlic cloves, through
  the press
2 tablespoons Italian to-
  mato paste
5 whole allspice, crushed,
  or 1 teaspoon ground allspice
1 teaspoon crushed mace
Salt and freshly ground
  black pepper to taste
Chili pepper or chili sauce
  to taste
½ cup chopped cilantro
  leaves

SERVES 4

Beans are so easy to dry and, when in that state, can be stored for so long a time that they have been carried far and wide in the world, settling down here and there as basic foods. Black beans are as popular for soups in Hungary as they are in Spain or Puerto Rico and the recipes are not that different. Considering the many kinds of beans, why is the black bean such a favorite for soups? We assume that it is due to the peculiarly meaty flavor and texture of this particular bean, which enables it to combine especially well with all kinds of meats and vegetables with the most satisfying results.

These Creole versions of Black Bean Soup are fine demonstrations of how a classic, basic recipe can be altered almost at will to produce many equally tasty variations. It is of practical significance as well, adjusting the use of different ingredients to changes in the seasons when the supplies of one or another become temporarily scarce and must be replaced. The use of island flavorants distinguishes these fine soups from those of the rest of the world.

1 Soak the beans in water overnight.
2 Drain the beans and place them in a casserole along with the ham hocks and cover with water. Simmer for 2 to 3 hours or until both the hocks and the beans are tender.
3 Remove the hocks to a plate and cut the meat from the bone, discarding the bone, skin, and fat. Cut the meat into small pieces and return it to the casserole. Remove any loose skin, fat, or bone from the liquid with a slotted spoon. The amount of liquid should be 3 to 4 cups depending on how thick you'd like the soup to be. Add as much water as you'd like to thin the soup.
4 Add the scallions, garlic, tomato paste, allspice, mace, salt, pepper, and chili. Simmer for 30 minutes, then check the seasoning and adjust, if necessary.
5 Simmer for a few more minutes, then spread the chopped cilantro on top of the soup and serve promptly.

Variations
Pureed Black Bean Soup   At step 5 add the cilantro leaves and allow the soup to cool. Working in batches, pour into a blender or processor bowl and spin for at least 10 seconds to produce a rich, smooth puree. Adjust the texture by adding water if needed. Bring the soup to a boil again before serving.
Black Bean Soup with Yam, Malanga, or Dasheen Tubers   At step 4 add 4 cups small-diced yam, malanga, or dasheen. When the dice is

cooked, if the soup is too thick, add a little water as needed, bring to a boil, and serve. The yield will climb to 6 to 8 servings.

Black Bean Soup with Calabaza   Simmer 4 cups cubed calabaza in a separate pot until soft. Drain and add to the soup at step 5 along with the cilantro. There will be enough for 6 to 8 servings.

Black Bean Soup with Lime   Delete cilantro from the ingredients. Instead, at step 5, float very thin slices from 1 lime on the servings.

N o t e

This is a very filling soup and the portions with French bread and a salad easily make a meal, and a very ample one, for 4.

T h i s very filling soup tastes much better when made with African or Spanish peanuts rather than American, because they possess a more insistent flavor. American peanut butter in containers is somewhat sweetened. We prefer, therefore, to use Spanish peanuts, which are smaller and rounder, or the butter made from them, now being marketed in the States.

Tortola

PEANUT SOUP

◆

½ cup Spanish-type pea-
nut butter *or* 1 cup un-
salted, roasted Spanish or
African peanuts
2 cups concentrated, low-
salt chicken broth
1 small onion *or* 2 scallions, chopped
1 cup half-and-half
Salt
Yellow bonney pepper
sauce or equivalent to
taste

S E R V E S 4

1   Process the peanuts until reduced to a buttery consistency. Skip this stage if using the packaged peanut butter.
2   In the processor bowl combine the peanut butter with ½ cup of the chicken broth and the onion. Spin for 10 seconds while gradually adding the remaining broth.
3   Transfer the puree to a casserole and heat to a simmer. Cook until the mixture slowly thickens, about 5 minutes. Then add the half-and-half slowly, stirring constantly. Stop adding liquid when the soup is the consistency of heavy syrup. There may be milk left over or a little more may be needed.
4   Salt to taste. Then stir in the chili sauce, drop by drop, until the flavor suits you.
5   Serve in cups or in shallow soup bowls with plantain chips or crackers.

St. Kitts

CHICKEN PEANUT SOUP

◆

½ of a 4- to 5-pound stewing chicken
1 cup roasted Spanish
  peanuts *or* peanut butter
½ teaspoon ground all-
  spice
½ teaspoon freshly grated
  nutmeg
5 leaves of mace, crushed
  in a mortar and pestle
1 tablespoon freshly grated
  ginger *or* 1 teaspoon
  ground ginger
1 tablespoon Bell's Poultry
  Seasoning
3 scallions, chopped in
  lengths
½ pint coconut milk or
  heavy cream *or* evapo-
  rated milk flavored with
  coconut extract
Salt and freshly ground
  black pepper to taste
Chili pepper or chili sauce
  to taste
1 egg yolk (optional)
2 jiggers dark rum
Croutons

SERVES 6

This recipe is one of the more unusual and delicious among the innumer-able chicken soup recipes. To be at its best, however, you must have a large hen, formerly at liberty to choose its diet. A real stewing chicken, these days is, alas, a *rara avis* except in such places as villages on the islands. Without it, the stock will be far too weak and you will have to compensate by using double-strength, low-salt chicken broth from cans. We also find Bovril chicken concentrate quite palatable when blended with other ingredients. The peanuts should be the round Spanish or African type, which are, luck-ily, not too hard to find. There are also butters of these on the market.

1 Simmer the chicken for 1½ hours in 4 cups of water with the cover on. Add extra water as needed.

2 Strain and reserve the liquid. Set the chicken aside to cool, then remove the meat, discarding the bones and fat.

3 Put the chicken meat into the processor bowl along with all the peanuts, allspice, nutmeg, mace, ginger, poultry seasoning, and scallions. Add ½ cup of the stock.

4 Process for 20 seconds or until thoroughly pureed.

5 Pour the remaining chicken broth into a saucepan. Add the paste from the processor and stir thoroughly. Simmer, covered, for 30 minutes.

6 Add the coconut milk and stir thoroughly, along with the salt, black pepper, and chili pepper.

7 If the soup is too thin and syrupy, stir the egg yolk rapidly in a cup with some of the soup, then pour slowly into the pan, stirring actively until it is fully absorbed and the soup thickens.

8 Just before serving, add the rum and stir. Place the croutons on top of the soup.

Variations

Beef Peanut Soup   Use a standard-size can of corned beef instead of the chicken. Eliminate the first cooking instructions. Add 1 tablespoon Colman's Hot English Mustard Sauce to the ingredients in the processor bowl.

Spicy Meat Peanut Soup   Instead of the chicken, process ½ pound spicy sausage without the casings before adding the other ingredients to the processor bowl.

The East Indians were relatively late arrivals in the islands, having been encouraged to emigrate there to augment the farming population and to provide small merchant businesses. They settled mainly in Guyana and Trinidad where they now form a large part of the population. Elsewhere in the islands they mostly became keepers of small and large shops. Some of the vegetables and fruits from their homeland preceded them, brought in first by the English and others. So, curries and masalas have become fairly common in the islands. In Trinidad, in fact, these flavors form the dominant cuisine.

Lentils, which are grown in Europe, the eastern Mediterranean, and southern Asia, are a staple legume for Indian communities. With additional water they make a nourishing soup. The brown, yellow, or grayish lentil of our markets are European, but, lately, Near Eastern and Indian lentils, which are orange or red, have been imported and sold in chain groceries, taking their place among the numerous dried beans of the Hispanic diet.

The following recipe takes long cooking. Lentils soften more quickly than other beans but the silky texture of a soup is improved by lengthy simmering. When cooked in heavy iron or ceramic-coated pots, the beans can be left unattended for many hours. The lentils can be any color. Read instructions on the package. Some packagers prepare the beans so that they do not require soaking. Indian recipes call for strong chili flavor. We keep it mild, as the amount can be adjusted at table.

1   If there are instructions for soaking the lentils, follow them. Otherwise, it's up to you whether to soak the beans overnight in water. Drain before using.

2   In a soup pot heat the butter and very gently fry the lentils and onion for 10 minutes, stirring frequently. Add 2 quarts of water and all the other ingredients except the salt, pepper, and chili pepper. Stir well. Bring to a boil, reduce the heat, and set to simmer as slowly as possible for at least 3 hours—the longer the better. If the pot is tightly covered and the heat very low, there should be no need for constant supervision.

3   When finished cooking, fish out the bay leaves with a slotted spoon and discard. Add enough water to make the texture you prefer, then season with the salt, pepper, and chili pepper. Simmer another few minutes and serve

LENTIL SOUP

◆

½ pound lentils
2 tablespoons butter or corn oil
1 medium onion, finely sliced
1 large garlic clove, through the press
¼ teaspoon ground ginger *or* ¾ teaspoon freshly grated ginger
1 teaspoon dry Colman's mustard
½ teaspoon ground coriander
4 bay leaves
¼ teaspoon dried thyme leaves
Salt and freshly ground black pepper to taste
Chili pepper to taste

SERVES 4

very hot. (A plate of thin lemon slices on the side and an Indian flat bread usually accompanies this soup.)

Variation

Mustard and coriander may be replaced by 3 teaspoons Madras curry powder of an Indian packer—French or American won't do. As curries vary in flavor, add them little by little to taste.

◆ Callaloo ◆

The eastern and least-populated part of little Tobago, next door to much bigger Trinidad, is the most scenic region of either island. Charlotteville, a sprawling village where we spent two months, is gloriously situated in a great amphitheater looking out on Man-O-War Bay. Widely traveled seamen have told us that nothing in the South Seas surpasses it.

Tobagans Sharon Eastman and friend Walter worked out a joint dinner with us. They provided the soup and fish and we brought the salad and dessert. Her callaloo was our magnificent starter. When we asked about the recipe we were surprised to learn that she used a processor. Those labor-saving gadgets turn up in some unlikely places. The old way was to cut up the meat and greenery and beat it with a looped-wire swizzle stick, which is a lot more work.

Callaloo, spelled a dozen different ways, is a true staple of Caribbean cuisine. Every island, every family, has its own way of preparing it and the formulas change with the seasons. However, the essential ingredient, dasheen, or taro leaves, remains the same. The plant is also known as elephant ear because of the shape of the leaves. Mature, they produce a large tuber which is cooked and eaten like potatoes. The young leaves, harvested for greens, are mucilaginous and so delicate that they almost dissolve when boiled.

The leaves have a slightly sour flavor that is appetizing and difficult to duplicate. With some addition of a meaty component, herbs, and spices, it makes a nourishing meal or a tasty first course. Mr. Williams, on St. Lucia, insisted that it gave him heartburn as a luncheon dish. We suspect that he invented that put-down for the occasion, which was when he and his wife were our guests at a local restaurant. He was not about to have us order a dish that they normally ate at home. Anyone else living in the islands would have done the same.

Dasheen leaves in bunches have turned up in ethnic vegetable markets for some time, especially ones that are Asian or Caribbean. Substitutes are not quite right but will do. Spinach is usually recommended, but we prefer Swiss chard to which the addition of Chinese parsley (cilantro) brings us near to a perfect match. A number of published recipes specify crabmeat, fresh or canned. The only crab one encounters in the islands is the Gray Crab, a land creature, which is served stuffed (*farci*) sometimes with enough pepper seasoning to fuel a rocket. Also, these crabs are becoming rare, and are not cheap. If they find their way into the pot they do little for the soup. A better idea is to use the broth from boiling shrimp, crayfish, or lobsters. Canned, unsweetened coconut milk is still hard to get, but island pepper sauce is usually on the grocery shelves. Gumbo filé, for thickening and flavor, is also becoming easier to find.

Tobago

CALLALOO SOUP 1

◆

12 fresh dasheen leaves *or* 1 standard bunch Swiss chard or spinach

15 small fresh okras *or* 1 package frozen whole or cut okras

2 tablespoons vegetable oil

1 5-ounce jar dried beef (Beardsley or other) *or* 1 8-ounce can corned beef

½ pound Japanese crab-style fish product

2 cups coconut milk (optional)

2 garlic cloves, through the press

1 large yellow onion, sliced and chopped

1 tablespoon dried parsley *or* ¼ cup chopped fresh parsley

1 tablespoon Garammasala powder (*or* 1 teaspoon tamarind concentrate and 1 teaspoon ground all-spice)

Salt and freshly ground black pepper

Chili pepper *or* chili sauce to taste

SERVES 4 TO 6

Callaloo Soup should be a thin, deep green, and velvety puree, like a rich sauce, not a watery soup. The texture is very close to that of a bisque.

The soup always contains some dried beef or the equivalent of canned corned beef. Land crabmeat was once also a persistent ingredient. When these were plentiful and the children of a family had fun catching them, it was a good idea, even if the crab flavor didn't amount to much. They were there and they enriched the pot. Nowadays, with the crabs close to extinction, one can use Japanese crab-style fish product as sold in the chain stores. It is a more than satisfactory substitute.

1 Shred the dasheen leaves and place in a casserole along with the other ingredients.

2 Cover with about 1 quart of water. Simmer, covered, for 2 hours. Add more water if the soup becomes very thick.

3 Strain the liquid into a bowl and process the contents remaining in the sieve for 15 seconds.

4 Return the broth and the puree to the casserole, reheat, and adjust the seasoning, if necessary. Simmer to reduce if the soup is too thin. If too thick, add coconut milk or more water and simmer until hot.

5 Serve in soup plates with croutons, dumplings, or cooked and sliced starchy vegetables.

1 In a large casserole or soup pot, gently fry the salt pork. When enough fat has been rendered to coat the bottom of the pot, add the onion and green peppers. Simmer until the onion is golden.

2 Slice the greens to a manageable size and pack into the pot. Add the okra. Stir well in the fat and cook over low heat, covered, for 3 to 4 minutes.

3 Add 2 quarts of water to the pot and bring to a boil.

4 Add the garlic cloves and thyme. Simmer until the onion, peppers, and okra are tender.

5 Strain the liquid into another pot or bowl and set the vegetables aside to cool for a few minutes. Skim the excess fat off the liquid in the bowl.

6 Put the vegetables into the processor bowl and reduce to a smooth puree. It may be necessary to load and unload the processor bowl a few times. If the mixture becomes too thick for handling, stir in a bit of the soup liquid and spin for a moment.

7 Return the strained liquid to the original pot and combine with it the puree, the chicken broth, the coconut milk, and the grated nutmeg.

8 Simmer, uncovered, for at least 1 hour.

9 At the end of cooking and just before serving check the texture of the soup. It should be the consistency of a light puree or a bisque. If too watery, gradually stir in the Gumbo filé powder or cornstarch dissolved in a little cold water until the desired thickness is achieved. The filé should not cook long as it will become stringy. Add salt, pepper, and chili pepper.

Just before serving add the cilantro leaves. Serve promptly. The soup should be very hot and accompanied by cooked island root vegetables or calabaza, a salad, and plenty of bread, croutons, or crackers.

Note

Store excess soup in containers in the freezer. To take up less space reduce the liquid by simmering. Omit the filé if you intend to freeze the soup. When ready to reuse, reheat and restore the proper consistency by adding sufficient water.

St. Lucia

CALLALOO SOUP 2

◆

½ pound diced salt pork
  or mildly smoked bacon
1 yellow onion, peeled and
  sliced
3 large green bell peppers,
  stemmed, seeded, and
  coarsely cut
1 large bunch dasheen
  leaves *or* 1 bunch Swiss
  chard and ½ bunch of
  fresh spinach
1 package frozen cut okra
  or ½ pound fresh okra,
  trimmed and sliced
3 large garlic cloves,
  peeled
6 fresh Spanish thyme
  leaves *or* 1 teaspoon
  dried oregano leaves
2 cans concentrated, low-
  salt chicken broth
1½ cups fresh or canned
  coconut milk
1 teaspoon grated nutmeg
Gumbo filé powder or
  cornstarch, as needed for
  thickening
Salt and freshly ground
  black pepper to taste
Chili pepper to taste
6 sprigs cilantro, snipped

**SERVES 4 AS A MEAL
OR 8 AS A FIRST
COURSE**

Martinique

CALLALOO SOUP (LE CALALOU) 3

◆

1 large bunch dasheen leaves, cleaned and de-veined, *or* 1 bunch spinach

6 fresh okras, trimmed, *or* ½ package frozen okras

8 ounces cubed salt pork

2 green bananas *or* 1 large green plantain, skinned and cut into pieces

1 tablespoon Spanish thyme leaves *or* 1 tea-spoon dried oregano

5 scallions *or* 1 large yellow onion, chopped

6 cloves pounded in a mortar and pestle *or* ¾ teaspoon clove powder

2 tomatillos, husked and quartered (optional)

2 garlic cloves through the press

1 pound yam, malanga, or dasheen root, peeled and diced

Salt and freshly ground black pepper to taste

Scotch bonnet chili pepper or chili sauce to taste

SERVES 6

1 Combine all but the last three ingredients in a pot with 2 quarts of boiling water. Simmer for 1½ hours.

2 Meanwhile simmer the yam in lightly salted water until just tender. Drain the water and reserve the vegetables.

3 Allow the soup in the pot to cool sufficiently for processing. Strain the liquid stock into a bowl and set aside. Place the solids in the processor bowl and reduce to a fine puree by spinning for at least 10 seconds.

4 Return the puree to the pot or casserole and add enough reserved stock for the combination to form an unctuous, syrupy consistency. In a small pan, reduce the remaining stock until thickened and add to the soup.

5 Add the salt, pepper, and chili pepper. Simmer the soup for about 1 hour until ready to serve. Five minutes ahead of time, add the diced vegetables to the pot. Heat through, then serve.

No other squash can match the calabaza as a base for soup. The fine grain, the definite, clean flavor unique to itself, and the rich color, all add to the pleasures of cooking with this great vegetable. Fortunately, it is becoming a familiar sight in the vegetable sections of mainland stores. The following recipes are only a sampling of the innumerable combinations with other vegetables, with meats, with seafood, and with spices that are possible.

 The basic recipes here are meant as first courses; those with additions of meat, fish, or beans become meals in themselves.

1 Simmer the onion in the butter until golden.
2 Add the chicken broth, calabaza, plantain, cilantro, nutmeg, and ginger. Bring the mix to a boil, then simmer until the squash and plantain are thoroughly softened, about 20 to 30 minutes.
3 Strain the liquid into a bowl and transfer the solids to another. Work the latter into a smooth puree, adding soup liquid when necessary. If lumps remain, allow the mixture to cool a bit and run it through the processor for 8 seconds.
4 Return puree and liquid to the original pot and check for texture. Stir well and add a little water if needed. Add the salt, pepper, and chili pepper. Reheat to the boiling point and serve.

Variation
The soup is wonderful with some water added (because, when cooled, the puree thickens) and served ice-cold with a big dab of sour cream in the middle of each serving.

Cuba

CALABAZA SOUP 1

◆

1 onion, finely sliced and chopped
2 ounces butter (½ stick), margarine, or oil
2 cans concentrated, low-salt chicken broth
1 to 1½ pounds calabaza, peeled, seeded, and cut into chunks
1 plantain, ripened between green and yellow, cut into slices
2 cilantro sprigs, finely snipped
½ teaspoon freshly grated nutmeg
½ teaspoon ground ginger
Salt and freshly ground black pepper to taste
Chili pepper to taste

SERVES 4 TO 6

Guadeloupe

CALABAZA SOUP 2 (SOUPE DE GIRAUMON)

◆

1 to 1½ pounds calabaza, peeled and seeded

1 green bell pepper, chopped

1 garlic clove, through the press

3 or 4 scallions, sliced

6 Spanish thyme leaves *or* 1 teaspoon dried marjoram leaves (optional)

4 whole allspice, crushed, *or* 1 teaspoon ground allspice

1 teaspoon ground cumin

1 teaspoon dried fenugreek leaves (optional)

1 large, ripe tomato, peeled and chopped

1 cup coconut milk or evaporated milk flavored with coconut extract (optional)

Salt and freshly ground black pepper to taste

Chili pepper or chili sauce to taste

SERVES 6 TO 8

As the sun goes down in the islands, the air quickly cools, and it feels even cooler if one has spent the day on the beach. Beach sun and the resulting dehydration makes soup our first choice to start a dinner, and because we are hungry, it often seems to be the best part of a meal. In Gosier, we sat out in the restaurant's garden, umbrella open over the table in case of a shower, and tucked away this magical Calabaza Soup that came piping hot to the table.

1 Simmer all the ingredients except the salt, pepper, and chili pepper in 6 cups of water for 1 hour.

2 Strain the liquid into a bowl. Allow the solids in the sieve to cool.

3 Put the solids into the bowl of the processor or blender and spin for 10 seconds.

4 Return the puree to the pot along with the strained liquid. Simmer, uncovered, until the mixture is reduced to a rich, syrupy-soupy consistency.

5 Add the salt, pepper, and chili pepper while simmering. Serve very hot.

Variations

A Add ½ pound fresh okra *or* 1 standard-size package of frozen okra at step 4. Simmer for 30 minutes before serving. This variation yields 7 to 9 servings.

B Simmer 2 strongly smoked pork hocks *or* bones and meat from a smoked ham butt in sufficient water to cover for at least 2 hours or until tender.

Cut the meat free, discarding the skin, fat, and bones. Cut the meat into chunks. Return to the pot and reduce the liquid to 1 or 1½ cups.

Add to the Soupe de Giraumon at step 5 and serve very hot.

This variation yields 8 to 10 servings.

The recipe uses all the ingredients of Calabaza Soup 1, (page 95) except that 2 cups of water replace the chicken broth. You may also use recipe of Calabaza Soup 2 (see page 96).

The additional ingredient, using either basic recipe, is ½ to ¾ pound prepared salt cod (see page 129), cut into 1½-inch chunks.

Cook the salt cod with the other ingredients for one hour; adjust the salt, pepper, and chili pepper, if necessary, and serve very hot.

Variation   **Pureed Calabaza Soup with Salt Cod**

1 Follow the basic procedure above, but, when the ingredients have been thoroughly cooked at the simmer, strain the liquids from the pot into a separate bowl. Reserve.

2 Put the solids from the sieve into a processor bowl. Add ½ cup of the strained liquid. Process for 10 seconds or until the mixture is thoroughly pureed.

3 Combine the puree and the remaining strained liquid in the pot and bring to a boil. If the soup is too thin, reduce by simmering. If too thick, add a little water.

4 Before serving adjust the salt, pepper, and chili pepper, if necessary, and bring to a boil. Serve very hot.

CALABAZA SOUP WITH SALT COD

◆

SERVES 6 TO 8

Guadeloupe

CRAYFISH OR SHRIMP BISQUE

◆

6 whole crayfish or large
  shrimp
Scotch bonnet chili pepper
  to taste
1½ pints half-and-half
2 tablespoons sweet butter
1 heaping teaspoon corn-
  starch
Salt and freshly ground
  black pepper to taste

SERVES 4

In islands where the French held sway in the past or in those that are still joined to the European motherland, Creole cookery, closely related to that of our own Louisiana, is the dominant cuisine. We have found it by far the most sophisticated of the different styles. Crayfish Bisque is just one item in an extensive repertory to which the ingenuity of island cooks is constantly contributing new, original dishes. Employing French techniques, the results are qualitatively far superior to imitations of "continental cooking" or the mixing of imports, alien to the islands' cookery, with local produce.

Bisque is a French cooking term that, historically, has gone through a number of transformations, starting with almost any kind of fowl or seafood meat pounded and floating in broth, to the present finely sieved, creamy soups of vegetables or shellfish. Island cooks, using French techniques, have adjusted recipes to fit local ingredients and traditions. The flavors are as varied here as they are in France.

Shrimp *(crevette)* and crayfish *(écrevisse)* are virtually interchangeable in soups but the former are less common than the latter in the French islands. There the crayfish is called *z'habitant* or *crebiche* and is cultivated artificially in inland ponds that look like swimming pools. If you cannot find this elegant shellfish in your market, shrimp can be substituted.

With a processor sparing us lengthy pounding of the ingredients, this is a very easy soup to make. However, the flavor of crayfish and shrimp is very delicate and succumbs to injudicious, lengthy cooking, herbing, or spicing. We preserve that flavor by using very fresh ingredients, by cooking a minimum of time, and by serving immediately.

1 In a saucepan bring 1 cup of water to a boil. Drop into it the crayfish and simmer for 3 minutes.

2 Turn off the heat and fish out the crayfish from the liquid. Set aside. Retain the water. Remove the body meat and set the shells and claws aside.

3 Put the crayfish meat in the processor bowl along with the chili pepper and enough of the half-and-half to moisten well. Reduce to a very fine puree. Add the butter and the remaining half-and-half. Process for another 15 seconds. Pour into a bowl and set aside.

4 Put the crayfish shells in the processor bowl and spin until finely ground. Add this to the water in the pot. Boil gently for 10 minutes. Strain the liquid into a bowl and discard any solids. Rinse out the pot.

5 Combine the pot water with the crayfish mixture. Add the salt and pepper. Put it all into the rinsed pot.

6 In a cup, mix the cornstarch with cold water, making a smooth slurry by stirring with a teaspoon. Bring the contents of the pot just to a simmer. Check quickly for consistency. If too thin, stir in a little of the cornstarch slurry, stirring with a whisk and allowing a moment for the starch to take effect. When the soup attains a rich syrupy consistency, turn off the heat and serve as soon as possible.

The amount of chili is a matter of taste. Have a bottle of yellow island chili sauce or Tabasco at table so that everyone can help themselves.

Variation

At step 5, add whipping cream (about ¾ cup) for 5 to 6 servings. Less cornstarch thickening will be required.

According to the French definition, court bouillon is an herbed and spiced broth that contains a tart juice—lemon or lime—and is then used for simmering seafood, vegetables, or meat. The recipes here are for the broth itself, which changes formula according to what will be cooking in it. In the French islands court bouillon stands for both the broth and the featured ingredient, such as court bouillon *de poisson* or court bouillon *de lambi*. The Creole dish is also tart but more highly spiced than the French versions. Down-islanders still call court bouillons of seafood, *macadam*. Less watery, with additional ingredients and served from the pan, it becomes a *trempage*, a soakage.

1 Fry the onions in the oil. When they turn golden, add the cod and the scallions. Continue to fry over low heat, covered, until the cod is cooked, about 10 minutes.

2 Add the tomato, garlic, and lemon juice. Simmer a few minutes longer, covered. Add the chili pepper and stir. Serve in soup bowls with a cooked root starch or rice. The rice may be added to the court bouillon just before serving.

Note

In the north we can cook shelled mussels or oysters in the court bouillon.

COURT BOUILLON CREOLE

◆

2 onions, thinly sliced
¼ cup vegetable oil
2 pounds salt cod, soaked, boned, skinned, but not fully cooked (see page 129), or other white-fleshed fish, cut into 1- to 1½-inch chunks
4 scallions, cut into small pieces
1 to 1½ pounds ripe tomatoes, peeled, chopped, and well crushed
3 garlic cloves, through the press
Juice of 1 sharp lemon *or* 2 mild lemons
Scotch bonnet chili pepper, very finely chopped, or chili sauce to taste

SERVES 6

Sint Maarten

TOMATO FISH SOUP

◆

1½ pounds fresh fish
  heads, tails, and fins
3 ripe, medium tomatoes,
  peeled and quartered
1 bunch scallions, finely
  minced or processed
½ cup snipped cilantro
  leaves
Salt and freshly ground
  black pepper to taste
Chili pepper or chili sauce
  to taste

MAKES 6 TO 8 CUPS

1 Cover the fish with a quart of water (or more, if necessary) and simmer for 1½ hours.
2 Strain and discard the solids.
3 Return the liquid to the pot and add the other ingredients except the salt, pepper, and chili pepper. Simmer for at least 20 minutes.
4 Reduce by simmering or add enough water to make 6 to 8 cups of soup. Add the salt, pepper, and chili pepper and simmer for a few minutes longer.
5 Strain the soup and serve piping hot.

Variations

A Do not strain the vegetables from the soup at step 5, but serve as is after checking the seasoning carefully. This variation yields 7 to 9 servings.
B To the other ingredients add sliced celery and/or green or red bell pepper, finely sliced. At step 3, simmer for 30 to 35 minutes instead of 20 minutes.
C At step 5, add to the original recipe, or either of the above variations, the juice of ½ to 1 whole lime, to taste.
D At step 5, to variation B add 1 teaspoon Angostura Bitters.
E In the islands, when the heads, tails, and fins are strained from the stock, the solids are usually picked over to salvage any pieces of fish meat. This is done since some fish heads are rated as delicacies on their own. Do the same and simply incorporate the meat with the other ingredients and finish up as suggested.

St. Thomas

SEAFOOD SOUP

◆

THE STOCK
1½ to 2 pounds fish heads
  and tails and/or shellfish
  legs, claws, and shells

This is a recipe for a very concentrated, typically Creole seafood soup with enough solids in it to make a meal. It consists of two parts. One is the stock or marinade made from fishy discards along with vegetables and herbs. After a lengthy simmer the liquid is drained and used for the relatively short cooking required by the boneless fish or shellfish meat. There is nothing like it on our northern menus.

1 In a large pot with 2 quarts of water, simmer the stock ingredients, covered, for at least 1 hour.
2 Strain the liquid into a bowl or another pot and discard the solids.
3 Return the strained liquid to the same or another pot. Add the fish and yam.

4 Reduce the liquid over low heat, uncovered, to 3 to 3½ cups maximum, by which time the fish and yam or malanga will have cooked.

5 Add the salt, pepper, chili pepper, and lime juice (we like it with plenty of lime). Serve in deep soup bowls with an ample supply of crisp French bread.

Variations

A At step 3, add the yam but *not* the fish. Simmer for 20 minutes. Remove the starch with a slotted spoon and put in the processor bowl. Process for 4 seconds.

B At step 4, to the liquid remaining in the pot, add the fish meat and yam puree. Add ½ cup coconut milk and ½ teaspoon grated nutmeg. Simmer, uncovered, until liquid is reduced to 3 to 3½ cups maximum.

C At step 5, add the salt, black pepper, and chili pepper. *Do not add lime.* Serve in deep soup bowls with an ample supply of crisp French bread.

4 tablespoons achiote oil (page 110)

5 whole scallions, minced, *or* 2 yellow onions, chopped

2 garlic cloves, peeled

3 largish tomatoes, peeled and quartered

3 fresh tomatillos, husked and quartered, *or* 3 canned tomatillos

6 whole allspice, crushed, *or* 1 teaspoon ground allspice

1 teaspoon tamarind concentrate

THE FISH AND VEGETABLES

2 to 2½ pounds fish, skinned and boned, or shellfish, shelled and cut, depending on thickness, into 1½-inch cubes. (For this purpose any of the common fish or shellfish of northern or Caribbean waters are suitable.)

½ pound yam or malanga, peeled and cubed very small

Salt and freshly ground black pepper to taste

Chili pepper to taste

Lime juice to taste

SERVES 4 TO 6

Tortola

BULLFOOT SOUP

◆

4 pieces bullfoot *or* 1
  smoked pork hock
1½ pounds short ribs of
  beef or shin with bone
2 tablespoons coconut oil
  or corn oil
1 can concentrated beef
  broth (optional)
3 garlic cloves, peeled
1 medium purple onion,
  peeled and chopped
1 bunch dasheen leaves,
  escarole, mustard greens,
  or spinach.
2 medium carrots, sliced
6 frozen or fresh okras,
  trimmed and sliced (op-
  tional)
2 cilantro sprigs (optional)
6 largish red potatoes (optional)
Salt to taste
Yellow island chili sauce
  or other chili sauce to
  taste.

SERVES 4 AS A MEAL AND 8 AS A FIRST COURSE

We had our first Bullfoot Soup at the second-floor Butterfly Bar & Restaurant, Main Street, Roadtown, Tortola, British Virgin Islands—a big, square, plainly furnished room where honest "home-cooked" island meals are served, mostly to local business people and to shoppers in town from other parts of the island.

The name bullfoot suggests to the imagination a more powerful concoction than, say, calf's foot or pork hock soup, a dish rich in beef flavor, boldly spiced, and sufficient in itself to make a meal. It can be all of that, although the bullishness of the spicing is easy to control. It is essential to make a very strong-tasting a beef broth as the base. That was taken for granted in olden days everywhere. Now it has become almost unattainable at home because our American beef is so pampered that it proves far better for steaks and roasts than for soups and stews. Like the ruins of old sugar mills, bullfoot is an authentic product of the past, with the important difference that it is very much alive and well today in the islands. It is virtually identical to oxtail soup, except that most of the meat in bullfoot soup is supplied by other cuts.

Island cattle, the statuesque Brahmin, are not pampered, being all range fed, and tasty but tough. The tender beef comes south by air from the States. So the problem of making a good bullfoot soup is doing the best one can with the meat cuts available. That is why we recommend a smoked pork hock, or we brown our short ribs or shin meat. To approximate island results we must go to some more trouble.

1 Slice away as much meat from the bones as you can and cut into small cubes. In a soup pot quickly fry the meat in the oil until browned. Place bones in a separate pan and broil until blackened, about 15 minutes.

2 Pour 3 quarts water plus the broth into the soup pot with the browned meat. Add the blackened bones, garlic, and onion.

3 Simmer slowly, covered, for 4 hours on top of the stove or in the oven. The meat must be very tender. With a slotted ladle remove the bones, gristle, and fat. Discard. Skim off fat floating on the surface.

4 Meanwhile, in a separate pot cook the dasheen, carrots, okra, and cilantro in a minimum of water for 5 minutes. Cool, drain, and reduce to a puree in the processor. Add to the soup pot.

5 Peel the potatoes, cut into chunks, and add to the soup pot. (The potatoes should *not* be added if serving the soup as a first course.)

6 Simmer for 40 minutes. Add salt gradually. Add drops of chili sauce very gradually. Keep it mild. You can serve more chili sauce on the side for individual choice.

7 Serve with hot, crisp French bread or island breads (page 265).

Variation

Add soup-green mixes and other vegetables at step 4.

Note

Extra soup can be cooled, poured into containers, and frozen for later use.

This is a quick soup, light yet rich, satisfying but not one to spoil appetites.

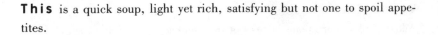

1 Combine the avocado, chives, half-and-half, and chicken broth in the processor bowl. Process for 10 seconds. Empty into an enameled soup pot and bring to a boil.

2 Mix the cornstarch with a teaspoon of cold water in a cup. Pour gradually, while stirring, into the simmering soup. Stop when a desirable syrupy consistency is achieved.

3 Stir in the nutmeg and lemon juice. Add the salt and pepper. Serve hot.

Note

Islanders use various nut and bean flours in place of cornstarch.

St. Barts

AVOCADO SOUP

◆

1 large, ripe avocado, pitted, peeled, and sliced
½ cup snipped chives
½ pint half-and-half
1 standard-size can low-salt chicken broth or the equivalent of fresh stock
1½ tablespoons cornstarch
½ teaspoon freshly grated nutmeg
Juice of ¼ lemon
Salt and freshly ground black pepper to taste

SERVES 4 TO 6 AS AN APPETIZER

COLD AVOCADO SOUP

◆

2 ripe avocados, pitted,
   peeled, and cut into
   chunks
1 cup low-salt chicken
   broth or stock
½ pint half-and-half
4 sprigs cilantro, snipped
Juice of ½ lemon
Salt and freshly ground
   black pepper to taste
Chili pepper or chili sauce
   to taste

SERVES 4

A very piquant and refreshing soup for hot weather lunches or dinners. Cold soups are delightful in summer yet mainlanders rarely serve them. They can be either light refreshers or main-course soups, containing a quantity of solids. Meant to be served very cold, they add variety to the rather limited choices of salads and meats that appeal to us during the dog days of summer. Creole cooks offer a number of these excellent dishes, and once one has become used to the soups, it is difficult not to return to them again and again.

1   Combine all the ingredients except the chili in a blender or processor bowl. Beat or process until a syrupy consistency is achieved.

2   Add the chili pepper carefully to taste. Stir thoroughly. Serve very cold.

Variation

Add 1/2 pint sour cream instead of the chicken broth to the recipe. Float rings of peeled, cored, and sliced cucumbers on the surface.

Note

The down-islanders usually make the chili very "hot."

Jamaica

PEPPERPOT SOUP

◆

1 to 1½ pounds lean stew-
   ing beef, cut into small
   cubes
½ pound corned beef,
   cubed
¼ pound salt pork or ba-
   con, cubed

The Jamaican version of pepperpot differs from the Barbados dish with the same name (page 202) because it is a soup and does not use casareep. Although most recipes call only for beef and/or pork, local recipes are a catchall, also using stewing chicken, goat, mutton, and any seafood that is handy. Seafood turns up when meat is scarce. The addition of small amounts of shrimp, frequently mentioned as an ingredient, does little for the flavor and serves only to increase the cost and volume of the dish.

1   Simmer the stewing beef and corned beef in sufficient water to cover for 1½ hours or until tender.

2 In a separate covered pot, with just sufficient water to cover, simmer the salt pork, callaloo, green pepper, scallions, garlic, cilantro, ginger, cumin, and yam for 30 minutes.

3 Allow the cooked vegetables to cool a bit, decant into a processor or blender bowl, and reduce to a puree.

4 Add the pureed vegetables and 1 quart water to the meat. Add the salt, pepper, and chili pepper, along with the okra and coconut milk, mixing well. Simmer for another 20 minutes, cover off. If the liquid is too thin, reduce over high heat or thicken with a small amount of cornstarch mixed with cold water stirred gradually into the soup. If too thick, add a little water. The end result should be a syrupy soup with intense flavor.

1 or 2 19-ounce cans cal-laloo *or* 2 bunches dasheen leaves *or* 1 bunch spinach, washed, cut, and coarsely chopped
1 large green bell pepper, chopped
1 bunch scallions, sliced
2 garlic cloves, through the press
½ cup chopped cilantro or parsley leaves *or* 2 table-spoons dried parsley leaves
1 teaspoon freshly grated ginger or ground ginger
1 teaspoon ground cumin
½ to 1 pound white yam, roughly cubed
Salt and freshly ground black pepper to taste
Scotch bonnet chili pepper or chili sauce to taste
½ pound okra, sliced
1 cup coconut milk (op-tional)
Cornstarch (optional)

SERVES 6 AS A MAIN COURSE OR 12 AS AN APPETIZER

Tobago

COLD PAPAYA SOUP

◆

1 ripe papaya, about 6
 inches long
Sugar to taste
Fresh lime juice to taste

SERVES 4

This is a soup in the style of a European fruit soup—one that requires no cooking, is served very cold, and is the most refreshing of all introductions to meals on hot summer days. Mainlanders are not accustomed to these light, sweet productions that are especially popular in eastern Europe where they are made with spring cherries. In the Caribbean they have even more reason for being, as there are so many fruits (many of which, being unavailable in the north, we do not mention here) to choose from.

The papayas on the southern Caribbean islands are huge. On Tobago we came across specimens fifteen to eighteen inches long, which supplied us with desserts for a whole week. The flesh is rich, reddish pink, and much sweeter than the fruit from Florida. Smaller, yellow papayas are now common in our markets. A six-incher is ample for four portions of soup. The fruit should be ripe but very firm.

1   Peel the papaya and cut in half. Spoon out the seeds, which look almost like caviar, and keep them in a small container in the fridge.
2   Cut the fruit into chunks and reduce to a liquid puree in the processor.
3   Add the sugar and lime juice. If the puree is too thick, stir in a little water. Be careful, because a very little can change the consistency of the puree.
4   Serve in fruit cups, with a dab of the reserved seeds in the center of each.

Variation

For a fruity custard, add milk instead of water to the puree. Adjust the flavor immediately after processing and add ½ teaspoon of a good vanilla extract. Pour into fruit cups and chill.

Five

HOT SAUCES

AND

INGREDIENTS

U ntil relatively recently there were not many prepared, bottled sauces on our grocery shelves. Worcestershire, A-1 Steak Sauce, and ketchup predominated. Tabasco Sauce, a Louisiana specialty, was the proper chili sauce for cold shellfish. Other sauces were mostly concoctions that made the way easier for would-be cooks who didn't know how to make sauces. We remember that it was a rare dinner party where a roast was served with a sauce resembling anything more than a bowl of slightly flavored water (except for lamb with the inevitable and ghastly "mint jelly").

In the islands, on the other hand, there have always been many sauces—both homemade and bottled—for sale. The two most common kinds have been mixes of herbs and spices in liquid form for meat and seafood dishes, and those sauces made up of chili peppers alone or with herbs, which are always very much "hotter" than the others.

On Tobago, Pat Turpin of Charlotteville makes bonnet pepper wine, the local name of which is Weary-Wearies, translated as Wary-Wary; and, indeed, Wary-Wary it is. To make it, break off the stems of bonnet chili peppers, being careful not to bruise the fruit. Half fill an empty wine bottle with them. Fill to the top with sherry or dry vermouth. Cork and let stand for 3 weeks. Add to sauces or serve at table. As the liquid fire is consumed replace with more wine.

To cook up and preserve sauce mixtures was a logical development on these islands where spicy flavorings are appreciated but the ingredients available only "in season." When the right materials came to market, down-island cooks always worked up batches of sauce and stored them for future use. Naturally, with time and the growth of towns, it became a business, supplying those who no longer had the means of making the sauces. Every island has its specialties, and Jamaica, Trinidad, and Barbados are the islands that now pack and export sauces in the greatest numbers. On local grocery shelves there are many more.

For example, we have a Trinidadian store in New York City, whose owner, an enthusiastic island cook, frequently introduces us to products from small island packers that are excellent additives to down-island cookery. His friends bring up packaged herbs and seeds. Through him we have learned about a number of natural culinary products that are difficult for mainlanders ever to discover while visiting. Whenever these items are available, we stock up with everything needed to carry us for the rest of the year.

ACHIOTE OR ANNATTO OIL

◆

1 cup vegetable oil
3 ounces achiote seed

MAKES 1 CUP

Achiote oil has made a major contribution to our own daily cooking. We do not hesitate to use it in many standard American household recipes. You will create a sensation by frying the breakfast eggs in the oil, for the coloring is spectacular and also enhances the flavor.

Just be cautious when handling—the color is virtually indelible when spilled on cloth. So take special precautions when you use good napkins or tablecloths. On second thought, it would be safer to substitute place mats and paper napkins.

1 Heat the oil in a saucepan over medium flame and stir in the seed. Immediately turn the heat down to low.

2 In less than 3 minutes the oil will turn a deep red. Remove instantly from the heat and allow to cool at room temperature. Strain into a screw-top jar. If cooked too long the color will fade.

3 The oil can be stored without refrigeration for at least 2 months and in the fridge indefinitely. When made with lard instead of oil, as is frequently done down-island, refrigeration is recommended.

Note

Usually in island Creole cooking, when saffron is listed as the coloring matter, achiote or turmeric is actually used. Though achiote oil is deep red, it colors bright yellow.

The powder is commonly sold in both chain and Hispanic groceries. The commercial product is usually loaded with salt and MSG, as are most of the other packaged sauce bases, especially sofrito and recaito. They are short-cuts to making sauces of any kind and are as inescapable as Maggi used to be. Adobo is simply sprinkled on meats, fish, vegetables, soup, rice, beans, or into sauces. The homemade powder below is less enticing than the store-bought product, but it allows natural flavors to survive the treatment.

Mix the ingredients thoroughly and store in a screw-top jar.

Puerto Rico

ADOBO

◆

1 tablespoon garlic powder
2 tablespoons ground
  cumin
2 tablespoons freshly
  ground black pepper
1 tablespoon dried parsley
  leaves, crushed
1 teaspoon dried sage
1 teaspoon dried thyme
  leaves, crushed
Salt and freshly ground
  black pepper to taste

MAKES ¼ CUP

French Islands

COLOMBO

◆

¼ cup finely ground cassava flour or plantain flour *or* 2 tablespoons cornstarch

1 teaspoon ground coriander

1 tablespoon ground turmeric

½ teaspoon ground anise

1 teaspoon garlic powder

1 teaspoon black mustard or dry English mustard

1 teaspoon ground clove

1 teaspoon amchur powder

¼ teaspoon salt

¼ teaspoon freshly ground black pepper

MAKES ½ CUP

Colombo is the standard curry powder mix of the French islands. It has as much resemblance to real East Indian curries as do the curries of France itself—namely, not much at all. The use of cassava meal as the filler or thickener material indicates that it was a very early introduction to island cookery. That too is not ideal, resulting in a sludge that never goes into solution.

The powder is available, packaged, in island groceries, notably in Guadeloupe. But the better local cooks use packaged Indian curry powders or combine their own formulas consisting of Indian herbs and spices along with local "bush." The resultant Colombo is mixed with oil and pan liquids to produce results that are rather different from traditional Indian cooking, totally individual and always a treat to the senses. Colombos are usually used in sauces for meats, beans, and rice.

Mix the ingredients thoroughly and store in a screw-top jar.

Note

Powdered, liquid, or fresh chili pepper is always added. But it is advisable to do this during the cooking, using care when adding.

We have always been tempted to consider roasted flour our own invention because so few cooks and professional chefs seem to know about it or use it. Yet it is no secret to French cuisine and is both a great convenience and a superior way to color flour for brown sauces. We make a supply that lasts us for six months at a time so that it is always handy to make sauces for meat and poultry.

Roasting avoids the mess of cooking flour in oil with its accompanying risk of producing either a pasty sauce or a bitter one. Making the brown flour requires a little experimenting and some practice. So, at the start, make small quantities until you have the right color firmly fixed in your memory. One can always keep a sample around so that new batches can be matched correctly. The timing of the operation might possibly be made exact for massive quantities under strictly controlled conditions but not for the small amounts used in a family kitchen. The process, on the other hand, is so easy that you will have no trouble mastering it.

1 Preheat oven to 250 degrees. Sift the flour into a thick iron or aluminum skillet and spread it evenly. Place in the oven.

2 Every 30 minutes remove the pan from the oven and sift the flour, which tends to cake a bit in the early stages of roasting. Discard any hard bits in the sieve.

3 Continue as above, for at least 1½ hours, until the flour starts to turn yellowish in the middle and brown along the edges. Raise the temperature to 350 degrees. Stir the flour thoroughly, scraping the bottom of the pan carefully and mixing the darker flour with the lighter. Continue to repeat this process at intervals of 10 minutes until the whole mass is light cocoa brown.

4 The flour is ready when ½ teaspoon mixed with a little cold water is absorbed, forming a slurry, and has turned from grayish brown color to the color of brown sauce. Do not expect the very dark color chefs achieve by using roasted bones to produce a stock. Keep a sharp watch on the whole process—if you fail to take charge at the right time your flour will be somewhat burned, resulting in very bitter sauces. When correctly done, your brown sauces will be superior.

5 When finished, simply store in a screw-top jar and use as needed. It keeps forever. Two pounds will last out the needs of a small family for months. The recipe can be doubled without problems.

6 Use the brown flour with liquids as well as pan oils. It is most commonly mixed with pan fats and thinned with water or wine. Being that it is properly cooked in the first place, the roasted flour will absorb less liquid than when browned in oil.

ROASTED FLOUR

◆

2 pounds unbleached all-purpose flour

PANADE SAUCE

◆

PANADE BASE
FORMULA 1

½ cup stale white bread
  crumbs
1 cup milk

In the French islands, as in France itself, bread is still the staff of life. The beautiful, long baguettes are seen everywhere being carried home daily without bagging by children and adults alike—afoot, on bicycles, or in cars. With so much bread there are always leftovers that dry in a basket until put to use feeding animals and birds or making croutons and bread crumbs.

Much more commonly than cookbooks would suggest, the bread is also substituted for flour to make the thickened sauce that binds all kinds of sausages, forcemeats, and pâtés, as well as for gratins, especially cheese sauces. Both dried and fresh bread may be used. In fact, trimmed American white bread is excellent for the purpose, so long as it has not been sweetened too much. Our recipes below describe the procedure for making these sauces. It is very simple with modern equipment. The time required is very short and the results are especially silky and suave.

1 Mix the bread and milk together in a saucepan and bring just to a boil. This should produce a thin sauce that can be thickened by continued boiling or simmering until it becomes a dough that can be shaped. For our recipes, this additional preliminary cooking (for making croquettes, quenelles, and meat loafs, see Formula 2) is unnecessary.

2 To this sauce, add the other ingredients of your recipe, be they vegetables, seafood, meats, or herbs and spices. Control the texture by thickening through heating or thinning by adding small quantities of oil, cream, water, or wine. This formula is a traditional panade. It can also be enriched and thickened by adding egg yolk mixed with a little water and stirring vigorously into hot, not boiling, sauce. It can then be smoothed by bringing *just* to the boil for a very short time while stirring.

We wish to emphasize the versatility of this and the following panade base. When the panade is thickened to the consistency of white sauce, the solid meat, seafood, or vegetables are incorporated and served in individual ramekins or in a casserole, baked in the oven, and then lightly browned under the broiler. When made into a nearly liquid dough, the panade is mixed with ground or pureed ingredients.

Some may find the panades a much easier way to make smooth and suave white sauces than working with roux made of flour.

Whereas Formula 1 is for sauces that start with the panade and to which other ingredients are added, Formula 2 is used as an extender and thickener for foods that are being fried or stewed with butter or oil, and vegetables, herbs and spices. It is like adding cornstarch or flour to a sauce in the later stages to give it body.

1 Process or blend the bread and liquid together for 10 seconds, forming a puree that is very smooth.
2 Add the pureed mixture by the tablespoon to pan gravies or stewing liquids, stirring vigorously while simmering. Control the texture of the sauce by adding more of the puree or a little more water, wine, or cream.

The yield of this sauce is rather large for smaller family courses; it can easily be halved or quartered. These sauces, like many of the other white sauces, can be extended both by using more of the starchy thickening ingredient and/or egg yolks. There is allowance for considerable flexibility in manipulating both texture and flavor.

1 Melt the butter gently in a saucepan. Add the cheese, half-and-half, and egg yolk, stirring well.
2 When the mix begins to steam, add the parsley and pepper.
3 Start adding the prepared panade a little at a time, stirring vigorously. As the panade content increases, the sauce will thicken.
4 The sauce is finished when the texture is right for the purpose to which it will be put—lighter for straight sauce use, heavier if the panade is to be mixed with other ingredients to make appetizers or entrées. Increase the volume by adding more half-and-half or some stock along with more panade.

PANADE BASE
FORMULA 2

1 cup compacted, trimmed, fresh white bread
½ cup water, milk, or beef or seafood stock

CHEESE PANADE SAUCE

◆

1 recipe Panade Base Formula 1 (above)
¼ stick butter or margarine
1 cup Mouli-grated cheese, such as Gruyère, Monsegur, sharp American, Sardo, Romano, or Pepato
1 cup half-and-half
1 egg yolk, at room temperature
1½ teaspoons parsley flakes, basil, or other herb leaves
Freshly ground black pepper to taste

MAKES 2 TO 2½ CUPS

LEMON OR LIME PANADE SAUCE

◆

1 recipe Panade Base Formula 1 (page 114)
½ stick butter or margarine
1 cup half-and-half
1 egg yolk
Juice of 1 lemon or lime
1½ teaspoons parsley *or* 1 teaspoon snipped cilantro leaves
Freshly ground black pepper to taste
Chili pepper to taste

MAKES 2 TO 2½ CUPS

This sauce is compatible with boiled or stewed poultry, veal, seafood, and vegetables.

1 Melt the butter in a saucepan.
2 Add the half-and-half, egg yolk, and lemon or lime juice, stirring well. Add the parsley, pepper, and chili pepper.
3 Stir in the prepared panade, a little at a time, until the sauce thickens as desired.

ROASTED GROUND PEANUTS

◆

1 pound raw African or Spanish peanuts

1 Preheat the oven to 300 degrees.
2 Process the whole batch in 3 or 4 lots. Do not overload the processor bowl each time. Run the processor for at least 10 seconds for each lot. If the grains mount the sides of the bowl, stop the motor and rock and bump the bowl gently to shake them down.
3 Spread the ground peanuts on a large baking sheet and roast for 30 minutes.
4 Spoon the grains around, breaking up any loose lumps.
5 Resume roasting until the nuts are medium brown and have lost their "raw" odor. When tasted, they should be nutty, crisp, and richly flavored.
6 Cool thoroughly and store in a screw-top jar until needed.

All through the Caribbean islands, the local cooks have used a small quantity of burnt sugar syrup to darken and sharpen the flavor of their meats, fish stews, and sauces, and to give a rich color to their cakes, particularly the Black Cake (page 284) of Trinidad and Tobago. Driving down a local road, the scent of browning sugar drifts through the flowering shrubbery surrounding a brightly painted house, and one knows that a fresh supply of burnt sugar syrup is being made in the kitchen. Bottled syrup can also be bought in local island stores. We have also found that Stateside Caribbean stores and some supermarkets now carry the bottled syrup.

1 Place the sugar and ¼ cup of the water in a heavy-bottomed stainless steel saucepan and mix together with a fork. Boil the remaining water.

2 Put the saucepan over medium heat; refrain from stirring until the sugar starts to liquefy. Tip the pan from side to side, to mix the liquid and the still unmelted sugar. Break up sugar lumps with the fork.

3 When the sugar has completely melted and is turning brown, lower the heat. Keep cooking the syrup until it smokes and turns black and solid. Take the pan off the heat, and, bit by bit, pour in the boiling water. For safety, pour the water into the molten sugar through a metal sieve anchored above the pan and stand back so you will not get splattered with hot water.

4 Return the pan to the heat and stir and scrape with a fork or metal tablespoon as you bring the liquid to a boil. Cook until the black sugar has been dissolved—or almost completely dissolved, as some will stick to the pan. The consistency should be that of a light syrup—adjust with more water to thin or reduce by boiling.

5 Pour the liquid into a heatproof bowl, through a fine-mesh, stainless steel sieve. When cool, check the consistency again, adding a little water if necessary. Pour into a screw-top jar and place in the fridge. This keeps for months.

BURNT SUGAR SYRUP

◆

1 cup white granulated sugar or island-style light-brown *granulated* sugar
1 cup water

MAKES 2 CUPS

Puerto Rico

RECAITO

◆

2 medium onions, cut into
  chunks
1 tablespoon vegetable oil
1½ cups snipped fresh
  cilantro leaves
1 teaspoon ground corian-
  der
2 tablespoons finely
  snipped Spanish thyme
2 tablespoons white
  vinegar
1 garlic clove, through the
  press
½ cup water
1 tablespoon cornstarch,
  as needed
Salt and freshly ground
  black pepper to taste
Chili sauce to taste

MAKES 1 CUP

Recaito is similar to Green Sauce (page 55), but it is based on the coriander (cilantro) leaves the islanders call "narrow-leaf coriander," which is similar to or the same as the narrow-leaf thyme of the islands. The latter is occasionally sent fresh in bunches to mainland stores. It has an individual, rather bitter flavor. At home, when the narrow-leaf thyme is unavailable we use ground coriander and some Spanish thyme.

The packaged sauce contains MSG in quantity plus preservatives and fillers. Its popularity seems only to be enhanced by these ingredients, yet the homemade sauce is far superior every time. Use it like Green Sauce.

1 Combine all the ingredients but the cornstarch, salt, pepper, and chili sauce in a processor bowl. Stir with a spoon. Process for at least 10 seconds.

2 Transfer to a saucepan and heat to the boiling point, then reduce to a simmer. Stir to prevent from sticking to the bottom.

3 The final consistency should be like ketchup. Stir the cornstarch with a little cold water in a cup. Mix spoonful by spoonful into the sauce, stirring constantly until the texture has thickened. Then cease adding the cornstarch. Simmer, stirring, for 5 minutes.

4 Set aside and add the salt, pepper, and chili sauce, stirring well.

5 Pour into a screw-top jar and store in the fridge until used.

STOCKS

◆

For the purpose of making many sauces very quickly in kitchens serving a large number of dishes, the French (or possibly the Italians) learned to make a separate stock of vegetables, beef, or seafood. These basics were slowly simmered in water for a very long time and then reduced to a gelatinous consistency that could also be used for glazing—a very thin, shiny, intensely flavored coating for foods. When traveling long distances to cook for banquets one famous French chef used to take along a quantity of solidified stock, ready to be cut and dissolved in numerous sauces, which lasted the entire journey.

Such stocks have become rare these days as methods have changed, although recipes still call for them. They are not usually made in Caribbean cooking. Instead, strong flavors for sauces are produced in the pot or pan during the cooking process and augmented by a wider range of spices and herbs than are usual in European cookery. Nevertheless, considering that the island chicken usually ranges for a living and acquires a richer-flavored meat than ours, canned, low-salt chicken broth or stock is a useful additive to some sauces. So is Bovril Beef Extract for some meat sauces. If you have time to cook up some discarded parts of fish (heads, tails, and fins) by all means do so. It makes a wonderful base for seafood soups.

Divide large batches into small containers and keep on hand in the freezer.

Sofrito is another immensely popular prepared sauce base, principally different from Recaito because it contains tomato paste. Again in the commercial product MSG is the primary flavorant, a convenient shortcut to appetizing sauces that are all dominated by its special effect on the ingredients. In our home MSG is rarely used, and the results, though less spectacular, are more wholesome. Sofrito is recommended for beans, yellow rice, soups, and stews, and it can also be used as a base for barbecue sauce.

Thoroughly combine all the ingredients together in a bowl.

Puerto Rico

SOFRITO

◆

2 tablespoons tomato paste
2 medium green bell peppers, cut into chunks
2 tablespoons vegetable oil
2 medium yellow onions, cut into chunks
1 teaspoon garlic powder
2 tablespoons ground coriander
Cornstarch, as needed
Salt and freshly ground black pepper to taste
Chili sauce to taste

MAKES 1 CUP

Trinidad and Tobago

BROWN SAUCE TRINIDADIAN

◆

½ cup chopped fresh
Spanish thyme leaves *or*
1 tablespoon dried oreg-
ano leaves
4 whole scallions, leaves
cut into 1-inch lengths
1 tablespoon ground
cumin
1 tablespoon ground cori-
ander
1 teaspoon tamarind con-
centrate *or* 1 tablespoon
amchur powder (see page
33)
1 tablespoon soy sauce
½ teaspoon freshly grated
nutmeg
1 large garlic clove,
through the press
1 celery stalk, cut into
1-inch pieces
1 teaspoon Burnt Sugar
Syrup (page 117)
¼ teaspoon salt

Similar to other prepared sauces based on local recipes, this is one that is best used as an additive to pan gravies or thinned and reinforced with other flavorsome ingredients. Note that the coloring matter is the Burnt Sugar Syrup, a staple in the islands and to be found here at island and Hispanic food shops.

Brown sauces enhance meat dishes. They are prepared in the pan using the fat, herbs, and spices involved in the early cooking of the meat. The meat is then divided into pieces or portions and allowed to simmer in the sauce and, eventually, to be served in it. Or the sauce is made when the meat is nearly ready for serving and then poured off into a sauce boat and served separately.

Our sauce should be stirred into the pan gravy and diluted with water and wine. The meat can be temporarily removed for this process or pushed to the side of the pan. Stir well and reduce, but add more liquid if the sauce becomes too thick.

The sauce can also be brushed or spooned onto a roast before or early in the beginning of cooking. As the liquid in the sauce evaporates it will cake on the surface. This is normal and enhances the flavor of the meat. The rest of the sauce can be liquid and made in the pan as above. The sauce can be stored for a considerable length of time in the freezer.

Process all the ingredients for a minimum of 10 seconds. This should make a thick syrup.

2 Pour into a saucepan and simmer for 30 minutes, being careful to prevent the sauce from becoming too thick. Add a little water as needed and stir well.

3 Store in a screw-top jar in the fridge. The sauce can also be frozen.

Note

The sauce may be made without the burnt sugar syrup, but is less authentic.

½ teaspoon freshly ground black pepper

¼ Scotch bonnet chili pepper or other chili pepper, seeded and forced through a garlic press

MAKES 1 TO 1½ CUPS

1 Put all the ingredients except the salt and chili pepper into a blender or processor bowl and reduce the mix to a textured puree, not a smooth puree.

2 Transfer to a saucepan and simmer, covered, for 30 minutes, stirring a few times.

3 Add the salt and chili. Simmer another 5 minutes. If the sauce is too thick add a bit of water.

4 Serve as a cold sauce for seafood, beef, and chicken in salads.

TOMATILLO SAUCE

◆

½ pound raw tomatillos, husked and simmered for 30 minutes, *or* 1 11-ounce can tomatillos

2 large garlic cloves, through the press

½ teaspoon ground all-spice

½ cup snipped fresh cilantro

1 medium white or yellow onion, cut into chunks

2 tablespoons vegetable oil

Salt to taste

Fresh chili pepper to taste

MAKES 1½ CUPS

VELOUTÉ SAUCE OR BÉCHAMEL SAUCE

◆

2 tablespoons butter, margarine, or vegetable oil
3 tablespoons all-purpose flour
2 cups water or chicken, veal, or seafood stock

MAKES 2 CUPS

The confusion of these two names has occurred because traditionally velouté was made only with chicken stock or boiled milk, while béchamel, which is now called cream sauce or sauce supreme, was made with double cream. On the mainland we call simpler sauces velouté, while in the islands they become béchamel, usually made simply with water or a chicken or seafood broth. The enrichment is lemon or lime, "bush," pepper, and chili. The more complex white sauces are rarely employed.

1   In a saucepan melt the butter. Stir in the flour with a wooden spoon and heat until it froths without turning color.
2   Promptly stir in the liquid and whip until it comes to a boil. Continue to whip for 1 minute.
3   Add flavorants and adjust the texture by reducing the liquid by simmering or by liquefying it through adding stock or water while stirring.

Note

The most common additional enrichment and thickener is egg yolk. Mix with a few drops of water and stir rapidly into the sauce.

· Six ·

SEAFOOD

here is no question that seafood dishes are the outstanding achievements of Caribbean cookery. The working settlers and later immigrants to the islands were very dependent on the products of the surrounding waters. Domestic animals had to be imported and did not flourish in the tropical heat and humidity. Those that did survive were found in the ovens or pots of the well-to-do, leaving only the poorest cuts for the rest of the population. But as long as the numbers of people were small, there was plenty of fish and other seafood, augmented by the crayfish of the streams and the land crabs of low-lying areas close to the sea. There are always families of fisherpeople, even to this day, bringing their catches to open-air stalls on the road near the shore in every coastal village. There you can still get the best seafood if you arrive early enough in the morning—before buyers from local restaurants and the big hotels snap up all the goodies.

Caribbean seafood cuisine is, in the main, a combination of Spanish, French, African, and Indian influences. In the big hotels and international restaurants you will find some good grilled and broiled seafood along with the stuffed fish and "Thermidors" that are standard fare in the States. There is some fresh fish, but to meet the tourist demand most places fly in frozen fish from the States and even Europe, where the supply is more dependable.

In the local Creole restaurants you will find preparations that are very different—stews, main-course soups, gratins, fritters, and *beignets*, along with grilled dishes, all of them with tart and spicy flavorings that are totally foreign to mainland experience and derived from the habit of cooking seafood almost daily. The recipes are by no means complicated, but they are, nonetheless, original and far more piquant than our own.

◆ Fish and Shellfish ◆

hough there are many excellent food fishes that inhabit the shallow waters and shoals of Caribbean islands, they are not as plentiful as the great schools of the north. Seafood supplies for greatly increased populations and waves of tourists are inadequate except in winter when some of the temperate-zone fishes migrate south. Formerly huge quantities of salt cod were imported from Nova Scotia and Newfoundland (see page 128) but that is somewhat reduced today. Replacing them on the tables of "better" hotels are imports from around the world.

Fish in Caribbean waters, as elsewhere, go by local names, which, with all those islands and dialects, can be an inextricable tangle. There is also the habit in every language of grouping fish by types, apparent or real, as in English we have groupers, sea breams, mackerels, snappers, etc., and then attaching nicknames to some in the bargain, just like the people along our own coasts.

For the cook there are a few basic, recognizable categories: bony fish to be filleted at any cost; fatty, gray-fleshed fish; and the coarse or fine white-fleshed fish. The last are the most versatile and usually the most desirable. A little experience teaches us to recognize the basic types and assess their potential for cookery. Comparable fish to be substituted in the north can be recognized by comparison with the local fish we list below.

It is important, especially in the tropics, to ensure the freshness of the fish you intend to cook. On the tables of the fishermen or -women set up at the little ports there is no protection from the sun and the natural slime on any fish rapidly becomes odorous. That, however, does not mean that the meat is becoming mushy or is risky. Down-islanders simply dissolve the slime in lime juice by rubbing and marinating for 30 minutes before cooking.

There is a much better method, which we learned in Italy, to test for real freshness than simply by checking surface odor. Lift up the fish's head and open the gill wide and smell. That will give you an unmistakable and perfectly reliable test of freshness or incipient spoilage.

Barracuda   Still not a food fish in the north but popular in the islands.

Bream, sea   There are a number of these with local names that are difficult to disentangle from each other. They are rather short, broad fish with projecting jaws. *Capitaine blanc* and *Capitaine rouge*, descriptive names from the French islands, are very similar in appearance.

Burgaux   Large sea snails, green in color. Common along the shores of the islands. They are always served au Nage (see page 145). In the States mussels may be substituted using the same sauce.

Ceviche   Creviche. Escabeche. See page 69.

Chadrons   Sea urchins.

Codfish, fresh   Not available in the islands.

Codfish, salt   A staple import from the north.

Crayfish Ecrevisse Z'habitants Ouassous   Crayfish are fresh-water shellfish related to lobster but with much smaller bodies and very long, inedible legs and claws. Wild, they inhabit streams and ponds and they are now being cultivated in artificial ponds in Martinique. The flesh is sweeter than shrimp. "*Z'habitants*" is Martinique's name for them, a joking suggestion that crayfish are the original people of the island. They are long-bodied and narrow. The *ouassous* of Guadeloupe are shorter and thicker but the appendages are just as long. These are the best of the breed—unforgettable. Basic cooking is a simple matter of boiling, steaming, or grilling for a few minutes.

Crayfish can be found in some unpolluted waters in the States, and farm-raised varieties are available in some gourmet markets. If one cannot find a source there is no other recourse except lobster, sliced or cut into chunks. Shrimp won't do.

Dolphin fish   Not to be confused with the mammals: Mediterranean dolphin or Caribbean porpoise. A medium-size fish, excellent for grilling, white fleshed, and very popular with visitors to the islands.

Flying fish   Not too common. Very firm, white fish and much esteemed locally.

Groupers   Bottom fish sometimes of great size, ranging from an extremely coarse-grained meat and good only for chowders to a relatively fine-grained meat. Names change from island to island. *Vieille Maconde* and *Vieille Rouge* and *Croissant* belong to the type but rarely appear on menus with these names. A fish soup or stew is just that and down-island cooks rarely reveal what fish has been used.

Kingfish   A large mackerel, cut into steaks and grilled or cut into chunks and stewed. The meat is grayish. Best when used for stews.

Lambi   French-island word for conch.

Langouste   The spiny lobster of the Caribbean. French for the clawed lobster is *hommard*.

Molocoye   Morocoy. Sea turtle.

Morue   See Salt Cod.

Mullet   Considered trash fish in the north until recently, but there are many kinds including the golden mullet. Good eating from the grill.

Ouassous   The crayfish of Guadeloupe.

Oursin Chadrons   Sea urchins.

Palourdes   Clams. But in the islands they are different.

Rabbitfish   Cordonier. A half-pound fish for frying.

Sea egg   Sea urchins.

Snappers   There are all kinds of snappers and they're not all red. And there are a number of red fish and they're not all snappers. Vara vara is a superior red snapper. By "superior" we mean finer in texture and firmer.

Soudons   Creole French for small edible bivalves. Small clams.

Titiris   French for one of the tiny fishes that looks and cooks like white bait. Considered a delicacy.

Tuna   The yellow variety comes south. A medium-large fish that makes good steaks for broiling or grilling.

Freshening Fish with Lime Juice.   Throughout the islands it is customary to marinate fish or at least wipe them thoroughly with lime juice. The reason for this is that it removes the slimy coating of the skin, which is most vulnerable to deterioration in the tropical heat. At the same time, it removes any trace of unpleasant fishy smell or taste. This practical solution to an ancient problem also led long ago to the discovery that the flavor of lime juice is in fabulously refreshing contrast to the mild taste of fish. Why we mainlanders have not emulated the Creoles is impossible to say. Ever since we started visiting the islands we always start our fish dishes with a bath of lime juice and consider it just about de rigueur. Of course, once the lime juice has done its work the fish is washed in water and the fishy lime liquid discarded. Lime may then be, and often is, added to a spicy marinade or a sauce. The recipe for Blaff (page 136) demonstrates this process.

◆ Fresh, Salt, and Packaged Fish ◆

Visitors to the islands who venture outside their hotel and villa colony compounds soon discover that local people consume a surprisingly large amount of imported salted or packaged fish, especially during Lent. Why, they wonder, would anyone wish to eat preserved fish when the waters at their doorsteps are teeming with gorgeous seafood of all kinds?

Actually, although the variety in tropical waters is greater, the numbers of fish are much smaller than in northern waters. This occurs because of the much higher oxygen content of waters in the colder latitudes. In addition, a great many of those pretty fish are not particularly good eating. Local fish, therefore, were never sufficient for the daily needs of the islands during that period of the year when meat was taboo in the Spanish and French islands. The true food fish of island waters are still the kingfish, dolphin fish, mackerel, red snappers, sea trout, and those varieties that migrate south in winter. Shellfish have been more relatively plentiful but are rapidly being depleted.

Salt cod comes down to the Caribbean from Nova Scotia and Newfoundland before Lent, by the boatload. Long ago in Long Island Sound one saw the dismasted hulks of big old four-masters being pulled along by tugs on the long journey south. Necessity made down-islanders expert in preparing this heavily salted fish and their ingenuity has resulted in some grand dishes.

◆ Salt Cod ◆

On the mainland, old-fashioned salt cod is plentiful in chain, Hispanic, and Mediterranean groceries. It is hard, bony, and reeks of salt and fish. The salt and the drying are such good preservatives that the fish keeps perfectly even in the hottest weather. Even when it has been boned and desalted it still does not return to the same texture or taste of the fresh. Instead, it acquires a new personality, which in some ways is much more interesting than the fresh fish. That probably accounts for the fact that, while there are very few recipes for cooking fresh cod, the number is very much increased for the salted product. Island homes all have their own ways of making salt cod fish cakes, soups and stews, marinades, salads, and salt cod with vegetables.

Recently a new product has appeared on the market—salt cod that is skinned, boned, and packed rather soft in plastic bags. The best we can say for it is that it is much easier to handle, but that it has lost some of the gutsy flavor along the way to the shelves.

◆ Preparing Salt Cod ◆

The slabs of dried and salted fish are sold by weight. Cut them up at home with a cleaver into convenient pieces and place them in a large pot. Fill the pot with water and bring it to a boil. Allow to cool overnight. Drain off the water and carefully remove bones and any skin from the meat. Shred the fish with the aid of two forks and again cover with boiling water. Allow to cool and drain again. By now the cod should be just faintly salty. If still too strong, soak again in boiling water.

Once thoroughly desalted, boil the fish for ten minutes. Allow to cool. Drain through a sieve once again. The fish will now keep in the fridge for several days or in the freezer compartment indefinitely.

The fish packaged in plastic is soft and less salty. It should, nevertheless, be soaked like the hard salt cod until it is thoroughly desalted. This will take place much more quickly.

Can fresh cod be substituted in the recipes? Not really. The results may be very pleasant but not at all the same as with the salt cod; in fact there is a considerable difference both in flavor and texture. For pure down-island richness, the traditional product is far superior.

Jamaica

SALT COD AND AKEES

◆

3 thick slices strongly
  smoked bacon, cubed
1 medium yellow onion *or*
  3 scallion bulbs, chopped
1½ pounds prepared salt
  cod (see page 129)
1 19-ounce can akees,
  drained (see page 228)
½ teaspoon oregano *or* 4
  Spanish thyme leaves or
  cilantro sprigs, chopped
Salt and freshly ground
  black pepper to taste
Scotch bonnet chili pepper
  chopped, or forced
  through a garlic press, to
  taste

The national dish of Jamaica. Conventional recipes are very much alike for this unusual specialty, whereas local cooks freely vary proportions and herbs and spices. We start with a simple, basic formula, not even including bell pepper, which we save for the variations.

The dish is often served at room temperature (which is not to our own taste.)

1   In a large pan gently fry the bacon cubes until golden and crisp. Remove with a slotted spoon and reserve.
2   Fry the onion in the bacon fat until soft.
3   Thoroughly shred the prepared salt cod with 2 forks.
4   Combine the cod, akees, oregano, and the reserved bacon cubes with the onion in the pan. Add the salt, pepper, and chili pepper, stirring the whole mixture well.
5   Adjust the seasoning, if necessary. Cover and simmer until pipping hot. Stir thoroughly with the cheese sauce and serve with a salad of tomatoes and peeled and cored cucumbers.

Variations

A   Add 1 large or 2 small green bell peppers, well chopped, to the onions at step 2.
B   Add ½ pound cubed, cured cooked ham (not the "water added" type) at step 4.

C The following is a sauce that may be served with the Salt Cod and Akees and prepared at the same time.

1 Make a roux of the butter and flour. Heat gently for 3 minutes. Add the milk gradually and stir until syrupy. And the cheese and nutmeg over lowheat. Rapidly stir in the egg yolk with a whisk or wooden spoon. Simmer and stir till smooth. Add more milk if needed. Simmer very gently for 5 minutes.

2 Pour over the hot salt cod and akees mixture in the frying pan. Stir well.

Variation

Add 1 tablespoon Madras curry powder to the sauce in step 1.

Note

This dish will serve 6 if you add rice or white or yellow yams as a side dish and thin the sauce somewhat.

½ stick butter or margarine
¾ cup milk, half-and-half, or diluted evaporated milk
1½ tablespoons flour
¾ cup grated Gruyère, Pepato, Romano, or good, sharp American cheese
¼ whole nutmeg, grated
1 egg yolk

SERVES 4

Trinidad

BAREFOOT RICE

◆

½ pound meaty salt pork or pigs' tails

3 tablespoons vegetable oil

2 medium yellow onions

½ to ¾ pound prepared salt cod, flaked (see page 129)

4 scallions, bulbs chopped and leaves minced

2 small garlic cloves, through the press

1 sweet red and 1 green bell pepper, seeded, cut into strips, and then cubed

1 tablespoon fresh or dried curry leaves, crushed, *or* 1 tablespoon dried oregano leaves

2 cups Basmati or long-grain Carolina rice

4 cups coconut milk or whole milk flavored with ½ teaspoon coconut extract

Salt to taste

Chili pepper to taste

SERVES 6 TO 8

This salt cod pellao from Trinidad is a fantastic dish. Pellaos using other meats and island flavorants are made in the same way. See our variations below. Keep in mind that the Caribbean housewife is no different from her counterpart anywhere else in the world. She obeys no strict rules of quantity and adjusts her formulas according to season and circumstance. Once the basic steps in this kind of cooking are understood, the rest can be adjusted to need, and the taste of the cook controls the flavoring, which is always different because ingredients are always changing—larger, smaller, more intense or less, and so on.

1   Cut the salt pork into small pieces, wash well, and desalt by soaking overnight, draining, bringing to a boil in water, and draining again. (If using pigs' tails follow the same instructions for salt pork.)

2   Heat the oil and fry the onions and the pork until the onions turn yellow and the pork is partly rendered.

3   Add the cod, scallions, garlic, red and green peppers, and curry leaves. Heat the cod gently until some of its moisture has evaporated.

4   Into the mixture stir the rice and the coconut milk. Bring to a boil. Cover pan tightly. Simmer on very low heat until the rice is just tender. Drain any excess liquid or add a little water if the mixture is too dry.

5   Check the seasoning for saltiness. Add salt, if necessary, and the chili pepper. Serve hot with a garnish of tomatoes and cucumbers.

Variations

A   Salt (dried) beef may be added at step 3 if salt pork is omitted.

B   Fried or roasted chicken, cooked beef, roasted or fried pork meat, and various kinds of seafood may be substituted for the salt cod in step 3. The amount of meat or fish added depends on the availability and the number of people to be served.

Note

If curry leaves cannot be found, substitute 1 to 3 tablespoons Madras curry powder or various masalas.

NOW that partially desalted salt cod is appearing in the markets, salt cod fish cakes are coming back. Northerners are rediscovering their distinctive and enjoyable flavor. The following recipe from the islands is certainly better than anything we can remember from a time when using Gorton's or Beardsley's packaged cod for cakes was essential for making this once-popular Lenten dish.

1 Stir the baking powder into the flour. Whip in sufficient milk for a dough just barely firm enough to form. Incorporate the egg and achiote oil.

2 Load the processor bowl with the cod, scallions, and bell pepper. Process for 5 seconds.

3 Add the chili pepper.

4 Decant the contents of the processor bowl into the bowl containing the dough. Stir them together thoroughly. The mixture should be firm enough to mold. Add salt if needed.

5 Heat the oil to 370 degrees. Form the cakes by hand or use heaping tablespoons of the mix. Drop into the oil one by one and brown on both sides. Drain on paper towels in a hot oven.

Serve a sharp tomato sauce or Sauce Chien (page 53) on the side. Leftover cakes can be stored in the freezer and reheated in a 400-degree oven.

Variation

The same formula makes up to 20 heaping-teaspoon-sized cakes or 30 ball-shaped tidbits for serving with drinks or as appetizers.

Jamaica

CODFISH CAKES STAMP AND GO

◆

1½ teaspoons baking powder

1 cup flour

1 cup milk

1 egg

2 tablespoons achiote oil (page 110)

½ pound prepared salt cod (see page 129)

2 whole scallions, leaves snipped and bulbs chopped

1 medium green bell pepper, seeded and chopped

Scotch bonnet chili pepper or yellow island chili sauce to taste

Salt to taste

Vegetable oil for frying

MAKES 6 TO 8 CAKES

RED SNAPPER CURAÇAO-STYLE

◆

2 pounds filleted snapper, red fish, dolphin fish, mackerel, firm sole, turbot, or kingfish
½ cup fresh lime juice
2 garlic cloves, through the press
½ Scotch bonnet chili pepper, forced through a garlic press, *or* 1 teaspoon yellow island chili sauce
Pinch of salt and freshly ground black pepper
All-purpose flour for dredging the fish
4 tablespoons margarine or butter

THE SAUCE

2 onions *or* 5 scallions, chopped
1 green or red bell pepper, seeded and chopped
1 garlic clove, through the press
4 large, ripe tomatoes, peeled and chopped
Salt and freshly ground black pepper to taste
Additional chili pepper or chili sauce to taste
1 tablespoon vegetable oil

SERVES 4 TO 6

Any number of filleted fishes can be cooked in the following way. We recall from years ago a "Spanish Sauce" on seafood or the Italian tomato preparation "Diavolo," but this version is both lighter and sharper—a real treat.

1   Marinate the fish in the lime juice, garlic, chili pepper, salt, and pepper for at least 2 hours.

2   Remove the fish to a plate, reserving the marinade. Cut the fish into serving pieces and coat well with the flour.

3   Fry the fish in the margarine over high heat until both sides are browned. Remove the fish to a shallow baking dish to be used for serving. Set aside.

4   Into the pan in which the fish has been fried, add the reserved marinade and the sauce ingredients, including the vegetable oil.

5   Simmer for 20 to 30 minutes to produce a thick sauce. Adjust the seasoning.

6   Pour the sauce over the fish and heat in the oven at 300 degrees. Serve with rice on the side.

One of the joys of island life is eating dinner in "full air," and St. Thomas was no exception. Our favorite place at Red Hook was right beside the marina, where tables were placed along two wide, roofed-over terraces, overlooking the boats moored to the wood-planked dock and walkways. It was a godsend one night when the town's lights went out—as the restaurant's kitchen stoves were gas fired. The staff quickly hung oil lanterns and Coleman lamps from the rafters, and placed candles on the tables. We took one of their packets of paper matches back to our studio apartment to light our own candles!

Here fish was king of the menu, and dolphin fish one of the best.

Dolphin fish (not to be confused with the much larger dolphin or porpoise that belongs to the mammal family) is understandably popular in the islands. It is a firm, white-fleshed fish that can be broiled, boiled, steamed, or fried in butter. Restaurants usually douse filleted dolphin fish in lime or lemon juice and plenty of butter and black pepper before broiling very quickly on a metal serving dish. That certainly can hardly be improved upon, but the following, more complicated recipe is a pleasant relief from the conventional way of preparing it. The Creole touch is marinating in lime juice and chili pepper. Any other white-meat fish fillets may be substituted.

1 Prepare the fish by soaking the fillets in the lime juice, salt, and pepper for at least 1 hour.

2 Fry the sauce ingredients in a large pan with half the oil for 20 minutes. Set aside.

3 Remove the fillets from the lime juice and dredge them thoroughly in the flour.

4 Fry the fillets in the remaining oil, or more if needed, until crisply browned. Drain them on paper towels or on a rack. Meanwhile, reheat the sauce.

5 Serve the fillets with a covering of sauce or serve the sauce on the side.

Note

We find that the custom in some of the islands of simmering the fried fish in the sauce is poor cooking practice, because the fish becomes soggy.

St. Thomas

DOLPHIN FISH FILLET

◆

2 pounds dolphin fish fillets
Juice of 2 limes
Salt and freshly ground black pepper to taste
All-purpose flour for dredging the fillets

THE SAUCE

2 large tomatoes, peeled and chopped
1 yellow onion, sliced
1 garlic clove, through the press
2 tomatillos *or* 1 cucumber, peeled, cored, and chopped
1 teaspoon ginger powder
2 large bell peppers *or* 4 sweet chili peppers, seeded and chopped
Minced Scotch bonnet chili pepper or chili sauce to taste
¼ cup vegetable oil

SERVES 4

Martinique

BLAFF

◆

1 pound firm, white-fleshed fish, filleted or cut into steaks or cut into chunks

THE MARINADE

6 tablespoons fresh lime juice
1 large garlic clove, cut into chunks and passed through the press
½ small Scotch bonnet chili pepper, forced through a garlic press
¼ teaspoon salt

THE COOKING

LIQUID

½ cup dry white wine
2 tablespoons white vinegar
½ teaspoon powdered allspice *or* 6 whole allspice, crushed, or bay rum leaves (optional)
4 whole scallions, the leaves snipped and the bulbs finely chopped
8 cilantro sprigs, finely snipped
Salt and freshly ground black pepper to taste

SERVES 2

There are various theories about how this traditional way of cooking fish got its name, none of which makes any sense. French chefs would probably call this a court bouillon. As far as we can judge, its special distinction is provided by the inclusion of cilantro. It makes all the difference. What we end up with is something to which mainlanders are totally unaccustomed and which, for that reason, is rarely served in hotels to tourists. It is a sour, watery, sharp sauce that doesn't look appetizing at all and offers no hope of becoming more decorative by means of ingenious changes in the recipe. It is only after the first few tastes of this blend of solid fish meat and the broth that we become addicted. Because in the climate of the Caribbean we realize that this is the way to achieve both substance and refreshment. If we tend to be lethargic, Blaff jolts us alive, simple, seductive, and stimulating.

1 Lay the filleted fish in a shallow dish and barely cover with the marinade. Fish cut into steaks or chunks should fit tightly in the bowl so as to use a minimum of liquid to cover. Marinate for at least an hour.
2 While the fish is marinating, prepare the cooking liquid.
3 Decant the fish and its marinade into a pan with high sides and add the cooking liquid.
4 Simmer, covered, for 12 to 15 minutes. When the fish is tender there should remain at least 1 cup of liquid in the pan. Remove the allspice berries or bay rum leaves with a slotted spoon. Skim off any foam.
5 Check the sauce for flavor and texture. It should be slightly syrupy. Add water if necessary.
6 Bring the sauce to a boil. If the flavor of cilantro is not sufficiently noticeable add more finely snipped leaves and simmer a little longer.
7 Divide the fish between 2 hot soup bowls and split the sauce between the servings. Serve with generous amounts of French bread.

Variations
A The fish and the sauce can be chilled in the fridge and served cold with a salad and plenty of bread.
B Mussels also are delicious with this marinade and cooking liquid and can be used in place of the fish.

Note
If fresh lime juice is not available for the marinade, use bottled. Do not substitute lemon for the lime.

The sauce should end up fairly hot because of the chili. But tolerance is uneven and the exact amount is up to the cook. One can simply soak the chili pepper in the marinade and then remove it. Or wait until the fish is cooked and add yellow chili sauce to taste.

This recipe is derived from Court Bouillon Creole (page 99). It requires one spacious pan for the cooking and another, at least 12 inches in diameter, for the serving.

1   Fry the onion in the oil. When it turns golden add the fish along with the scallions. (If using shrimp, crayfish, mussels, or oysters, do not cook at this time; they should be saved for step 5.) Continue to fry over low heat, covered, until the fish is cooked.

2   Add the tomato, garlic, juice of 2 lemons, and parsley to the contents of the pan. Simmer, cover on, for 6 minutes.

3   Cut the bananas into pieces about an inch long. Put into a separate covered pan with a very little water and the remaining lemon juice. Cook for a few minutes until the bananas are soft. Set aside.

4   Soak the bread in water. Squeeze out as much liquid as possible. Divide the lump of bread, place on a carving board, and flatten with a cleaver or roller until you have enough thin sheets to cover the bottom of a clean 12-inch pan. Cover it completely, and discard any extra bread.

5   If using shrimp, crayfish, mussels, or oysters, add them to the simmered tomato mixture now, because they require less cooking than the other fish. Be ready to serve in 5 or 6 minutes.

6   There should be at least 2 cups of liquid sauce, including the tomatoes. Bring the contents to a boil. With a slotted spoon remove the solids and spread them over the prepared bread in the second pan. Pour the sauce over the bread.

7   Bring the contents of the second pan to a simmer and add the salt and pepper. Arrange the pieces of banana along the edge of the pan and serve. Guests should be provided with soup bowls.

TREMPAGE OF SEAFOOD

◆

2 onions, finely sliced
¼ cup vegetable oil
2 pounds boned and skinned white-fleshed fish or prepared salt cod, cut into chunks, *or* 2 to 2½ pounds shelled shrimp *or* 18 shelled crayfish *or* 1 quart shucked mussels or oysters
4 scallions, finely chopped
1 pound ripe tomatoes, peeled, chopped, and crushed
2 garlic cloves, through the press
Juice of 3 lemons or limes
1 tablespoon dried parsley leaves
4 large or 10 mini ripe bananas
10 slices white bread, crusts trimmed
Salt and freshly ground black pepper to taste

SERVES 6

◆ Conch (Lambi) ◆

The Conch, *Strombus gigas*, pronounced "conk," is the biggest and heaviest shell found in Caribbean waters. The outer lip or wing is huge. The exterior is yellow and there is a strong suffusion of red on the enamel interior of the lip. The snail that lives inside has a substantial "foot," a muscle that closes the opening of the shell and also acts as a means of moving along the bottom in shallow waters. It is this muscle that is cooked and listed as conch or lambi (Creole) on menus. Lambi is a gourmet treat, and the conch shell is a beautiful souvenir for tourists to carry home, so naturally these splendid creatures are approaching extinction. Nevertheless, better fish stores on the mainland still supply the meat throughout the year.

The white and rubbery conch muscles weigh from one-quarter to three-quarters of a pound. The conchs in our markets, fresh or canned, have been cleaned and skinned.

Conchs have a surprisingly sweet and seductive flavor—a great delicacy. But they can also be very tough, like gristle, unless properly prepared and cooked. In the islands the tenderizing is not always performed as thoroughly as it should be, and conch is served to tourists who are not aware that it can be a great deal better. Hence come chewy crumbs in accras or rubbery slices when barbecued or spitted. Do it right for full enjoyment.

To preserve conch for posterity, attempts are being made to farm them in salt-water compounds like crayfish in fresh-water ponds.

◆ Conch: Preparing and Basic Cooking ◆

The difficulty of tenderizing conch has been greatly exaggerated. It requires little preparation effort, and the cooking that follows, preceding its use in various dishes, is shortened considerably if a pressure cooker is available.

1 Lay a whole conch on a cutting board and pound it with a tenderizing hammer, a carpenter's mallet, a meat mallet, or a hard rubber mallet used in craft work. We do not recommend using the side of a cleaver because it lacks balance, making it difficult to control.

2 Hit the muscle with short, light smacks. It will start to flatten almost immediately. Continue pounding from one end of the muscle to the other. It will spread considerably just like a piece of veal when pounded. The process will be finished when there are no more thick, hard lumps. It takes 4 or 5 minutes at most.

3 Cut into 2- × -¾-inch strips. Pieces may be irregular, no matter.

4 Following manufacturer's recommendations (adding more or less water if so specified), cook the conch in a pressure cooker with ¾ cup water for 20 minutes. When the pressure cooker is opened, test the meat for tenderness. If it is not sufficiently tender add more water and resume cooking until the desired results are achieved. We have found that some lime juice in the water speeds the tenderizing process.

Without a pressure cooker, the conch should be simmered in shallow water for about 40 minutes, possibly more, until it becomes tender.

5 When the conch is tender, and not before, drain it and either use immediately or keep covered in the fridge. The small amount of liquid should also be saved for flavoring sauces.

We have also experimented with unpounded conch as follows: Do not pound the conch but cook it for 25 minutes with as much water in the pressure cooker as instructions allow. Remove the conch, reserving the liquid in the pressure cooker. Test the conch for tenderness.

If the conch is tender it can be added as is to stews, accras, and salads, or it can be skewered and grilled. If not, try cooking another 20 minutes with additional water added to the pressure cooker. That should do it. One thing we have learned is not to freeze the conch after cooking, for it loses all its sweetness, which is its main attraction. Skillful cooks can also slice the pieces of conch horizontally into thin strips that can be cut into bite-sized pieces for various purposes. Try it.

Martinique

BROCHETTE DE LAMBI (SKEWERED CONCH)

◆

3 thick slices cured and smoked bacon, cut into 1-inch squares
1 medium yellow onion, bulb "leaves" separated
1 garlic clove, through the press
2 tablespoons minced celery leaves
6 Spanish thyme leaves *or* ½ teaspoon dried oregano leaves
½ teaspoon snipped parsley leaves or dried parsley
Salt and freshly ground black pepper to taste
Chili powder or chili sauce to taste
1 small chayote (christophene), cut into 8 1½-x-½-inch slices
1 medium prepared conch (see page 139), cut into 1-inch pieces
Juice of ½ lime

SERVES 2

Brochette de Lambi in most island restaurants consists of small pieces of very tough conch spread apart by seared raw onion and green pepper. Skewered conch is a great dish when the fish, as well as any vegetable accompaniment, is tender, appropriately spiced, and, above all, cooked on a charcoal grill. Cooking skewered meats and seafood at home under a broiler does not, as we all know, yield the same incomparable results as cooking on a grill, but conch is very special and, made the following way, a wonderful novelty to serve special guests at lunch, dinner, or even supper. This recipe can be multiplied to serve as many as necessary.

1 Fry the bacon gently until cooked but not crisped. Remove from the pan to a plate and reserve.

2 Sauté the onion leaves in the fat. Add the garlic, celery, thyme, parsley, salt, pepper, and chili pepper. Mix the chayote in with the other ingredients. Cover and simmer until the onion is golden and soft.

3 Stir the prepared conch into the pan and sprinkle with lime juice. Check the sauce to taste. Cover and simmer for 2 minutes. Allow to cool.

4 This step is messy but unavoidable. When the mixture in the pan has cooled, arrange the conch, bacon squares, chayote, and onion leaves on 2 6-inch skewers for each portion.

5 Place the skewers on a grill over a charcoal fire or at an angle in a pan under a preheated broiler. Grill the food well so that it is slightly blackened on both sides. Serve immediately.

Guadeloupe

COLOMBO OF CONCH (LAMBI)

◆

1 Cut the prepared conchs into strips about 1 inch wide and 1½ inches long.

2 Stir together all the ingredients except the cornstarch, and put in a pressure cooker with ¾ cup water.

3 Cook under pressure for 20 minutes.

4 Decant the contents of the cooker into a pan. There should be 2 cups of syrupy sauce if you have used the yam. If not, mix the cornstarch with a little water and thicken the sauce. If the sauce is too thick add a little water. Stir the sauce as it simmers. Adjust the spicing.

5 Serve with molded rice on the side and French bread.

4 medium prepared conchs (see page 139)

4 scallions, bulbs chopped and leaves snipped

Juice of ½ very sharp lime or lemon *or* juice of 1 whole mild lime or lemon

2 small yellow onions, finely chopped

1 garlic clove, through the press

1 tablespoon tomato paste (optional)

4 cilantro sprigs, finely chopped

4 tablespoons Colombo powder (page 112) *or* 2 tablespoons mild Madras curry powder

Salt and freshly ground black pepper to taste

Chili pepper to taste

1 cup diced yam (optional)

Cornstarch (optional)

SERVES 4

◆ Spiny Lobster ◆

We have just one name for lobster, whereas the French differentiate between *hommard*—similar to our clawed lobsters of the northern Atlantic coast—and langouste, the spiny or rock lobster of Florida, the Antilles, and southern Europe. The meat of the spiny lobster is reputed to be less sweet than the Maine or clawed lobster. If the usual restaurant lobster in Florida is any guide, one would certainly judge that to be the case. Even the better hotels in the Caribbean manage to ruin them quite reliably. It is another matter when one finds a down-island restaurant that has access to a good supply of the spinies. Such a place is Stanley's at Cane Garden Bay in Tortola. On good days Stanley's 50-gallon drums are loaded with big spinies in plenty of sea water and spice. In the evening his shed is crowded with visitors and locals feasting on them and a first-rate potato salad. Fresh from the sea and done "Stanley's" way they are as fine as lobsters can possibly be. In Martinique the lobsters are justly famous and are exported to the Continent.

The popular way with lobsters in the islands is to boil them. But hardly anyone bothers with a recipe, for into the boil goes anything in the way of "bush," spices, and other flavorants that happen to be seasonal and strike the fancy of the cook. A Creole restaurant with a good regular supply of "spinies" will fill a fifty-gallon drum, maintained for that purpose, with sea water and the flavorants, especially plenty of chili pepper. A good fire beneath brings it all to a boil, and in go the lobsters. What comes out shortly is heaven.

1 Combine all the ingredients except the lobsters in a pot large enough to later hold the lobsters. Cover with a quart of water.

2 Bring to a boil and simmer, tightly covered, for 30 minutes. Strain the liquid into a bowl and return it to the pot. Discard the solids.

3 Kill the lobsters by *cutting them* lengthwise, clean the heads, and remove the back vein. Your fish store can do this for you if you are squeamish.

4 Check the flavor of the liquid—it should be tart and sharp. Toss in the lobsters and simmer, covered, for 10 minutes.

5 Remove the lobsters to a colander. Place the colander on top of the pot and reduce the sauce (if necessary) to 1½ cups.

6 Serve the lobster in large, shallow soup bowls with the sauce.

SPICY BOILED SPINY LOBSTER

◆

¼ cup vegetable oil
4 yellow onions, peeled and quartered
Juice of 4 limes
3 tomatoes, peeled and quartered
1 Spanish thyme branch *or* 1 tablespoon marjoram leaves
4 bay rum, allspice, or laurel bay leaves
1 celery stalk, cut into pieces
1 small Scotch bonnet, *jalapeño*, or other chili pepper
Salt and freshly ground black pepper to taste
4 whole, live lobsters

SERVES 4 AS A MAIN COURSE OR 8 AS AN APPETIZER

French Islands

LANGOUSTE FRICASSEE

◆

1 3-pound live spiny or Maine lobster

THE SAUCE
Reserved lobster shell, legs, and scraps
½ stick butter
3 cloves, crushed
1 garlic clove, through the press
Salt and freshly ground black pepper to taste
Pinch of saffron threads (optional)

◆

2 medium yellow onions, finely chopped or sliced
½ cup vegetable oil
2 scallions, leaves snipped and bulbs chopped
2 garlic cloves, through the press
4 sprigs parsley, snipped, *or* 1 tablespoon dried parsley leaves
6 Spanish thyme leaves, snipped, *or* 1 teaspoon dried thyme leaves
4 large, ripe tomatoes, peeled
Salt and freshly ground black pepper to taste
Juice of 1 lemon
Chili pepper or chili sauce to taste

SERVES 4

This is not a fricassee by any known definition, but that is what it is called in the French islands and no worse for that. It is very important that the lobster itself be cooked for a minimum of time to preserve the juices and enchanting sweetness.

1 Kill the lobster by popping it into boiling water for 3 minutes.

2 Allow to cool before removing the meat from the back and claws. Cut into small chunks. Reserve the shell, legs, and scraps and start the separate sauce.

3 To prepare the sauce simmer the lobster shell, legs, and scraps, covered tightly, for 30 minutes in 1 cup of water. Strain the liquid and return it to the pot.

4 Add the remaining sauce ingredients to the strained liquid.

5 As there must be 1 cup of sauce at the end, add more water, if necessary, and set aside while you complete the lobster dish. Bring to a boil before serving.

6 While the separate sauce is cooking, gently fry the onion in the oil until golden brown and soft. Add the scallions, garlic, parsley, Spanish thyme, tomatoes, salt, and pepper. Stir. Simmer for 10 minutes.

7 Toss in the lobster and lemon juice along with the chili pepper and adjust the spices to taste. Have your guests ready at table because this dish must not wait.

8 Simmer no more than 4 minutes and serve promptly with rice, French bread, and the separate sauce.

◆ Grilled Langoustines ◆

Langoustines are saltwater relatives of both lobster and crayfish. In the French islands they have long and narrow bodies with lengthy legs and antennae. The flesh is sweet. Though very costly, their preparation is of the simplest.

Sprinkle the fresh langoustines with salt and a peppery spice mix equivalent to the mainland Old Bay or crab-boil powders. Grill very quickly over high heat. In the islands they are served with Sauce Chien (page 53). They make a superb meal starting with accras followed by the langoustines with sauce, french fries, a mixed salad, and a sorbet for dessert.

◆ Seafood au Nage ◆

In the French islands seafood of any kind may turn up on the menus as *au Nage*, most frequently as *Poisson au Nage*. It is a favorite dish on Guadeloupe. Like the word *z'habitants*—the name for crayfish on Martinique—the term *au Nage* is an example of the Creole sense of humor, for *nage* means "swimming." It is a neat way of saying that the fish is swimming in its cooking liquid. Actually the cooking broth is lime-tart and chili-hot. Nonetheless, it is surprising how the best of the sea flavor comes through, making a most satisfying dish.

The court bouillon (for that is what it is) used for *au Nage* dishes may be described as a modified and diluted Sauce Chien (page 53). The concentration of vinegar and lime and chili is left very much to the taste of the individual cook. It is a simple and superb way of preparing shellfish or most any fish.

Au Nage, then, is a formula applicable for most fishy comestibles. Our recipe for *ouassous (ecrevisse)* is basically the same as for other seafood.

Guadeloupe

OUASSOUS AU NAGE

◆

THE BROTH

1 medium yellow onion,
   very finely sliced and
   then crosscut into minute
   bits
1 small green or red bell
   pepper, seeded and finely
   cubed
6 cilantro leaves, snipped,
   or Italian parsley leaves,
   finely snipped
4 tablespoons fresh lime
   juice *or* 7 tablespoons
   bottled lime juice
½ teaspoon sugar
½ cup white vinegar or
   white wine vinegar
Salt and freshly ground
   black pepper to taste
¾ to 1¼ cups water
Chili pepper or yellow island chili sauce to taste

◆

10 fat crayfish, in their
    shells, *or* 2 split lobster
    tails, meat cut into
    chunks and returned to
    the shells

SERVES 2

1   Combine all the broth ingredients except the water and chili pepper in a pot large enough to later hold the crayfish. Add ¾ cup of the water. Then add the chili pepper very carefully, testing for balance of flavor with the vinegar and lime. Add more of the remaining water to dilute further, if necessary.

2   Heat the broth to simmer and cook very gently for 20 minutes. Then drop in the crayfish and simmer gently, covered, for 5 minutes.

3   Decant the crayfish into deep soup bowls, and portion out the broth with a ladle. Serve with French bread, croutons, or dry crackers and a salad.

Variations

Poisson au Nage   This is the dish most commonly served in the islands. Any white fish from cod to flying fish will do. But *only* white-fleshed fish should be used. At step 2, cut the fish into chunks and simmer in the broth for 10 minutes.

Palourdes au Nage   These are Lucine clams, Great White Lucines *(Codakia orbicularis)*. They have pretty, 2-inch shells, entirely white, with a ¾-inch "clam" inside. They are invariably tough, but impart a strong flavor to the broth.

Plan to serve 10 to 12 clams per portion. At step 2, pop the clams into the simmering broth, cover tightly, and cook over low heat for 5 minutes, presuming that the clams have come cold from the fridge. Room temperature clams need only 3 minutes, if that. Serve with lots of fresh French bread and an avocado, tomato, and lettuce salad.

As substitutes for the Lucine clams, hard shell northern clams will do. We believe that soft shell clams would very possibly be best of all if the clams were very clean. Don't steam but simmer just like the clams.

Moules au Nage   *Au Nage* makes a *Moules Mariniere* with zip and our northern mussels are superb when cooked this way. Reckon 15 large mussels per serving. Scrub well and check each one for tight-fitting top and bottom shells before using. Open shells should be discarded. After cooking, the mussels with closed shells are the ones that should not be eaten. Because of pollution this must be a winter dish in the north.

◆ Sea Urchins or *Oursins* ◆

These spiny shellfish are widely eaten in the French islands, because the supply is very large and the tradition derived directly from France where they are plentiful along the Mediterranean coast. Down-islanders eat them raw as they do in Marseille. It is not a practice advisable in these hot climates where fresh seafood can become spoiled extremely quickly.

Creole restaurants serve sea urchins in a number of ways, but, at least in our experience, always with the snippets of meat inside the shell removed and the shell discarded. What one sees is a piled collection of brown, crumbly objects, irregular in shape and less than one inch long, usually drowned in plenty of zesty sauce. The urchins are boiled for a very short period, the tops of the shells where the mouth is cut out and the little pieces of meat inside, after draining thoroughly, removed and served separately in the broth.

In addition to the recipe below, the reader can follow the recipes for Court Bouillon Creole (page 99) or Blaff (page 136), substituting sea urchins when the broth is finished cooking, and thereby enjoy the same delicacies we have enjoyed in Creole homes and restaurants. The recipes also are worth knowing because sea urchins are available everywhere in tropical waters and they may come in handy during your travels.

French Islands

SEA URCHINS OR *OURSINS* AU NAGE

◆

SERVES 2

Follow the recipe for *Ouassous au Nage* (page 146), until the broth has simmered for twenty minutes.

1 Substitute 24 whole sea urchins for the crayfish. Place them in the broth and cook, covered, for 5 minutes.
2 Fish out the sea urchins, one by one, with a slotted spoon. Allow to cool at room temperature or run cold water over them. Open the tops with a small knife and remove the little pieces of flesh to a plate. Discard the shells.
3 Drop the sea urchins into the broth, bring to a boil, and simmer for 2 minutes.
4 Lift out the sea urchins with a slotted spoon and divide between the soup bowls, then pour the broth into the bowls.

Note
We recommend using less vinegar and chili, as the flavor of the sea urchins is very delicate.

French Islands

SEAFOOD PANADES, OMNIBUS RECIPE

◆

½ cup chopped scallion
  leaves
1 tablespoon dried parsley
  leaves
1 teaspoon dried thyme
  leaves
1 garlic clove, through the
  press
½ bottled or canned pi-
  miento, sliced and diced
Yellow island chili sauce
  to taste
½ teaspoon sugar
½ cup water
6 large clams or medium
  oysters *or*
1 cup crabmeat *or* 2 prepared conchs, (see page
  139) *or* 1 cup lobster or
  crayfish meat, sliced or
  cubed, *or* 1 cup shelled
  shrimp *or* 1 cup bay scallops or quartered sea

**SERVES 2 AS A MAIN
COURSE, 6 AS A
FIRST COURSE, OR
12 TO 15 AS AN
APPETIZER**

1   To prepare the marinade, combine in a pot the scallion, parsley, thyme, garlic, pimiento, chili sauce, sugar, and water. Simmer the seafood in the marinade for 6 minutes. Remove from the heat.

2   Remove the seafood from the marinade with a slotted spoon and chop, slice, cut, or process for just 3 seconds to achieve a coarse fineness. Reserve the marinade in the pan.

3   Soak the bread in water and squeeze out the excess moisture. Process for 10 seconds. Decant and reserve 1 cup of the puree. Set the remainder aside.

4   Chop or finely slice the onion and simmer in a saucepan with the butter until soft.

5   Add the cooked onion and butter to the marinade. Gently heat the mixture and gradually add the bread puree, a spoonful at a time, stirring with a wooden spoon. The sauce will thicken and become silky. Produce 1½ cups of sauce, adding both water (or milk) and more puree, if necessary, stirring constantly.

6   When the sauce is sufficiently thick, return the seafood to the pan and stir together thoroughly. Heat the seafood through.

7   Butter 2 gratin dishes or 6 large or 12 to 15 small scallop shells. As soon as the seafood mixture is piping hot, fill the serving dishes close to the brim.

8   Serve with fresh French bread or crisp crackers and a salad.

Variation

If using scallops, grate Gruyère cheese over the filled dishes and color quickly under the broiler before serving.

Note

The sauce and seafood can be kept in the fridge for up to 2 days. Before serving, preheat the oven to 300 degrees, and reheat the panade in a covered container, filling the dishes when it has become piping hot. Serve immediately. The excess cooking may cause the seafood to lose its pristine fresh taste.

scallops *or* 1 cup
firm white-fleshed fish
or ½ pound Japanese
crab-style fish product
1½ cups cubed white

bread, crusts trimmed
1 medium yellow onion,
  finely sliced and diced
4 tablespoons butter or
  margarine

The very mild flavor of akees is a perfect foil for shrimp, lobster, or any more delicate fish.

1 Simmer the shrimp in lightly salted water for 3 minutes. Cool, shell, and reserve the shells. If using lobster, cook for 10 minutes, remove the meat from the back and claws, cut into bite-sized pieces, and reserve the shell.

2 Drain the liquid from the akees through a strainer into a pot and reserve the akees. To the liquid add the shrimp shells, lobster shell , or the reserved head, tail, and bones from the fish. Add 1 cup of water and simmer, covered, until reduced to 1½ cups of liquid. Strain into a bowl and reserve.

3 Melt the butter in a heavy skillet and sauté the onion and garlic until the onion is golden. Add the reserved stock and tamarind concentrate. Stir in the rum, raise to a boil, and burn off the alcohol. Reduce to a simmer, and add the salt and pepper. Add the chili pepper carefully.

4 Mix the cornstarch in a cup with just enough cold water to liquefy. Add to the contents of the skillet very gradually, stirring constantly, until the texture is a syrupy sauce. If the sauce becomes too thick, add a bit of water and stir. Allow the sauce to cool until no more than 10 minutes before serving.

5 Bring the sauce to a boil and add the akees and seafood. Bring to a boil again, reduce to a simmer, and check the seasoning. Be prepared to serve in no more than 5 minutes.

Serve with Basmati or long-grain rice cooked with a little salt and turmeric or achiote oil (page 110) for color. Make a ring of rice with the seafood in the center, arranging on individual plates or a separate platter.

Variation

One or 2 whole bottled pimientos or roasted red sweet peppers cut into thin slices adds a decorative note to this dish.

Jamaica

SEAFOOD AND AKEES

◆

1 to 1½ pounds shrimp *or*
1 2½-pound lobster *or*
1½ pounds white-fleshed fish fillets, cut into chunks, and head, tail, and bones reserved
1 19-ounce can akees
½ stick butter
1 medium yellow onion, chopped
1 large garlic clove, through the press
½ teaspoon tamarind concentrate or amchur powder (optional)
¼ cup golden Jamaica rum
Salt and freshly ground black pepper to taste
Chili pepper or chili sauce (Matouk's) to taste
3 tablespoons cornstarch

SERVES 4

Martinique

GRILLED OR BROILED SHRIMP

◆

As shrimp is no match for island crayfish, the only excuse for this recipe is the consolation of serving a shellfish with Sauce Chien, thus imparting Caribbean flavor.

Use medium to large shrimp, with their heads and shells on. Dip in vegetable oil and salt and pepper the surfaces. Grill quickly over a very hot fire or toss in a pan with very good butter. Three minutes over heat is sufficient. Serve with Sauce Chien (page 53) on the side.

FRIED SHRIMP AND AKEES

◆

This is a favorite dish which takes a bit of doing to organize but only five minutes of cooking at the end. The flavoring is subtle so that the taste of both the shrimp and the akees is enhanced.

½ teaspoon Colman's dry mustard
½ teaspoon ground all-spice
½ teaspoon ground ginger
½ teaspoon mace, crushed with a mortar and pestle
½ teaspoon ground cassia or cinnamon
½ teaspoon paprika
1½ pounds headless shrimp, shelled, *or* 2 pounds with heads on
1 19-ounce can akees, drained
1 small chayote or ½ large one, boiled, peeled, pitted, and julienned
5 tablespoons achiote oil (page 110) or vegetable oil
Salt to taste
Chili pepper to taste (optional)

SERVES 4

1 In a small container mix together all the spices except the chili pepper and salt.

2 Arrange separate bowls containing the shrimp, akees, chayote, and spices close at hand for quick cooking.

3 Spread the achiote oil in the bottom of a large frying pan. 10 minutes before serving, heat the dinner plates in the oven.

4 At about 7 minutes before you plan to serve, turn up the heat under the pan to high.

5 When the oil begins to smoke slightly toss in all the shrimp. Fry until the shrimp changes color to pink. Add all the spices.

6 Immediately add the akees and stir. Then spread the chayote evenly on top. Add the salt and chili pepper. Cover the pan and cook for 2 minutes, shaking the pan several times.

7 Turn off the heat and serve with rice on the side.

Variation

At step 5 add 4 tablespoons lemon juice.

Shrimp can be deliciously sweet *and* chewy or just chewy. The way to preserve the sweetness is to cook the shrimp quickly. Long cooking is fatal. But, alas, much of the shrimp on the market is not very fresh and so has lost its sweetness for good. The cure? As for sweet peas—add a bit of sweetener.

1   In the butter gently sauté all the ingredients except the coconut milk, shrimp, and sugar for 6 minutes, covered.
2   Add the coconut milk and bring to a boil. Test for seasoning. Set aside, covered, to cool, then store in the fridge until 10 minutes before serving.
3   With guests seated at table, reheat the mixture over low flame. Add the shrimp and sugar, stirring well. Bring to a boil. Cover and turn off the heat. Wait 3 minutes before serving on rice with suitable condiments, chutneys, and other relishes.

Variation
Add 2 tablespoons rum to the sauce and stir just before serving.

Trinidad

CURRIED SHRIMP WITH COCONUT MILK

◆

½ stick butter or margarine
1 garlic clove, through the press
½ the leaves of a scallion, finely minced
2 tablespoons freshly grated ginger *or* 1 tablespoon ground ginger
2 tablespoons Colombo (page 112) or Madras curry powder
Salt and freshly ground black pepper to taste
1½ cups coconut milk
1½ pounds raw shrimp, shelled and deveined
½ teaspoon sugar (optional)

SERVES 4

Puerto Rico

SHRIMP AND RICE

◆

6 tablespoons achiote oil
  (page 110)
2 medium onions, peeled
  and finely sliced
1 garlic clove, through the
  press
2 very ripe, medium toma-
  toes, peeled
2 bay rum leaves *or* 4
  whole allspice, crushed,
  or ½ teaspoon ground
  allspice
1 teaspoon dried parsley
  leaves
Salt and freshly ground
  black pepper to taste
Chili pepper to taste
1 cup long-grain or Bas-
  mati rice
1 pound medium shrimp,
  peeled and deveined.

SERVES 2 TO 4

1   Using 2 tablespoons of the oil, slowly simmer the onions. When they are golden and soft add the garlic, tomatoes, bay rum, and parsley. Cover and simmer for 15 minutes. Season with the salt, pepper, and chili pepper.

2   Meanwhile, boil the rice until just done. Strain into a sieve and keep warm over a pot of boiling water.

3   Add the shrimp to the tomato mixture and cook, covered, over high heat for 3 minutes.

4   Quickly toss out the water in the rice pot, spoon the remaining 4 table-spoons of oil into the pot, and, over low heat, stir the rice in the oil until it is evenly colored.

5   Serve immediately, arranging the rice in a ring on plates and placing the shrimp in the middle.

N o t e

If you wish to add more servings, do so by increasing the number of shrimp rather than the amount of rice. The coriander in some versions of this combination drowns out the flavor of shrimp.

Tobago

SHRIMP AND RICE

◆

1 Boil the rice to slightly underdone. Drain it and reserve.

2 While the rice is cooking, blanch the shrimp in a minimum of water for 3 minutes. Drain and set aside.

3 Sauté the bell peppers, carrots, scallions, celery, and parsley in the butter until tender. Add the nutmeg and the salt, pepper, and chili pepper

4 Preheat the oven to 350 degrees.

5 Combine all the ingredients, stir well, and pack into a straight-sided baking dish. Heat in the oven for 15 minutes and serve.

Variation

This recipe can be made into a shrimp pellao with the addition of Indian spices. The simplest is Madras curry powder, but Samber, Tandoori, and other curry mixtures are suitable. Or, make your own mix of turmeric, coriander, cumin, garlic powder, amchur powder, and fenugreek leaves.

2 cups long-grain or Basmati rice
1 pound small shrimp, shelled
2 large red or green bell peppers, seeded and chopped
2 large carrots, scraped and thinly sliced
3 scallions, finely sliced and chopped
1 cup finely sliced celery
1 tablespoon minced fresh or dried parsley leaves
½ stick butter or margarine
½ teaspoon freshly grated nutmeg
Salt and freshly ground black pepper to taste
Chili powder or chili sauce to taste

SERVES 6

Curaçao and
Sint Maarten

KESHY YENA
WITH SHRIMP

◆

1 4-pound Edam cheese
   wheel
4 scallions, chopped
3 tablespoons butter
1 ripe, medium tomato,
   peeled and chopped
Salt and freshly ground
   black pepper to taste
Bonney Pepper Sauce or
   other chili sauce to taste
1 pound cooked shrimp,
   cut into small pieces
1 cup packaged bread
   crumbs
½ cup sour gherkins
¼ cup seedless raisins
½ cup chopped green ol-
   ives, with or without pimiento stuffing
2 eggs

SERVES 8

Though the name is from one of the Creole dialects, Keshy Yena is among the few dishes that can be identified with certainty as of Dutch origin. It is a relic that is rapidly disappearing, but still served as an exercise in nostalgia and a test of digestion. We have never made it ourselves, after suffering through one island experience. However, this recipe comes from our reliable down-island sources.

This is also one of the few times we consciously list ingredients foreign to the islands. Stuffed olives, sweet gherkins, and seedless raisins are as non-Creole as imported bottled sauces; they just don't belong.

Among our informants there has been general agreement that baking and serving this dish without making an unholy mess is a challenge.

Our recipe takes into account that, to counteract the tasteless cheese, strong accents are necessary. We have substituted sour for sweet gherkins. The sweet raisins and the olives must be suffered. See Note at end.

1 Cut the wax coating off the cheese and peel it away.

2 Slice a 1-inch-thick round from the top of the cheese and set it aside.

3 With a melon cutter, scoop out all but a ½-inch shell of the cheese. Set the cheese balls aside. Be careful not to punch a hole in the shell, or you will have to start all over again with a new wheel of cheese. Put the shell and the lid in a bowl and cover with very cold water. Let stand for at least 1 hour.

4 Grate 2 cups of the cheese balls and store the rest for other uses.

5 Preheat the oven to 350 degrees. Butter a baking dish, deep and wide enough to just fit the cheese shell. Place the baking dish in the oven. If you haven't got a dish that size, you'll have to face the messy consequences.

6 In a large frying pan, fry the scallions in the butter, then add the tomatoes, salt, pepper, and chili sauce. Cook until the mix can be stirred smooth; then add the shrimp, bread crumbs, pickles, raisins, olives, and grated cheese. Stir together well. Heat and stir continuously until the cheese is thoroughly melted and mixed into the rest of the ingredients. Beat the eggs and stir into the pan. Reduce the heat to low.

7 Remove the cheese shell and lid from the water. Dry the interior and exterior and the lid with paper towels. Stuff the cavity with the contents of the pan. Cover with the cheese lid and place in the baking dish in the oven.

8   Cook for 30 minutes. It is important that the cheese soften, but *not* disintegrate.

9   Remove from the oven; slip onto a serving dish (and not onto the floor) and serve by cutting this extraordinary object into wedges.

Variation

The basic recipe may be used in various ways by substituting other seafood, fowl, or meat for the shrimp. In each case 1 pound is sufficient. The stock from the different ingredient will change the flavor of the mixture. Green pepper or celery, well chopped, are suitable additions and onions can replace the scallions.

Note

A lady in Sint Maarten told us that she never bothered to stuff a cheese. Instead, she purchased the cheese, sliced it, and lined a baking dish of the right size for her number of guests. She filled it with fried seafood or meat mixture (like our recipe), and covered it all with a layer of sliced cheese. She then baked it in the oven and served with a large spoon . . . without risk of disaster. We approve.

・・*・*・*・*

◆ *Seven* ◆

POULTRY

・・*・*・*・*

Chicken cookery is not as common in the islands as on the mainland. There are fewer large poultry farms, and they are mostly on the bigger islands, such as Puerto Rico and Jamaica. Barbados, though small, has excellent roasting chickens. But down-islanders habitually cut them up. The reader will notice the absence of roasts in general, which is due to the previous lack of ovens.

Among the differences in mainland and Caribbean chicken cookery is the number of pieces one gets from a "cut-up" chicken. Instead of four, six, or eight pieces, the number should be twelve to fourteen. Namely, the breast is divided into six pieces, thigh and drumstick into two pieces, and the same for the wings. Butchers call this the Chinese cut. These smaller, more numerous pieces mix better in rice dishes and are easier to distribute among guests.

Guadeloupe and French Islands

AROMATIC SPICED CHICKEN (CHICKEN COLOMBO)

◆

1 3½- to 4-pound chicken, cut into 12 to 14 pieces
¾ stick butter or margarine
1 teaspoon ground ginger *or* 1 tablespoon grated fresh ginger
1 tablespoon ground turmeric
1 teaspoon ground cumin
2 tablespoons mild Madras curry powder

SERVES 4

Our first Colombo on Guadeloupe was at a small restaurant with a second-floor dining porch. After a hair-raising drive in the dark, from the airport to Gosier, *sans* map or sensible directions, we finally found our small hotel, dumped our bags, and got back into the car to find a restaurant. Luckily for us, the nearest one was only two blocks away, and it was very good. Later on in the week, we found packets of Colombo powder at the *supermarché* on the main street. These we brought back home to try out the flavor.

This is the dish most chicken Colombos attempt to be but fail because of the poor quality of Colombo powders sold in island grocery stores. Good Creole cooks know better and either make their own Colombo or buy the imported Indian curry powders. When the chicken is cooking in our home-made sauce, the house is filled with appetizing odors and the resulting dish comes up to the expectations they arouse.

½ teaspoon ground cinnamon *or* 2 inches cinnamon bark
6 cardamom seeds *or* 1 teaspoon ground cardamom
5 whole allspice, pounded, *or* 1 teaspoon ground allspice
Salt to taste
Scotch bonnet chili pepper or other chili pepper or yellow island chili sauce to taste
2 large garlic cloves, through the press
4 medium yellow onions, finely chopped or sliced

1   In a deep frying pan or casserole fry the chicken with half the butter. Once the chicken is heated, sprinkle it with the ginger and turmeric and stir well. Continue over moderate heat to brown the chicken on all sides, stirring occasionally. Fry for 10 to 15 minutes.

2   Add the other spices, salt, chili, pepper, garlic, and onion. Add the rest of the butter and stir. Cover and simmer for 30 minutes or until the chicken is tender. Stir again.

3   Just before serving add sufficient water to make a rich, syrupy sauce and heat thoroughly.

Serve with rice colored with turmeric or achiote oil (page 110).

N o t e

The dish may be served immediately or stored for a day or two in the fridge, which can only improve the flavor. Reheat very gently.

In the islands, where whole, roasted chickens are of rare occurrence, there is no need for true stuffings. This dish, which is served as an accompaniment to poultry, also makes a very tasty and different stuffing. Cold, it can be sliced like a pâté for an hors d'oeuvre or snack.

1 Fry the pork and chicken livers gently in the oil. Add the scallions when the meat is about halfway to being cooked through. When the meat is completely cooked, remove from the heat and allow to cool for a few minutes.
2 Decant the contents of the pan into a blender or processor bowl along with the breadfruit nuts, garlic, poultry seasoning, and egg. Process for about 8 seconds.
3 Place in a larger bowl and add the salt and pepper. Stir in the chili pepper. Add enough milk, if needed, to make the mixture soft but not fluid.
4 Use the stuffing for poultry, or cook the mixture in a double boiler, covered, for about 30 minutes. Serve in a ceramic casserole.

Guadeloupe

BREADFRUIT NUT CASSEROLE AND STUFFING

◆

½ pound pork sausage, sliced and casings removed
½ pound chicken livers
3 tablespoons vegetable oil *or* ½ stick butter
3 scallions *or* 2 onions, coarsely chopped
1½ to 2 cups peeled breadfruit nuts (see page 45)
1 garlic clove, through the press
1 tablespoon Bell's Poultry Seasoning *or* ½ teaspoon each dried sage, parsley, savory, and basil
1 egg
Salt and freshly ground black pepper to taste
Chili pepper or Bonney Pepper Sauce to taste
Milk, as needed

SERVES 4

Hispanic Islands

ARROZ CON POLLO

◆

1 3½- to 4½-pound chicken, cut into 14 pieces

3 tablespoons vegetable oil

1 medium yellow onion, chopped

1 green bell pepper, seeded and chopped

1 large tomato, crushed and chopped

4 bay rum leaves *or* ½ teaspoon ground allspice

4 strips thick-cut bacon, cubed, *or* ½ cup smoked ham or sausage, cubed

8 Spanish thyme leaves *or* 1 teaspoon thyme or marjoram

1½ cups long-grain or Basmati rice

2 tablespoons achiote oil (see page 110)

Salt and freshly ground black pepper to taste

SERVES 4 TO 6

Arroz con Pollo is a basic Spanish recipe, so common that the better cookbooks either don't list it at all or offer it apologetically. It is simple and inexpensive. That being the case, it is a frequent dish on Caribbean island tables, becoming pilau or pellao (or other spellings of the same) when Indian cooks have influenced the spicing.

It is, in reality, a dish that can be made in many ways, some of which are delicious even when they lack a specific name. It all depends on the seasoning and whether it is prepared by a talented or indifferent cook. Chicken and rice are cooked together in this recipe; in other words the meat and rice are mixed together early on. Other dishes of exactly the same character but hiding under different names are merely the chicken and rice cooked and served separately. The main thing is to have well-balanced and interesting flavors and textures. The best of these stews are made by imaginative island cooks rather than by following a Spanish model, for the sufficient reason that the islands have available many more unusual ingredients to add to it. Saffron, the most typical Spanish flavoring, can be had in the islands but costs a lot and is usually replaced by turmeric or achiote (annato), which add coloring but lack a distinctive taste.

1 In a moderately deep skillet or in a casserole fry the chicken gently in the vegetable oil, about 15 minutes, or until tender.

2 In the same pan with the chicken, fry the onion and pepper over moderate heat until the onion is golden, about 10 minutes.

3 Add the tomato, bay rum leaves or allspice, bacon or ham, and thyme or marjoram. Stir well over low heat.

4 Pour in the rice and stir well. Allow to cook for 4 minutes.

5 Add enough water to cover the mixture, then stir in the achiote oil.

6 Simmer gently until the rice is cooked and the water absorbed. If needed, add a little more water. Absorption depends on the type of rice used and the other liquids in the pan.

7 After the rice is cooked add the salt and pepper. Cover the casserole or pan and allow to stand, without heat, for 5 minutes before serving.

Variations

A Many island cooks add chili pepper according to taste at step 3.

B Do not cut the chicken into so many pieces. At step 1, fry until tender, bone, cut into smaller pieces for serving, and return to the pan.

C The rice at the end of cooking need not be dry. Hispanic cooks prefer it rather moist or mushy, like risotto. That is not the way we like it, but you may continue to add water a little at a time as cooking continues.

D   The recipe can be turned into an excellent curry simply by adding 3 tablespoons of Madras or other curry or local Colombo powder (page 112) when the water is added. Note that the curry powder thickens the sauce considerably and more water may be needed. The rice can also be cooked separately, colored with turmeric or saffron, and the chicken served on a mound or in the middle of a ring of rice with the sauce poured over it.

N o t e

We do not recommend such Hispanic ingredients as capers, olives, sherry, pimiento, or even green peas, although they are common elements of this dish.

Trinidad

CHICKEN WITH BEANS AND RICE

◆

1   Fry the chicken gently in achiote oil until tender. Add the salt, pepper, and chili pepper.

2   Stir the chicken into the cooked beans and rice mixture and serve.

V a r i a t i o n

A colorful and tasty addition to the mixture is a whole red pimiento, finely cubed.

1 small chicken, cut into
 12 to 14 pieces
Achiote oil (page 110) for
 frying
Salt and freshly ground
 black pepper to taste
Chili pepper to taste
1 recipe Black Beans and
 Rice (page 233)

SERVES 6

Guadeloupe

CHICKEN FRICASSEE CREOLE

◆

1 4- to 4½-pound chicken, cut into 12 to 14 pieces

8 whole allspice, well crushed in a mortar and pestle, or *malagueta* seeds (see page 38)

3 whole scallions, leaves snipped and bulbs chopped

Juice of 2 lemons

1 tablespoon dried parsley leaves

3 Spanish thyme leaves *or* 1 teaspoon ground oregano

1 teaspoon yellow island chili sauce

Salt and freshly ground black pepper to taste

3 tablespoons margarine, butter, or vegetable oil

1 cup dry white wine

1 jigger of good Jamaican or Martiniquan rum

SERVES 4

This is not at all like the fricassee for which the Hungarians are justly famous. It is entirely in the island tradition and a joy for the casserole cook.

1 Stuff the chicken pieces into a bowl small enough to crowd them. Mix the allspice, scallions, lemon juice, parsley, thyme, chili sauce, salt, and pepper in a separate bowl. (Go easy on the chili, which can be increased later if you so choose.) Add to the bowl with the chicken and stir the pieces thoroughly so that they are well coated.

2 Marinate the chicken, covered, for at least 2 hours. Down-islanders let it stand overnight at room temperature if cool, in the fridge if hot.

3 Remove the meat and reserve the marinade. Fry the chicken in the margarine for at least 20 minutes over moderate heat, turning at least once.

4 Reduce the heat, add the marinade to the pan, and stir together thoroughly with the chicken. Simmer, covered, for 15 minutes. Add the wine and rum and burn off the excess alcohol. Cover and simmer for another 15 minutes.

5 When the chicken is well cooked and tender, adjust the seasoning once again and serve.

Variations

A At step 4, add 4 tomatoes, peeled and cut into chunks. Simmer, with the cover off, and reduce the sauce to a thick, syrupy consistency. Add the wine and rum and simmer again, with cover off.

B At step 4, add 1 teaspoon Burnt Sugar Syrup (page 117). Some down-islanders make the syrup right in the pan with the chicken but there is no advantage whatsoever to that.

This dish, a Creole interpretation, is as different from typical English cookery as from Continental models. Paprika, reminiscent of Hungary, is included. But flour thickening is replaced by more ground spices which are quite sufficient to make a syrupy sauce of considerably greater potency.

1 Pile the pieces of chicken in a narrow bowl so that a minimum of liquid need be used to marinate the chicken.

2 Pour in the coconut milk along with all the other ingredients except the salt pork with the caution to use only part of the chili, which you can add later on.

3 Cover and leave in the fridge for 1 or 2 days, turning at least twice a day.

4 An hour before serving, render the pork or bacon cubes; remove the bits with a slotted spoon and reserve.

5 With a fork or slotted spoon remove the chicken pieces from the marinade, reserving the liquid, to the pan and fry until nicely golden and almost cooked through.

6 Add the marinade to the pan, stir well, and simmer until the sauce is a thick-textured consistency. Additional coconut milk or water can be added if more sauce is preferred. Check the seasoning and add the remaining chili sauce if needed. Serve sprinkled with the salt pork and with mashed yam on the side.

Variation

This is an easier method but not as satisfying.

1 Fry the salt pork till almost crisp. Remove the bits with a slotted spoon and reserve.

2 Fry the chicken along with the onions for 20 minutes, covered, over medium heat.

3 Add the rest of the ingredients except the celery leaves and coconut milk. Simmer, covered, for another 20 minutes.

4 Add the celery leaves and coconut milk. Reduce the sauce to a syrupy consistency. Adjust the seasoning. Add water to thin the sauce if needed. Serve with the salt pork sprinkled over the top.

Jamaica

CHICKEN FRICASSEE

◆

1 4- to 4½-pound chicken, cut into 12 to 14 pieces
½ cup coconut milk
3 medium yellow onions, chopped fine
2 garlic cloves, through the press
1 teaspoon ground cardamom
1 teaspoon freshly grated nutmeg
½ teaspoon ground cumin
1 tablespoon paprika
2 medium tomatoes, crushed and chopped
½ cup snipped celery leaves
Salt and freshly ground black pepper to taste
½ teaspoon yellow island chili sauce
6 ounces salt pork, cubed, *or* 4 thick strips bacon, cut into small bits *or* 3 tablespoons vegetable oil

SERVES 4

Guadeloupe

FRIED, BROILED, OR GRILLED CHICKEN COLOMBO

◆

1 3½- to 4-pound chicken, cut into 4 pieces
½ lime
Colombo powder (page 112), as needed
Vegetable oil or butter
Chili powder to taste

SERVES 4

1 Rub the chicken with the lime or squeeze the lime and baste the chicken with the juice.

2 Dust the chicken—the top and bottom of each piece—with Colombo powder. Be liberal and rub the powder into the meat with your hands.

3 Cook the chicken in any of the following ways.

Fry the chicken pieces skin side up in oil, covered, for 20 minutes over moderate heat. Turn the pieces and fry, covered, for 15 minutes. Finish by cooking with skin side up, uncovered, until the meat is tender. Sprinkle with the chili powder.

Or, broil the pieces, about 2 inches from the flame, with the skin side down for 25 minutes. Turn skin side up and, with reduced flame, broil until the skin is crisp but with care not to burn. Immediately turn the pieces again and continue cooking until the meat is tender. Finish with the skin side up and sprinkle the pieces with chili powder and more Colombo powder 5 minutes before serving.

Or, grill with skin side up over coals for 15 minutes. Then turn for just sufficiently long to crisp the skin. Turn again and cook till tender with the skin side up. Before serving sprinkle with chili powder and more Colombo powder.

Court bouillon, according to Larousse, is "an aromatic liquid in which meat, fish, and various vegetables are cooked." Seafoods cooked *au Nage* (pages 145–47) are really simmering in a court bouillon. But in the islands the term means any dish that is a combination of a meat, fish, or vegetable with lots of sauce. For this recipe we recommend a good, fat stewing chicken.

1 Stir each of the meats in the juice of 1 lemon and season with the salt and pepper.

2 Fry the chicken and pork with 2 tablespoons each of the oil in separate pans. Fry the pork for only 8 minutes over moderate heat. The chicken will take longer to turn golden.

3 Combine the chicken and pork in a large pan or casserole. Add the remaining ingredients except the bananas and chili sauce. Simmer, covered, for 30 minutes.

4 Peel the bananas and cut them into thick slices. Add to the pan with the chili sauce and the juice of the remaining 2 lemons.

5 Simmer everything together for another 30 or more minutes, until the chicken, pork, and bananas are well cooked. The sauce should be fairly thick but flowing. If needed, add a bit of water at the very end and stir well to mix. Serve hot.

Martinique

COURT BOUILLON OF STEWING HEN

◆

1 4- to 5-pound stewing chicken, cut into 12 pieces
2 pounds lean pork, without bones, cut into 1-inch cubes
Juice of 4 lemons
Salt and freshly ground black pepper to taste
4 tablespoons vegetable oil
1 pound ripe tomatoes, peeled and crushed
4 garlic cloves, through the press
5 whole scallions, chopped
1 tablespoon fresh or dried parsley
1½ teaspoons dried thyme
4 cloves, crushed
6 whole allspice, crushed
4 pounds small or normal-size bananas (somewhat green), unpeeled
Yellow island chili sauce to taste

SERVES 6

Sint Maarten

CHICKEN SANCOCHO

◆

Juice of 2 limes or lemons
4 to 5 pounds chicken
 parts

THE MARINADE

1½ cups chopped celery
 with leaves
3 whole scallions, chopped
 or sliced
1 large, green bell pepper,
 seeded and chopped
2 medium yellow onions,
 sliced
2 ripe tomatoes, peeled
 and chopped
½ tablespoon poultry sea-
 soning
½ teaspoon freshly grated
 nutmeg
3 mace leaves, pounded or
 grated
1 tablespoon ground
 cumin
Salt and freshly ground
 black pepper to taste

THE VEGETABLES

2 cups sliced carrots
2 green plantains, peeled
 and sliced

SERVES 6

This sancocho provides an example of the diversity of recipes disguised by the names used in the Antilles. Each island and every family seems to have its own way of cooking and naming basic dishes. Quality depends very heavily on the ability to afford plenty of superior ingredients and a cook with talent. Down-island there is no lack of the latter commodity, but don't expect down-island cooks to be able to give you an accurate description of what they do to turn out their creations. Practice and instinct are rarely mated to an ability to communicate systematically.

1 Using your hands, work the lime or lemon juice into the chicken meat.
2 Make the marinade by mixing together all the ingredients.
3 Stir the marinade together with the chicken parts in a large bowl, cover, and store in the fridge overnight.
4 Empty the chicken and marinade into a pot, stir well, and add water just to cover. Simmer until the meat is tender, about 30 to 45 minutes.
5 Remove the chicken from the broth and set aside. Strain the broth into a bowl, discarding the solids.
6 Return the broth to the pot. Add all the vegetables except the cabbage and corn. Mix in the chili pepper.
7 Thirty minutes before serving, heat the broth and vegetables and bring to a simmer. Add the cabbage, corn, and chicken. Simmer until ready to serve.
8 Serve in a soup tureen or large vegetable dish or in individual soup plates.

Note

This list is divided into three parts: the chicken, the marinade, and the vegetables. In practice there is a large degree of flexibility, for this is one of those ragouts into which the down-island cook tosses just about anything that is at hand and reasonably compatible with the chicken. Quantities of the vegetables can be shifted and the dish will not suffer if different ones are used. Also, islanders complicate matters by timing the cooking of the vegetables at different intervals; at least some are said to do it. This is quite unnecessary.

½ pound calabaza, diced
¾ pound white yam,
 peeled and cut into chunks
½ small white cabbage,
 shredded

3 fresh corn cobs, kernels
 stripped
Chili pepper, chili pow-
 der, or chili sauce to
 taste

Tortola

COLD CHICKEN WITH TOMATILLO WHITE SAUCE

◆

1 Simmer the chicken in a pot along with the herbs and spices, the salt and pepper, and a minimum of water for about 30 minutes or until tender.

2 Remove the chicken from the broth and let cool. Separate the meat from the bones (unless boneless) and cut into bite-sized chunks. Meanwhile, boil down the poaching liquid to no more than a few tablespoons. Place the chicken in a bowl and pour the remaining liquid over it. Store in the fridge, preferably overnight.

3 Mix the sauce ingredients together thoroughly.

4 Drain the bowl with the chicken of any remaining stock. If jellied, it can be kept cold and served separately on the plate. Mix the sauce with the chicken in the bowl. Serve.

Note

The chicken can be served with potato salad, tomato salad, cucumber salad, or celery salad on lettuce.

THE SAUCE

½ cup Tomatillo Sauce
  (page 121)
½ cup sour cream
  Chili powder or chili
  sauce to taste
1 whole chicken breast,
  split, with bone in, *or* 2
  boneless breast pieces
¼ to ½ cup herb and
  spice mix of large
  pinches of parsley flakes,
  dried sage, ground coriander, and ground cumin
Salt and freshly ground
  black pepper to taste

**SERVES 2 AS A MAIN
COURSE OR 4 AS A
FIRST COURSE**

Jamaica

JERKED CHICKEN, PORK, LAMB, OR BEEF

◆

THE MARINADE

¼ cup whole allspice crushed or grated, *or* 3 tablespoons ground all-spice

1 teaspoon ground cinnamon *or* 1½ teaspoons cassia powder

½ teaspoon freshly grated nutmeg

1 tablespoon ground coriander

4 whole scallions, the leaves minced and bottoms chopped

2 garlic cloves, through the press

1 teaspoon tamarind concentrate

¼ cup red wine or water

¼ cup vegetable oil

Salt and freshly ground black pepper to taste

Scotch bonnet chili pepper or other chili pepper or chili sauce to taste

The sudden popularity of jerk in the United States is a continuation of the recent craze for Cajun, Texan, and Mexican dishes. It is no more than a combination of two meats marinated in fiery hot chili sauce and grilled. As noted elsewhere, real aficionados of chili peppers can munch a Scotch bonnet pepper (10,000 units of chili heat) as if it were a spoonful of green peas, and they, of course, adore this dish. We sensitive souls have to take it easy.

Like all such fads this one will probably be short lived and will have faded before this book is published. Really hot chili food has never caught on for long in the north. No skill at all is required to make this dish, and anyone with a supply of chili powder or bottled sauce can make it as easily as making a hamburger with ketchup. Most island cooking is a bit hot by our everyday standards, but it is not usually in a class with jerk. Fortunately, most island cooking is also much more sophisticated and subtle.

There is nothing special about the Jamaican dish except the story that the original jerk was prepared in pits with hot charcoal or other burning material placed over the meat. That approximates the New England clambake idea applied with less reason, for the same results can be achieved by simply marinating and grilling. Popularity has brought to the market several bottled hot sauces bearing jerk labels. These can be used for the marinade and basting the meat by diluting as advised on the labels. The following recipe is less one-sided in its spicing.

Jamaicans usually cook only pork and chicken together, but other combinations, including goat, are equally good. Hence we have here a true omnibus recipe where there are usually several meats, each one no different from the others except in some minor detail. The frequent suggestion of using all kinds of ordinary mainland bottled meat sauces along with the chili is to deprive this exotic oddity of any merit. Each of the meat amounts is calculated for six servings. A combination of two meats makes twelve servings. There is no taboo against making the dish with just one kind of meat or with the chicken alone.

The marinade is for twelve servings of six half chickens and six pounds meat or six pounds each of two kinds of meat. Amounts of meat and marinade can be halved for six servings.

1 Combine all of the marinade ingredients into a light, spreadable paste.
2 Place all the meats in a large container and using rubber gloves (do not touch with the fingers!) mix the marinade with the meats until every piece is completely covered.

3 Cover and store in the fridge overnight.

4 The best way to cook the meats is over a charcoal grill, browning the pieces on all sides. Otherwise, do the same under a preheated broiler. Pay attention to the fact that the chicken will take somewhat longer than the meat.

5 Serve hot with Fried Plantain (page 262), plenty of mixed salad, and cold drinks to quench the internal flames.

Note

Any of a number of Jamaican jerk sauces can be substituted for the above marinade. Usually the concentrate is diluted with twice the amount of water. It still remains indescribably hot, so look out. We prefer simply to add chili powder or a yellow chili sauce according to taste.

THE MEATS

3 3½-pound chickens, split

6 pounds tender, lean, boneless pork, stewing lamb, mutton, goat, or beef, cut into pieces 1 to 1½ inches thick and 4 to 6 inches long

SERVES 12

St. Thomas

CHICKEN LIVERS WITH ACHIOTE OIL

◆

1 Place the livers in a bowl and stir in 1 teaspoon of the vegetable oil. Then stir in the parsley, anise, Tabasco sauce, salt, and pepper.

2 Stir the bread crumbs and the livers together. Make sure that the livers are fully coated. Use more bread crumbs if needed.

3 Heat the remaining oil in a skillet over medium heat until frying hot. Add the livers one by one. The trick is to brown the bread crumbs without burning them. Turn frequently. When the livers are cooked halfway through, add the achiote oil and swirl the livers around to give them color.

4 When cooked through, remove the livers from the heat and serve immediately with a vegetable or salad.

¾ to 1 pound chicken livers

3 tablespoons vegetable oil

¼ cup fresh chopped or snipped parsley

1 teaspoon anise or star anise powder or grated nutmeg

Tabasco sauce or dried chili pepper flakes to taste

Salt and freshly ground black pepper to taste

¾ cup bread crumbs

1 tablespoon achiote oil (page 110)

SERVES 2

St. Martin

DUCK CREOLE

◆

2 small duck breasts *or* 1
large duck breast, split
and boned
1 tablespoon vegetable oil

THE SAUCE

2 tablespoons vegetable oil
1 large shallot *or* 3 small
shallots, peeled and
chopped, *or* 4 whole
scallions, leaves minced
and bulbs chopped
1 garlic clove, through the
press
5 whole allspice, crushed
in a mortar and pestle, *or*
½ teaspoon ground all-
spice
4 Spanish thyme leaves,
minced, *or* 1 teaspoon
dried thyme leaves
½ cup white wine *or* 2
jiggers rum
Salt and freshly ground
black pepper to taste
Chili pepper to taste
½ teaspoon Burnt Sugar
Syrup (page 117)

The French duck is thin skinned, lean, and solid. American and English ducks are fat and mushy. Hence the difference in cooking methods as well as the astonishing difference in the finished product. On the mainland we quarter our ducks because there is no other way of serving them. The French slice the breasts and thighs vertically. We cook our ducks until they are dry and stringy to get rid of the fat. The French can serve theirs slightly or more than slightly rare. French-style ducks are raised in the Caribbean islands. These superior birds make a superior dish that cannot be duplicated on the mainland.

As we are obliged to work with overly fat duck, we make the best of it in the following recipe, by achieving a crisp skin and a relatively underdone meat. Handled in this way, with extra effort, we admit, even our ducks become satisfactorily edible . . . and effectively Caribbean.

This is a combination dish. The mango is cooked and served along with the duck meat in the sauce and the yam is served separately in the sauce.

1   To prepare the duck, remove the skin of the breasts and their layers of fat with a very sharp, thin knife. Cover the breast meat with aluminum foil and store in the fridge until ready to use.

2   Gently fry the skin with the fat side down in the oil in a covered pan, until it is well rendered and crisp. Set the skin aside and discard the rendered fat.

3   Meanwhile, make the sauce. Combine the sauce ingredients in a large pan. Simmer, stirring occasionally, for 10 minutes. Set aside.

4   Meanwhile, prepare the vegetable and fruit. Boil the yam, in salted water to cover, until tender. Remove from the heat and keep warm. Use a melon cutter to scoop out 10 mango balls and set the mango aside in the fridge.

5   Thirty minutes before serving, remove the duck meat from the fridge. Lay the breasts in the sauce, add the mango balls, and simmer, covered, for 10 to 15 minutes. Add a little water to the sauce if needed. Meanwhile, heat the duck skin and the serving plates in a low oven.

6   When ready to serve, remove the breast meat from the sauce and slice it vertically across the grain.

7   Arrange the meat neatly on the plates and cover with the sauce. Cut the crisped skin into strips and lay over the meat. Distribute the yam slices and mango balls and cover with the remaining sauce from the pan.

Note

If the amount of sauce is inadequate or too thin, mix 1 tablespoon cornstarch in a cup with a little water. To thicken the sauce add a little at a time stirring briskly. To produce more sauce add water to the thickened sauce.

THE VEGETABLE AND FRUIT

1 white yam (batata), cut into 4 to 6 slices
1 green mango or other tart Caribbean fruit, peeled

SERVES 2

On menus in the islands, scrambled eggs are uncommon but there are plenty of chickens and, therefore, eggs around, so some of the latter receive the scrambled treatment.

It is a deceptive dish, seeming so easy yet in reality a challenge to any chef. Escoffier's scrambled eggs were famous and the exact secret of their preparation has never been discovered. As French for scrambled eggs is *oeufs brouillis*, anyone not speaking the language perfectly (and make the distinction clear to the waiter) will usually receive *oeufs bouillis*, boiled eggs; and they're not even soft but boiled hard, hard!

At any rate, we discovered that a variety of island ingredients are a wonderful addition to basic scrambled eggs. Try it.

An eight and a half inch pan will accommodate four eggs.

ISLAND-STYLE SCRAMBLED EGGS

◆

¼ stick butter or margarine
4 large eggs
3 tablespoons half-and-half or cream
Salt and freshly ground black pepper to taste

SERVES 2

1   Heat the butter in the pan over low heat until all hissing ceases.
2   Meanwhile, whip the eggs in a bowl with the half-and-half and salt and pepper.
3   Raise the heat to medium and pour the eggs into the pan. Allow the eggs to coagulate around the edges. Tilt the pan toward you and then tilt it away from you so that the liquid occupies the open space. Stir lightly with a wooden spoon.
4   When the eggs are half coagulated, turn off the heat. Allow to stand for a moment. The heat from the pan will continue to cook the eggs, but there should remain some liquid egg on the surface. Quickly, with a fork, fluff the

eggs thoroughly and serve immediately on warm (not hot) plates. Serve with fried bacon, ham, sausage, chicken livers, or leftover meats.

Variations

A   At step 2, add finely snipped cilantro or parsley leaves. Proceed as in the basic recipe.

B   To variation A add ¼ cup snipped scallion leaves.

C   Scramble the eggs in 1 to 2 tablespoons achiote oil (page 110).

D   Take from a can of akees ¾ cup of the vegetable. Drain. Pour the remaining akees in the can into a screw-top jar and place in the freezer for future use. Fry the akees in achiote oil for 3 minutes or until all signs of moisture have disappeared. At step 2, pour into the egg mixture and proceed as in the basic recipe. Super!

E   Add finely minced cooked shrimp, lobster, fish, conch, sea urchins, or other seafood to the egg mixture at step 2. Proceed as in the basic recipe.

F   To the egg mixture at step 2, add ½ teaspoon mild Madras curry powder or 1 teaspoon Colombo powder. Proceed as in the basic recipe.

G   Add a pinch each of ground allspice, cumin, coriander, and turmeric at step 2. Proceed as in the basic recipe.

Notes

If using extra-large or jumbo eggs and a large frying pan, more butter may be required, up to double the amount.

Instead of half-and-half or cream, down-islanders will usually substitute evaporated milk.

This is a lovely and different way of serving poached eggs. For more on dion-dion, see page 46.

Haiti

POACHED EGGS WITH DION-DION

◆

1 In a small saucepan heat ½ cup of the chicken broth. Stir in the dried mushrooms. Simmer gently until the liquid turns nearly black.

2 Strain the mushroom liquid into a shallow pan large enough to fry 4 eggs. Discard the mushroom residue.

3 Heat the mushroom liquid and add the butter, scallions, salt, pepper, and chili pepper. Bring to a boil.

4 Break the eggs into the pan, spacing them apart. Reduce the heat to low and cover the pan tightly.

5 Simmer until a white film has formed on the egg yolks. There should be at least ½ cup of liquid. If not, add more chicken broth to make ½ cup.

6 Serve on slices of white toast bathed in the dion-dion sauce.

Note

Other dried mushrooms, soaked overnight and very finely snipped, then cooked as for dion-dion (but retaining the mushroom residue), may be used for the same general effect.

½ to ¾ cup low-salt
  chicken broth or water
2 tablespoons dried dion-
  dion mushrooms
½ stick butter or marga-
  rine
1 tablespoon snipped scallion leaves
Salt and freshly ground
  black pepper to taste
Chili pepper to taste
4 eggs

SERVES 2 TO 4

✦✦✦✦✦✦✦✦✦

• *Eight* •

SELECTIONS

FROM THE

RIJSTAFEL

✦✦✦✦✦✦✦✦✦

◆ Rijstafel ◆

The Rijstafel is part of a separate cuisine transplanted from Indonesia by Holland to its possessions in the Caribbean, namely Sint Maarten, Sint Eustatius, Curaçao, Aruba, and Surinam, the last a country on the mainland of South America. Rijstafel literally means "rice table," and the menu consists of fourteen to twenty dishes of condiments, soup, meat, fish, vegetables, rice, and fruits, brought to the table all at once. The hot dishes are perched on square grills over fat, short candles that keep the food hot. In one particular Sint Maarten restaurant, the dancing light from these candles on all the tables was reflected on the overhanging roof of the outside porch, with the garden plantings of the back garden coming right up to the floor's edge, the soft night breezes mingling the scent of flowers with the spicy fragrance rising from the steaming sauces.

This festive individual buffet is an enjoyable experience, though the food can be a shade monotonous because of repetitions of the bland flavorants usually served to tourists. We have the impression that they are move lively in the Pacific islands using local ingredients. Nevertheless, we present a number of these very different recipes here which have world-wide popularity.

Condiments for the Rijstafel   Many of the small side dishes forming part of the Rijstafel are filled with various thickened condiments that are used for dipping pieces of meat or seafood between bites, even though the foods already have sauces. The condiments are also eaten with plain rice, or the rice is eaten with food from one of the dishes and some of the condiment. Pretty much a free-for-all.

These condiments can be made at home and stored, but unless you use them frequently, it is advisable to buy them in Asian foodshops that usually carry a plentiful supply. The Conimex brand is the most common. The quantities are usually quite small, and the flavors rather mild. However, when served, they mostly become violently hot as chili is added to the mixes. This you can do yourself, a little at a time.

If the packaged condiment is already overly seasoned with chili, the sauce can be diluted with finely chopped and boiled cabbage, chopped eggplant, chopped carrots, cooked beans and lentils, and other fillers, along with oil and liquid as needed. Many of the condiments are called sambals.

As all the substantial dishes of a Rijstafel are served in a sauce the only use for a separate sauce is with rice. This type of sauce follows a rule, very similar to that prevalent in other countries and known as drowning everything in a "cream sauce." It must be mild, look nice, and be fundamentally tasteless. The island-Indonesian version is invariably sweetened with sugar and perhaps has some vinegar and soy sauce added. The thicker condiments are usually equally tasteless but are loaded with very salty fish sauces and chili.

A typical peanut sauce that is very popular is Gado Gado, which can be bought under the Conimex label—a mix of ground roasted peanuts, tamarind powder, sugar, paprika powder, shrimp extract (very salty), and "herbs and spices." It comes in the form of a yellow powder, to which one adds water and then simmers for a while. What isn't mentioned is the chili powder or the whole chilis that are usually tossed into the pot and change a very mild sauce into a pretty violent one.

The following recipe made from scratch is similar, and a welcome change from the habit of combining rice and soy sauce.

Mix the ingredients in a pot and simmer, covered, for 15 minutes. If too thick, add water as needed.

Note

Coconut milk can be replaced by evaporated milk mixed with ½ teaspoon coconut extract.

Curaçao

PEANUT SAUCE

◆

¼ pound Spanish or African peanuts, roasted and ground
1 yellow onion, finely chopped
1 cup coconut milk
½ teaspoon concentrated tamarind paste
1 tablespoon molasses or dark-brown sugar
1 teaspoon Sereh powder (lemon grass) *or* 1 teaspoon grated lemon zest
1 garlic clove, through the press
2 dried curry leaves *or* ½ teaspoon Sambar powder
Salt and freshly ground black pepper to taste
Chili pepper or chili sauce to taste

MAKES 2 CUPS

Dutch Islands

RUDJAK SALADS

◆

RUDJAK VEGETABLE SALAD

1 2-quart mixture of cauliflower florets, cut small,
white cabbage, finely
shredded, carrots, cut
into very thin strips and
diced, bean sprouts, and
cucumbers, peeled,
cored, and cut into strips
Juice of 1 lemon
¼ teaspoon sugar
1 teaspoon grated blachan
or anchovy or shrimp
paste
1 chili pepper, finely
chopped, or chili sauce
to taste
1 tablespoon water
Salt to taste
½ cup Spanish or African
peanuts, grated and
roasted, *or* 1 jar Gado
Gado (dry peanut sauce)

SERVES 4

One of these salads is made with vegetables, the other principally of fruits; one sour and the other sweet. They should be strongly spiced with chili, which restaurants in the Caribbean usually tone down considerably. At table chili can be added to one's heart's content.

Blachan or trasi, an essential ingredient of both, is made of salted and dried shellfish and smells to high heaven. It is sold in jars or cans by Asian food shops. Before using, it must be heated in aluminum foil (to confine the odor) until dried and rather hard, whereupon it is grated and mixed with other spices in a recipe. The quantities used are not large and we suspect that restaurants avoid the material when serving tourists. If you are unable to find this condiment, substitute shrimp or anchovy paste. We think the latter is closer in flavor. Another ingredient, southeast Asian fish sauce—dark, watery and very salty—is much more commonly available.

1   Combine the vegetables in a salad bowl.
2   Mix the remaining ingredients except the peanuts in a jar. Seal and shake well.
3   Pour over the vegetables and stir. Cool in the fridge.
4   Before serving, sprinkle the grated peanuts or Gado Gado over each portion.

1 Combine the fruits in a bowl.

2 Mix the remaining ingredients in a jar. Seal and shake thoroughly.

3 Pour the dressing over the fruit and stir. Cool in the fridge for 1 hour or more before serving.

RUDJAK FRUIT SALAD

1 2-quart mixture of green mangoes, sliced, bananas, sliced, pineapple, diced, cucumbers, cored and sliced, and papaya or other tropical fruits, sliced
1 teaspoon grated blachan or anchovy or shrimp paste
Juice of 1 lemon
1½ tablespoons brown sugar
2 tablespoons Indonesian bottled fish sauce
Chopped chili peppers or chili sauce to taste

SERVES 4 TO 6

These crisps have much the shape of fortune cookies but their surfaces shine like plastic. They are sold in cellophane bags in most Asian stores. They are the southeast Asian and Indonesian equivalent of potato chips and plantain chips. There they are almost weightless delicacies to be nibbled while eating the daily meals. Here they make excellent snacks with drinks, or as an accompaniment to soups or salads.

1 Heat the oil in a frying pan until it begins to smoke ever so slightly, then reduce the heat by half and toss in the crisps. They will promptly increase considerably in size. Cook them and turn them as they change color. When they are golden, approaching brown, take them out with a slotted spoon and drain them on paper towels.

2 Serve hot or keep for future use. They will keep very well in a tightly sealed metal cookie box or a screw-top jar. The flavor is pleasantly indefinable; the texture is the thing.

Dutch Islands

KRUPUK UDANG (SHRIMP CRISPS)

◆

1 package shrimp crisps
1 to 2 cups vegetable oil for frying

SATÉS

◆

SKEWERED LAMB SATÉ

1 large yellow onion, sliced
2 garlic cloves, through the press
Juice of 1½ lemons
1 teaspoon tamarind concentrate
1 tablespoon brown sugar
4 curry leaves (optional)
¼ cup dark soy sauce
4 thin slices fresh ginger *or* 1 teaspoon ginger powder
1½ teaspoons ground cumin
½ teaspoon caraway seeds (optional)
1 tablespoon chunky peanut butter *or* 2 heaping tablespoons chopped cashew nuts
½ cup boiled coconut milk
Freshly ground black pepper to taste
Chili pepper to taste
2 pounds lean lamb, cut into ½-inch cubes (shoulder or leg cuts work best)
3 tablespoons vegetable oil

SERVES 4 AS A MAIN COURSE OR MAKES 72 HORS D'OEUVRES

Saté denotes any meat, seafood, or vegetable, marinated then skewered and fried, broiled, or grilled. The Antillean versions are not "authentic" Indonesian, but adaptations using local flavorants with results that possess their own charm. We prefer satés to those many skewered meat dishes that alternate the meats with half-cooked vegetables. Whether we've had them in Sicilian hill towns or in the Caribbean islands, we consider the skewers loaded only with deliciously spiced meats to be infinitely superior. Satés can be made with any meat and any firm fish (if the flesh is soft it will fall off) or shellfish. You will need plenty of bamboo saté sticks or thin metal skewers.

Party givers long ago discovered that satés and other skewered dishes make ideal hors d'oeuvres. The cooked meats are simply slipped off their skewers, pierced with toothpicks, and served to guests either hot or at room temperature.

1 Combine all the ingredients except the meat and oil in a blender or processor and reduce to a slurry.
2 Put the meat in a bowl just large enough to hold it and thoroughly stir in the marinade. Cover the bowl and let stand for 2 hours, turning the meat at least twice.
3 Thread the meat on very sharp, 6-inch bamboo saté sticks or metal skewers. Add the vegetable oil to the remaining marinade.
4 Cook the skewered meat over a charcoal fire, under the broiler, or in a heavy frying pan with some oil, basting with the marinade to prevent the meat from drying. Serve with condiments and vegetables and/or salad, either as part of the Rijstafel or featured in another meal.

Variation

Skewered Beef Saté   At step 1, add 1½ teaspoons coriander powder instead of the cumin powder. At step 2, substitute 2 pounds lean, tender beef for the lamb and proceed in the same way.

It is as easy to skewer sausages inside their casings as it is pieces of meat. However, doing the same thing with ground meat enclosed in a bacon casing is a much more difficult matter. Indonesians are said to wrap the soft mixture in sheeps' cauls, which we doubt. More likely they use the casings or intestines which are much more plentiful and have been used everywhere for stuffing (some casings available today are made of an edible synthetic). We believe that we have made the task easier by hardening the mix through cooling in the fridge.

1   Brown the onion and garlic in the oil. Be careful not to overheat and burn them. Remove with a slotted spoon. Bring the coconut milk to a boil and set aside.

2   Combine the onion, garlic, tamarind, coriander, sugar, and coconut milk in a blender or processor bowl. Process until it becomes a paste.

3   Add the lamb to the contents of the processor bowl. Process for 15 seconds. Remove the cutter blade. The mix should be very finely ground and very firm.

4   Transfer the lamb mixture to another bowl. Stir in the pepper and chili pepper. Mix thoroughly.

5   Set the lamb mixture, uncovered, in the fridge for at least 1 hour. This will further harden the mixture.

6   Lay out the bacon and cut each strip into 3 3½-inch lengths. Remove the lamb mixture from the fridge. With a spoon or melon cutter, scoop out small amounts of the lamb mixture. Lay 1 scoop on each bacon strip. Roll the bacon strips around the lamb and thread them on six-inch metal or bamboo skewers, about 3 or 4 to a skewer. Do this as rapidly as possible while the mix is cold. Leave portions of the lamb mixture in the fridge while you work, if necessary.

7   Wrap each prepared skewer very tightly in aluminum foil.

8   Broil for 6 minutes on each side.

9   Remove the foil and serve the lamb on the skewers.

Variation
Skewered Pork Saté   At step 2, add 1½ teaspoons shrimp paste and 1½ teaspoons freshly grated ginger *or* 1 teaspoon ground ginger. At step 3, substitute pork for the lamb and proceed in the same way.

Serve with a garnish of cucumber slices.

GROUND LAMB SATÉ

1 yellow onion, sliced
2 garlic cloves, peeled
¼ cup vegetable oil
½ cup canned coconut milk, boiled
½ teaspoon tamarind concentrate
1 tablespoon ground coriander
4 tablespoons dark-brown sugar
1 pound boned, fatty lamb, cut into ½-inch cubes
Freshly ground black pepper to taste
Chili pepper to taste
1 1-pound package thinly sliced, cured smoked bacon (each strip should be at least 1½ inches wide)

SERVES 2 AS A MAIN COURSE OR MAKES 36 HORS D'OEUVRES

TAHU GORENG (FRIED BEAN CURD OR TOFU)

◆

8 squares soybean curd
Vegetable oil for frying
½ pound fresh bean
 sprouts
1 red bell pepper, finely
 chopped
¼ cup soy sauce
2 garlic cloves, through
 the press
1 scallion, finely minced
1 teaspoon sugar
½ Scotch bonnet chili
 pepper or other small
 chili pepper, forced
 through a garlic press or
 minced
Juice of 1 small lemon
1 cucumber, thinly sliced

**SERVES 6 AS A
SALAD**

1 Cut the bean curd into 6 cubes each.

2 Deep fry in vegetable oil heated to 370 degrees until crisp and browned on all sides.

3 Heat water to boiling in a small pot and toss in the sprouts. Boil for 30 seconds. Drain. Cool in the fridge.

4 Put the remaining ingredients except the cucumber in a blender or processor and process for 4 seconds.

5 Spread the bean curd on a serving plate or distribute among 4 to 6 plates. Spread the sprouts and the cucumber over the bean curd. Pour the sauce over all. Serve very cold.

The tomatoes in this recipe were not, of course, an original ingredient back in Indonesia. It is a New World fruit which has spread everywhere since Columbus. In the Dutch islands they liven up the traditional formula, which, as usual, contains the inevitable trilogy of sugar, soy sauce, and vinegar.

1 In a bowl, stir the chicken pieces in the vinegar and sprinkle salt thoroughly over them while stirring.

2 Deep fry the chicken in the oil at 370 degrees until brown but not cooked through, about 5 minutes. (Deep frying is best, but frying over medium-high heat in ¼ inch of oil is adequate.) Drain the chicken on paper towels and reserve the oil.

3 Blend or process the onion, garlic, and Laos into a fine paste. Fry in 1 tablespoon of the reserved chicken oil until it acquires a "roasted" odor.

4 Add 2 cups of water to the pan along with the soy sauce, brown sugar, tomato, chili pepper, and extra salt to taste. Stir the chicken pieces into the mixture and finish cooking, about 10 minutes. Do not allow the sauce to dry out. Add a little water as needed and stir well.

AJAM OR AYAM SEMUR (FRIED CHICKEN)

◆

1 4-pound chicken, cut into 12 to 14 pieces
3 tablespoons white vinegar
Salt
Peanut or vegetable oil for frying
1 yellow onion, finely sliced
2 garlic cloves, through the press
2 teaspoons Laos powder
2 tablespoons soy sauce
1 tablespoon brown sugar
1 large, ripe tomato, chopped
Chili pepper to taste

SERVES 2 TO 4

SPICY CHICKEN OR DUCK

◆

RECIPE 1

3 tablespoons coriander
seeds *or* 2 tablespoons
ground coriander

1 tablespoon black cumin
seeds or ground cumin

1 tablespoon Laos powder
or 1 teaspoon ground
ginger

1 teaspoon ground tur-
meric

½ cup peanuts *or* 8
cashew nuts, grated or
processed

1 stalk fresh lemon grass,
sliced, *or* 1 tablespoon
grated lemon zest

2 or 3 medium yellow on-
ions, sliced

2 garlic cloves, through
the press

1 teaspoon tamarind con-
centrate (optional)

1 cup coconut milk, boiled

Salt and freshly ground
black pepper to taste

1 3- to 4-pound chicken *or*
4- to 6-pound duck, flat-
tened (butterflied)

1 small Scotch bonnet
chili pepper or other chili
pepper, forced through a
garlic press, to taste

SERVES 4

Here are two related recipes that are both superb. There is no reason whatsoever why they should not be standard ways of serving festive chicken or duck in American homes.

The Indonesian—and island—way is to cut the chicken or duck down the back and flatten it out, then spit it, and put it over a grill or turn it over a fire. This is not practical in most homes, but the flattening is convenient for carrying out the important continuous basting this recipe requires. Ask your butcher to split and flatten the bird (butterfly) without halving it. A couple of whacks with a heavy cleaver will flatten the carcass. Then you can roast the bird in the oven on a simple grill in a roasting pan or, alternately, set under the broiler for at least part of the cooking. The result is a richness of flavor, accompanied by a mouth-watering aroma, with which our normal roasting methods can't compete.

The first recipe has fewer ingredients and is milder in flavor than the second. The second recipe has more ingredients but lacks two of those in the first. Both recipes use the same method of preparation.

1   To prepare either recipe preheat the oven to 350 degrees.

2   In a processor bowl combine all the ingredients except the meat and chili pepper. Process for at least 15 seconds. A paste, just short of flowing, should be the result. It can be adjusted with a few more nuts to thicken or a little water to thin.

3   Decant into another bowl and stir in the chili pepper to taste

4   Place the meat on a rack in a roasting pan, skin side up, and spread part of the paste completely over it. Reserve enough paste for additional layers.

5   Roast the bird until tender, allowing about 18 minutes to a pound. When the heat has caked (solidified) the first layer of paste, spread another layer and repeat in this way until the paste is used up. Three bastings will probably be required.

6   When the meat is tender, if the surface of the basting paste is still dull in color, place the roasting pan under the broiler and broil until it turns brown.

7   Remove immediately from the broiler and keep hot in a 200-degree oven.

8   Bring in the bird whole on a platter and carve at table.

9   Provide a brown sauce or fruit sauce or condiments on the side.

RECIPE 2

3 tablespoons coriander seeds *or* 2 tablespoons ground coriander

1 tablespoon black cumin seeds or ground cumin

1 teaspoon ground turmeric

1½ tablespoons fennel seeds

4 mace blades, crushed in a mortar and pestle

1 teaspoon freshly grated nutmeg

1½ teaspoons ground cinnamon

1½ teaspoons ground cloves

1 teaspoon ground cardamom

1½ teaspoons freshly ground black pepper

1 1-inch piece peeled ginger, crushed with a mallet

1 tablespoon grated lemon zest

3 medium yellow onions, sliced

2 garlic cloves, through the press

1 teaspoon tamarind concentrate (optional)

1 cup coconut milk, boiled

Salt to taste

1 3- to 4-pound chicken *or* 4- to 6-pound duck, flattened (butterflied)

SERVES 4

NASI GORENG

◆

2 eggs
Vegetable oil for frying
1 onion, finely chopped
1 garlic clove, through the
  press
¼ small chili pepper,
  forced through a garlic
  press, or chili pepper to
  taste
¾ pound tender steak
  meat, cut into very thin
  strips, ⅜ inch wide and
  2½ inches long
10 raw shrimp, peeled
2 cups cold, cooked rice
1 tablespoon soy sauce
1 tablespoon sugar
Salt and freshly ground
  black pepper to taste

SERVES 5 TO 7

This is among the most famous, and common, of Indonesian dishes—very appetizing and easy to make. We find the sweetening and the soy sauce cloying when repeated and use other mixes of spices and herbs. However, this is the way it is prepared in the islands and in the Far East.

1 Beat the eggs and pour into a hot pan with the vegetable oil to make a thin omelet. Turn over once, using a plate to help flip it over in one piece. Remove and slice into thin strips. Reserve.

2 Using the same pan, gently fry the onion, garlic, and chili pepper until soft.

3 Add the meat and shrimp along with a little extra oil. Cook for 3 minutes.

4 Combine the rice with the contents of the pan and add the salt and pepper. Stir well while heating thoroughly. Serve with the shredded omelet piled on top.

Variation

Onion flakes (toss commercial dried onion flakes over medium heat, optionally in oil, until they turn light brown) and sliced tomatoes can be added as garnishes.

''**Rendangs**'' are very dry and very hot Indonesian meat curries. It is rare to meet up with them in mainland restaurants. Readers of this recipe may easily be confused by the absence of oil from the list of ingredients, despite the "frying" that follows. The mystery is solved when one knows that it is the coconut milk that supplies the fat. As the liquid evaporates, the thick lump of coconut fat that rises to the surface after cooling in the fridge is simply released into the pan. Tricky.

As canned coconut milk is thinner than fresh coconut milk, it may be necessary to add a little vegetable oil to the pan.

It seems like an awful waste of "tender steak," but the result, especially with somewhat reduced use of chili, is astonishingly enjoyable. It should be served with quantities of rice to quench its fires.

DAGING RENDANG (SLICED SPICED BEEF)

◆

¼ cup very thinly sliced fresh ginger
1 yellow onion, chopped
2 cups canned coconut milk
1 tablespoon ground coriander
1 teaspoon ground turmeric
1 large garlic clove, through the press
1½ teaspoons grated lemon zest *or* 1 teaspoon lemon grass powder
1 pound tender steak, cut into thin strips or bite-sized cubes
Chili pepper to taste
Salt and freshly ground black pepper to taste

SERVES 6

1 Blend or process the ginger and onion with 1 or 2 tablespoons of the coconut milk in order to make a paste. Then add the coriander, turmeric, and garlic. Add the rest of the coconut milk and blend or process completely.

2 Decant the mix into a frying pan and add the lemon zest. When the mix begins to boil, stir in the meat and coat it thoroughly. Add the chili pepper, salt, and pepper.

3 Continue cooking over high flame until the sauce is very thick.

4 Turn the heat to low but continue cooking. Soon the sauce will disappear and the oil from the coconut milk will be the only liquid in the pan. The meat will turn dark brown without burning (if the heat is sufficiently low). It is, obviously, dried out and thoroughly impregnated with the flavorants.

5 Serve the meat as a main course with rice or as individual snacks. The meat, though dry, will be crisp and tender as well as intensely flavorsome and sharp.

PISANG GORENG (BANANA FRITTERS)

◆

1 egg, beaten
4 tablespoons sugar
½ cup all-purpose flour
Salt to taste
4 to 5 ripe bananas, thoroughly mashed with a potato ricer or a fork
Vegetable oil for frying
¼ cup confectioners' sugar
1 teaspoon cinnamon powder

MAKES 8 TO 12 FRITTERS

1 Mix together the egg, sugar, flour, and salt. Then blend in the mashed banana very thoroughly.

2 Add ¼ inch of the oil to a skillet and heat to 370 degrees. Drop heaping tablespoons of the mixture into the oil and fry until well browned and crisp. Remove with a slotted spoon and drain on paper towels in a hot oven. Meanwhile, mix together the confectioners' sugar and cinnamon.

3 Serve with a generous coating of the confectioners' sugar and cinnamon mix. The fritters are delicious served with a tart apricot sauce.

• Nine •

MEATS

Empanadas, Empanditas, Patties,
◆ and Pastechis ◆

Throughout the Caribbean islands, small and large "turnovers," called *empanadas*, *empanditas*, patties, and *pastechis*, are made of thinly rolled doughs that enclose spiced meats, seafood, or vegetable fillings. The small are eaten out-of-hand as snacks or appetizers; the large are meal size and served at luncheon or dinner. They can be fried in shallow or deep oil or baked in the oven.

Empanadas are circles of dough folded over soft, spicy mixtures of meat and/or vegetables. They are big enough to make light meals. *Empanaditas* are smaller versions that are appetizer size and for snacks. Patties are much the same except that a flaky, crisp dough is used. *Pastechis* are Dutch but are called patties on some islands. Two circles of dough enclose the filling. No matter how they are cooked, they are, with their crisp golden crusts and savory fillings, one of the most appetizing treats that one can devise.

Disks of fresh, frozen, or precooked doughs for stuffing with fillings are sold by Hispanic and Indian groceries in the States. Even regular grocery chains are beginning to carry them. Not as good as homemade, they are a convenience as they need only to be fried or moistened and heated, filled, and folded.

1 Measure the *masa harina* into a bowl and pour the boiling water over it, stirring vigorously with a wooden spoon. Let cool.

2 When cool, sift in the flour, salt, and turmeric. (If using achiote oil and not ground turmeric, wait until the end of step 2 to add the oil.) Mix well into the *masa harina*. Add half the beaten egg. When the egg has been incorporated, add the melted butter and achiote oil.

3 Knead briefly to blend the dough. Roll out between sheets of floured wax paper to a thickness of ⅛ inch. Using a glass or cookie cutter, cut into 3-inch circles. Place the filling in the center of each circle. Brush the remaining beaten egg around the edges of the circles. Fold the circles in half over the filling and firmly press the edges together. Brush the top of the joining edge with the beaten egg, fold the edges over, and press down to seal. Flute the edges.

4 Fry in deep oil heated to 370 degrees until they are golden brown. Remove from the oil with a slotted spoon and place them in a hot oven on paper towels to drain. Keep in a hot oven until all the *empanadas* have been fried, then serve. They can be made earlier in the day and reheated in the oven just before serving.

Variation

Try Flaky Pie Crust, page 298, as an alternative dough for baking *empanadas*.

Note

If baking the *empanadas* in the oven instead of deep frying, place them on a buttered 11-x-17-inch baking pan. Brush the tops completely with the beaten egg and bake in a preheated 375-degree oven for 30 to 35 minutes or until the tops are golden brown.

DOUGH FOR EMPANADAS

◆

½ cup *masa harina* (fine cornmeal flour)
½ cup boiling water
½ cup all-purpose flour, plus additional flour for rolling out the dough
½ teaspoon salt
1 teaspoon ground turmeric or achiote oil (page 110)
1 egg, beaten
1 tablespoon butter, melted
Filling (pages 194–197)
Vegetable oil for frying

MAKES 12 3-INCH EMPANADITAS OR 4 6-INCH EMPANADAS

Jamaica

DOUGH FOR PATTIES

◆

½ cup water
⅛ teaspoon salt
1½ tablespoons butter
1½ tablespoons vegetable
 oil
1 teaspoon achiote oil
 (page 110)
1¼ cups all-purpose flour,
 plus additional flour for
 rolling out the dough
1 egg, beaten
Filling (pages 194–197)
Vegetable oil for frying

**MAKES 12 3-INCH
PATTIES OR 4
6-INCH PATTIES**

This is a cream puff–type dough, but thinly rolled out, as it contains more flour.

1   Put the water, salt, butter, and oils in a saucepan. Heat until the butter has melted. Turn off the heat, quickly stir in the flour, then add half the beaten egg. Beat the dough well with a wooden spoon, adding a little more flour if sticky.

2   Cover the saucepan, and let the dough stand for 30 minutes.

3   Roll out the dough, very thin, between sheets of floured wax paper.

4   Using a glass or cookie cutter, cut the dough into 3-inch circles. Gather the dough scraps, roll out, and cut into circles. Repeat until all the dough has been used.

5   Place 2 teaspoons of filling in the center of each circle. Brush the remaining beaten egg around the edges of the circles. Fold the circles in half over the filling and firmly press the edges together. Brush the top of the joining edge with the beaten egg, fold the edges over, and press down to seal. Flute the edges.

6   Fry the patties in 1-inch deep oil heated to 370 degrees, until well browned. Remove the patties from the oil with a slotted spoon and place them in a hot oven on paper towels to drain. Keep in a hot oven until all the patties have been fried, then serve.

Variation

Try Flaky Pie Crust, page 298, as an alternative dough for baking patties.

Note

If baking the patties in the oven, place them on a buttered 11-x-17-inch baking pan. Brush the tops completely with the beaten egg and bake in a preheated 375-degree oven for 30 to 35 minutes or until the tops are well browned.

1 Sift the 3 cups of flour into a bowl and set aside.

2 Cream the butter and shortening together in a mixing bowl. Add the salt and 1 egg. Mix well.

3 Slowly add 1 cup of the sifted flour, beating vigorously to incorporate.

4 Add ½ cup of the water and mix into the dough. Then add a second cup of flour and mix. When well incorporated add the third cup of flour. If the dough is too stiff, gradually add ¼ cup more of the water until the mixture holds together when kneaded.

5 Beat the remaining egg in a small bowl, and mix in the 1½ teaspoons cold water. Set aside.

6 Divide the dough into 2 pieces. Roll out half of the dough between sheets of floured wax paper until very thin. Using a glass or cookie cutter, cut out 3-inch circles and place them on a strip of wax paper. Cover with a second strip to keep the dough from drying out. Gather the dough scraps, roll out, and cut into circles. Repeat until all the dough has been used. Repeat with the remaining piece of dough. You must have an even number of circles in each lot.

7 Line up half of the pastry circles on a working surface and put a tablespoon of the filling in the center of each circle. Brush the edges with the beaten egg. Cover the filling with a second circle and press the edges together. Moisten the top edge with the beaten egg, fold the edges over the moistened surface, and press hard to seal. Flute the edges. Repeat with all the circles.

8 Drop a few *pastechis* at a time into deep oil heated to 370 degrees. Fry until golden brown. Remove with a slotted spoon, and place them in a hot oven on paper towels to drain. Keep in a hot oven until all the pastechis have been fried, then serve. The *pastechis* can be made earlier in the day and reheated in the oven just before serving.

Variation

Try Flaky Pie Crust, page 298, as an alternative dough for baking *pastechis*.

Note

If baking the *pastechis* in the oven, place them on 2 11-x-17-inch buttered baking pans, brush the tops completely with the beaten egg, and bake in a preheated 375-degree oven for 30 to 35 minutes or until the tops are golden brown.

Dutch Islands

DOUGH FOR *PASTECHIS*

◆

3 cups all-purpose flour, plus additional flour for rolling out the dough
2 tablespoons butter
2 tablespoons solid shortening
½ teaspoon salt
2 eggs, at room temperature
½ to ¾ cup plus 1½ teaspoons cold water
Filling (pages 194–197)
Vegetable oil for frying

MAKES 24 3-INCH PASTECHIS

FILLING 1 FOR *EMPANADAS, PATTIES, AND PASTECHIS*

◆

½ pound finely chopped or processed beef, lamb, mutton, or pork
2 tablespoons achiote oil (page 110) or margarine
2 tablespoons finely chopped scallions
1 garlic clove, through the press
1 tablespoon thinly sliced celery
2 tablespoons chopped green bell pepper
1 tomato, peeled and chopped, *or* 1 tablespoon tomato paste
½ teaspoon mustard seeds
½ teaspoon ground clove
Salt and freshly ground black pepper to taste
Chili pepper to taste
1 cup water

MAKES ENOUGH FILLING FOR 1 DOUGH RECIPE

The recipes that follow make enough filling for four six-inch *empanadas* or pastries or twelve three-inch *empanaditas* or small patties. Double the recipes for twenty-four three-inch pastries.

1 Fry the meat in the oil, stirring until lightly browned.

2 Add all the other ingredients to the pan.

3 Stir thoroughly and simmer on very low heat, covered, for at least 40 minutes, adding more water if needed.

4 Reduce the sauce so that the mix is soft but not runny, being careful not to burn the ingredients.

5 Remove the pan from the heat and follow the directions for filling *empanadas*, patties, or *pastechis* (pages 190–193).

Note

The filling can be made in advance, placed in a bowl in the fridge, and reheated with a little water when needed.

FILLING 2 FOR *EMPANADAS*, PATTIES, AND *PASTECHIS*

◆

1 Fry the meat in the oil, stirring until lightly browned.

2 Add all the other ingredients to the pan.

3 Stir thoroughly and simmer on very low heat, covered, for 1 hour, adding more water if needed. Stir occasionally.

4 Reduce the sauce so that the mix is soft but not runny.

5 Remove the pan from the heat and follow the directions for filling *empanadas*, patties, and *pastechis* (pages 190–93).

Variation

At step 4, before the mixture has been reduced to a soft but non-liquid consistency, add 1 beaten egg over low heat and stir very rapidly into the mix. The egg should absorb most of the excess liquid, if any, immediately.

Note

The filling can be made in advance, placed in a bowl in the fridge, and reheated with a little water when needed.

We find that long, patient simmering improves the texture and flavor immeasurably. It is such details that account for the differences between mediocre cooking and a truly savory production of distinction.

½ pound finely chopped or processed lamb, mutton, pork, or beef

2 tablespoons achiote oil or margarine

1 yellow onion, finely chopped

1 garlic clove, through the press

6 Spanish thyme leaves or small-leaved thyme, snipped, *or* 1 teaspoon dried marjoram leaves

1 teaspoon amchur powder *or* ½ teaspoon tamarind concentrate

1 tablespoon lemon juice

1 teaspoon ground allspice

Salt and freshly ground black pepper to taste

Chili pepper to taste

1 cup water

MAKES ENOUGH FILLING FOR 1 DOUGH RECIPE

FILLING 3 FOR *EMPANADAS, PATTIES, AND PASTECHIS*

◆

½ pound finely chopped or
  processed pork, beef,
  lamb, or mutton
¼ pound smoked ham or
  bacon, finely chopped or
  minced
1 yellow onion, finely
  chopped
1 garlic clove, through the
  press
2 tablespoons achiote oil
  (page 110)
½ cup snipped cilantro
  leaves
1 small green bell pepper,
  seeded and finely
  chopped
1 tomato, peeled and
  chopped
¼ cup cooked, crushed
  chick peas (optional)
¼ cup seedless raisins
  (optional)
Salt and freshly ground
  black pepper to taste
Chili pepper to taste
Water or chicken stock as
  needed

**MAKES ENOUGH
FILLING FOR 1
DOUGH RECIPE**

The following recipe is of a type that recently has been corrupted from the original down-island simplicity by the inclusion of European herbs, capers, olives, almonds, and canned pimientos, even raisins—imported ingredients that have begun to appear on store shelves. We have kept the original down-island recipe, except for the inclusion of raisins, which is due more to oddity than our taste. We have left it optional.

1 Fry the pork, ham, onion, and garlic in the oil until the meat is lightly browned.

2 Add all the other ingredients plus sufficient water or stock to cover.

3 Simmer, covered, for 40 minutes. Uncover and reduce the liquid so that the mix eventually becomes a soft paste. During the last 10 minutes cook over low heat and stir frequently until most of the liquid has evaporated.

4 Remove the pan from the heat and follow the directions for filling *empanadas*, patties, and *pastechis* (pages 190–93).

Note

With the additional ingredients, the yield of this recipe may be increased by about one-quarter, enough to fill a large *empanada* or patty.

The filling can be made in advance, placed in a bowl in the fridge, and reheated with a little water when needed.

The recipes for chicken fillings for *empanadas* and the like are very often filled with imported ingredients and not at all the way a down-islander, for whom the ingredients are alien, would make them. The resources of most of the islands are more than ample to turn out more tasty formulas, of which ours is only an example.

1   Sauté the chicken breasts in the vegetable oil, covered, over very low heat, until cooked, about 15 minutes. (If using chicken parts, sauté in the oil, covered, until cooked, about 25 to 30 minutes.)

2   Dice the cooked chicken breasts. (If using chicken parts, bone and dice the cooked chicken.)

3   In a large frying pan, combine all the ingredients except the diced salt pork. Add 1 or 2 tablespoons oil.

4   Fry the mixture gently for about 5 minutes. Mix in the salt pork at the end.

5   Remove the pan from the heat and follow the directions for filling *empanadas*, patties, and *pastechis* (pages 190–93).

Note

The filling can be made in advance, placed in a bowl in the fridge, and reheated with a little water when needed.

FILLING 4 FOR *EMPANADAS*, PATTIES, AND *PASTECHIS*

◆

¾ pound boned chicken breasts, cut into small pieces, *or* 1½ to 2 pounds chicken parts, with bones

2 tablespoons vegetable oil or margarine, plus additional oil as needed

1 teaspoon ground cardamom

½ teaspoon freshly grated nutmeg

½ teaspoon ground cinnamon *or* 1 teaspoon ground cassia

¼ cup chopped scallion leaves

Salt and freshly ground black pepper to taste

Chili pepper to taste

¼ pound diced salt pork, fried crisp and rendered fat discarded

MAKES ENOUGH FILLING FOR 1 DOUGH RECIPE

*Trinidad,
Tobago,
Tortola, and
Barbados*

DHAL (SPLIT PEA PUREE)

◆

¼ cup dried yellow split
   peas
1 2-inch scallion top
³⁄₁₆ teaspoon Madras curry
   powder
Coarsely ground black
   pepper
Salt to taste

◆ Roti ◆

Roti pancakes are always served with a filling of pureed meat, seafood, or vegetables and can be made into any size. As three-inch rounds they make ideal party snacks; as four- or five-inch rounds they make a satisfying light lunch; and as nine- to twelve-inch rounds they are a dinner course. As the pancakes increase in size they must be made thicker, so that a twelve-inch round is somewhat puffy and soft and folds four ways over the filling. The smaller rotis, folded only once, are quite thin. The amount of the filling increases with the size of the pancakes.

The dhal used in making the pancake itself, diluted and with extra ingredients, is the basis of our roti fillings.

Wherever East Indians have settled in the Caribbean islands, you will find roti as a staple meal. A large, rolled or folded whole wheat "pancake"— dhalpourri or paratha type—contains a thin, interior layer of split pea puree (dhal). After frying, the "pancake" is folded over a meat, fish, or vegetable curry containing potato as well as dhal.

We have seen these made over coalpots on the street corners in Port of Spain in Trinidad, at a tiny counter in a shack in Tobago's Charlotteville, at a sprawling beach-shack restaurant at Cane Garden Bay in Tortola, and at an upstairs restaurant overlooking the bay at Philipsburg on Sint Maarten—and we've enjoyed all the variations of fillings.

It was a Trinidadian friend who told us just how to make the island version of paratha. We have used her mixture of spices to flavor the dhal, but ground cumin can be substituted for curry powder; garlic for scallions; and sometimes a dash of chili powder is added to the mixture for spiciness.

1   Measure the split peas into a small bowl and wash thoroughly until the water is no longer cloudy. Cover the peas with water to a depth of ½ inch above the surface. Let soak for 2 hours.

2   Pour off the soaking water, rinse the peas, and pour them into a small saucepan. Add ¾ cup of water, the scallion top cut into ⅛-inch-thick slices, ¹⁄₁₆ teaspoon of the curry powder, and 2 turns of freshly ground black pepper. Bring to a boil and reduce the heat. Bring to a simmer and cover the pot. Cook for 40 minutes, stirring occasionally.

3   Remove the cover, turn up the heat, and stir with a long-handled spoon, for the puree will spatter as it thickens. After 10 minutes the puree should be the right thickness.

4 Remove from the heat and press the puree through a fine metal sieve into a small bowl. Add the remaining curry powder, or to taste, and the salt. Add more pepper to taste. Place the bowl in the fridge to cool the puree.

Note

This recipe will make more puree than you will need for 6 rotis, but any leftover puree can be added to the curried fillings or to additional rotis if you are doubling the dough recipe (below).

We've developed our own rhythm of forming, rolling, and frying each roti in succession. The balls of dough are first folded around the dhal. After placing the rolled roti dough on the hot pan, start filling and rolling the next ball of dough, keeping an eye on the griddle and turning the roti over as it browns. The newly rolled-out roti should be ready by the time the cooked one is done. If you try to fill all the balls at once with the dhal before rolling them out, the dough will have softened and the dhal will spurt out immediately upon rolling.

1 Mix the dry ingredients together in a mixing bowl. Add the butter and blend it into the flour mixture with your fingertips until smooth. Gradually add the water, stirring the dough with a wooden spoon. The dough will be slightly soft. Knead the dough in the bowl for 5 minutes, turning, folding, and punching it with clenched fists. (This whole procedure can also be done in a processor.)

2 Divide the dough into 6 equal parts, and roll each part into balls between the palms of your hands. Set aside on a lightly floured sheet of wax paper. Cover with a slightly dampened piece of cheesecloth or clean dish towel. You will be working with 1 ball at a time, and the dampness will prevent the surfaces of the dough from drying out.

3 Cup a ball of dough in the palm of your hand, and open the ball up around the edges, spreading it but *not thinning the center section too much*. Smooth a tablespoon of split pea puree (dhal) into the opened area. Fold the edges of dough over the puree, overlapping sections as you work around the circle, dipping a finger in water to help seal the overlapping folds. Roll the dough lightly between the palms of your hands to shape the ball.

4 Put the ball on a floured sheet of wax paper on a pastry board. With your fingers, lightly press it into a disk about 4 inches in diameter. Cover the disk with a second sheet of floured wax paper, and carefully roll out a thin 9-inch

DOUGH FOR ROTI

◆

1 cup all-purpose flour
1 cup whole wheat flour
¼ teaspoon salt
1 teaspoon baking powder
1½ tablespoons butter, cut
 into small pieces
1 cup warm water
6 tablespoons Dhal
 (page 198)
Vegetable oil for frying

**MAKES 6 ROTIS, 9
INCHES IN DIAMETER**

disk. Roll the dough from the center without rolling over the edges. If you thin the edges too much and too quickly, the filling will spurt out. As you reach the 9-inch size, a certain amount of filling will ooze out, but just scrape it off.

5   While you are rolling out the first roti, heat a large, heavy frying pan or griddle on top of the stove until a few drops of water sprinkled into the pan will bounce. Brush the pan very lightly with the oil and transfer the roti to the pan. Lightly brush the top of the roti with oil and turn it over. Cook on each side until browned in small blisters, smoothing the top with the back of a table-spoon. Exact cooking time has too many variables—the moistness of the roti dough, the heat of the pan. Too long a cooking time will toughen the roti; you also will be reheating the roti just before folding it around the curried filling.

6   Transfer the cooked roti to a paper towel and repeat the process of forming, rolling, and frying the dough.

7   When cool, layer the rotis between sheets of clear plastic wrap, one on top of the other. Place the pile on a plate and put into the refrigerator until needed. Reheat in a hot frying pan or on a griddle just before serving.

ROTI FILLING 1

◆

1 cup Dhal (page 198)
2 cups water
¾ pound beef, goat, lamb, pork, or chicken, cut into very small cubes, *or* ½ pound raw or cooked shelled shrimp, chopped into small pieces
1 medium potato, yam, or malanga, sliced and diced small
Salt and freshly ground black pepper to taste
Chili pepper to taste

1   In a casserole, stir the dhal paste with the water. Bring to a boil and reduce to a simmer.

2   Add the meat. (If using shrimp, do not add until after step 3 is completed.) Stir well. Cover and simmer gently for 2 to 3 hours, being careful to add more water if the mixture becomes too thick or begins to stick to the bottom of the casserole.

3   Adjust the texture, which should be a thick puree, slightly flowing. Adjust the seasoning by adding the salt, pepper, and chili pepper to taste.

4   Add the potato and simmer for 15 minutes. (If using shrimp, add here, after the potato has simmered, and cook for 3 minutes.)

5   The filling can be refrigerated until needed. Reheat, if necessary. It should be piping hot, ready to fill the roti pancakes (page 199) as they come off the griddle.

6   Place a quantity of filling in the center of each roti. Small rotis should be simply folded over once; large rotis may be folded 4 ways. This should be done quickly so that, whatever the size, the stuffed rotis are very hot when offered at the table.

MAKES ENOUGH FILLING FOR 4 TO 6 9-INCH PANCAKES, 20 TO 24 4-INCH PANCAKES, OR 26 TO 30 3-INCH PANCAKES

The following recipe employs the same basic ingredients as Roti Filling 1, but with typical additions.

ROTI FILLING 2

◆

¾ pound beef, goat, lamb, pork, or chicken, cut into small cubes, *or* ½ pound raw or cooked shelled shrimp, chopped into small pieces
1 garlic clove, through the press
1 onion, chopped, *or* 3 scallions, sliced fine
1 green bell pepper, seeded and chopped
1 tablespoon fenugreek leaves (optional)
3 tablespoons Colombo powder (page 112) or Madras curry powder, mild or hot, to taste
1 teaspoon ground turmeric
1 tablespoon ground cumin
1 teaspoon freshly grated ginger *or* 1½ teaspoons ground ginger
Salt and freshly ground black pepper to taste
Chili pepper to taste
1 large potato or medium yam or malanga, sliced and diced
1 cup Dhal (page 198)
2 tablespoons vegetable oil

1   In a casserole mix together all the ingredients except the potato and the dhal paste. (If using shrimp, do not add until 5 minutes before serving.)
2   Pour in the vegetable oil and stir the meat and spices thoroughly together over moderate heat. Keep stirring for 4 minutes as the meat becomes thoroughly impregnated with the oil and spice mixture.
3   Cover the mix with water, bring to a boil. Cover and reduce heat to a minimum for simmering.
4   Simmer for 2 to 3 hours, checking the liquid from time to time. Add more water if needed to prevent from becoming too thick or sticking to the casserole.
5   Thirty minutes before serving, check the seasoning, then add the potato and dhal, stirring well. The mixture will thicken and the liquid should be of a barely flowing puree consistency. Add water or reduce through heating to maintain it that way. (If using shrimp, add here 5 minutes before serving.)
6   When ready to serve, take the hot roti pancakes out of the oven and place a dab of the mixture in the middle of each one. (Use more filling for large rotis, less for small rotis.) Fold the small ones over once and the large ones 4 ways. Serve hot.

MAKES ENOUGH FILLING FOR 4 TO 6 9-INCH PANCAKES, 20 TO 24 4-INCH PANCAKES, OR 26 TO 30 3-INCH PANCAKES

◆ Beef ◆

St. Kitts

PEPPERPOT

◆

1 to 2 pounds oxtail
1 to 2 pigs' or calves' feet, halved or quartered
1 pound lean beef, cut into cubes
1 stewing chicken, cut into 12 or more pieces
1 to 2 4-ounce jars of salt beef, cut into 1- to 2-inch pieces (substitute corned beef if necessary)
½ cup casareep (see page 34)
Salt to taste
Scotch bonnet chili pepper or other chili pepper to taste

SERVES 8 TO 12

This famous recipe attributed to Guiana or some of the more southerly islands is quite possibly of ancient Indian origin. It has spread notably to St. Kitts as well as Barbados, Jamaica, and other islands. Certainly casareep is local. As for the other ingredients, they are simply a mélange of meats, such as any down-island cook might put together from whatever happens to be available in sufficient quantity for a family get-together. It is also laced with plenty of chili pepper, which can be compromised but never to the point of blandness.

Meals such as this, common everywhere down-island, have been largely banished from the menus of restaurants that serve nouvelle cuisine. But in doing so, they have lost foods of character, blanketing the meats in mild sauces instead of enhancing them with contrasting flavors. Much the same effect is achieved by sauces that are strained, eliminating all those different textures of their ingredients in favor of unchanging silkiness.

Casareep, being reputed a preservative, allows leftovers of Pepperpot to be added to other leftovers and stored indefinitely, despite the tropical temperatures, to be available in emergencies and on special occasions. We do not recommend trying it.

1   Put the meats and casareep in a large casserole. Add water to cover.
2   Simmer 2 or more hours until the meats are tender.
3   Fish out any loose bones with a slotted spoon. Add the salt and chili pepper. The chili pepper should be as strong as you can stand it. The sauce should be syrupy. Simmer, uncovered, or add a little water to make it just right.
4   Serve in soup bowls with separately cooked slices or cubes of yam, malanga, dasheen root, or cassava.

Note

As the simple combination of sweet (casareep) and very hot (chilis) may be cloying for some, we suggest the addition of tomatoes, dried tomatoes, onions, scallions, garlic, green mango, papaya, carrots, celery, chopped dasheen leaves, green peppers, and more, individually or together to enrich the dish according to your own taste or to increase the total number of servings. This is exactly what a down-island cook would do.

This traditional recipe should be hot and spicy, but for many it will be just as tasty if milder. It is best served as a lunch dish. Handling the plantain takes a bit of practice.

Down-island, this dish is made with any leftover meats whatsoever, cooked or uncooked. If no meat is available cooked beans take its place.

1   Slice each of the plantains lengthwise into 3 or 4 strips, depending upon the thickness, and fry gently in the vegetable oil until golden. Remove to drain on paper towels and set aside.

2   Add the achiote oil to the pan and stir in the beef, frying until browned but not crisp. Break up any lumps carefully.

3   Add the scallions, bell pepper, and garlic. Stir well. Follow with the ham, cornstarch, tomatoes, capers, and tamarind. Finally, add the salt, pepper, and chili pepper.

4   Stir in a few tablespoons of water and simmer until the mixture is moderately firm and the flavors are blended, about 4 minutes.

5   Heat the oil for deep-fat frying in a pan to 365 degrees.

6   Coil each plantain slice into a circle 3 inches across with vertical sides and hold the overlap together with pieces of toothpicks. On a flat surface, stuff the rings with the meat mixture. Pat it in firmly and flatten the top to form fairly solid patties.

7   In a wide, shallow bowl, beat the eggs with a whisk. Slip each patty into the egg mixture, turning so that it is completely covered, and drop into the heated oil. Brown the patties, about 4 minutes, and drain on paper towels.

8   The patties can be served immediately, reheated in an oven and served later, or frozen for future use.

Puerto Rico, Cuba, and the Dominican Republic

PIONONOS (STUFFED PLANTAINS)

◆

2 to 3 ripe plantains, peeled

3 tablespoons vegetable oil, plus additional oil for frying

2 to 3 tablespoons achiote oil (page 110)

1 pound lean ground chuck or sirloin

¾ cup chopped scallions

½ green bell pepper, seeded and chopped

1 garlic clove, through the press

¼ pound diced ham or spicy sausage

2 tablespoons cornstarch

3 medium tomatoes, peeled and chopped

1½ tablespoons capers

1 teaspoon tamarind concentrate

Salt and freshly ground black pepper to taste

Chili pepper to taste

3 to 4 eggs

SERVES 4 TO 6

St. Martin

BEEF SHORT RIBS

◆

THE MARINADE

4 tablespoons tomato
  paste, preferably im-
  ported
2 tablespoons red vinegar
  or white wine vinegar
2 garlic cloves, through
  the press
1 tablespoon dried basil
  leaves
1 teaspoon dried parsley
1 tablespoon strong dry
  mustard
¼ teaspoon grated clove or
  ground clove
¼ teaspoon freshly grated
  nutmeg
1 teaspoon ground cumin
1 teaspoon Bonney Pepper
  Sauce or fresh chili pepper, forced through a
  garlic press, to taste
Salt and freshly ground
  black pepper to taste
2 tablespoons vegetable oil

THE BEEF

4 beef short ribs, consisting of 3 to 4 sections of
  bone with a thick covering of meat

SERVES 2 TO 3

I t is unfortunate that most mainland homes cannot use charcoal grills except for occasional summer barbecues. What a difference they make with almost any meat or fish! The finest sauces in the world can hardly compete with, say, the flavor of charcoal flame on sirloin steaks in a woodsy setting. Much of the best island cooking comes off grills in restaurants and coalpots in local homes. Instead of charcoal, the fuel is brushwood or huge bean pods and the results are quite stupendous without any frills. The ladies of St. Martin have it down to a science on their grills and quite outdo the cooking of the restaurants close by. It will be a sad day when bottled gas and electric hot plates (to say nothing of the microwave) replace this perfect way of cooking so many good things.

This marinade and sauce, which is a typical island mix, is equally good with chicken, pork spareribs, and boned breast of goat and lamb.

Finally, we specify *strong* mustard. At present, the only mustard on our shelves is the Chinese mustard. American versions of European mustards are a travesty. A good bet is to mix Colman's dry mustard with a good wine vinegar; it's easy to make and tastes much better than the prepared mustard available in bottles.

1 Mix all the ingredients of the marinade together in a bowl except the oil. When the mix thickens, add a little water until it becomes like a heavy syrup. Allow to stand for about 1 hour, during which the ingredients will continue to absorb more of the moisture. Then stir in the vegetable oil and as much water, a little at a time, to cause the marinade to become just barely flowing.

2 Stand the meat up in a long narrow dish or hold together with skewers on a pan.

3 Spoon or brush half the sauce over the meat, making sure that it is all covered. Allow to stand at cool room temperature for 2 to 4 hours.

4 Place the meat under a preheated broiler and cover with a sheet of aluminum foil.

5 Broil for 20 minutes, then reduce the thermostat to 300 degrees and continue cooking for another 20 minutes.

6 Remove the foil and spread the rest of the marinade over the meat and cook, uncovered, for another 20 minutes at the same temperature.

7 Remove from the oven and serve at least 3 sections of bone and meat for each portion.

This is not a traditional down-island recipe for the reason that tender steaks were virtually unknown there until recently. They are more common now, and since the recipe originates in Martinique, it merits the epithet "Creole." Besides, it's a very snappy way of making a quick and piquant steak.

1 Heat the butter in a pan and fry the scallion for not more than 1 minute. Remove with a slotted spoon to a plate.

2 Raise the heat to high and allow the pan to become smoking hot.

3 Toss in the steak and fry no more than 1½ minutes on each side. (If using 2 thin steaks, allow 45 seconds for each side.)

4 Flip the steaks. Quickly add the salt, pepper, and chili pepper to the surface, spread the mustard mixture on it, and at the last moment, sprinkle the scallion over the surface.

5 Serve immediately on a preheated plate with Sauce Chien (page 53) on the side.

Note
This recipe can be multiplied as necessary to produce a larger yield.

Martinique

MINUTE STEAK CREOLE

◆

1 to 2 ounces butter or margarine
1 whole scallion, snipped and chopped
1 ¾-pound well-hung, lean, boneless shell steak (New York cut) *or* 2 thinner steaks, approximately ½ pound each
Salt and freshly ground black pepper to taste
Chili powder or chili sauce to taste
1 teaspoon French or dry English mustard mixed with ¼ teaspoon ground coriander or ground allspice

SERVES 1

French Islands

DAUBE OR MATETÉ OF BEEF

◆

½ pound diced salt pork
2 pounds lean bottom
 round of beef (chuck or
 eye-of-round will do but
 is inferior)
2 cups dry red or white
 wine or water
2 medium yellow onions,
 peeled and quartered, *or*
 4 scallions, coarsely
 chopped.
2 celery stalks cut into
 pieces
1 cup sliced carrots
1 large green bell pepper,
 seeded, sliced, and
 coarsely diced
½ cup canned or fresh
 tomatillos (optional)
10 dried tomatoes *or* 2
 large fresh tomatoes,
 peeled and quartered
1 teaspoon tamarind con-
 centrate
2 teaspoons ground cumin
½ cup snipped cilantro
 leaves
1 pound yam, yautia, or
 dasheen, cut into small
 cubes

SERVES 4

In the French islands the local word *matete* is used for ragout. A ragout may be a fricassee, and a fricassee may be any mixture of vegetables and meat, and daube is a stew or pot roast.

Under any name, the preparation of large pieces of beef, lamb, goat, or pork is a production as exotic as it is seductive, as appetizing as any pot roast you are likely to experience anywhere else. Prepare a day or two ahead for maximum goodness and serve with rice or one of the splendid root starches for which there is rich sauce aplenty.

1 In a casserole fry the salt pork until golden. Remove the cubes with a slotted spoon and reserve.

2 Fry the meat in the oil left in the casserole until lightly browned. The meat can be left whole or cubed in bite-size pieces.

3 Add the wine, onion, celery, carrot, bell pepper, tomatillo, tomato, tamarind, cumin, and cilantro. Add sufficient water just to cover.

4 Simmer for a minimum of 2 hours, adding liquid when the depth of the sauce in the casserole becomes less than 2 inches. Simmer until the meat is tender.

5 Add the yam and simmer 20 minutes longer. This should help thicken the sauce.

6 Add the salt, pepper, chili pepper, and the burnt sugar syrup for coloring. Toss in the reserved salt pork.

7 The amount of sauce should be at least 1½ cups. Reduce by simmering, uncovered, or add a little water or wine to thin the sauce. It should contain solids from the vegetables and should not be strained.

8 If the meat has been cubed it can be served immediately with the sauce. If cooked whole, remove the meat, allow to stand for a few minutes, and then cut into slices across the grain with a very sharp knife, applying minimum pressure. Reheat in the sauce and serve with the sauce on the side.

Salt and freshly ground
 black pepper to taste
Chili pepper to taste

1 teaspoon Burnt Sugar
 Syrup (page 117)

Until meats started to be imported from the mainland, beef, lamb, goat, and pork were usually very tough indeed. Even now that mainland meats are available, the quality, except for the more expensive restaurants, remains poor. In the old days the best meat went to plantation owners. So down-islanders are experienced in making the best of what is available—the more inexpensive cuts. Of beef these are chuck, round, flank, and shin. The poorer lamb and pork cuts are from the shoulder. All these meats, and the tough goat (euphemistically called kid), can be cooked in a casserole on top of the stove and made into very tasty meals. Moreover, the islanders use papaya fruit, which contains the enzyme papain—a tenderizer that breaks down meat fibers. The fruit, when in season, is widely used for this purpose.

1 Spread the papaya on a plate, cover with the meat, and lay the rest of the papaya on top. Place in the fridge for 2 to 3 hours.

2 Spread the oil in the bottom of a pan or casserole. Spread the onion on the bottom and lay the steaks over the onion. Cover the steaks with papaya and spread the tomato over all.

3 Simmer, tightly covered, for 30 minutes or until the meat is tender. Check the liquid. The meat, onion, and tomato should supply enough. If not, a little water should be added.

4 Spread the lentils over the casserole. Cover.

5 Simmer for 15 minutes longer. Remove the cover and add the tamarind and papaya seeds. Season with the salt, pepper, and chili pepper. Adjust the thickness of the liquid and serve.

St. Thomas

PAPAYA BEEF STEAK

◆

1 small papaya, peeled, sliced, and seeds removed and reserved

1½ pounds beef, lamb, or pork suitable for potting

3 tablespoons achiote oil (page 110)

3 medium yellow onions, sliced

1 large tomato, peeled and chopped

1 cup cooked lentils or small beans

1 teaspoon tamarind concentrate (optional)

Salt and freshly ground black pepper to taste

Chili pepper to taste

SERVES 2

Tobago

PLANTAIN MEAT PATTIES

◆

1 yellow plantain, peeled and cut into chunks
½ teaspoon ground all-spice
¼ teaspoon freshly grated nutmeg
1 teaspoon Colombo powder (page 36) *or* ½ teaspoon mild Madras curry powder
Chili pepper to taste
1 egg
¼ teaspoon salt
1 pound ground beef
All-purpose flour for dredging the meat patties
Vegetable oil for frying

MAKES 6 PATTIES

These exotic patties should be served with typical island bottled sauces, such as Pickapeppa (Jamaica), the Matouk sauces from Trinidad, Green Sauce (page 55), or one of the mild yellow island chili sauces now being distributed through larger mainland chain groceries and Hispanic and island shops. One can also make a brown sauce in the pan with Roasted Flour (page 113).

1   Put all the ingredients but the meat, flour, and oil into a blender or processor and spin for about 8 seconds.
2   In a bowl combine the meat and the contents of the processor bowl, mixing well with a spoon.
3   Form into 3-inch patties. Dredge in the flour to cover completely.
4   Fry in shallow oil or deep fat heated to 365 degrees until the surfaces are crisp.

Sancocho appears to be an ancient name for stew in northern South America and the Antilles, although less commonly found in the French-speaking islands. It is a catch-all whose charms derive from a great mélange of seasonal local products cooked with the basic meats. We have followed local custom in our kitchens on various visits to the islands and come up with different results every time—though with what we may legitimately call "island taste," derived from the exotic quality of some spices, the local squash, greens, and starches, and the never-failing chili pepper. In short, one improvises according to the season.

We give several versions of this recipe (see Goat Sancocho and Lamb Sancocho, page 213), allowing great freedom. However, we do not recommend what is often described as authentic—namely mixes of all four major starches. These may happen occasionally because quantities of each are in short supply, but the usual combination is a squash and a starch. All of them makes less culinary sense. Mainlanders will have fun experimenting with other ingredients. A little daring will produce a rich stew-like soup, ideal for those wretchedly cold days of winter, especially after sports or other physical activity when one's appetite is keen.

1 Fry the meats and onion in a large casserole until lightly browned.
2 Add the peas, cover with water, and simmer for 1 hour.
3 Add the remaining ingredients except the plantain, salt, and pepper. Simmer until the meat is tender.
4 Meanwhile, boil the plantain in its skin until it is softened. Cool slightly, remove the skin, and cut into thick slices. Add to the casserole.
5 Season with the salt and pepper and check if other seasonings are needed.
6 Store in the fridge for reheating later or serve promptly in soup bowls.

Variation

Add 2 peeled tomatoes, cut into chunks, a few minutes before serving.

Note

The procedures are really essentially the same for all sancochos and the above is hardly, if at all, different from goat sancocho.

Trinidad

BEEF OR OXTAIL SANCOCHO

◆

½ pound pigs' ears, jowls, or tails, cut into chunks
2½ pounds boneless beef, cubed, *or* 5 pounds meaty oxtail
2 yellow onions, chopped
1 cup split yellow peas or lentils
2 pounds yam, cut into thick, large cubes
1 tablespoon amchur powder *or* 1 teaspoon tamarind concentrate
1 teaspoon ground anise
1 tablespoon ground coriander
1 teaspoon dried mace
1 tablespoon ground turmeric
2 cups coconut milk (optional)
1 whole chili pepper
1 green plantain, unpeeled
Salt and freshly ground black pepper to taste

SERVES 6 TO 8

◆ Goat, Lamb, and Mutton ◆

Goat stews are still common in the islands both at home and in restaurants. The tropical climate has never been hospitable to domestic animals, except the goat, which survives in most situations. They can be seen everywhere in the Antilles, usually tethered to prevent them from consuming whatever vegetation remains in the wild. One can see the down-islanders careening home on bicycles balancing loads of grass and weeds on the handlebars for the goat tied close to the house.

In the Spanish islands one is offered *cabrito*, or kid, and you can almost imagine the cute little fellows gamboling around their parents. But their appearance on the table is illusory. One is reminded of D. H. Lawrence *(Sea and Sardinia)* sitting, exhausted from a day's hiking, in front of a Sardinian hearth, tantalized unbearably by the sight and tantalizing odor of kid roasting on the spit, and then being served old goat in a stew while the host family regales itself with the pièce de résistance.

Yes, the goat will usually be mature and strong flavored, but if cooked long enough it will be tender and altogether appetizing if prepared with down-island combinations of spices and bush. Results are a revival of taste sensations we no longer experience with our pampered, tender, but often bland and insipid, meats.

One lunchtime we stopped at Eunice's Terrace, near the turn off for Coral World. Eunice is the ultimate island cook, and her tiny restaurant of weathered wood, with a porch-like dining room crowded with chairs and tables, is easily passed by. Here, for the first time, we ate a goat stew flavored with allspice, and we quickly made notes to try this ourselves.

This Creole stew of goat is distinctive and fit for a feast. We particularly recommend it to those who, like ourselves, were brought up on white Irish-style lamb stew with potatoes, a dish that sticks in the memory as a test of endurance.

1 If the raw meat is difficult to cut, indicating that it is tough, place the pieces in a bowl, and interlayer with the papaya. Set aside at room temperature for 3 hours.

2 Separate the papaya and the meat and reserve the fruit. In a casserole, brown the meat with the achiote oil and onion for about 6 minutes.

3 Add the wine and enough water to cover. Stir in the remaining ingredients except the salt, pepper, chili pepper, and burnt sugar syrup.

4 Simmer, covered, at least 2 hours or until the meat is tender.

5 Remove the bay leaves with a slotted spoon. Carefully season with the salt, pepper, and chili pepper. Add the burnt sugar syrup. The sauce should be plentiful and fairly thick. Reduce through further simmering or add a little water if necessary.

6 Serve with your favorite starches and green vegetables. Or, store for 1 or 2 days in the fridge. When reheating, you will find that the sauce has thickened and that it is necessary to add some wine or water to make a sauce that flows but does not run.

Variation
Substitute the same amount of lamb or mutton for the goat.

St. Thomas

GOAT RAGOUT

◆

2½ pounds goat stewing meat, with bone, *or* 1½ pounds lean, boneless meat

½ unripe papaya, finely sliced and seeds removed

3 tablespoons achiote oil (page 110) or plain vegetable oil

1 large yellow onion, chopped

2 cups dry red or white wine or water

1 large green or red bell pepper, seeded and cut into pieces

1 celery stalk, cut into small slices

1 large garlic clove, through the press

4 bay leaves

5 whole allspice, crushed in a mortar and pestle, *or* ½ teaspoon ground allspice

1 teaspoon tamarind concentrate (optional)

Salt and freshly ground black pepper to taste

1 small chili pepper, seeded, cut into pieces, and force through a garlic press

1 teaspoon Burnt Sugar Syrup (page 117)

SERVES 2

French Islands

COLOMBO OF GOAT, MUTTON, OR LAMB

◆

3 tablespoons vegetable oil
or 6 ounces cubed salt
pork
1½ to 2 pounds lean goat,
mutton, or lamb, cut into
1½-inch cubes
2 medium yellow onions,
peeled and chopped
1 large green bell pepper,
chopped
1 tablespoon freshly grated
ginger *or* 1½ teaspoons
ground ginger
1 tablespoon dried fenu-
greek leaves
1 teaspoon ground cinna-
mon *or* 1 1-inch cinna-
mon stick
3 tablespoons Colombo
powder (page 112) *or* 2
tablespoons Madras curry
powder
2 cups water
½ pound white yam, cut
into small cubes
1 teaspoon Burnt Sugar
Syrup (page 117)
Chili pepper to taste
Salt to taste

SERVES 2

This Colombo recipe is just one of the many possibilities for ingredients and proportions which occur in every Creole household according to the changing seasons. Having made it once, you can launch on all kinds of quite safe experiments. The Colombo or curry powder blankets all the other flavors, which break through only as nuances, but can make interesting differences just the same. Try other vegetables and spices.

This recipe is for two servings but such curry ragouts are frequently made for large parties. Just multiply everything accordingly and cook slowly. The ragout can be prepared a day in advance and stored in the fridge. The delay improves the flavor. When reheated, additional water usually has to be added.

1   In an enameled casserole heat the vegetable oil or fry the cubed salt pork until golden.
2   Add the meat, onions, green pepper, ginger, fenugreek, cinnamon, and Colombo. Stir thoroughly. Cover and simmer for 30 minutes.
3   Add the water and stir well. Simmer for 1½ hours. Add more water if the sauce becomes too thick.
4   Add the yam and simmer the stew for 20 more minutes or until the meat is thoroughly tender.
5   Add the burnt sugar syrup, chili pepper, and salt. Simmer for at least another 5 minutes. Serve hot with rice or root starches.

Variation

The servings can be increased to at least 6 by adding 3 cups of cooked split peas, lentils, or beans to the stew 10 minutes before serving. Additional water may be required to thin the sauce.

In a restaurant the menu may list a sancocho of kid or kid stew, but we have never seen a young goat served anywhere in the islands. They exist, of course, and are consumed by local families on very special occasions, but the usual victim is one of those nannies tethered beside the road as you enter town. She's tough but well seasoned—by nature and a vegetable diet. As a stewing animal they don't come better, reviving intense flavors that have almost entirely disappeared from modern meats.

This recipe is also a sort of basic model on which, with all the repertory of Caribbean meats, vegetables, and cooking fruits, one can develop a host of variations. In short we treat sancocho as the essential basic stew of the islands, and the following ingredients are only the ones which one cannot well do without. Other stewed meat recipes will fill in the picture.

Note the sancocho is not treated as an entrée or first course but as a meal. A portion is the whole dinner.

1   Heat the oil or rendered fat in a large casserole. Add the meats and onion and fry, stirring, for 5 minutes over high heat.

2   Cover with water, reduce the flame to a minimum, and simmer until the meat is tender, 2 to 3 hours.

3   Add the remaining ingredients except the salt and cilantro. Simmer for another 30 minutes.

4   Fish out the bay leaves with a slotted spoon. Do the same with the chili pepper if you have used a whole one. Salt to taste.

5   The stew is ready to serve but will only improve if stored in the fridge overnight.

6   Twenty minutes before serving, reheat the stew, being careful to prevent it from sticking to the bottom of the pot. Add water if needed to prevent the mix from solidifying. There should be plenty of liquid sauce.

7   Six minutes before serving, add the cilantro. Sprinkle with cracklings on serving.

Variation

Lamb Sancocho   This is a Trinidadian dish that calls for lamb in place of the goat. It is less intensely flavored, so we suggest adding 1 tablespoon ground cumin and 1 tablespoon fenugreek (optional).

Proceed with the basic recipe directions.

Note

If the goat is tough, tenderize by marinating with green papaya slices for 3 hours before cooking.

Jamaica

GOAT SANCOCHO

◆

3 tablespoons vegetable oil or fat rendered from diced salt pork, cracklings reserved

3 to 4 pounds goat meat with bone, cut into manageable chunks

½ pound pigs' ears, jowls, or tails, cut into small pieces

2 medium yellow onions, coarsely chopped

2 garlic cloves, peeled

1 tablespoon dried sage leaves (optional)

4 bay leaves or bay rum leaves

6 crushed malagueta or whole allspice

1 teaspoon tamarind concentrate (optional)

½ pound peeled calabaza, cut into chunks

½ pound peeled yam, dasheen, or malanga, cut into chunks

1 teaspoon Burnt Sugar Syrup (page 117)

1 green plantain, peeled and cut into thick slices

1 Scotch bonnet chili pepper or other chili pepper

Salt to taste

½ cup snipped cilantro leaves

SERVES 6 TO 8

St. Thomas

LAMB WITH BEANS AND RICE

◆

1 pound boneless stewing
  lamb
1 garlic clove, through the
  press
2 tablespoons vegetable oil
Sofrito powder or liquid to
  taste
Chili pepper to taste
½ cup water
1 recipe Black Beans and
  Rice (page 233)

SERVES 6

This is a natural development of the beans and rice theme, so popular in island cooking and spawning endless small changes of ingredients as various vegetables and fruits become available during the year.

1 Simmer the lamb and the garlic in the oil for 20 minutes, covered. Add the sofrito, chili pepper, and water. Cover and simmer for 30 minutes. Reduce the liquid to a syrupy sauce. Add more water if needed.

2 Serve the meat and its sauce in the center of a ring of the beans and rice or stirred in with it.

Variation

Any other cooked beans may be substituted for the black beans.

We stayed in one of several six-sided cottages on St. Lucia, and, even though we had a kitchen, we often ate at the rambling, palm-frond-roofed, open-air dining room at the edge of the beach, with a small water garden in the middle of all the chairs and tables. One of Marguerite's special appetizers was small skewered meats broiled over a clay coalpot set on a long table. Piping hot, the skewers were quickly transferred to a plate and rushed to the table.

Down-island, whole or large pieces of lamb, mutton, and goat are thickly coated with marinades such as the one below, before being roasted on a spit over an open pit. We have reduced the amount of meat and the size of the pieces so that they can be broiled and served on small skewers. The meat is not divided on the skewers by the usual onions, green pepper, and mushrooms, as is customary on the mainland. The rich spicing is similar to the spice used on skewered meats in Portugal, Spain, and Italy, but more exotically flavored.

1   Cut the meat into 1-inch-or-smaller cubes.

2   Combine the meat and the remaining ingredients in a bowl. Stir well and leave in the fridge to marinate for 2 days, turning the meat over a few times.

3   Thread the meat on 12-inch skewers or on 6-inch skewers that can be served on plates.

4   Broil until the meat is browned and no longer moist on the outside. The meat is remarkably good even when it contains very little moisture. Serve promptly and very hot.

Note

The meat can also be served as cocktail snacks. Spear them with toothpicks. They can also be cut into smaller cubes after cooking for this purpose.

St. Lucia

SPICY SKEWERED LAMB, MUTTON, OR GOAT

◆

3 pounds lean lamb, mutton, or goat shoulder or other more tender cut
1 yellow onion, finely chopped
3 garlic cloves, through the press
6 cloves, grated or crushed
6 whole allspice, crushed, *or* 1 teaspoon ground allspice
1 teaspoon ground cardamom
1 teaspoon ground cumin
1 teaspoon ground ginger
1 teaspoon fenugreek leaves (optional)
½ cup white wine vinegar
Salt and freshly ground black pepper to taste
Yellow island chili sauce to taste

SERVES 6

Barbados

BARBECUED LAMB OR PORK CHOPS

◆

1 garlic clove, through the press

1 teaspoon tamarind concentrate

1 tablespoon strong English or Dijon mustard

4 meaty, lean shoulder lamb or pork chops

Achiote oil (page 110) or vegetable oil as needed

1 medium yellow onion, sliced

1 large *or* 2 small, very ripe tomatoes

½ cup water or dry red wine

Salt and freshly ground black pepper to taste

Chili sauce or fresh chili pepper to taste

SERVES 4

''Barbecue'' applies here to the sauce and seasoning rather than to the method of cooking. The recipe produces tender as well as tasty results with all pork chops, but is preferable for shoulder chops of both lamb and pork. These cuts must be simmered to preserve their juices. Down-islanders know this and you will find tender lamb and pork almost exclusively in their homes and restaurants rather than in the typical tourist places.

1 Mix together and make a paste of the garlic, tamarind, and mustard. With a broad knife, spread the mixture over one surface of the chops.

2 In a 10-inch-or-larger pan put oil to cover the bottom. Spread the onion slices in the pan. Lay the chops, *coated side up*, on the onion.

3 Simmer gently for 40 minutes, covered. Turn the chops over.

4 Chop the tomato and add it to the pan along with the water. Shake well. Cover and simmer for another 15 minutes.

5 Before serving, readjust the thickness of the sauce by reducing or by adding a little more water. Adjust the seasoning with salt, pepper, and chili pepper.

Note

Two tablespoons tomato paste may be substituted for the fresh tomatoes.

◆ Pork ◆

One Saturday at Charlotteville on Tobago, the cottage colony where we were staying held a pig roast. We all chipped in, and Charles, our host, went down to Scarborough to buy a small pig. Very early on Saturday morning he dug a pit and started the fire; then, with help, metal uprights and crossbars were set up and the pig laboriously pierced by a huge spit. All day it cooked slowly, the spit occasionally turned and wood added to the fire, until nightfall. Then a long table was set with locally baked bread, salads, and drinks. Guests had contributed cooked yams, boiled rice, and fruits for dessert. George did the carving of the tender, juicy, flavorsome meat. What a feast that was!

Our most vivid memory was of the several impish children, perched on the thick, sprawling branches of a sea grape tree, plates in hand. Lanterns on the ground and on the two long tables cast stage lighting up into the tree, picking out the children gesticulating, making faces, and joking about the adults below. It was a perfect, still, moonlit night with the dark mountain of the cacao plantation rising behind us and the calm waters of glorious Man O' War Bay in front.

Island cooks understand very well that pork must be cooked slowly and under cover if the meat is to remain juicy and tender. It is true that the pig is blessed with a thick layer of fat (encasing it for roasting whole) but the meat itself is rather dry and becomes tough if exposed to high heat and dehydration. It is for this reason that fried pork chops in restaurants are usually tough. The same rule applies to loins and larger roasts as to cutlets. When larger pieces are roasted slowly there is the bonus of a considerable amount of tar in the drippings, which is an ideal stock for intensely flavored sauces.

Grenada

PORK CHOPS OR CUTLETS IN CINNAMON

◆

4 pork loin chops or boneless cutlets
1 small garlic clove,
  through the press
3 tablespoons achiote oil
  (page 110)
1 tablespoon ground cin-
  namon or cassia (see
  page 34)
Salt and freshly ground
  black pepper to taste
½ cup water
Chili pepper to taste

SERVES 4

The difference between pork chops and cutlets is that the chops come from the cuts nearer the neck with bone attached, while cutlets, larger and farther down the back, are offered without bone. We always prefer the latter, especially in this cinnamon-spiced recipe.

Americans associate cinnamon with sweets just as they do chocolate. But the Mexicans make a marvelous chicken mole loaded with chocolate and prove to us that the candy flavoring is a wonderful, rich, bitter condiment. Peppermint leaves are an ingredient of North African stews. And in the islands cinnamon is a spice that is used freely in cooking just like cloves or nutmeg. See page 34 for more about the difference between cinnamon and cassia.

1 Simmer the pork and garlic over low heat in a covered pan with the achiote oil for ten minutes.

2 Sprinkle with the cinnamon and the salt and pepper. Stir in about ¼ cup of the water.

3 Continue simmering very slowly for at least 15 minutes. Add more water if too much liquid evaporates. When ready to serve, there should be at least 4 tablespoons of liquid sauce. Add the chili pepper and serve.

Antigua

SPICY PORK CHOPS

◆

1 Fry the chops in the oil over moderately high heat until they show a bit of color on each side. Then reduce the heat immediately.

2 Add all the other ingredients except the chili pepper, salt, and water. Stir thoroughly with a wooden spoon. Cover the pan and reduce the heat to as low as possible.

3 Simmer for at least 45 minutes. Then add the chili pepper and salt.

4 Crush the chunks of tomato that have not cooked down and reduce the sauce to a thick consistency. Moisten with a little water or white wine if the sauce seems too thick.

5 Serve each chop with a dollop of the sauce on top.

4 pork loin chops, well marbled and trimmed of excess fat
2 tablespoons achiote oil (page 110) or vegetable oil
1 teaspoon grated nutmeg
½ teaspoon powdered sage or several dried leaves
1 teaspoon ground coriander
½ teaspoon ground allspice *or* 4 whole allspice, crushed
8 dried tomatoes *or* 2 large, ripe tomatoes, peeled and cut into chunks
1 garlic clove, through the press
1 fresh tomatillo, husked and sliced, *or* 1 canned tomatillo
Chili pepper or yellow island chili sauce to taste
Salt to taste
Water or white wine as needed

SERVES 4

Trinidad

EXOTIC PORK ROAST

◆

THE PORK

2 tablespoons Colman's
  dry mustard
1 tablespoon ground ginger
  or freshly grated gingerroot
2 tablespoons Madras
  curry powder
2 tablespoons ground
  cumin
1 tablespoon ground tur-
  meric
1 tablespoon ground cori-
  ander
6 whole allspice, crushed
  in a mortar and pestle, *or*
  1½ teaspoons ground
  allspice
1 tablespoon dried fenu-
  greek leaves *or* 8 cilantro
  leaves, snipped (optional)
3 garlic cloves, through
  the press
1 tablespoon tamarind
  concentrate
Salt and freshly ground
  black pepper to taste
Chili pepper to taste
Vegetable oil
1 4- to 6-pound pork roast
  or fresh ham, rolled and
  tied

The pork roast is one of those sumptuous dishes in which succulent meat is mated with richly flavored sauce in the process of cooking. The principle underlying this goodness is the same as for all large cuts of meat. Very slow, lengthy cooking causes the juices of the meat to blend with the surrounding liquid containing a mix of spice and herbal flavorants. Once the meat has been deprived of most of its moisture, a reverse process begins and it becomes permeated with the taste of the surrounding sauce. It is because island cooks have always understood this that their daubes and *matetés*, ragouts and fricassees are so magnificent.

This is a typical way of making island brown sauce, colored with burnt sugar syrup in place of browned or roasted flour. The syrup also possesses a bitterness which gives the sauce a flavor different from our mainland sauces. Thickening is partly provided by the ground spices and herbs in the solution that we used on the roast itself.

1 Preheat the oven to 350 degrees and place a large roasting pan or casserole in the oven to heat.

2 To prepare the pork, stir together all the ingredients except the salt, pepper, chili pepper, oil, and pork in a bowl. Add cold water, 1 tablespoon at a time, while stirring, to make a syrup.

3 When the mixture has become a thick syrup, set it aside for at least 30 minutes while the pan is heating in the oven.

4 The mixture will have thickened more. Add more water, very slowly, while stirring until the mixture is nearly but not quite a fluid paste.

5 Add the salt and pepper. Mix in the chili pepper. It is all right to use up to 1 whole chili pepper if you are accustomed to it. Otherwise, stir in the chili pepper a little at a time and test carefully.

6 Remove the pan from the oven and pour enough oil into it to cover the bottom. Place the meat in the container and roll it around with a fork.

7 Brush the paste thickly over the top of the roast, reserving 2 to 4 tablespoons.

8 Cover the pan with aluminum foil if it does not have its own cover. Allow enough cooking time for 30 minutes to the pound.

9 During the last 10 minutes remove the cover. Reduce the temperature to 250 degrees and roast for another 10 minutes. Remove the pan from the oven and place the meat in another pan. Return the pork to a 200-degree oven to keep warm.

10 Ladle from the pan all but ½ cup of the fat and any solids. Make the sauce, described below, immediately.

11 Place the pan in which the pork has been roasted, with the drippings, over low heat.

12 Stir the flour thoroughly into the fat. (If you object to the pork fat in the pan, skim it off carefully, leaving all the solids and tars, and replace it with butter or margarine.)

13 Add the water, the burnt sugar syrup, and the remaining pork coating. Stir very thoroughly and scrape up any solids adhering to the bottom of the pan with a metal spatula. Stir until well blended.

14 As it heats, the sauce will thicken. Because of the uncooked flour in the sauce it must simmer for at least 15 minutes. During this time it may thicken excessively, in which case add a little water to thin and stir well. If it is too liquid just simmer to reduce the mixture to a thicker consistency. Finally, check the salt, pepper, and chili concentration for taste. Add more if needed.

Serve the roast on a platter and slice at table or do this in the kitchen and distribute the portions on the plates. Serve the sauce in a separate sauce bowl. We recommend a good serving of a starch—rice, one of the root starches or breadfruit—and a light and refreshing salad for contrast. A superior Burgundy is called for.

Variation

Instead of using white flour in the sauce, add 6 tablespoons Roasted Flour (page 113) and stir well. The mixture need not be cooked as long because the flour is already prepared. You can also safely eliminate the burnt sugar syrup as the roasted flour provides enough coloring. But you will miss out on the additional, desirable flavor of the syrup.

Note

Some may judge the spices to be excessive. Wrong. Most of the spices are quite mild in flavor and a truly rich sauce demands more than is usually assigned for the purpose. Another reason is that the packaged spices we buy in the stores are not nearly as flavorful as freshly ground spices. The islander who grinds spice from the local bush or tree needs considerably less to produce the results that we so admire in their cuisine.

THE SAUCE

3 tablespoons butter (optional)

3 tablespoons all-purpose flour

1 cup water

2 to 4 tablespoons of the mixture used to coat the pork

1 teaspoon Burnt Sugar Syrup (page 117)

SERVES 6

◆ Pork Variety Meats ◆

The principal pork variety meats are the head, ears, snout, jowls, tail, and feet. France's great charcuterie is based on these meats with the addition of internal organs. In the United States, except for pigs' feet and sauerkraut, a favorite German dish, variety meats have been disdained for a long period. It was the African-Americans who, deprived of the "finer" cuts of meat, made a virtue of necessity and developed wonderful ways of preparing the variety meats. On the English islands, Souse, which employs the whole pig's head, became traditional. In most of the islands, ears, jowls, tails, and feet are cooked or marinated and end up as ragouts. The salt-brine jar was a means of preserving these meats in a climate that took its toll very quickly.

Salt pork from the belly and other parts is the principal cooking fat for baking. The solid fat with occasional meaty streaks is cubed and rendered in the pan. Crisp cubes make a splendid garnish for meats and stews and even eggs. The fat is either poured off and stored or used in the pan for frying vegetables or meats. Producing fresh lard in this way was preferred to packaged lard in the old days, preventing the risk of rancidity.

Boudin, blood pudding, is big in France, an essential of charcuterie and eaten in various combinations with meats as well as making a meal in itself. Surprisingly, it is equally or more popular in the islands and not just the French ones. Pudding and Souse is a famous down-island meal on Barbados and few restaurants of quality fail to list it. That is surprising because the sausage is made of pigs' blood and one would expect the problem of keeping the product fresh to be rather difficult. And yet the sausages are good everywhere.

Our recipe is our own, for it does not call for the stuffing of intestines and is properly a meat loaf rather than a sausage. We do this because few people in the States can find intestines in the butcher shops. Without stuffing the result is just as good. Our one objection to blood sausage in the islands has been when the casing has been tough and the filling soft, so instead of cutting through in slices, one had to press out the soft puree with one's fork. Our loaf pan is easier to handle and easier to serve.

Homemade *boudin* is better but you can usually buy blood sausages in chain groceries as well as butcher shops during most of the year.

It is worth mentioning that some recipes for the sausages recommend using "sweet potato," which we consider a travesty. They also call for boiling the sausages, which is the reason for the toughness of the casings. The sausages should always be grilled before serving.

1   Thoroughly mix all the ingredients in a large bowl. Meanwhile, oil a bread pan and preheat the oven to 250 to 300 degrees.

2   Divide the contents of the bowl into convenient amounts for processing. Process each amount evenly for 6 to 10 seconds.

3   As each lot is finished, pack it into the bread pan.

4   When finished loading the bread pan, smooth the surface and cover with aluminum foil.

5   Place the pan in the oven and bake for 40 minutes. Remove the foil and bake for another 10 minutes.

6   Take the pan from the oven and pour off any excess liquid.

7   Prepare immediately for serving or cover with aluminum foil and store in the fridge.

8   Cut into 1-inch-thick slices and slice these into 1-inch-thick sticks. Fry gently in margarine or vegetable oil until lightly browned. Serve.

Tobago and Guadeloupe

BOUDIN

◆

1 pound desalted salt pork, diced

2 cups finely chopped yellow onion

½ stick margarine

1 pound white yam, peeled and grated

1 pound calabaza, peeled and grated

¼ cup snipped Spanish thyme leaves *or* 1 tablespoon dried thyme leaves

1 tablespoon dried marjoram leaves

1 teaspoon grated cloves or ground clove

1 teaspoon freshly grated nutmeg

Juice of ½ lemon

½ Scotch bonnet chili pepper or other chili pepper, seeded and forced through a garlic press, or to taste

½ teaspoon freshly ground black pepper

½ teaspoon salt

2 cups pig's blood *or* 1 pound cubed calves' liver

SERVES 8 TO 10

Barbados and Jamaica

SOUSE

◆

5 to 6 pounds fresh pork jowls, tails, feet, or ears, in any combination
2 celery stalks, thinly sliced
2 medium yellow onions, peeled and quartered
5 cilantro sprigs, snipped
5 Spanish thyme leaves *or* 1 teaspoon dried thyme leaves
3 garlic cloves, peeled and crushed
1 ripe cucumber, peeled and cored
½ cup lime juice
Scotch bonnet chili pepper or other chili pepper or chili sauce to taste
Salt to taste

SERVES 4

Souse, a special occasion dish, employs a whole pig's head and the feet. Similar parts of goats, sheep, and beef receive the same treatment. We suppose that a majority of Stateside people would not know where to acquire a pig's head and are not at all inclined to tackle so formidable an object.

On the other hand, the variety meats, already cut to more convenient sizes, are sold throughout the country in butcher shops and the meat departments of grocery chains. It should be obvious that we are dealing here with the makings of head cheese, without the casing stuffed with chopped meat or the liquid stock that becomes gelatinized as it cools. A good head cheese reminds us of how delicious these meats can be. We, therefore, present the recipe that uses the precut meats.

Often, it is not sufficiently emphasized that the boiling liquid should be reduced to a concentrated stock if possible, for that is responsible for the richness of flavor. Furthermore, the dish can be served hot or cold—splendid for a salad lunch or dinner in summer and even better as a hearty, warming dish on cold winter days.

In Barbados, Souse is mated with black pudding for celebratory occasions.

Because of the large amounts of fat and bone in the cuts that are used for Souse it is shooting in the dark to aim at estimating just how much to provide for each portion. The ¾-pound rule is no help. We judge that a minimum of 1¼ to 1½ pounds is closer to reality if the meat has to suffice for the meal. When blood sausage is served with it or as an appetizer, the amount of pork may be reduced to 1 pound per serving. The other ingredients need not change.

1 Wash the meat well and put in a pot with enough very lightly salted water to cover. Cook over very low heat for at least 2 hours. Remove the meat to a platter to cool.

2 Bring the water in the pot to simmer and skim off as much fat as possible. Continue to simmer until the liquid is reduced to 5 cups.

3 Add the remaining ingredients except the lime juice, chili pepper, and salt. Simmer, covered, until the celery and onion are tender. Then reduce the stock to not more than 1½ cups.

4 Add the lime juice, chili pepper, and salt.

5 Cut away the meat from the bones and excess fat or gristle. Discard the bones and fat. Cut across the grain of the meat to make thin slices.

6 Put the meat into a large bowl and cover with the stock from the pot. Marinate overnight in the fridge. (The reader, at this point if not sooner, will become aware that what is being made is an unshaped head cheese. In fact the marinade may well become jellied in the fridge.)

7 If the Souse has jellied in the cold do not remove from the fridge until ready to serve. Then slice or break up into chunks and serve as the center-piece of a salad or separately with cold potato or other salad. If not jellied, heat and serve in soup bowls or on flat plates with the sauce served hot on the side.

Ten

VEGETABLES

As a rule it is more difficult to maintain domestic animals for food in the tropics than in the north. Even in comparatively rich tropical societies vegetables are more important in the diet. Typically, individual meat and seafood servings are small and highly spiced. It is customary to eat them sparingly along with large quantities of starches and vegetables. Many of the down-island dishes are served to tourists with far more meat or seafood than is customary in homes.

There is also more cooking of meat or seafood right along with the vegetables and serving them that way. While the variety of vegetables is greater than in the north, usage has been dictated by the seasons, for lack of refrigeration. For this reason the variety of vegetable treatment in menus is greater. However, as hotels import more of their supplies, vegetables are losing this seasonality. These are only some of the reasons why vegetable cookery is a more complicated affair in the Caribbean than it is with us.

We describe the starchy vegetables in some detail because there is such an array of them that the bins of an island store are utterly confusing when encountered for the first time. The same is true of squashes. Note also that vegetables going by the same name are different in appearance, texture, and flavor depending upon the island of origin. In our recipes we have felt obliged to confine ourselves to listing those that are more accessible in our stores on the mainland.

◆ Akee (Ackee) ◆

Seed of akee, *Blighia sapida*, the national tree of Jamaica, was brought there from Africa in 1778 by Captain Bligh of *Mutiny on the Bounty* and breadfruit fame. It is a handsome small tree whose vegetable-yielding fruits bear the same name.

The flowers are small and greenish but the fruit is handsome—about three inches long, colored orange to red. As it ripens the rind splits into three parts revealing three large, plum colored, round seeds, nestled into a thick, soft, fleshy, yellow column, the aril. It is this aril which is collected and cooked as a vegetable—also nicknamed vegetable scrambled eggs—a real curiosity that is as delicious as it is unusual.

About fifty years ago an investigation of unsolved deaths of children and adults in Jamaica was traced to the eating of akee and the specific cause was a lethal poison in the unripe fruit. Ripe arils proved to be perfectly safe when cooked. Akee is now sold in nineteen-ounce cans here on the mainland, although fresh fruit is nearly impossible to find. Akee and salt cod is now the most famous Jamaican dish.

The cooked akees in the cans look like lumps of scrambled eggs floating in water. The consistency is soft yet brittle and the mild flavor as nearly neutral as eggs, making it easy to adapt to many kinds of foods, from fabulous real scrambled eggs to seafood and meat dishes . . . a challenge for gourmet experiments in the kitchen.

Akee adds a distinction to scrambled eggs that quite sets them apart, imparting a flavor and texture that is unrivaled. As akee cans are large (nineteen ounces) and scrambling more than four eggs at a time is impractical, figure on using about one-third of a can per recipe. Store the remaining akees in their liquid in a screw-top jar in the fridge.

1   In a bowl beat all the ingredients except the butter vigorously with a fork.

2   Over high heat melt the butter in a frying pan and continue till it stops sputtering. Pour the egg mixture into the frying pan and stir instantly with a wooden spoon. Turn off the heat as soon as the egg has partly coagulated. Continue to stir. Serve as soon as the eggs are cooked but still fluffy.

Variations

A   Substitute 3 tablespoons achiote oil (page 110) for the butter or margarine.

B   Add 3 tablespoons of any of the following: finely chopped, sautéed mushrooms; minced smoked ham; or finely chopped, cooked spicy sausage— Italian, Spanish, Hungarian, or other.

Jamaica

AKEE AND SCRAMBLED EGGS

◆

4 large eggs
1 cup canned akees,
   drained
Parsley or cilantro to taste
2 tablespoons half-and-half
   or cream
Salt and freshly ground
   black pepper to taste
3 tablespoons (1½ ounces)
   butter or margarine

SERVES 4

Jamaica

AKEE SOUFFLÉ

◆

1 cup canned akees, drained

3 tablespoons unsalted butter

3 tablespoons all-purpose flour

1½ tablespoons chicken stock concentrate (optional)

1 cup half-and-half

5 eggs

2 tablespoons chopped fresh or dried parsley (optional)

½ teaspoon dried thyme

½ teaspoon masala or turmeric (optional)

¼ teaspoon freshly ground black, white, or pounded green pepper

Salt to taste

SERVES 4 FROM A LARGE SOUFFLÉ DISH OR 8 FROM INDIVIDUAL RAMEKINS

The delicate texture and very slight sweetness of the akees are ideal for luncheon soufflés baked in large bowls, or as hot appetizers in small ones. The standard deluxe Jamaican recipe is flavored with Worcestershire sauce, which is not only objectionably sour but curdles the eggs! It is unfortunate that, in a desire to emulate or satisfy English standards of cookery, Jamaicans frequently spoil the best down-island dishes with bottled sauces that in no way conform to Caribbean taste. We believe the following recipe makes more culinary sense.

1 Dry the akee thoroughly by heating very gently in a pan and constantly shaking. Allow it to cool for a moment, then give it a very short spin in the processor, just enough to reduce it to fine crumbles.

2 In a saucepan make a light roux with the butter and flour. Stir in the chicken stock. Gradually, over low heat, add the half-and-half while stirring. Once you have a thick, stable sauce stop mixing in the liquid.

3 Separate the eggs into 2 bowls, placing 4 egg yolks in 1 bowl and 5 egg whites in the other. Reserve the remaining egg yolk for another use.

4 Remove the pot from the stove and beat in the egg yolks with a whip or hand beater. Add the herbs and spices and, finally, the akee. If the mix becomes too thick, add a little more half-and-half.

5 Preheat the oven to 375 degrees. Butter the bottom and sides of a 1½-quart soufflé dish.

6 Beat the egg whites until they are very stiff. Fold the egg whites into the egg mixture and decant into the soufflé dish.

7 Bake in the oven for approximately 40 minutes or until the soufflé climbs above the rim of the bowl and becomes appetizingly light brown. Test with a straw or metal skewer, which should be quite dry when withdrawn from the soufflé. Be ready to serve instantly.

Variation

At step 3, add ¾ cup freshly grated Gruyère or Parmesan cheese.

Note

The soufflé mix may also be poured into small, deep, buttered ramekins. Cooking time is no more than about 12 to 15 minutes.

◆ Beans and Rice Dishes ◆

This combination, which was introduced by the Spaniards, has spread through most of the islands, becoming virtually customary everywhere. One should not forget that, for many island people, fresh food has in the past been seasonally difficult to come by. Dried beans and rice can be stored for long periods.

In *Moros y Cristianos* we have an ancient Hispanic combination of black beans and rice with vegetables. Depending on the seasonal availability of produce, different kinds of beans may be used and cooked with seasonal vegetables. What distinguishes the island dishes is the use of local vegetables, unripe fruits, herbs and spices, and small quantities of highly spiced meat on special occasions.

COOKING DRIED BEANS

◆

Except for lentils, which do not require it, soak all beans overnight in cold water. Drain the water and sort through the beans. Put in a pot with just enough water to cover. Do not add salt or anything acidic while the beans cook because they will shed their skins and turn mushy.

Most beans must be simmered in slow boiling water for about 1 to 1½ hours. Lentils and split peas require 35 to 45 minutes. Chick-peas take 3 hours or more with ½ teaspoon baking soda added to the water. Large red beans take about 2 hours.

The yield of cooked beans is usually 4 cups cooked to 1 cup dried. Large lima beans yield only 2½ cups cooked to 1 cup dry.

RICE

◆

The most popular rice in the islands is Uncle Ben's long-grain rice. The French and English like it dry and fluffy, the Spanish-speaking islands prefer it mushy like risotto. Indian descendants on Trinidad prefer Basmati, a small-grain, Persian-type rice that is almost immune to overcooking. So do we.

One cup dry rice produces about three cups cooked rice, sufficient for three to five servings.

After washing the rice, pour into lightly salted boiling water and stir once. Allow to simmer for fifteen minutes, then test. The rice, to be fluffy, must be a bit firm. Drain the rice and keep warm over steaming water in a sieve or double boiler.

Turmeric adds an excellent color to rice, imparting a clear, bright yellow. Use one tablespoon of the powder for each cup of dry rice. Stir into the boiling water before adding the rice. Saffron supplies a unique flavor but has become very expensive. It is hardly an island ingredient but is imported from Europe. Most island cooks avoid it except the Indians of Trinidad and elsewhere who are very partial to it. Finally, there is annato (achiote) oil that can be mixed with the cooked, drained rice as needed, which also supplies a rich yellow color.

In the Spanish-speaking islands black beans are the most popular combination with rice. The combination, except for tomato, probably goes back to the medieval rivalry of the Spaniards and Moors. We usually avoid recipes that have a completely off-island origin, but this is an exception. Our excuse is that it is so pervasive. For our own taste, black beans, so good in some European and island soups, are very rich and filling in this combination. Relatively small portions should satisfy most appetites.

1 In a casserole heat the oil and gently fry the onion and pepper until tender. Add the tomato and garlic and simmer until they are tender.

2 Add the rice, toss to coat, and cover with the water. Simmer, stirring from time to time, until the rice is overcooked and mushy.

3 Add the cooked black beans and mix with the rice. Simmer until the beans are thoroughly heated through. Add the salt, pepper, and chili pepper. Stir constantly to prevent it from sticking to the casserole. Add a little water if needed. The consistency should be thick but not dry.

4 Serve piping hot.

Variations

A In Tobago, when the beans and rice are ready, it is customary to add a fried egg to each portion. Make a ring of the beans and rice on each plate and place a fried egg in the middle. To decorate the dish, fry in achiote oil (page 110) instead of butter.

B While preparing the beans and rice, sauté a chicken breast in butter, then slice it into bite-sized pieces. Return to the pan and sprinkle with poultry seasoning. Simmer, covered, for 2 minutes. Then stir into the mixture of rice and beans. Serve.

C Other frequent additions to the rice and beans are boneless pieces of fried fish, shrimp (St. Martin), or small pieces of leftover beef, goat, or pork.

Puerto Rico

BLACK BEANS AND RICE (MOROS Y CRISTIANOS)

◆

3 tablespoons vegetable oil
1 yellow onion, finely sliced
1 green or red bell pepper, seeded and sliced
1 large tomato, peeled and cut into wedges (optional)
1 garlic clove, through the press
¾ cup long-grain Carolina rice
3 cups water
1½ cups cooked black beans (page 45)
Salt and freshly ground black pepper to taste
Chili pepper to taste

SERVES 4

Trinidad

HOLIDAY RICE AND BEANS

◆

½ cup chopped red and green bell pepper
½ stick butter or margarine
1½ cups Basmati or long-grain Carolina rice
2 cups coconut milk
1 can low-salt chicken broth
1½ cups minced or cubed cooked chicken
1 cup minced smoked ham (optional)
1 can green pigeon peas
1 to 2 tablespoons ground turmeric
1 teaspoon ground ginger
5 scallion tops, snipped
Freshly ground black pepper to taste
Chili pepper to taste
Salt to taste

MAKES 4 LARGE PORTIONS OR 8 SIDE DISHES

This is a super dish for those who love their rice as we do.

1 In a large pan sauté the bell pepper in the butter until tender.
2 Stir in the rice along with the coconut milk, chicken broth, meats, drained beans, the turmeric and the ginger. Stir together well.
3 Simmer very gently until the rice is just barely tender. Stir in the snipped scallion leaves. Add water if needed to prevent sticking.
4 Start a pot that can be fitted with a colander, sieve, or steamer partly with water and bring to a boil.
5 When the rice is ready and all the liquid has been absorbed, correct the seasoning with the pepper and chili pepper. Add salt if needed.
6 Transfer the contents of the pan to a colander, sieve, or top of a steamer. Set on top of the pot of boiling water, lower the heat, and reduce to a simmer. Place a cover over the colander. Steam the mixture in this way until you are ready to serve.

Note

Before serving, you may enrich the rice and beans by adding some more melted butter.

We have seen as many as half a dozen different printed recipes attributed to other islands that merely list slightly different proportions for this basic recipe. Such simple, standard, frequently served dishes are rather flexible.

1 Simmer the rice in 1 quart lightly salted water with the onion, garlic, and bay rum for 15 minutes or until the rice is cooked but still firm. Add a little more water if needed. Drain thoroughly.

2 Remove the bay rum leaf and add the cooked beans. Season with the cilantro, salt, pepper, and chili pepper. The mix should be dry and fluffy. Serve hot.

Variation

Cut 2 ounces salt pork into very small dice. Fry until golden and add to the rice and beans. The dish can be further enriched with butter. Fried diced bacon is a good substitute for the salt pork.

St. Barts

BEANS AND RICE (POIS ET RIZ)

◆

1 cup long-grain Carolina rice
1 small onion *or* 1 scallion, finely chopped
1 garlic clove, through the press
1 bay rum or allspice leaf *or* ½ teaspoon ground allspice
1 cup cooked red, pink, or other beans (page 44)
2 cilantro sprigs, snipped
Salt and freshly ground black pepper to taste
Bonney Pepper Sauce or other chili pepper to taste

SERVES 6

Haiti

RICE AND BEANS WITH DION-DION MUSHROOMS

◆

½ package (¼ ounce)
  dion-dion mushrooms
½ 9- or 10-ounce package
  frozen lima beans
1 medium yellow onion *or*
1 whole scallion,
  chopped
1 cup long-grain Carolina
  or Basmati rice
1 tablespoon butter or
  margarine
Salt and freshly ground
  black pepper to taste

SERVES 4

Dion-dion is the common name of very small, long-stemmed, dried black mushrooms, one of the delights of Haitian cuisine. They are used to flavor plain rice and also rice with beans. This wonderful fungus can be used wherever a strong meaty-mushroom flavor is desirable. The dried dion-dion is sold in half-ounce packages at Creole grocery stores in the islands and, more recently, on the mainland. One package is ample for two to three cups or rice. The combination of rice and beans serves four. Leave out the beans and the rice will serve two.

1   In a pot bring 2 cups of water to a boil and stir in the mushrooms. Simmer for 8 minutes. Drain the liquid through a sieve into a bowl and discard the mushroom residue.

2   Meanwhile, in another small pot, cook the lima beans, in the amount of water specified on the package, and the onion. Simmer gently for about 15 minutes. Then drain and transfer the beans to another pot.

3   Pour the mushroom liquid, which will be quite black, into the pot, add 1 cup of water, bring to a boil, and stir in the rice. Lightly salt the water.

4   Simmer until the rice is tender. Add a little more water if needed as the rice expands. (The object is to cook with a minimum amount of water so that the mushroom liquid remains concentrated.)

5   When the rice is done, drain any liquid through a sieve, add the butter, salt, and pepper, and serve.

Variation

At step 2, substitute any small, cooked beans for the frozen lima beans. If the liquid from the cooked beans is thick, add ¼ to ½ cup water. Heat the beans, add the onion, and simmer for 15 minutes. Then drain and transfer to another pot. Proceed with the remaining steps.

Note

For those who wish to add chili pepper, it can be added in any form desired at the end.

This is a neat and decorative way of serving a very tasty rice dish.

Martinique

1 Pour the rice into 1½ cups boiling water and stir. Add the bell pepper and scallion. Salt the water lightly.

2 Simmer gently until the rice is just tender, about 15 minutes. Drain through a sieve. Set the sieve over a pot of simmering water and steam until ready to serve. Add the salt and pepper.

3 Fill a small, round ramekin or a round-bottomed tea cup with the rice mixture. Press down. Then unmold onto the serving plate. Repeat this for each serving.

MOLDED RICE

◆

½ cup Basmati or long-grain Carolina rice

2 small bell peppers, 1 red and 1 green, seeded and chopped into small bits

1 scallion, tops only, finely snipped

Salt and freshly ground black pepper to taste

MAKES 6 SMALL RICE MOLDS

Variation

Add color to the rice with 1 teaspoon turmeric *or* 1 tablespoon achiote oil in the cooking water. The rice will turn a pleasant yellow.

Curaçao

RICE WITH VEGETABLE SAUCE

◆

2 cups long-grain Carolina or Basmati rice
½ stick butter or margarine *or* 4 tablespoons vegetable oil
2 medium yellow onions, finely sliced
2 green or red bell peppers, seeded and cut into dice
2 tomatoes, peeled and cut into chunks
½ teaspoon freshly grated nutmeg
½ cup minced cilantro leaves
4 to 6 cabbage leaves, finely shredded
Salt and freshly ground black pepper to taste
Chili pepper to taste

SERVES 6

Most mainlanders are traditional potato eaters. In recent years they have become accustomed to pasta, but rice remains a starch reserved for special menus culled from cookbooks and originating in Italy, Mexico, China, or India. In the islands, rice is a staple which is freely combined with other vegetables, including beans, as a normal accompaniment to meats, poultry, and seafood. The following is another such recipe that varies from island to island.

1 Simmer the rice in 2 quarts boiling water until just tender. Drain in a sieve and keep hot over a pan of simmering water.

2 Heat the butter or oil in a large pan. Fry the onions and the bell peppers. As soon as the onions turn yellow and the peppers are partly tender, add the tomatoes and crush them in the pan. Shake the pan well. Add the nutmeg, cilantro, and the cabbage. Season with the salt, pepper, and chili pepper. Cover and simmer for 3 minutes.

3 Shortly before serving, combine the rice and the vegetable mixture in the pan. Stir the contents well and serve hot.

◆ Breadfruit ◆

Native of the Malay Archipelago, the edible breadfruit tree, *Artocarpus altilis*, was brought to the Caribbean by Captain Bligh on the voyage following his miraculous survival from the Mutiny on the Bounty. The fruit was intended as a cheap, starchy food for workers on the sugar plantations of the English possessions. They grew very well in their new home and are still seen everywhere in the islands. Although some food experts because of its flavor have taken a dislike to the fruit, the fact is that it is enjoyed by the population. The white flesh retains its color if boiled with a little vinegar and the texture is firm and fine grained. Hence there are numerous recipes.

The tree is one of the most beautiful in the tropics, a magnificent giant with huge, long-fingered, decorative leaves. Few sights match them when the six-inch or larger, round, green, pimply fruits hang down from the branches in considerable numbers. All the recipes we supply for breadfruit can be used for cassava, malanga, taro, and yam.

The French introduced the smaller, inedible variety of the fruit because the tasty seeds which stuff the inner cavity reminded them of chestnuts. In fact they call them *châtaigne*, French for chestnut. The nuts (see page 45), available here in cans, are a culinary challenge and a gastronomical delight.

St. Lucia

BAKED BREADFRUIT

◆

On St. Lucia, one still sees outdoor working people roasting their luncheon breadfruit on small grills or coalpots beside the road—as it has been done for centuries. Allowed to cool a bit, the breadfruit is cut up into chunks and distributed, making a nourishing though hardly luxurious meal. It tastes better at home with seasoning and butter.

The easiest way to cook breadfruit is to bake it. Be careful to choose one that is firm and without any spots on the skin. When overripe, the cooked starch becomes oddly mushy.

Just wrap the whole fruit in aluminum foil and place in a 350-degree, preheated oven for thirty to forty minutes. Test with a fork for tenderness. Remove the skin by peeling with a sharp, small knife. Slice into a warmed serving dish and dab with butter. Sprinkle with salt and pepper to taste.

One large breadfruit serves four.

Tobago

BREADFRUIT CROQUETTES

◆

1 just-ripe breadfruit,
  peeled, halved, cored,
  and cut into chunks
3 cups milk
2 eggs
Salt and freshly ground
  black pepper to taste
½ cup all-purpose flour or
  ¾ cup bread crumbs for
  dredging the croquettes
1 stick butter or margarine

SERVES 4 TO 6

Breadfruit tends to be a bit of a problem because of its dense texture, which makes it "heavy," even when mashed. This recipe displays the vegetable's best qualities.

1 Boil the breadfruit in lightly salted and vinegared water until soft. While still warm, pass through a potato ricer into the top of a double boiler with water already boiling below.

2 Immediately beat the milk into the breadfruit puree with a whisk and then add the eggs, salt, and pepper while beating some more.

3 Simmer, covered, for 8 to 10 minutes. Remove the top of the double boiler from the water bath and set aside.

4 Spread the flour or bread crumbs on a large plate; form croquettes with your hands and roll in the flour or crumbs.

5 Fry the croquettes in the butter. When crisp and browned, remove to paper towels or a sieve placed over a bowl to drain. Reheat gently in a covered pan or the oven before serving.

Variations

A Add ½ cup minced scallion leaves to the puree as it cooks in the double boiler.

B Other additions, which will occur to any even modestly experienced cook, are usual in the islands—fresh or dried herbs, finely chopped or ground spicy meats, or seafood

C For the breadfruit, substitute ¾ pound cassava, malanga, taro, or yam.

This is one of the scrumptious lunch choices prepared on little open grills by the ladies at the dock in Grand Case. There, down-island cooking in all its purity competes successfully with a whole row of little, deluxe, international restaurants on the beach road.

1 Boil the breadfruit in lightly salted and vinegared water until tender.
2 Slice very thin.
3 Fry in shallow vegetable oil in a pan or deep fry in oil heated to 370 degrees, as for potato chips, until quite crisp.
4 Remove the slices with a slotted spoon as they turn golden and drain on paper towels. Salt liberally and serve.

Variation

Pepper lovers can shake dry chili pepper over the chips in addition to or in place of the salt.

St. Martin

FRIED BREADFRUIT

◆

1 ripe breadfruit, peeled and cored
Vegetable oil for frying
Salt

This is one of those recipes that fits a number of related vegetables. Soufflés can be made this way using yam, malanga, taro, or cassava, to say nothing of our mainland potatoes. But it is typically an island production, simply because we mainlanders tend not to make potato soufflés, while down-islanders do utilize their splendid island starches for the purpose. One advantage to using breadfruit is that the soufflé doesn't collapse.

1 With a wooden spoon stir the egg yolks and the softened butter or margarine into a bowl along with the breadfruit puree. Add the salt, pepper, and nutmeg. The consistency should be thick but just barely flowing. If too firm, beat in the half-and-half, 1 tablespoon at a time, to loosen the mix.
2 Heat the oven to 325 degrees and butter a 1-quart soufflé bowl.
3 Beat the egg whites until stiff, then fold into the breadfruit puree. With the aid of a plastic spatula, pour the mix into the soufflé bowl, smooth the surface, and cook in the oven for about 30 minutes or until a thin skewer or table knife inserted in the center comes out clean. Place the bowl under the broiler for a moment to color. Serve immediately.

Variations

A In St. Vincent, achiote oil (page 110) is substituted for the butter or margarine.
B In Guadeloupe, chopped cilantro leaves are added to the puree.
C Substitute 1 pound of any root starch for the breadfruit.

Martinique

BREADFRUIT SOUFFLÉ

◆

3 eggs, separated
½ stick butter or margarine, softened
3 cups cooked breadfruit, pressed through a potato ricer
Salt and freshly ground black pepper to taste
Grated nutmeg to taste
Half-and-half as needed

SERVES 4

◆ Breadfruit Nuts ◆

The seeds that fill the inner cavity of the smaller type of breadfruit, whose flesh is inedible, are one of the most interesting vegetable products of the Caribbean and could some day become a gourmet ingredient of northern cuisine.

This smaller fruit, about five inches in diameter, was brought to the islands earlier than the large, edible, seedless kind introduced by Captain Bligh on his second voyage. Now grown principally in the Dominican Republic and Guadeloupe, it contains a number of fat seeds, approximately one and a half inches long, covered with a thin brown skin, rather like chestnuts. Spanish-speaking islands call them *pana de pepita*. In the French islands they are called *chataigne*, which is the name of the chestnut tree rather than of its nut, which is called *marron*. In the farmers' markets the ladies pile them up on their tables next to the coconuts, plantains, vanilla beans, and other local products.

Goya Foods, packers of Hispanic and Creole products, sells the nuts in ten-ounce cans through grocery chains. The texture of the nuts is quite similar to that of chestnuts and can be used for many of the same purposes in cooking. We use them for stuffings and as a very appetizing, not at all cloying, vegetable. Guests usually ask for seconds.

Guadeloupe

PUREED BREADFRUIT NUTS

◆

1 10-ounce can breadfruit nuts
1 tablespoon dried parsley leaves
1 tablespoon ground cumin
¾ stick butter or margarine, softened
½ pint half-and-half

SERVES 2

1 Drain the nuts. With a small paring knife, slice off a bit of the base of each nut. Insert the knife under the brown skin and lift. Part of the skin will come off and the rest can be peeled by inserting the knife along the cut edges.

2 Put the nuts into a processor bowl along with the other ingredients except the half-and-half. Process for 10 seconds.

3 The consistency should be rather like nutty or grainy mashed potatoes. Add the half-and-half gradually, while stirring, until you achieve a desirable texture.

4 Heat the mix in a double boiler and serve.

Variation

The mix can be enriched with fried bacon bits, finely chopped sausage or bell peppers, curry powders, and more. The vegetable is delicious with brown meat gravies.

◆ Calabaza ◆

Calabaza, or Giraumon, the West Indian pumpkin (on English islands) or squash (on our mainland), whose origins are lost in an uncertain past, is a favorite vegetable on all the islands. Understandably so, for it is the king of the orange- or yellow-fleshed, meaty, slightly sweet squashes. So tasty is this vegetable that it can be eaten more often with enjoyment than other squashes and can be cooked in more ways.

Calabazas are now so common in our vegetable markets that it is unnecessary to suggest substitutes such as butternut or hubbard squash, both excellent but not to compare. It is large and melon shaped, with a somewhat flattened top and bottom. The skin is greenish and spotted with white or yellow. The flesh is yellow to orange, firm and crisp, and the core is filled with seeds. It is usually sold quartered, each piece weighing about one to one and a half pounds, sufficient for three to five servings. Buy a somewhat larger piece than seems necessary, because of the waste from discarding the skin, seeds, and pulp. Test for hardness, as soft-fleshed pieces are overripe or have been on the shelf too long; the cooked result may be mushy.

To prepare the calabaza for cooking, clean out the seeds and soft integument and then attack the skin—carefully. It is thin but hard. Use a large, sharp knife and lay a cut side of the squash on the cutting board. Chip downward and away. With a little practice, the removal will proceed rapidly. Cut the flesh into thick or thin slices, remaining on your guard because this is also tough to cut. Always make certain that the piece is steady on the board before attempting to cut. This is the same care required in handling most of the hard squashes.

BOILED CALABAZA

◆

1 Scoop out the seeds and cut the squash into convenient pieces. Boil in lightly salted water for at least 10 minutes or until soft.
2 Drain and cut the flesh away from the skin.

Note
Boiling is the best way to cook the squash if you intend to use it for soup or to mash it.

2 pounds calabaza, unpeeled

SERVES 3 TO 5

Sint Maarten

MASHED CALABAZA

◆

1 2-pound-section cala-
baza, unpeeled
2 tablespoons butter or
margarine
2 sprigs fresh parsley,
snipped, *or* 1 teaspoon
dried parsley
Freshly grated nutmeg (optional)
Salt and freshly ground
black pepper to taste

SERVES 3 TO 5

1   Scoop out the seeds and cut the squash into convenient pieces. Boil in lightly salted water for at least 10 minutes or until soft. Drain and cut the flesh away from the skin.

2   Force the squash through a potato ricer or puree with an old-fashioned wire masher or spin for a very short moment in the processor. (In the islands an ingenious swizzle stick consisting of 3 rows of wire circlets is used. The stick is rubbed between the hands or handled with a beating motion.) Reheat the squash gently over low heat.

3   Add the butter, parsley, nutmeg, and the salt and pepper. Stir these in with a wooden spoon or whisk by hand. Serve immediately. The vegetable can be reheated.

Sint Maarten

FRIED CALABAZA

◆

2 pounds calabaza
Butter or margarine or
vegetable or achiote oil
(page 110) for frying
Ground coriander to taste
Salt and freshly ground
black pepper to taste

SERVES 4

1   Scoop out the seeds and peel the squash as described on page 243.

2   Cut the flesh into ¼- to ½-inch-thick slices.

3   Fry gently in the butter until lightly browned on both sides, about 5 minutes for each side, turning only once.

4   Season with the coriander, salt, and pepper. Serve hot.

This is a delicious way to prepare the best of squashes. It is very easy to extend the cooking time and reduce the squash to a puree which many people prefer. We do, however, maintain that the calabaza always tastes best when it is a little firm. This is not exactly easy to accomplish because the transition period between just tender and mush in cooking is very short. Nevertheless, one must try not to overcook the squash, as it both looks and tastes better.

1　In a large pan, fry the salt pork cubes gently until golden. Remove the cubes with a slotted spoon and set aside.

2　To the pan add the onion, bell pepper, and garlic. Fry gently, covered, until the bell pepper begins to soften. Then stir in the calabaza and simmer, covered, very gently for 5 minutes.

3　Add the nutmeg and Colombo, then add the salt, pepper, and chili pepper. Test the squash to see that it has not overcooked. Stir carefully to prevent the contents from sticking to the bottom of the pan. A metal spatula is also useful for this purpose.

4　Continue cooking over very low heat until the squash, when tested, is just cooked. Serve promptly with the cubed pork fat sprinkled over or keep warm in the oven.

Variation

The mix can be enriched by the addition of a small amount (¼ to ½ pound) of spicy meat or sausage, finely ground. Stir in at step 2 with the squash.

Note

Adding tomato, although fine in some recipes, is not advisable here, as the mix will then definitely stick to the pan.

French Islands

COLOMBO DE GIRAUMON (CALABAZA)

◆

½ pound salt pork, cubed
1 medium yellow onion, sliced
1 large bell pepper, seeded and chopped
1 garlic clove, through the press
1½ pounds very fresh, firm calabaza, cubed
½ teaspoon freshly ground nutmeg
1½ tablespoons Colombo powder (page 36) *or* 1 tablespoon mild Madras curry powder or garam masala powder to taste
Salt and freshly ground black pepper to taste
Chili pepper to taste

SERVES 6

St. Martin

DAUBE DE GIRAUMON (CALABAZA)

◆

½ pound salt pork or
  boneless jowl, ears, or
  tail meat, cut into cubes
3 tablespoons vegetable oil
2 pounds calabaza, peeled
  and seeds removed
1½ to 2 tablespoons all-
  purpose flour for dredging
  the calabaza
1 teaspoon tamarind con-
  centrate
2 medium garlic cloves,
  through the press
1 tablespoon snipped
  Spanish thyme leaves or
  local small-leaved thyme
  or dried marjoram leaves
4 allspice or bay rum
  leaves *or* 1 teaspoon
  ground allspice
Salt and freshly ground
  black pepper to taste
Chili pepper to taste

SERVES 4

''**Daube**'' (French for "stew") is inappropriate here, because this dish is not truly a stew. But such matters are not important in the islands. Daube is used to name a variety of dishes, we suspect, more for its sound than its meaning. The dish is what counts, though, and this is a beauty.

1 Fry the salt pork for 10 minutes in the oil over moderate heat.

2 Cut the calabaza into cubes and roll in the flour until well coated. Add the calabaza to the salt pork and continue frying for another 10 minutes, turning the squash at least twice.

3 Preheat the oven to 180 degrees.

4 Remove the salt pork and calabaza to a small baking pan. Cover with aluminum foil and place in the preheated oven.

5 Pour ¼ to ½ cup of water into the frying pan and scrape with a spatula. Stir in the tamarind concentrate and the other herbs and spices. Adjust the flavor and seasoning to taste and simmer 4 to 5 minutes until reduced to a syrupy sauce consistency.

6 Serve the squash covered with the reduced sauce.

For recipes containing cheese we sometimes specify a superior Italian grating cheese where down-islanders might use a rather plain, tasteless product, enhancing the flavor instead with chopped spicy meat, sausage, or simply additional spices and herbs. Anyone can do the same.

1   Cook the squash till tender in lightly salted water.

2   Cut into convenient pieces and pass through a potato ricer.

3   Beat in the milk and eggs with a wooden spoon or whip along with ½ cup grated cheese and the salt and pepper. Add butter and garlic.

4   Preheat the oven to 350 degrees. Spoon the squash into a buttered baking dish and spread the remaining grated cheese on top.

5   Bake in the oven until the surface has browned lightly. Serve promptly.

Variation

The puree can be flavored with grated nutmeg, fresh snipped parsley, finely chopped scallions, or all three.

Trinidad

GRATIN OF CALABAZA

◆

1 to 1½ pounds calabaza, peeled and seeds removed

½ pint milk

2 eggs

1 cup grated cheese, such as pepato or aged provolone

Salt and freshly ground black pepper to taste

½ stick butter

1 garlic clove, through the press

SERVES 4

◆ Chayote (Cho-cho) ◆

Chayote is the Spanish name for a New World squash, called christophene in the French islands and cho-cho in Jamaica and other English islands. It is a staple vegetable throughout the Caribbean, followed in favor by the very different calabaza (see page 45). Pear shaped in outline, five to seven inches long, and oval in cross-section, it is regularly grooved from top to bottom. Thin skinned, with slippery flesh when green, it becomes yellow, thicker skinned, and firmer when ripe. They are now a common feature of our vegetable markets for most of the year. Although the green fruits are excellent, we much prefer, as do down-islanders, the ripe ones for all purposes, especially for stuffing. They weigh a maximum of twelve ounces apiece.

Cut the vegetable along the narrow axis, revealing very white flesh and a single, very large, thin white seed that is soft and edible in the unripe fruits but removed and discarded before cooking in the ripe ones. The vegetable can be cooked, whole or peeled and cut into chunks, cubes, or slices, in ten to fifteen minutes. The flesh is crisp, nutty, and juicy; not at all sweet like calabaza. In season, it is one of our favorite vegetables to cook in the Creole manner, or according to both American- or European-style recipes. This is certainly the prize winner among white squashes.

Large, ripe, ten- to twelve-ounce chayotes make a portion for two. The smaller, green fruits must be judged by eye, as a whole fruit per portion may be needed. Be careful when cutting this vegetable vertically. Because it can slip under the knife, we recommend removing a slice from the top and bottom before halving.

1 Cut a thin slice off the top and base of the chayote. Cut in half along the narrow side and remove the seed if the vegetable is ripe.

2 Peel the skin with a flexible peeler. Lay the halves flat and cut crosswise into thin slices.

3 Melt the butter in a skillet and toss in the chayote. Shake well and simmer, covered, until tender, about 10 to 15 minutes. Do not overcook. The flesh should be crisp, not mushy. Add the salt and pepper before serving.

Variations

A Thinly slice a medium yellow onion. Simmer in the covered pan with the butter for 8 minutes before tossing in the chayote and continuing.

B In a separate small pan render a cup of cubed salt pork. Toss in with the onion and chayote just before serving.

C Along with the partly cooked onion add 1 cup cubed *queso blanco* (see page 41) to the pan with the chayote shortly before serving.

D Substitute achiote oil (page 110) for the butter or margarine.

E Add 1 tablespoon Madras curry powder near the end of cooking.

F In a separate pan with 1½ tablespoons oil, heat chopped chorizos or spicy Hungarian or Italian sausage (casings removed) and add to the onion and *queso blanco* five minutes before serving. Simmer for 4 minutes and then mix with the chayote in the other pan. Serve with beans, pasta, or rice.

G To any of the above, add chili pepper, fresh or powdered, to taste.

Puerto Rico

BUTTERED CHAYOTE

◆

1 large chayote
2 tablespoons butter or
  margarine
Salt and freshly ground
  black pepper to taste

SERVES 2

Guadeloupe

CHRISTOPHENE (CHAYOTE) AU GRATIN 1

◆

2 ripe christophenes (chayotes), unpeeled
2 small onions, peeled and finely sliced, *or* 2 scallions, tops only, finely snipped
1 small, green bell pepper *or* ½ large, green bell pepper, seeded and finely chopped
1 tablespoon finely snipped parsley *or* 1 teaspoon dried parsley leaves
Pinch of freshly ground nutmeg
½ garlic clove, through the press
1 cup grated, sharp cheese, such as Romano, aged provolone, or Pepato
4 tablespoons bread crumbs
Butter

SERVES 4

1   Slice the christophene in half vertically and remove the seeds. Simmer in lightly salted water for 15 minutes.

2   Meanwhile, in a covered pan, simmer the onion and bell pepper until soft. Add the parsley and nutmeg at the end.

3   Gently flush the christophene with cold water to cool. Then scoop out the flesh from each half, using a curved grapefruit cutter or a small paring knife, leaving a shell about ¼ inch thick. Set the shells aside.

4   Preheat the oven to 350 degrees.

5   Slice the scooped-out flesh of the christophenes into thin, narrow strips no more than 1½ inches long.

6   Combine the christophene slices with the onion mixture in the pan. Add the garlic. Simmer for 1 minute.

7   Stuff the christophene shells by alternating layers of the mix and the grated cheese, leaving a few tablespoons of the cheese for the topping. Mix the remaining cheese, or more if needed, with the bread crumbs. Spread over the stuffed christophenes and place on each a dab of butter.

8   Bake in the preheated oven until the cheese and crumb topping turns golden, about 15 minutes. Serve immediately.

Martinique

The only really basic difference between these recipes is that in this one we use a béchamel-cheese sauce rather than simply spreading grated cheese between layers of the vegetables.

CHRISTOPHENE (CHAYOTE) AU GRATIN 2

◆

1   Slice the christophenes vertically and remove the seeds. Simmer in lightly salted water for 15 minutes.

2   Gently flush the christophenes in cold water to cool. Using a curved grapefruit cutter or a small paring knife, scoop the flesh out from each half, leaving a shell about ¼ inch thick. Set the shells aside.

3   Preheat the oven to 350 degrees.

4   Slice the scooped-out flesh of the christophenes into thin, narrow strips no more than 1½ inches long. Set aside.

5   Heat the béchamel. Just before the simmering point, stir in all the grated cheese and half the butter. Then add, stirring vigorously, the egg yolk. Raise the temperature to simmer for a moment and allow the sauce to thicken to a Welsh rarebit consistency. Then set aside.

6   In a saucepan melt the remaining butter, add the scallion, garlic, and cilantro and heat gently for 1 minute.

7   Stir in the sliced christophene and the béchamel. Season with the pepper, adding the chili pepper if desired.

8   Set the christophene shells on a baking sheet and fill the cavities with the christophene mixture, forming a mound.

9   Sprinkle a thin coating of bread crumbs over the filling and set the baking pan in the preheated oven.

10   Bake for 20 minutes or until the surface turns golden. Serve piping hot.

Variations

Panade Sauce Formula 1 (page 114) or Cheese Panade Sauce (page 115) may be substituted for the béchamel at step 5. The panade sauce is firmer and more velvety when the gratin is served in large shells or ramekins.

Christophene Farci   In Guadeloupe salt beef is added at step 5. We use Beardsley Sliced Dried Beef, which is sold in a 5-ounce jar, but similar products will do as well.

With a very sharp knife, reduce 2½ ounces of salt beef to a mass of fine snippets. (This may also be done with scissors.) Mix the beef into the béchamel. Allow to simmer on low heat for 5 minutes, stirring continuously, before adding the egg yolk. Proceed with the remaining steps.

Note

Canned corned beef may be substituted for the salt beef.

2 ripe christophenes (chayotes), unpeeled
¾ cup Béchamel Sauce (page 122)
1 cup grated, sharp cheese such as Romano, aged provolone, Pepato, or a superior Grùyere
½ stick butter
1 egg yolk
2 scallions, tops only, finely snipped
½ garlic clove, through the press
¼ cup finely snipped cilantro leaves
Freshly ground black pepper to taste
Chili pepper to taste (optional)
4 tablespoons bread crumbs

SERVES 4

Jamaica

STUFFED CHO-CHO

◆

1 pound tender boiled
  beef, such as bottom
  round
2 red bell peppers, seeded
  and boiled until tender
½ cup concentrated beef
  stock *or* 1 tablespoon
  Bovril Beef Extract
2 tablespoons tomato paste
1 tablespoon dried parsley
  leaves
1½ teaspoons Pickapeppa
  Sauce (optional)
1½ tablespoons vegetable
  oil
Salt and freshly ground
  black pepper to taste
Chili pepper to taste
4 large, ripe chayotes or
  cho-chos

SERVES 8

The combined meat and vegetable filling makes a dinner course that is unfailingly appreciated.

1   Cut the beef into cubes and process for 12 seconds. Leave in the processor bowl.

2   Cut the bell peppers into thin slices. Put in the processor bowl along with the beef extract, tomato paste, parsley, Pickapeppa Sauce, and oil.

3   Process all for 10 seconds. It should form a sticky mass. If too dry add water, 1 tablespoon at a time.

4   Add the salt, pepper, and chili pepper. The mixture should be fairly hot.

5   Meanwhile, boil the chayotes, whole, for 20 minutes. Drain and flush with cold water to cool. Slice each chayote in half, remove the seed, and cut out the flesh with a grapefruit cutter or small knife, leaving a shell about ¼ inch thick. Set the shells aside and cut the scooped-out flesh into cubes.

6   Preheat the oven to 350 degrees.

7   Decant the contents of the processor bowl into a mixing bowl. Stir the chayote together with the meat mixture and fill the shells. Place them on a baking sheet and bake for 30 minutes. Serve hot.

Mainland and Island Root Starches:
◆ The Differences ◆

Before we present some root starch recipes we must clarify the confusion that exasperates everyone who attempts to understand the various types of tubers that are staples in the islands. To do that we must first separate the identity of our mainland staples, potatoes and sweet potatoes.

The white or Irish potato belongs to the same family, the Solanaceae, that produces chili peppers, tobacco, petunias, and eggplants.

The sweet potato belongs to the morning glory family, the Convolvulaceae. When their flesh is pale yellow and only moderately sweet, we usually call them sweet potatoes. When they are quite orange and soft-fibrous we call them yams. They are only different types of the same vegetable, just as there are big, mealy baking potatoes and much moister, smaller red potatoes. The rest of the world uses the word yam for a different vegetable.

The point we are making is that neither the white potato nor sweet potato, or yam, as mainlanders know it, is grown to any considerable extent in the tropics. And the second point is that what we call a yam is unrelated to the vegetable called by that name throughout the islands. When we talk island Creole cooking, we mean the local tubers that we describe below.

The following are the local starchy vegetables of the Caribbean. Although they are botanically different from each other, all have similar uses in the kitchen and can, to a considerable extent, be substituted one for another. This happens quite naturally because their seasons do not overlap completely, harvesting is irregular, and different ones store better than others.

A serious problem is keeping the names straight as each vegetable is known by more than one name depending on the place where it is grown or used. Besides, the spelling is far from standardized. Finally, these tubers have never been seriously cultivated systematically, selected, bred, and "improved" the way we do with all the northern vegetables. Differences in quality abound and are due to place of origin, climate, and the chance strain that is grown in any one place. For example, an island friend on St. Thomas brought us taro (dasheen) roots that he claimed to be very superior to those sold in local markets. His friend on Domenica gathers them in the swamps where they grow wild and sends them to him. Everyone seems to have a favorite, but mainlanders find it extremely difficult to memorize the differences. Most root starches are of excellent quality and can be cooked and served like potatoes. The roots, nevertheless, possess a degree of individuality that makes the exploration of this aspect of Caribbean cooking an adventure.

Cassava Euphorbiaceae *Manihot esculenta* **and** *Manilot dulcis*   This relative of the poinsettia grows up to nine feet tall and has tuberous roots in clusters that are a staple starch throughout the American tropics. They were the basic food of the native populations when the Spanish explorers first arrived.

The spindle-shaped roots are about ten inches long and two inches in diameter; the surface is shiny brown and flaky, and marked by thin rings. The flesh is blindingly white, hard, and brittle. During cooking it tends to split apart into wedges. The flavor is nutty and the texture smooth. The processed flour from the roots is made into the tapioca of commerce and a gritty flour for crisp and tasty cassava bread that can be bought in the States from Hispanic and island groceries. Cassava flour for making bread is sold in mainland health stores. In the islands it is often sprinkled on ragouts or on gratins as a contrasting texture.

Bread is sold in small (10-inch) or large (18-inch) thin, round sheets, like matzohs. It is dry and gritty. Heated in the oven and brushed with butter it is a crisp snack. Moistened and heated it softens and is a good accompaniment to meats with sauces. See page 268 for more about this. Hermetically sealed the dry bread keeps indefinitely without refrigeration.

There are two species of the tubers. *Manihot esculenta*, the bitter cassava, no longer sold in northern markets, contains poisonous prussic acid which is eliminated by cooking for at least an hour and a half in lightly salted water which is later discarded. *Manihot dulcis*, the sweet cassava, sold in northern markets, is virtually free of acid and requires boiling for only twenty minutes (or until tender) in plenty of water.

Dasheen Taro Kalo Eddo Araceae *Colocasia esculenta*

The plant grows worldwide in the tropics. Both tubers and leaves are edible. The tubers are generally stubby but roundish and roughly lined with horizontal ridges. The flesh color is variable: white, bluish white, grayish, or white with purplish threads of color. To choose the best varieties for cooking one needs the advice of an island-born cook. At Hispanic and island vegetable stores the differences are often known and available for the asking.

The triangular, arrow-shaped leaves which grow directly from the tuber on long stalks are called dasheen (da chine, from China) or callaloo in the islands, the latter being also the name of the greatest of island soups (page 91). You may also hear them called dasheen bush.

Dasheen bush is being shipped fresh to market on the mainland and sold in plastic bags. Cans of dasheen leaves (Goya and Roberts, nineteen ounces) are labeled callaloo on one side and *epinards* (French for "spinach") on the other. Callaloo soup is also available in cans. Like all commercial soups it requires fortifying with processor-ground spicy sausage, crab meat, Japanese crab-style seafood product, and herbs and spices, especially cumin and fenugreek.

Malanga Yautia Tannia Tanier Tanyah Ocumo Belembe Tiquisque *Xanthosoma sagittifolium* or *Xanthosoma violaceum*

The tubers are dark brown, rough skinned, three to four inches thick, and twelve inches or more long. They are often marked with circular ridges. The flesh is white or light purple and very juicy. Both types cook fast and are fine textured. If mashed, the result is moister than potatoes. The tubers are especially popular in Puerto Rico and other Spanish islands.

Yam Batata Yampi Cush-Cush Name Igname *Dioscorea batatas Dioscorea esculenta Dioscorea alata*   The yam, of the Dioscoriaceae family, is a vine that grows everywhere in the tropics, sprawling along the ground or climbing high into forest trees, but always bearing large roots that, in some varieties, are edible. It is probable that more down-islanders eat yams than any other root starch.

These tubers assume many shapes and sizes. They can be huge and round and white, or long and rough and brown or black. The flesh is usually white or yellow. In our U.S. markets the imported yam most closely resembling the white potato, is a long, cylindrical kind with very white flesh. These usually come in from Colombia or Brazil. They can be boiled, fried, or mashed and are closer to our potatoes than any of the other root starches.

Yellow-fleshed yams are, in our opinion, less attractive. In cooking, they color the water very strongly as they, too, turn nearly white. But they are rather tough, not woody but somewhat hard, and they do not fry or mash easily.

Very popular with Hispanics are the batatas which are rather angular, bumpy, and pink, weighing at least one-half pound each. These are the yams the islanders refer to as sweet potatoes. But they are not at all like our sweet potatoes and yams of the South. The skin is thin and the flesh is white. The texture is similar to and almost as mealy as a potato. But they possess, for our taste, a peculiarly cloying mild sweetness. We avoid them, but others should try them before taking our word.

It is impossible to predict how many other types of yams will turn up in our markets. For the mainlander, keeping island root vegetables straight is difficult enough as it is, there being so many different types compared with our simple choices of potatoes. Yams have not been bred and selected like potatoes. If that were done systematically there is no telling what other excellent-quality starches might be developed to offer even more variety.

◆ The Preparation of Island Root Starches ◆

We offer recipes only for malanga and yam because these vegetables, as well as taro and cassava, are prepared no differently in the islands than our potatoes on the mainland. It would be redundant to offer more of what is amply covered in any American or European cookbook. The usage differences are implicit in the recipes in which they are combined with other ingredients. We are more specific in respect to breadfruit and bread-fruit nuts because these starches are rather different from those to which we are accustomed.

The following recipes can serve as models of the plain cooking of all the island root starches.

*Puerto Rico and
Tortola*

MALANGA, PLAIN AND FANCY

◆

1½ pounds malanga or
  any other root starch or
  breadfruit
2 scallions, finely chopped
1 tablespoon fresh, minced
  parsley leaves or dried
  parsley leaves
¼ to ½ stick butter or
  margarine
¾ cup sharp cheese,
  grated with a Mouli
  grater
1 egg
Big pinch of freshly grated
  nutmeg
Milk or half-and-half, as
  needed
Salt and freshly ground
  black pepper to taste

SERVES 4

1 Peel the tuber with a sharp knife or swivel peeler and cut into ¾-inch slices or cubes.

2 Simmer in lightly salted water for 20 minutes or until tender. Drain. (The vegetable may be served now, as cut, or mashed simply with butter, salt, and pepper to taste.)

3 Mash the malanga thoroughly with a wire potato masher, or pass through a potato ricer.

4 Place the malanga in the top of a double boiler set over boiling water. Add the remaining ingredients except the milk, salt, and pepper. Stir thoroughly.

5 Add the milk, stirring thoroughly, to achieve a light, nonflowing texture. Season with the salt and pepper.

6 Heat to the boiling point and serve.

Use the same ingredients as for Malanga, Plain and Fancy (above), with the addition of a little flour for dredging and vegetable oil for frying.

1 Follow the recipe through step 4.
2 At step 5, add only enough milk to the malanga to achieve a texture that will hold its shape.
3 Form the malanga into 4-inch cakes and dredge thoroughly in the flour.
4 Fry with vegetable oil in a pan until crisp and browned on both sides.

Variation

Add finely chopped onion or scallion tops to the mashed potato mixture before making the cakes.

FRIED MALANGA CAKES

◆

SERVES 4

Tobago

YAM FRITTERS

◆

½ to ¾ pound white yam
  or any other root starch
2 eggs
1 tablespoon dried parsley
  or 4 cilantro sprigs,
  snipped
1 scallion, tops only,
  finely snipped, *or* ½
  small onion, finely
  chopped
1 teaspoon mild curry
  powder (optional)
Salt to taste
Chili pepper, fresh or
  powdered, to taste
Vegetable oil for deep frying

**MAKES 10 TO 15
FRITTERS**

1 Peel and roughly cut up the yam. Boil for 30 minutes or until tender. Press through a potato ricer.

2 Add the rest of the ingredients except the chili and oil and mix thoroughly in a bowl. Stir in the chili pepper.

3 Heat the oil to 370 degrees in a small pan. It should be about 2 inches deep.

4 Shape heaping tablespoons of the yam mixture into small, flattened cakes. Drop one by one into the oil. Cook until golden and crisp, turning only once. Remove with a slotted spoon and drain on paper towels in a hot oven.

Serve as an appetizer with a hot or cold dip or as a side dish with a tomato sauce or brown sauce.

YAM PANCAKES

◆

MAKES 8 TO 10 PANCAKES

1 Proceed as for Yam Fritters (below) through step 3.
2 At step 4, form flat 3-inch cakes and pat each pancake all over with flour. Cassava flour is excellent for the purpose.
3 Brown on both sides in a pan with butter or oil. Serve hot.

Variation
At step 2 of the fritter recipe, add ¼ stick butter and 1 cup grated sharp cheddar cheese to the mixture. Proceed as above.

Tobago

PORK AND VEGETABLE SANCOCHO

◆

1 bunch spinach or dasheen leaves, shredded
4 large cucumbers, peeled, cored, and sliced
1 additional cup lentils or split peas, uncooked, or other cooked beans
½ pound spicy sausage, cut into chunks and processed for 5 seconds (optional)
4 large tomatoes, peeled and cut into chunks

Leave out the beef from Beef Sancocho (page 209) but retain the pork meats. To the remaining ingredients add:

1 Add 1 quart of water and the spinach, cucumber, beans, and sausage to the fried onion and pork. Add the peas and follow original recipe steps 3 and 4.
2 Simmer for 2 hours. Then add the tomatoes and the cooked plantain.
3 Test for seasoning.
4 The stew can be served immediately or stored overnight in the fridge. Alternatively, allow the sancocho to cool and strain out the liquid into a large pot. Remove any pork bones and process the solids for ten seconds. Return the puree to the vegetable liquid and simmer, reducing the mix to a rich thickness. Serve hot.

◆ Coo-coo or Fungi ◆

Whether fungi and coo-coo are the same, and if not, where the precise difference lies, is rather a mystery. Both are like our soft cornmeal recipes from the South but are made with a finer-milled meal *(masa harina)*. Barbados claims that coo-coo is the name of the swizzle stick or stirrer used to mix the meal with water. There is no question that cornmeal mush is fungi with or without okra. So we have made the arbitrary decision to call mushes made with other starches—breadfruit, plantain flour, or cassava flour—coo-coo, including those with vegetables other than okra added.

Cassava flour can be bought in the States from island groceries. Plantain flour is carried by health food stores. It is similar to cornstarch but slightly sweet. Cassava flour is decidedly, but pleasantly, gritty.

PLAIN FUNGI

◆

2 cups chicken broth or
  water
1 cup very fine yellow
  cornmeal *(masa harina)*
¼ stick butter or marga-
  rine
Salt and freshly ground
  black pepper to taste

**SERVES 2 AS A
SINGLE SIDE DISH
OR 4 ACCOMPANIED
BY ANOTHER
VEGETABLE**

The following is the basic recipe for this universal island starch dish. As a breakfast cereal it is made with water (or, occasionally, with milk) but is tastier if chicken or other stock is used for luncheon or dinner.

1 In a saucepan or small pot bring the chicken broth to a boil.
2 Gradually pour in the meal in a thin, steady stream while stirring rapidly with a wooden spoon.
3 Cook to a creamy consistency, about 3 or 4 minutes. Add the butter, salt, and pepper. Stir well and serve.

Variation
When made with chicken broth as a dinner dish you may wish to add 1 tablespoon Madras curry powder at step 2.

1 In a saucepan or small pot bring the chicken broth to a boil.

2 Gradually pour in the cornmeal in a thin, steady stream while stirring rapidly with a wooden spoon.

3 Follow immediately by stirring in 2 tablespoons of the achiote oil and the herb leaves.

4 Cook to a creamy consistency, about 3 to 4 minutes. Add the salt and pepper.

5 Pour the mixture onto an oiled baking sheet to a thickness of ¾ inch. Allow to harden in the air. Then cut into 1-x-3-inch rectangles.

6 Fry the rectangles in a skillet with the remaining achiote oil. They should be somewhat browned and crisp on both sides. Serve hot with meat dishes.

Almost everywhere in the islands fungi is preferred with okra at dinner. It is one of those ideal relationships that are so generally liked that they become a staple of regional cookery.

1 Drop the okra into boiling water and cook until barely tender.

2 Meanwhile, pour the chicken broth into a pot. Mix in the parsley. Slowly pour in the cornmeal in a thin, steady stream while stirring constantly.

3 Drain the okra through a strainer and immediately stir together with the cornmeal. Add the butter, salt, and pepper. Simmer for another 5 minutes while stirring. Serve hot.

FRIED FUNGI

◆

2 cups chicken broth or water
1 cup fine yellow cornmeal *(masa harina)*
4 tablespoons achiote oil (page 110)
2 tablespoons snipped Spanish thyme leaves *or* 1 tablespoon dried marjoram leaves
Salt and freshly ground black pepper to taste

SERVES 4

St. Thomas

FUNGI WITH OKRA

◆

½ 10-ounce package frozen okra pieces
1 10¾-ounce can low-salt chicken broth concentrate
1 tablespoon parsley flakes
¾ cup fine yellow cornmeal
¼ stick butter or margarine
Salt and freshly ground black pepper to taste

SERVES 4

St. Lucia

CASSAVA COO-COO (FUNGI)

◆

1 cup cassava flour
3 cups water
Butter to taste
Salt to taste

SERVES 4

The cassava version of fungi is neither as common nor as popular as the cornmeal fungi, but it may well be the original aborigine recipe.

Add the flour slowly to the boiling water while stirring with a wooden spatula. Cook about 10 minutes or until the mixture is smooth and fairly firm. Add the butter and salt.

Note
With the exception that cassava flour requires 3 cups of water instead of 2 to 1 cup of cornmeal, the recipe for Fungi with Okra (page 261) can be used.

Tobago

FRIED PLANTAIN

◆

Vegetable oil for frying
2 large plantains, peeled and sliced
Salt and freshly ground black pepper to taste

SERVES 2

Ripe plantains are used for frying. At this stage they are yellow and the firm flesh is slightly sweet. They do not become mushy when heated as do bananas. Plantains are peeled and then thinly sliced on the bevel in order to have larger pieces.

1 Heat the oil, using just enough oil to leave a filmy coat on the bottom of the pan.
2 Distribute the plantain evenly over the whole surface.
3 Simmer, covered, for 6 minutes.
4 Turn with a spatula and simmer, covered, for another 6 minutes.
5 Sprinkle with the salt and pepper. Serve hot on a warmed plate.

Variations
A At step 4, add a bit of Scotch bonnet chili pepper, forced through a garlic press, *or* a few drops of yellow island chili sauce to taste.
B Cook in achiote oil (page 110) instead of vegetable oil.
C At step 4, sprinkle with a mild curry powder.
D Sprinkle with grated nutmeg to taste.
E Add 2 tablespoons concentrated beef stock at step 4.

Antigua

OKRA COLD SPICED

◆

1 A. If using fresh okra, remove the hard, broad tip on each stalk. Boil in lightly salted water until just tender. (The time will vary considerably depending on the particular lot of the vegetable, as some take a longer time than others.) Remove from the heat and drain as soon as the vegetable offers little resistance to a fork. Overcooking makes okra soft and slimy. Better a little crisp than mushy.

B. If using frozen okra, pour undefrosted, into a colander or sieve placed over boiling water. Cover loosely. Remove from the heat as soon as the okra has reached the condition described above. Note that frozen okra cooks very quickly.

2 Pour the okra into a bowl, cover, and cool in the fridge.

3 When the okra is cool, squeeze the lime and mix the okra thoroughly with the juice. Then, an ingredient at a time, add first the parsley and then the remaining ingredients, stirring with each addition. The salt, pepper, and chili sauce should be added last.

4 Allow to cool and marinate in the fridge, covered, until ready to serve.

5 Spread the okra neatly on the plates. If used in a salad, cut into small pieces and mix with the salad ingredients.

1½ pounds fresh okra or 1½ packages frozen, whole okra
1 very juicy lime
½ cup chopped fresh parsley *or* 1½ tablespoons dried parsley flakes
1 tablespoon ground cumin
½ teaspoon ground allspice
½ teaspoon garlic powder *or* 1 garlic clove, through the press
4 sprigs cilantro leaves, finely chopped (optional)
1 teaspoon vegetable oil
Salt and freshly ground black pepper to taste
Yellow island chili sauce to taste

SERVES 4

Puerto Rico

ROASTED MASHED TOMATOES

◆

3 pounds ripe beefsteak
  tomatoes
½ stick butter or marga-
  rine *or* 4 tablespoons
  vegetable oil
2 tablespoons freshly
  grated green ginger *or* 1
  tablespoon ground ginger
1 tablespoon ground
  cumin
1 tablespoon ground cori-
  ander
6 whole allspice, crushed,
  or 1 teaspoon ground allspice
Juice of 1 lemon
Salt and freshly ground
  black pepper to taste
Chili pepper to taste

SERVES 4

A lively recipe for tomatoes is hard to find. This one was given to us by a hostess in Puerto Rico. It's terrific with steaks and chops. See below for other uses.

1 In a preheated 450-degree oven, bake the whole tomatoes until the skins crack and they sizzle and pop.
2 Allow to cool a bit and then mash them a couple at a time with a potato masher or with a fork and knife in a large bowl. Remove the skins and ends.
3 When the skins and ends have been removed and the tomatoes have cooled sufficiently, put 2 or 3 cups of the tomato at a time into a blender or processor bowl and whip for 3 or 4 seconds. Decant into a large saucepan. Before whipping the last amount of tomato, add all the other ingredients except the salt, pepper, and chili pepper.
4 Heat the processed tomato. Simmer, uncovered, until the mixture is reduced to a thick consistency. As the sauce thickens increase the frequency of stirring. At the end, season with the salt, pepper, and chili pepper.
5 Spoon into bowls or onto plates.

Variations

This recipe has many potentials. The following may be of interest.
A Use as a barbecue sauce, coating meat under the broiler. Especially good with meaty short ribs.
B Thin with white vinegar or white wine vinegar, turning the sauce into a ketchup. Store in a screw-top jar in the fridge. Unless frozen, it will not keep safely for more than 2 weeks.
C Add horseradish to taste and serve cold with cold fish, shrimps, clams, or oysters.
D Spread on canapés, crackers, or cassava bread as party snacks.
E Dilute with oil and red wine to make an excellent pasta sauce.

* * * * * * * * * *

• Eleven •

BREADS,

JAMS, AND

CHUTNEYS

* * * * * * * * *

◆ Breads ◆

In the small island villages, there always seems to be an outside bread oven, shaded by trees beside a part-time baker's house. It is a large, beehive-shaped affair of hard brown clay, scarred with black streaks from the smoke of many fires, medieval in appearance. Sometimes the oven is fired only once a week, and the villagers gather nearby on that day, baskets over their arms, waiting to buy a loaf or two. We have often, when housekeeping on an island, wanted to try the freshly baked bread, but somehow, we felt an intruder on this very local, almost mystic rite, in which the number of baked loaves is nicely balanced to the number of people who always gathered at the baking oven.

But a loaf of yeast bread does not begin to fill the needs of a starch at meals, so quick breads are made in every household kitchen on top of the stove or in the oven, or cooked outside on a grill or coalpot. Depending on the island, the breads are variously known as bakes, floats, johnny cakes, cassava bread or bang-bang, banana bread, butter bread or *pain beurre*, all smelling wonderful as they cook.

We, too, have made these breads on the islands and on the mainland. But often, when we are baking a regular loaf bread, we think of the beehive ovens perched on their stilts, and the trees that overhang them.

CASSAVA BREAD

◆

¾ cup cassava flour, plus additional for flouring pastry board (see Note)
⅓ cup all-purpose flour
½ teaspoon baking powder
Pinch of salt
¾ cup water plus 3 tablespoons
1 tablespoon corn oil, plus additional for cooking

MAKES 2 6- TO 8-INCH ROUNDS

Thin round sheets of cassava bread are probably the earliest of the island breads, handed down from the original Arawak and Carib Indians. In its pure form it is made of grated cassava root, wrung out in a thin cloth. The damp shreds are pressed together on a sheet of metal and "baked" over an outdoor fire. Served hot, it is soft; but once cold, the thin bread hardens and will keep for weeks. One of our St. Thomas friends says that her best breakfast is cassava bread, broken into pieces in a bowl and covered with milk.

There are many recipes for the bread in the islands, and cooks tend to be indefinite on proportions and exact procedures. There is a fuzzy area between the wringing out of the fresh cassava root and the drying and sifting of the shreds, mostly because no one will exactly admit to using cassava flour! Also, some will add grated coconut, white flour, and other refinements. From all these half-descriptions we've worked out a bread that can be made in mainland kitchens with available products.

Cassava Bread also is imported from the islands in six- to ten-inch rounds or from the Dominican Republic as quarters of much larger rounds. Both types are one-quarter to one-half inch thick, white, very dry, hard, brittle, and grainy. There are two principal ways to prepare it for the table

For soft cassava bread, hold the sheets under the water faucet and soak them only long enough to sponge up the moisture. Then place on a pan in a 350-degree oven and heat for about ten minutes. It should then be soft, flexible, and tender but no longer moist. Cut into sections, it is delicious with butter, soft cheeses, jams, and canapé-type spreads. It can also be folded over spicy ground meat or fish mixtures. The bread must be eaten hot because it toughens as it cools.

For crisp cassava bread, heat the round in a 350-degree oven until the color turns an appetizing yellow. This is the finest of crisp breads: very slightly sweet, crackly, and nutty. A true luxury bread. You can brush the bread with a mixture of butter or olive oil and crushed garlic before crisping in the oven.

1 Mix the dry ingredients together in a bowl. Slowly add ¾ cup of the water, stirring and smoothing the dough with a wooden spoon. Stir in the corn oil. If needed, add the remaining 3 tablespoons of water (more or less), depending on the texture of the dough. It should hold together so it can be rolled out to a thin disk.
2 Divide the dough into 2 pieces. Store 1 piece in a plastic bag to keep it from drying out. Sprinkle the pastry board with cassava flour and roll the dough out to a ¼-inch-thick 6- to 8-inch irregular circle.

3   Heat a griddle or heavy frying pan large enough to hold the rolled-out dough. When hot, brush very lightly with the corn oil.

4   Transfer the dough to the hot griddle, bottom side down. Cook for 3 to 4 minutes. Sprinkle the top with cassava flour and turn the bread over. Cook again for 3 to 4 minutes. The surfaces on both sides should be dotted with light-brown spots. When this occurs, the dough should be cooked. If not, cook a little longer on both sides.

5   When the bread is done, transfer it to a cake rack to cool. Repeat the procedure with the second ball of dough. Reheat in the oven to serve.

N o t e

Cassava flour can be bought in island shops and some health food stores.

St. Lucia

On two different occasions, we stayed in one of a group of six-sided cottages scattered under the trees, at the edge of a quiet bay with a long sandy beach. At the relaxed, open-sided dining room covered with a palm-thatch roof, we had a super banana bread, a specialty of the owner, who was generous with the recipe.

Then one day, while shopping for supplies in Castries, we joined everyone else in a search for bread. No bread anywhere—and no explanation. We ran into a friend who called out cheerfully that Charles's store had flour. We rushed over, knowing that we could make baking powder biscuits without a recipe. And then, there was that newly acquired recipe for banana bread. We picked up extra bananas at the market, and on the way home to our cottage borrowed enough potato flour and powdered buttermilk from the originator of the recipe—and life settled back to island normal.

1   Preheat the oven to 400 degrees. Butter and flour a 7½-x-3¾-x-2¼-inch loaf pan.

2   Sift together the flours, buttermilk powder, baking soda, salt, and nutmeg into a small bowl and set aside.

3   Slice the banana into a large mixing bowl and mash with a fork. Add the sugar and beat with a wire whisk. Beat in the egg and vegetable oil.

4   Stir in the flour mixture until just mixed. Add the water and mix.

5   Pour the batter into the prepared loaf pan and smooth the surface. Bake for 40 minutes at 400 degrees, then reduce the heat to 350 degrees for 10

BANANA BREAD

◆

1⅛ cups all-purpose flour
4 tablespoons potato flour
1 tablespoon cultured buttermilk powder (see Note)
¾ teaspoon baking soda
Pinch of salt
Pinch of grated nutmeg
1 very ripe banana, about 8 inches long
½ cup light-brown *granulated* sugar
1 egg
2 tablespoons vegetable oil
¼ cup water

MAKES 15 PORTIONS

minutes. The loaf is done when a small thin skewer inserted into the center comes out clean. Remove from the oven, let cool in the pan for 5 minutes, then turn out to cool on a rack. The banana bread will be a golden brown and will have risen to 4 inches in the center. The center will have split lengthwise. When cool, place in a plastic bag and store in the fridge overnight, allowing the bread to mellow and the flavor to intensify.

Note

We like using buttermilk powder, as most recipes call for 1 cup or less of buttermilk—and *what* does one do with the rest of the quart! At least it can be a problem for those of us who are not buttermilk drinkers.

Cultured buttermilk powder can be purchased from Saco Foods Inc., P.O. Box 5461, Madison, Wisconsin 53705.

Another bread, made throughout the islands is called floats, an obvious descriptive name, as the thin rounds of yeast dough are cooked in deep oil, and they float to the surface when done. The characteristic of local breads is that they have developed from hundreds of years of outdoor cooking: Grills, placed over wood or tree bean-pod fires, were balanced on low walls of stone or placed on top of clay coalpots (open-sided sheds protecting the fires from rain), and deep-fat frying was done in iron kettles containing coconut oil or lard. So that even now, when these familiar breads are made indoors on more modern stoves (bottled gas or electric), the style and procedures remain the same, though many houses in the outlying hills or rural areas are still without electricity. For instance, it was only in the mid-1950s that the first electric wires were installed on Tobago.

1 Measure ¼ cup of the warm water into a small bowl, stir in the sugar, then sprinkle the yeast over the surface. Keep the bowl in a warm place until the yeast foams.

2 Meanwhile, measure the flour and salt into a mixing bowl. Cut the shortening into ½-inch dice and blend into the flour with your fingers. Stir in the yeast and mix, adding extra warm water if needed to make a moist but not sticky dough.

3 Lightly flour a pastry board and knead the dough for 15 minutes.

4 Place the dough in a lightly oiled bowl, cover with a clean dish towel, and place in a warm area until the dough doubles in size, about 1 hour.

5 When the dough has risen, transfer it to a floured pastry board, punch down, and form it into an 18- to 20-inch-long roll. Cut into 1-inch slices. Roll each slice into a small ball. Place the balls on a lightly oiled baking pan. Cover with a clean dish towel and let the balls rise to double their size, about 30 minutes.

6 Heat the corn oil in a deep frying pan or pot to 370 degrees. The oil should be deep enough to cover the floats.

7 Flour the pastry board again, and roll out, into round, thin circles, 3 to 5 balls (or however many will fit into the pan of hot oil). Fry for 3 to 5 minutes or until the floats are a light, golden brown on both sides. Drain on paper towels in a 150-degree oven. Repeat with the remaining dough until all the balls have been cooked. Serve hot. These can be reheated in the oven.

FLOATS

◆

¼ cup lukewarm water, plus additional water for the dough
½ teaspoon sugar
1 packet dried yeast
3 cups all-purpose flour, plus additional for flouring pastry board
½ teaspoon salt
6 tablespoons solid vegetable shortening
Corn oil for deep frying

MAKES 18 TO 20 PORTIONS

Martinique

PAIN BEURRE (BUTTER BREAD)

◆

1 tablespoon dry yeast
2½ teaspoons sugar
6 tablespoons milk or half-and-half
1 stick unsalted butter
1½ cups plus 2 tablespoons all-purpose flour
¼ teaspoon salt
2 eggs

MAKES 8 PORTIONS

During one of our stays on Martinique, we spent a long weekend at the Leyritz Plantation. Driving north on the middle-of-the-island road, we caught a tantalizing glimpse, high up through the trees, of the soaring white domes of a Sacré-Coeur look-alike. Climbing steadily, the blue hills peaked on our left, changing their shapes with each curve of the road. After passing banana and pineapple plantations, we forded a shallow stream and drove up the winding road to the plantation entrance, royal palms thrusting upward like pillars of gray concrete topped by green rubber tubes holding the palm fronds.

We ducked into a low-ceilinged, tropical cabin furnished with colonial mahogany pieces. Then we settled down on our roofed porch, enjoying the cool rain-forest air after days on the sun-soaked Saline beach. Lush, green exotic fruit trees and flowering tropical bushes were scattered over the lawns, and off to our right was the rounded, tree-covered hump of Mt. Pelée. It is now an inactive volcano since its devastating eruption in 1902 that covered the town of St. Pierre with ashes, leaving only one person alive.

One of the highpoints of that weekend was breakfast, partially because of our discovery of *pain beurre*, a buttery loaf cut into inch-thick slices and stacked in a glass-fronted warming oven. It was warm and light, yet dry enough to blend with the tropical jams. The dough is a variation of brioche, but it is baked in a long loaf pan. In subsequent years we were to buy *pain beurre* at bakeries in France and compare them to that first taste in Martinique, and to our own *pain beurre*.

1   In a small bowl mix the yeast and ½ teaspoon of the sugar together. Heat 5 tablespoons of the milk to lukewarm and stir it into the yeast. Place the bowl in a warm place until the yeast foams.

2   Cut the butter into slices and let it come to room temperature on a small plate.

3   Sift the flour, salt, and the remaining sugar into a mixing bowl.

4   Beat the eggs in a small bowl. Reserve 1 tablespoon of the beaten egg in a small ramekin and add the remaining milk to it.

5   Blend the yeast into the beaten eggs. Stir half of this liquid into the flour with a wooden spoon. Mix, and slowly add the rest of the liquid until the flour and liquid are blended.

6   Gradually add the butter slices, 2 at a time, smoothing them into the dough before adding more slices. When all the slices have been added, beat the dough vigorously to be sure all the butter has been incorporated.

7 Transfer the dough to an oiled, straight-sided bowl, deep enough to allow the dough to rise two to three times its bulk. Cover the top of the bowl with a clean dish towel, and place the bowl in a warm place for 1¼ hours.

8 Butter an 8⅜-x-4⅜-x-2½-inch loaf pan.

9 When the dough has risen, turn it out onto a lightly floured board and punch down. Form the dough into a rectangle the size of the loaf pan. Slip the dough into the buttered pan, cover the top with the folded dish towel, and place the pan in a warm place for 1 to 1¼ hours. Fifteen minutes before the dough has completely risen in the pan, preheat the oven to 375 degrees (see Note). When risen, brush the top with a thin layer of the reserved egg mixture.

10 Bake the bread for 25 minutes, brush the top again with the remaining egg mixture, and continue to bake for 15 more minutes. Turn the loaf out of the pan and bake for 5 more minutes to crisp the outside. Place on a cake rack to cool.

11 Serve for breakfast or lunch cut into 1-inch-wide slices that are warmed in the oven.

Note

The dough will not continue to rise in the oven.

St. Martin

JOHNNY CAKE OR BAKES

◆

2 cups all-purpose flour, plus additional for flouring pastry board
2 teaspoons baking powder
¼ teaspoon salt
1½ teaspoons sugar
2 tablespoons butter or margarine
2 tablespoons solid vegetable shortening
¼ to ½ cup water, milk, or coconut milk
Corn oil for frying

MAKES 10 TO 12 PORTIONS

One noontime at Grand Case on St. Martin, we did not feel like going inside to an enclosed restaurant, especially after smelling the aroma of chicken and spare ribs wafting up from the lineup of charcoal grills beside the road at the pier, each one tended by a local lady. On the flanking tables were stuffed christophenes (chayote), sliced steamed yams, sliced cold cucumbers and tomatoes—and just hot-off-the-griddle johnny cakes. When our plates were full, we were motioned to the open-sided wooden building at the water's edge where there were tables, chairs, and a small bar. A cold beer and a magnificent view of the water completed our sense that all was right with the world.

Johnny cake or bakes are interchangeable names for approximately the same formula, depending on the island and the cook. The dough is sometimes fried in shallow oil on a griddle or in a heavy frying pan in deep oil, or baked in the oven. Mainland cooks will recognize this formula as one for baking-powder biscuits.

1   Measure and sift the dry ingredients into a mixing bowl.
2   Cut in the butter and shortening until achieving a cornmeal consistency. Add the liquid slowly, beating the dough with a wooden spoon until it is moistened enough to form a soft but not sticky ball.
3   Turn the dough out onto a floured board and knead a bit. Roll out to a ½-inch thickness and cut out rounds with a floured biscuit cutter.
4   In a large, heavy frying pan, heat ⅛ to ¼ inch of the oil, almost to the smoking point. Lower the heat to medium and slip some of the rounds into the pan using a broad spatula, leaving space between them. Fry until both sides are a golden brown, turning only once. When cooked, drain on paper towels in a 150-degree oven. Repeat with the remaining rounds until all have been cooked. Serve hot.

Variations

A   Deep-fat fry in 4 inches of oil heated to 375 degrees.
B   For bakes, place the rounds on an oiled baking pan and bake in a 350-degree oven, about 20 to 25 minutes or until the tops are a golden brown.

◆ Jams and Chutneys ◆

Making jams and chutneys is one of the islands' culinary traditions, as, contrary to northern beliefs about the ever-warm tropics, fruits are seasonal, and their season of eating is extended through jams, preserves, and chutneys.

All island fruits are jam possibilities, as bread, jam, and coffee are the breakfast staples. Jams are often not as strongly flavored as the northern ones, but their unexpected freshness is tantalizing, especially when used as a filling between cake layers.

Mangoes are in season in late spring through early fall, depending on the variety and the island's location. Papayas and bananas, since they are herbaceous plants rather than trees, have an extended season. Other fruits, including citrus, come and go throughout the year. In the Virgin Islands, limes are used for jelly, marmalade, and pickling, as are orange slices. Genips, available from late summer into fall, are turned into jelly, as are the long bunches of sea grapes. Guavas are made into jam, jelly, paste, and shells. For the shells, the thin skin is peeled away, the pink interior pulp and seeds scooped out of the halved guavas, and the thin shells of fruit boiled down with water and sugar until they turn an appetizing golden brown. Tamarind pulp is prepared by slow cooking when the trees hang heavy with the tan pods.

We have chosen a few jam recipes of fruit available in the States—jams and chutneys that we make and store to use in the cold Stateside winter, to remind us that somewhere there are palm trees, sweet air, and blue-green water.

Sugar is the preservative for jams and chutneys, and its concentration during the boiling down to reach the "jam" stage is part of this process. Follow the formulas in the following recipes to eliminate any chance of spoilage. Most homemade jams will keep from four to six months, but usually have been eaten well before that time! Chutneys are made for particular meals, and therefore are usually made in small quantities for immediate use; store any leftovers in the fridge. These directions apply to both jams and chutneys.

While the jam or chutney is boiling, wash the glass jars in hot water and detergent; rinse with clean, hot water. Slip the flat blade of a metal knife part way under the bottom of a jar to slightly lift it from the working surface. This will prevent the jar from cracking as you fill it with clean boiling water. Repeat with the rest of the jars. Let the jars stand until ready to fill with jam; then pour out the water.

Cover the working surface with several sheets of newspaper to protect the surface from hot spilled jam as well as hot paraffin wax. Place the jars upright on the newspaper. Fill the jars with jam to one-quarter inch from the top edge. While the jam is cooling in the jars, melt the paraffin wax in a small pot, following the manufacturer's directions.

When the jam has slightly cooled, and a skin has formed on the top, wipe off any jam on the inside and outside of the top one-quarter inch of the jar as well as any jam which has dripped down the outside of the jar. Use a damp, paper towel for this purpose.

Spoon the hot paraffin wax into each jar, filling the one-quarter-inch space to the top edge. Let the jars stand until the jam is cold, then screw on the metal tops, label the jars, and store them in a cool dark place.

St. Lucia

BANANA JAM

◆

1½ limes
6 ripe bananas
1 cup water
3½ cups sugar
½ vanilla bean
1 teaspoon banana extract

MAKES 3 10-OUNCE JARS

St. Lucia's money crop is now the banana. The plants are grown on the moist, flat land between the central mountains and the Caribbean coast and on the hillsides overlooking the Atlantic, with their large fruit bunches swathed in bright, transparent blue plastic. One's life in an automobile is at peril on the days when the Dutch fruit ship is anchored at Vieux Fort, for then the trucks, loaded with bananas, barrel down the winding road to the southern port, racing against time to get the fruit aboard ship.

We used to buy the tree-ripened fruit at the Castries market, and take it home and make our own homemade jam.

1 Squeeze the limes and set the juice aside in a bowl large enough to hold the sliced bananas.

2 Peel the bananas, removing any "strings." Cut them into ¼-inch-thick slices, for a total of 3¾ cups. As the measuring cup is filled, empty the slices into the bowl, stirring them with a fork to distribute the lime juice. Repeat with the remaining bananas, then set the bowl aside.

3 Put the water and sugar in a stainless steel pot and bring to a boil. Stir until the sugar has dissolved, then add the vanilla bean and the lime juice and banana mixture. Bring the contents to a boil, then lower the heat and bring to a lively simmer. Stir with a wooden spoon so that the bananas will not sink to the bottom. Skim off any foam that rises to the top. The juice will thicken and the fruit will become transparent after about 20 to 25 minutes. Check for the jellying stage by dropping ½ teaspoon of the liquid onto a saucer and putting it in the fridge for 1 minute. If the liquid has jellied, remove the pot from the heat, scoop out the vanilla bean, and stir in the banana extract. If the liquid has not jellied, cook until it does and follow the above instructions.

4 Ladle the jam into the hot, sterilized jars, evenly distributing the bananas. Fill the jars to within ¼ inch of the top of the jars. Let cool, and cover the top of the jam with melted paraffin (see page 275). When the wax is hard, put on the metal tops and place the jars on a cool, dark shelf to ripen for a week before using.

Throughout the islands there is a steady cooking-up of small and large batches of jam, jelly, and condiments as fruits ripen seasonally. Wherever there is a particularly fine cook, her jams, with handwritten or locally printed labels, will turn up on the local grocery shelves, and one looks for these special few. This is very noticeable in the French islands as jam is a way of breakfast.

When the mangoes are full grown, but before they begin to turn yellow or red, they are picked for jam. Their flesh is firm but full of flavor. If mangoes are too ripe, the flesh of some varieties turns stringy and disintegrates into juice, unsuitable for jam.

1   Squeeze ½ of the lemon and the lime to make 2 tablespoons of juice, reserving the lime skin. Set the juice and lime skin aside.

2   Peel the mango, or mangoes, and rub the exposed surface immediately with the remaining lemon as you remove the mango skin. Cut the mango into ½-inch-thick slices, then cut the slices into ½- to ¾-inch dice. Trim the fruit from around the pit and cut into pieces. You should have about 1 pound of fruit.

3   Put the fruit in a large stainless steel pot with water to cover, approximately 3½ cups. Bring to a boil. Lower the heat, bring to a slow boil, and cook for 20 minutes. Remove the pot from the heat and strain the contents through a stainless steel sieve into a bowl. Empty the fruit into another bowl and set aside.

4   Measure the juice back into the pot, making sure that you have 2 cups of liquid. Add more water if needed. Add the sugar and bring to a boil, stirring to distribute the sugar. Lower the heat and bring the liquid to a slow boil. Cook about 10 minutes. Add the reserved lemon and lime juice, lime skin, and the cinnamon, cloves, and partially cooked mango dice. Bring to a boil. Lower the heat and bring to a slow boil, skimming off any foam that rises to the surface. After 5 minutes, coarsely mash the fruit with a potato masher.

5   Continue to boil the jam, stirring with a wooden spoon, for 20 to 25 minutes. After 20 minutes, check for the jellying stage by dropping ½ teaspoon of the juice onto a saucer and putting it in the fridge for 1 to 2 minutes. If the juice thickens to jelly, remove the pot from the stove. If not, continue to boil, checking again at 10-minute intervals for jellying.

6   When the mixture has jellied, remove the pot from the heat and scoop out the cinnamon stick, cloves, and lime skin. Ladle the jam into 3 sterilized

Martinique

GREEN MANGO JAM

◆

1 lemon
¼ lime
1½ pounds green mango
2½ cups sugar
1 2¾-inch cinnamon stick
4 whole cloves

MAKES 3 6-OUNCE JARS

jars, filled to within ¼ inch from the top. Set the jars aside to cool, wiping the edges and outside to remove any jam from the glass. When the jam is cool, melt paraffin wax and pour on top of each jar, filling the space up to the edge (see page 275). When the wax has hardened, put the covers on the jars, label them, and store on a cool, dark shelf.

Martinique

LIME MARMALADE

◆

6 limes
6 cups water
Granulated sugar
Yellow and green food
  coloring (optional)

MAKES 5 10-OUNCE JARS

Throughout the Caribbean islands the pale-skinned limes are unique: They are almost round, and not more than 1½ inches in diameter, with an unbelievable concentration of lime flavor. In Martinique some limes are turned into marmalade that is spread on warm *pain beurre*, accompanied by French-roast coffee. It is a wake-up breakfast that could only happen in the French Caribbean.

Each morning at Leyritz Plantation in northern Martinique we looked forward to our leisurely breakfast. After settling in at an outdoor table facing the tree-shaded lawn, we'd listen to birds sing and watch the sunshine come and go as clouds blew over from Mt. Pelée. Each morning we helped ourselves from the line-up of mason jars filled with homemade tropical fruit jams. Then, over this lazy breakfast we would plan our day's expedition: a trip to the market in St. Pierre, or a hike through McIntosh's in Morne Rouge—a combination of greenhouses filled with tropical green and bright-red flowering plants and jungle-like trails under tall trees.

While the making of lime marmalade is scattered over three days, each day's preparation or cooking time is very short, but all this is necessary to soften the lime skins.

1 Cut 1 lime in half, and squeeze out the juice into a 1-cup measuring cup, removing any seeds. Remove the membrane from inside each half of the lime skin and cut the skin into narrow strips, no more than ⅛ inch wide. Cut the strips in half and add them to the juice in the measuring cup.

2 Cut the other 5 limes into quarters, remove any seeds, and put through a food grinder or processor with a steel blade, until the limes have been reduced to a pulp. Add enough of the pulp to the juice and skin strips to fill the measuring cup. Pour the contents into a large bowl. Measure the rest of the pulp—there should be another cupful—and add to the contents of the large bowl. If there is any pulp left over, put it in the cup to measure it and pour into the bowl.

3   Add 3 times the quantity of water to the pulp—6 cups if you have 2 cups of pulp. If you have more pulp, then add the additional proportion of water. Cover the top of the bowl with clear plastic wrap and a large plate. Place the bowl in the fridge for 24 hours.

4   The next day, pour the contents of the bowl into a large pot and bring to a boil. Boil for 10 minutes. Pour the pot's contents back into the rinsed bowl. Allow the liquid to cool to room temperature and cover the bowl as before. Place the bowl in the fridge for another 24 hours.

5   On the third day, measure the contents of the bowl, pouring each cupful into a large pot. Add cup for cup of sugar, plus 1 extra cup of sugar. Stir, and bring the liquid and sugar to a boil. Lower the heat and bring to a slow boil. Skim off any foam that rises to the top. Stir deeply from time to time to keep the fruit from settling and sticking to the bottom of the pot.

6   After 20 minutes, check for the jellying stage by dropping ½ teaspoon of the liquid onto a saucer and putting it into the fridge for 1 minute. If a jelly forms, remove the pot from the heat; if not, continue to cook the marmalade until the liquid has jellied, approximately 5 to 10 minutes more, then remove the pot from the heat.

7   In cooking, the fruit will lose its green color, turning a pale caramel. If you like, mix together a few drops of the yellow and green food coloring— more yellow than green. With a toothpick add a little color to a tablespoon of hot jam, then stir it into the contents of the pot. Check for color, adding more if needed. But add only in small quantities—you want just a pleasing and sparkling, light yellow-green marmalade.

8   Spoon the hot marmalade into sterilized glass jars, filled to within ¼ inch of the top. Let the hot marmalade cool, then cover the top surfaces with melted paraffin (see page 275). Label the jars and store on a dark shelf.

Trinidad

MANGO CHUTNEY

◆

2 large, semiripe mangoes,
  approximately 14 ounces
  each
1¼ cups white vinegar
¾ cup dark brown sugar
1 large garlic clove,
  through the press
½ green *jalapeño* pepper
  (1½ inches of the
  pointed end), forced
  through a garlic press
½ cup dark raisins
3 ounces (½ cup) crystal-
  lized ginger, cut into
  ½-inch chunks
¼ teaspoon ground all-
  spice
1 teaspoon whole allspice
½ teaspoon black mustard
  seed
½ teaspoon ground cumin
½ teaspoon ground ginger
½ teaspoon salt
¼ cup hot water (optional)

**MAKES 3 8-OUNCE
JARS**

Mango Chutney from India has infiltrated the cuisine of most of the Caribbean islands. There are as many formulas as there are cooks, but the constants are mangoes, raisins, brown sugar, vinegar, hot peppers, and garlic or onions. But, from then on, individual tastes prevail as to the spices and herbs used and the quantities of all the ingredients. Even the quantity of hot pepper is a matter of choice, and you might want to start with a small amount, and, through tasting, add the amount that suits your taste buds. We like to make a small quantity of chutney at a time, so that we can vary the spices with each batch.

We were served this chutney at an Indian restaurant in Trinidad with dining rooms scattered over the ground floor of an imposing old house. By careful tasting and experiments we worked out the balance of spices—though we will admit that the Trinidadian chutney was a lot hotter than this one!

1 Peel and cut the mangoes into ⅜-inch-thick slices, then into 1- to 1¼-inch squares. Cut and scrape the flesh from the pits. Set the fruit aside in a bowl.

2 Into a stainless steel pot, measure the vinegar and brown sugar. Add the garlic and the *jalapeño* pepper. Add the raisins and the ginger. Next add the allspice, mustard seed, cumin, ginger, and salt. Place the pot over high heat and bring to a boil, stirring to mix all the ingredients. Add the mango chunks to the pot and bring to a boil.

3 Lower the heat so the chutney is just under the boiling point. Stir often with a wooden spoon so that the fruit will not stick to the bottom of the pot. Cook until thick, approximately 1 hour. If, toward the end of that time, the chutney seems too thick, add the hot water, stirring it into the mixture.

4 Remove the pot from the heat, and ladle the chutney into 3 8-ounce sterilized glass jars. While the chutney is hot, screw on the lids and set the jars aside to cool. When the chutney is cool, label the jars, and place them in the fridge—though anything this good will not stay in the fridge for long.

Note

If fresh mangoes are unavailable, use an equal quantity of canned mangoes, partially drained of the juice, or substitute fresh peaches or nectarines.

A few years ago, in the northern part of Tobago beside spectacular Man-O-War Bay, we settled for two months into a local way of life—the Caribbean of many years ago, with overlays of the late twentieth century.

Vegetables were bought from local ladies who set up a small stand for the overflow from their backyard gardens; fish was bought at the local fishermen's cooperative where the day's catch (mostly kingfish) was brought in; and avocados dropped from the large tree beside our cottage and breadfruit, limes, and lemons from a neighboring one.

A neighbor from the cluster of houses nearby brought over a monster papaya which we promptly bought. It was over a foot long and eight to nine inches in diameter, red fleshed and sweet. We put it in the refrigerator and feasted on slices as the papaya slowly ripened. We made generous cuts at each end, and turned the fruit into a golden jam, accented with its own black, spicy seeds.

1   Cut the papayas in half. Scoop out the seeds into a small bowl and reserve. Remove the bits of stringy flesh from the seed cavity and cut away the thin outside peel. Cut the halves lengthwise into ½-inch-thick slices, then crosswise into ½-inch dice to equal 8 cups.

2   Put the papaya into a large, stainless steel pot with the water, lime juice, and vanilla bean. Bring to a boil, lower the heat, and lightly boil for 10 minutes. Add the sugar and bring to a boil again. Lower the heat to a light boil, cover the pot, and cook for 15 minutes longer. Remove the vanilla bean. (Wash the vanilla bean in cold water and dry it on a paper towel. When dry, it can be put into a metal shaker with confectioners' sugar for vanilla sugar.)

3   Mash the fruit coarsely with a potato masher, add the reserved seeds, and continue to cook until the jelly stage is reached, which should be approximately 20 to 25 minutes. Check for the jellying stage by dropping ½ teaspoon of the juice into a saucer and putting it in the fridge for 1 minute. If the juice thickens to jelly, remove the pot from the stove. If not, continue to cook, checking again at 10-minute intervals for jellying.

4   When the jellying stage has been reached, ladle the hot jam into hot sterilized jars. Fill the jars to within ¼ inch of the top. Let the jam cool, then cover the tops with paraffin wax (see page 275). When the wax has hardened, put on the jar tops and store the jam on a cool dark shelf.

Tobago

PAPAYA JAM

◆

4 1¼-pound papayas
6 cups water
Juice of 6 limes
1 vanilla bean
6½ cups sugar
8 tablespoons papaya
  seeds

**MAKES 5 10-OUNCE
JARS**

• Twelve •

DESSERTS

Many of the island desserts are simply fresh or cooked fruits in season and puddings, with the more elaborate cakes and tarts made for a joyous spread at special celebrations and holidays—weddings, church, village, and family get-togethers. Some desserts are found only on one island, and others turn up on several islands, as various cultures island hopped and recipes were adapted to their products. The Spanish flan assumes as many guises as there are islands!

It was surprising one year, in the first week in January, to pass a bakery shop in Fort-de-France, Martinique, and to see the French Three Kings' Cakes filling the window, interspersed with the classic accompaniment of gold paper crowns. And in November in Gosier, on Guadeloupe, the local baker was suggesting, via a large sign, that his customers order their Three Kings' Cakes *now*.

Even on those islands which grow cacao beans as a crop, either as formal plantations or gathered haphazardly from scattered trees, we have yet to find chocolate used in desserts. According to local superstition the eating of chocolate was taboo. Or perhaps it was that through the years cacao beans were so much a needed money crop, that none of the small supply was kept for island use. We did find a bitter, grainy bar of chocolate in St. Lucia's market, but it was just for making a hot breakfast beverage.

We acquired some recipes from local cooks, or made careful notes of desserts we were eating, then tested them to match our recollections of the unforgettable tastes and textures. The recipes we have included were carefully chosen to feature ingredients easily obtainable in the States.

Tobago

BLACK CAKE

◆

1 stick unsalted butter

6 ounces dried mango, papaya, pineapple, raisins, and crystallized ginger

1½ cups plus 1 tablespoon all-purpose flour

1 teaspoon baking powder

¼ teaspoon ground cinnamon

Pinch of salt

3 eggs, at room temperature

¼ teaspoon lemon juice

1 tablespoon sugar

¾ cup light-brown *granulated* sugar

2 teaspoons vanilla or essence (see Note)

2 tablespoons Burnt Sugar Syrup (page 117)

5 tablespoons dark rum

MAKES 15 PORTIONS

Black Cake is an exotic island version of English fruit cake, with clever adaptations to the climate and supplies. There is no cool pantry in which to store a cake for two or three months as it mellows and receives that dollop of rum each week; in the tropics one cooks and eats. Dark rum is added while mixing the cake batter, which itself is darkened with burnt sugar syrup; while candied fruits are tropical—papaya, mango, pineapple, and ginger.

Our recipe comes from Sharon Eastman who lived near our beach cottage at the edge of Tahiti-like Man-O-War Bay at the east end of Tobago, where we spent two winter months. Her recipe was enough for a number of cakes, so that back in the States we had to adjust the quantities as well as her proportion of baking powder (which quickly deteriorates in the moist tropical climate.) Her flavorant was "Essence," the name on the label of the bottles at the grocery store. We finally tracked it down as a mixture of vanilla, almond, and anise extracts.

Burnt sugar syrup is sold in bottles and is a thin, black, bitter liquid which is used both for cake coloring and in meat dishes for a dark brown gravy. One can find it in Caribbean grocery stores or make one's own from the recipe on page 117. The rum is always dark and is the liquid of the cake batter. A Trinidadian friend laughingly describes her experience, when growing up, of beating black cake as her mother added more and more rum for moisture, "I got dizzy just smelling all that rum!"

1 Preheat the oven to 350 degrees.

2 Butter a 9-x-3¾-x-2¾-inch loaf pan and cover the bottom with wax paper. Butter the wax paper and dust the bottom and sides with flour.

3 Cut the butter into slices, place in a large mixing bowl, and let come to room temperature.

4 Cut the dried fruit into ¼- to ⅜-inch pieces. Place the fruit in a small bowl and stir in the 1 tablespoon of flour with a fork to separate the pieces.

5 Sift the 1½ cups flour, the baking powder, cinnamon, and salt into a small bowl and set aside.

6 Separate the egg yolks and whites into 2 bowls. Beat together the whites and lemon juice, then add the tablespoon of sugar and beat in until the whites hold peaks. Set aside.

7 Cream the softened butter and gradually add the light-brown sugar, beating all the while with a wooden spoon. Beat in the egg yolks and, when well mixed in, add the vanilla or essence and burnt sugar syrup. Mix until the batter, which will be very dark, is evenly colored.

8 Gradually beat in the flour mixture, alternating with the rum. When all the flour and rum have been blended into the batter add the egg whites.

Spoon a third of the batter into the prepared loaf pan. Mix the chopped fruit with the remaining batter, then fill the pan, smoothing the top. This will keep the fruit from sinking to the bottom.

9 Bake the cake for 50 to 55 minutes or until a thin skewer inserted into the center of the cake comes out clean. Remove the pan to a cake rack. Let the cake cool for 5 minutes, then turn out of the pan. Peel off the wax paper, turn the cake upright, and let cool on the rack.

Note

Two teaspoons of essence is made up of 1 teaspoon vanilla extract, ½ teaspoon almond extract, and ½ teaspoon anise extract.

WHIPPED EVAPORATED MILK AND CAKE ICING

◆

1 5-ounce *or* 12-ounce can evaporated milk,

Before widespread refrigeration and the availability of fresh, heavy cream, island cooks ingeniously worked out a method of whipping evaporated milk. A can of evaporated milk triples in quantity when whipped, whereas regular heavy cream only doubles in bulk.

1 Bring a pan of water to a boil. The water should be deep enough to cover the can. Place the entire can in the water, boil for 15 minutes, and remove the can from the water. Let it cool to room temperature, then place in the fridge to chill the evaporated milk inside. The can may be chilled overnight or for 24 hours.

2 To whip, pour the contents of the can into a chilled bowl and whip as you would any heavy cream. It will be a little "softer" than whipped heavy cream.

3 For a soft icing to be applied just before serving a cake, sweeten the whipped milk with confectioners' sugar, in the approximate proportion of 4 tablespoons to 1 cup of whipped milk, or to taste. Add the flavoring extract of your choice—coconut, vanilla, almond, lemon, or other. Spoon over cake or other desserts just before serving. The top of the whipped milk can be sprinkled with sweetened, flaked or grated coconut—a *mont blanc*, in island parlance.

Note

When using whipped evaporated milk in place of heavy whipping cream (rather than as an icing), add 1 to 2 teaspoons of granulated sugar to a cup of whipped evaporated milk, plus flavoring extracts of your choice.

PAPAYA UPSIDE-DOWN CAKE

St. Lucia

1 very ripe, 6-inch pa-
paya, about 9 ounces
1 tablespoon lime juice
3 teaspoons dark rum
2 tablespoons butter
1¼ cups light-brown *granulated* sugar
½ cup all-purpose flour
¼ teaspoon baking powder
1⁄16 teaspoon salt
¼ teaspoon ground clove
1 egg
1 teaspoon vanilla extract
2 tablespoons boiling wa-
ter

SERVES 4

During an afternoon visit with one of the local families on St. Lucia, we were served a delicious tropical version of a more northern dessert—a papaya upside-down cake. Our hostess told us that it was a family recipe passed down through generations, and we could only imagine a homesick planter's wife adapting one of her favorite home recipes to the available island fruits and spices.

Papaya plants, with tall, straggly stems and large sheltering leaves, bear hanging green to yellow fruit at all times of the year, with new plants constantly appearing in gardens and along the roadsides. Cloves (flower buds) are gathered from low trees or shrubs growing wild in the hilly country, then dried on a sunny windowsill. Sugar is nearly always light-brown granulated rather than white, and is sold in brown paper bags in one- or two-pound quantities. (Everyone peers into the bags to find the lightest color.) At one time sugar was a major crop on St. Lucia. Driving along the dirt sideroads one comes upon the remains of stone sugar mills, deserted now, with gaping holes in their walls and overgrown with vines and small trees—a Piranesi scene.

1 Preheat the oven to 350 degrees.

2 Cut the papaya in half lengthwise and scoop out the seeds and "stringy" area around the seed cavity from half of the fruit. Reserve the other half for another use. Remove the skin, wasting as little fruit as possible. Cut the fruit in half lengthwise, then slice each piece crosswise into ¼-inch-thick slices. Place the slices in a small bowl and sprinkle with the lime juice and 1 teaspoon of the rum. Set aside.

3 Melt the butter and set aside to cool slightly.

4 Pour ¾ cup of the sugar into an *unbuttered* 3⅝-x-7⅜- or 4-x-8-inch loaf pan. With a fork, mix in the melted butter. Set aside.

5 Measure the flour, baking powder, salt, and ground clove into a sifter. Mix and set aside.

6 In a mixing bowl, beat the egg, then gradually add the remaining sugar, beating all the while with a wire whisk. Add the vanilla, the remaining rum, and the boiling water.

7 Sift the flour mixture over the egg and sugar mixture, beating with a wire whisk. This is a thin batter.

8 Scatter the fruit over the sugar in the pan and lightly stir with a fork to mix together. Pour the batter over the fruit and sugar and place the pan in the preheated oven. Bake for 55 to 60 minutes or until a thin skewer stuck into the center of the cake comes out clean.

9 Transfer the loaf pan to a cake rack and let cool in the pan until just warm. Turn it out onto an oval platter and serve. If making the cake well in advance of serving, do not remove the cake from the loaf pan. Fifteen minutes before serving, warm in a 300-degree oven, then turn out onto an oval serving dish.

Note

This cake can be served with sweetened whipped cream or whipped evaporated milk (page 285) flavored with vanilla extract.

One evening, after a long day at the beach, we picked up a drink at Sebastian's bar and settled at a table to watch the scene. Here, we knew we would have island food, cooked by the island staff, or Viennese food, the recipes supplied by the owners. The chef came over to talk and make suggestions, and just then the lady who made all the desserts came by with a large, dark cake on a footed cake stand. She set it down on the serving stand, and began to ice it from the contents of the bowl in her hand. The thick white icing, which slowly cascaded over the sides of the robust Spice Cake made from her local recipe, was island-style whipped evaporated milk (page 285). We've cut the recipe down here from her restaurant-size cake.

Tortola

SPICE CAKE

◆

1 cup all-purpose flour
1½ teaspoons ground ginger
½ teaspoon each ground allspice, clove, and cinnamon
1 tablespoon butter
½ cup white or light-brown *granulated* sugar
1 teaspoon baking soda
½ cup Barbados molasses
½ cup half-and-half
1 egg, beaten

SERVES 6

1 Preheat the oven to 375 degrees. Butter either a 6-inch springform pan or 2 6-inch cake pans. Line the bottom of the pan or pans with wax paper, and butter it as well.
2 Mix together the flour, ginger, and spices into a sifter, slightly mixing them together and set aside on a small plate.
3 Cream the butter and sugar in a mixing bowl and add the baking soda.
4 Measure the molasses into a measuring cup wiped with vegetable oil to prevent the molasses from sticking. Pour it into the creamed mixture, beating with a wire whisk, then slowly add the half-and-half, and then the beaten egg, beating all the time.
5 Sift the flour mixture into the batter, lightly beating it in with the wire whisk. This will be a thinnish batter.
6 Pour the batter into the pan or pans. Bake for 50 minutes for the springform pan and 30 minutes for the cake pans or until a thin metal skewer stuck into the center of the cake comes out clean.
7 When the cake is done, remove from the oven to a cake rack. Loosen the top edge with a knife, let the cake cool for 10 minutes, and then turn out, removing the wax paper. If the bottom seems moist, put the cake under the broiler to dry out the surface. Turn the cake right side up to cool completely.
8 Ice the cake with sweetened and flavored Whipped Evaporated Milk

Icing (page 285) Sprinkle the surface of the icing with sweetened, flaked or grated coconut.

O n Guadeloupe, *Pain Doux* is the local "plain" cake, whose seductive sweetness permeates the whole house while it is baking. We knew of it before we went to the island and searched out a local bakery in Gosier. Theirs was a delicious plain cake, moist and light; ideal, too, as the basis for many types of decorated cakes. It is also one of the components of a variation of *tourment d'amour*, the island's special sweet with its subtle blend of flavors and textures. We had several versions of *tourment d'amour* while we were on Guadeloupe and the recipes follow.

When we returned to the States, the proprietor of our local Trinidadian grocery shop asked us if we had had *pain doux*, and did it have coconut in it as it does in Trinidad? So we now make it both ways, and both are matchless.

Following is an old recipe in which the flour and sugar were measured by weight, the quantities based on the weight of the eggs. This sensibly took care of the differences between small and large eggs, and their liquid effect on flour and sugar. The formula was for equal weight of brown sugar and half their weight of flour. We've worked it out on the basis of 3 eggs equaling 6 ounces.

Guadeloupe and Trinidad

PAIN DOUX (SWEET BREAD)

◆

¾ cup all-purpose flour
¼ teaspoon baking powder
¼ teaspoon freshly grated nutmeg
½ teaspoon ground cinnamon
Pinch of salt
1 tablespoon grated lemon zest (½ to 1 lemon)
3 eggs (2¼ x 1¾ inches)
1 cup dark-brown sugar
1 teaspoon vanilla extract
¼ teaspoon lemon extract
¾ teaspoon orange-flower water (optional)
1 tablespoon dark rum
¼ teaspoon cream of tartar

SERVES 5 TO 10, DEPENDING ON SIZE OF PAN

1 Butter either a 6-x-3- or 10-x-1½-inch springform pan. Fit a circle of wax paper to the bottom, butter it as well, then flour the bottom and sides of the pan.

2 Preheat the oven to 350 degrees.

3 Measure and mix the flour, baking powder, nutmeg, cinnamon, and salt and pour into a flour sifter. Set aside.

4 Grate the lemon zest and set aside.

5 Separate the eggs, putting the yolks into a mixing bowl and the whites into another bowl.

6 Beat the egg yolks with a wire whisk, gradually beating in the sugar. Smooth out any lumps with the back of a metal spoon. Add the vanilla, lemon zest, lemon extract, orange-flower water, and rum. Mix well.

7 Beat the whites with the cream of tartar. When stiff, lightly fold a quarter of the whites into the egg yolk batter, then fold in the remaining egg whites. Sift the flour mixture over the top of the batter and lightly fold in.

8 Spoon the batter into the prepared springform pan. The 6-inch pan will be half-filled, but in baking, the cake will rise to the top of the pan. The

10-inch pan forms a wide shallow cake. Bake for 35 to 40 minutes for the 6-inch pan, testing the cake with a thin metal skewer inserted into the center after 35 minutes. Test the 10-inch cake after 25 minutes. In both cases, when the skewer comes out clean, remove the cake from the oven.

9 Place the springform pan on a baking rack and run a thin knife blade around the top edge to release any cake attached to the pan. Allow the cake to cool for 5 minutes before removing the side of the springform, the bottom metal disk, and the wax paper. Cool the cake, top side up. The cake will shrink a little but will not sink in the middle. The top surface will pull together into an "alligator skin" pattern, brown and appetizing in appearance.

10 Serve the cake plain or dusted with vanilla confectioners' sugar (see Step 2 on page 281). The 6-inch cake can also be iced with a lemon juice and confectioners' sugar icing and heavily covered with sweetened coconut flakes. This combination too is often called *mont blanc* in the French islands. Or ice with Whipped Evaporated Milk Icing (page 285).

Variation

For the Trinidadian version, fold ½ cup sweetened, flaked coconut into the batter after the flour mixture has been blended in at step 7.

Guadeloupe

BREADFRUIT NUT COOKIES (PETIT PAINS DE CHÂTAIGNES)

◆

1 10-ounce can breadfruit nuts (pana de pepita)
1 stick butter
1 to 1 ¼ cups all-purpose flour
1 cup confectioners' sugar
1 egg, beaten
Pinch of salt
1 teaspoon vanilla extract
2 teaspoons rum
Demerara cane sugar crystals (coarse crystals)

MAKES 30 TO 35 COOKIES

Walking down the one-way main street of Gosier, on Guadeloupe, with its small stores crowded together in a helter-skelter pattern of food and houseware stores, clothing shops, tiny restaurants, gift and tourist stores, we were surprised to see a tiny open-sided, covered farmers' market. Several ladies were behind tables of vegetables and fruits, and the nearest table to the sidewalk contained a pyramid of shelled nuts, which we did not recognize. Asking questions, we were told they were breadfruit nuts—*chataigne*—local "chestnuts." The islanders boil and puree them as a starch and use them in pastries, in the same way as the French use chestnuts. The local baker confirmed that these nuts were used in cookies, similar to the chestnut cookies of France. And, when we returned home, we found that our local island store had canned breadfruit nuts (see page 45)—so we proceeded to make the same goodies we had eaten on Guadeloupe.

1 Drain the breadfruit nuts. Remove the thin shells and brown skin from the nuts with a paring knife. (Since the nuts are cooked, this is a little easier than removing the shells and skins from chestnuts.) For the cookies you will need 6 ounces of the shelled and skinned nuts.

2 Put the nuts into a food processor and puree them with half of the butter, using the metal blade.

3 Sift together 1 cup of the flour and the confectioners' sugar into a mixing bowl, and form into a "well." In the middle of the fountain, put the remaining butter, cut into ½-inch dice, the nut puree, half of the beaten egg, the salt, vanilla, and rum. With a wooden spoon, blend and smooth everything until the butter and nut puree are completely incorporated into the other ingredients. If the dough seems too soft, sift in up to ¼ cup more of the flour. The dough should not be dry and stiff.

4 Form the dough into a 1-inch-thick disk, wrap in clear plastic, and place on a small plate. Refrigerate for 3 hours to stiffen.

5 At the end of the 3 hours, preheat the oven to 375 degrees. Lightly butter 2 11-x-17-inch cookie sheets.

6 Remove the dough from the refrigerator and place it on a pastry board between two sheets of floured wax paper. Roll the dough to a little over ⅛ inch thick, dusting with more flour if needed to keep it from sticking to the wax paper. Dip a fluted or plain oval 3⅛-x-1¾-inch cookie cutter into flour and cut out the cookies, transferring them to the cookie sheets. Leave ½ inch between each cookie. Gather the dough scraps and repeat the process until all the dough has been used.

7   Add 1 teaspoon of cold water to the remaining beaten egg. Brush the cookie tops with the beaten egg and sprinkle the tops with the cane sugar crystals, slightly pressing the crystals into the dough.

8   Place the pans in the preheated oven and bake the cookies for 15 to 20 minutes or until crisp and the tops slightly golden. Remove the cookies from the oven and transfer to cake racks to cool. When cool, store in an airtight metal box.

Driving through the interior of St. Martin, this French side of the Caribbean island has acquired an unexpected resemblance to a French countryside, with its neatly stone-fenced fields and hilly forests along the inland road, totally transforming a Caribbean island tropical ambience. Stopping at a small grocery store for bottled water, we saw a box of homemade coconut cookies on the counter, their tops shiny with golden egg yolk. We immediately bought half a dozen to take along to the beach for an afternoon snack. They were classic drop cookies with a crisp surface, and were redolent of coconut flavor with the added crunch of coconut flakes.

   When we returned to the States, we worked out the recipe, and in making a large batch, found that they froze beautifully. They only needed a quick warming through in a 350-degree oven to come right back to their original crispness. We also like to measure all the ingredients first, then smoothly mix the batter so it stays light and fluffy.

1   Butter an 11-x-17-inch cookie sheet and preheat the oven to 350 degrees.

2   Cut the butter into slices and soften to room temperature in a mixing bowl.

3   Place a fine sifter on a plate, and measure the confectioners' sugar into it and set aside.

4   Beat the egg in a small bowl and set aside.

5   Measure the flour, baking powder, and salt into a second sifter and set aside.

6   Measure the coconut flakes into a small bowl and set aside.

7   Cream the butter with a wooden spoon. Sift the confectioners' sugar over the butter and cream until smooth.

8   To the butter mixture add 3 tablespoons of the beaten egg (reserve the

St. Martin

COCONUT DROP COOKIES

◆

½ stick butter
½ cup confectioners' sugar
1 egg
½ cup all-purpose flour
½ teaspoon baking powder
⅛ teaspoon salt
½ cup sweetened coconut flakes, lightly packed
1½ teaspoons dark rum
½ teaspoon coconut extract

MAKES 15 COOKIES

rest to brush the tops of the cookies), the rum, and coconut extract. Beat with a wire whisk until light and fluffy.

9 Sift a third of the flour mixture over the batter and mix well with a wooden spoon. Add another third and mix, then add the rest of the flour. Beat with the wooden spoon until all the flour is well incorporated. Fold in the coconut flakes. Add up to 1 teaspoon of the reserved beaten egg if needed.

10 Drop the batter by heaping teaspoons onto the prepared cookie sheet, approximately 2 inches apart, as the cookies will flatten during baking.

11 Bake for 15 to 20 minutes or until the edges and bottoms are dark brown. Brush the tops of the cookies with the reserved beaten egg and put them under the broiler for 3 to 5 minutes or until the tops are golden. Remove the pan from the broiler and transfer the cookies to a cake rack to cool. When cool, store in a covered metal box. If you can wait that long, the cookies are better the next day as the flavors have blended. They will stay fresh for several days in the metal box, or can be frozen for up to several weeks.

Th   crisp, brown cookie, redolent of island spices, was
brou   land by early Dutch settlers. It is doubly appreciated,
becat   ay crisp even in the warm, often humid air of the
island.   ho served them to us said she decorates them in two
ways. On some she sprinkles raw cane sugar crystals—Demerara—and on
others she presses in a pattern from a cut glass pitcher. "In the old country
they say they use special molds, but cut glass works fine for me," she said.
And so we make them both ways, using Grandma's cut glass sugar bowl as
a pattern. But, somehow, we prefer the crunch and sweetness of the sugar
crystals on top.

Sint Maarten

SPICE COOKIES (SPECKULAAS)

◆

6 tablespoons unsalted
  butter
1½ cups all-purpose flour
¼ rounded teaspoon bak-
  ing powder
¼ teaspoon freshly grated
  nutmeg
¼ teaspoon ground clove
1 teaspoon ground cinna-
  mon
⅔ cup light-brown *granu-
  lated* sugar
¾ teaspoon lemon extract
1 egg
3 tablespoons coarsely
  chopped cashew nuts
Demerara cane sugar crys-
  tals

**MAKES 19 TO 20
COOKIES**

1 Slice the butter into a mixing bowl and let soften to room temperature.
2 Place a sifter on a small plate and add the flour, baking powder, nutmeg,
clove, and cinnamon, stirring lightly together with a fork, and set aside.
3 Add the sugar to the butter and cream with a wooden spoon. Add the
lemon extract and egg and beat with a wire whisk until well blended and
light.
4 Sift a quarter of the flour mixture into the creamed butter mixture and stir
with a wooden spoon. Add the rest of the flour mixture, a quarter at a time,
beating after each addition. When well incorporated, add the cashew nut
pieces and mix well. This will be a soft dough.
5 Pat the dough into a 5-inch circle, then wrap in clear plastic. Place the
dough on a small plate and refrigerate for 4 hours.
6 At the end of 4 hours, preheat the oven to 400 degrees and butter 2
11-x-17-inch baking pans.
7 Roll out the chilled dough between 2 sheets of floured wax paper, adding
extra flour during the rolling. The final thickness of the dough should be a
little more than ⅛ inch but not as much as ¼ inch. Cut out the cookies with
a 3-inch scalloped, round cookie cutter and transfer them to the baking
sheets, leaving ½ to ¾ inch between each cookie. Gather the dough scraps
into a ball and repeat the process until the dough is used up. Generously
sprinkle the cookies with the sugar crystals, slightly pressing them into the
dough, or decorate them with a pattern.
8 Bake the cookies for 7 minutes at 400 degrees, then turn the oven
temperature down to 350 degrees, and continue to bake for 25 to 30 minutes
more; the tops should be golden brown. Remove the pans from the oven and
transfer the cookies to a cake rack to cool. When cool, store in an airtight
metal box.

St. Lucia

COCONUT MACAROONS 1

◆

7 ounces sweetened,
   flaked coconut (see Note)
2 egg whites
½ cup superfine sugar
5 to 6 teaspoons canned
   guava paste

**MAKES 20 2-INCH
MACAROONS**

Coconuts are a basic staple throughout t̶ source of "milk" before the days of refrigeration (for cooking; and grated flakes for texture and flav Lucia, the first of many islands where we stayec many uses of this nut.

At a small luncheon, our hostess's cook had made macaroons to accompany her soursop sorbet. We were enchanted, and, having acquired the recipe, decided to try it out in our small kitchen. The next day at the large covered market at the edge of Castries, we bought a coconut. Knowing the limitations of our kitchen equipment, we looked for a grater and found the local variety. It was simply a large, metal juice can cut in half lengthwise (paper label removed), with nail holes punched through the metal from the inside, so sharp points stood up all over the curved outside surface.

We took both coconut and grater back to the cottage, and soon had enough flakes for the macaroons.

In the States we make these macaroons with packaged, sweetened flaked coconut.

1 Butter an 11-x-17-inch cookie sheet, cover with aluminum foil, and butter the foil as well. Preheat the oven to 350 degrees.

2 Place the coconut flakes and the egg whites in a saucepan and mix together with a fork. Stir in the sugar. Place the saucepan over low heat for 1½ to 2 minutes, stirring the mixture all the time to distribute the heat and to keep the coconut flakes from browning. Remove the saucepan from the heat.

3 Scoop up ½ tablespoon of the coconut mixture and place it on the buttered foil. Add ¼ teaspoon of the guava paste in the center and cover with another ½ tablespoon of the coconut mixture. Repeat until all the coconut mixture has been used, leaving space between each mound. Tuck in any stray strands of coconut as you even the edges with the flat side of a table knife. Smooth the mounds without pressing down on the mixture.

4 Bake on the middle rack of the oven for 25 minutes, then put the pan under the broiler for 1 or 2 minutes to brown the tops. Remove from the broiler and quickly transfer the macaroons to a cake rack, using a wide cake turner and wiggling it under each macaroon. If they start to stick, put the pan back into the oven to heat the bottom and the foil.

5 When the macaroons are cool, store in an airtight tin. They will keep for several days.

Variation

For plain coconut macaroons, omit the guava paste and use 1 heaping tablespoon of the mixture for each macaroon.

Note

Sweetened coconut flakes are sold in 7-ounce packages. If the coconut is unsweetened, then increase the superfine sugar to 1 cup, or to taste.

In spite of the daytime heat and the humid tropical air, these macaroons stayed crisp, the formula balanced just so to fit the climate of this coral island with its sugar fields and coconut palms. On this very British island, macaroons turn up at tea time—a very refreshing British habit and doubly welcome here—whether served in the shade of a cool porch, or under the trees in a garden.

1 Preheat the oven to 300 degrees. Butter 2 11-x-17-inch cookie sheets.
2 Put the coconut into a small bowl and sift in the flour, mixing thoroughly.
3 Beat the egg whites until they are stiff. Gradually sift in the confectioners' sugar, 2 tablespoons at a time, beating after each addition. Halfway through adding the sugar, beat in the vanilla and coconut extracts. Continue to add the remaining sugar, 2 tablespoons at a time, beating after each addition.
4 Fold the coconut mixture into the beaten egg whites, until well incorporated.
5 Drop by heaping teaspoonfuls onto the prepared baking sheets, placing spoons of the dough approximately ¾ inch apart. Bake for 30 to 40 minutes, depending on the thickness of the baking pan. When the macaroons are done, the bottoms should be light brown and the tops just beginning to color. Put the pans under the broiler until the tops are a golden brown.
6 With a wide, metal spatula, carefully remove the macaroons to cake racks to cool. Store in an airtight tin.

Note

The macaroons will be slightly chewy. If you like a crispier macaroon, bake them for an extra 10 minutes.

Barbados

COCONUT MACAROONS 2

◆

1½ cups sweetened, flaked or shredded coconut, lightly packed
6 tablespoons all-purpose flour
3 egg whites, at room temperature
½ cup confectioners' sugar
1 teaspoon vanilla extract
½ teaspoon coconut extract

MAKES 32 2-INCH MACAROONS

Puerto Rico

GUAVA PASTE TURNOVERS (*EMPANADAS*)

◆

1 cup all-purpose flour
2 teaspoons sugar
Pinch of salt
½ teaspoon baking powder
1/16 teaspoon freshly grated
  nutmeg
4 tablespoons butter
2 teaspoons water
1 egg yolk
¼ teaspoon vanilla extract
12 tablespoons canned
  guava paste
1 tablespoon butter, cut
  into 12 ¼-teaspoon
  pieces
Cinnamon

**MAKES 12 3-INCH
HALF-MOON
TURNOVERS**

Driving along the south coast of Puerto Rico to Parguera, on Phosphorescent Bay, is to see a landscape in sharp contrast to the northern coast. It is a dry area—the scarred stone and dirt cliffs covered with tall organ cacti, and century plants raising their once-in-a-lifetime flower stems that start out looking like ten-foot-high stalks of asparagus. The few beaches are covered with water-smoothed pebbles, but with enough interesting shapes and colors to lure a beachcomber the length of the water's edge.

Behind the cliffs is a flat plain of scrub grass, high hedges of *Euphorbia*, like great, green clusters of candelabras, and flat-topped trees of the pea family, for all the world like an African veld interspersed with sugar cane fields.

After a number of exploratory detours, we finally arrived at the old and rambling inn at the edge of Phosphorescent Bay. Here the setting was end-of-the-world tropics: cool and shaded rooms with shadowy corners and slow-turning ceiling fans, the tiled floors a hit-and-miss sampling of many designs and colors. After relaxing from the strangeness and hot sun of our drive with a long, cool sundowner drink, we went into dinner, which ended with crisp, warm *empanadas* filled with guava paste as accompaniments to orange sorbet.

1   Sift into a bowl or processor the flour, sugar, salt, baking powder, and nutmeg.
2   Cut the butter into the dry ingredients with two knives, or spin in the processor with the dry ingredients.
3   Mix the water with the egg yolk in a small bowl and add *half* of this liquid to the dry ingredients. Reserve the other half of the egg for brushing the turnovers. Add the vanilla. Stir the egg and vanilla thoroughly into the dry ingredients with a fork, then add enough cold water, up to 2 tablespoons, to make a dough that is just moist enough to hold together. Knead to form a ball.
4   Slightly flatten the ball of dough and place in a plastic bag. Let stand at room temperature for 30 minutes, then put in the fridge for 10 minutes.
5   Preheat the oven to 350 degrees and butter an 11-x-17-inch baking pan. Open the can of guava paste.
6   Pinch off pieces of dough the size of a walnut. Roll each piece into a 3-inch circle between floured sheets of wax paper.
7   Spread up to 1 level tablespoon of the guava paste on half of each circle, leaving a 3/8-inch border around the edge. Dot the paste with ¼ teaspoon of

the butter and a dash of cinnamon. Brush the edges with the egg wash and fold over the other half. Press the edges tightly to seal. Brush the sealed edges with the egg and fold the edge over onto itself, pressing tightly with the tines of a fork to seal. Brush the top surface with the egg. Prick the tops with the fork tines and place the turnovers on the buttered baking pan.

8 Bake for 15 minutes or until the tops are golden brown. Remove from the baking pan to a cake rack. Reheat the turnovers slightly just before serving.

Throughout the islands, fruit fritters are a quick and simple dessert: use whatever fruit is in season, cook on top of the stove, and serve piping hot. Wherever we went, we tried them and made notes for future duplication in our own kitchen.

1 Stir together the flour and baking powder in a large bowl. Beat the milk in to make a smooth mix.

2 Add the eggs and mix well for a smooth batter.

3 Add the sugar, lemon juice, vanilla extract, nutmeg, salt, and vegetable oil. Beat well.

4 Mash the mango thoroughly and add to the batter. Mix well.

5 Heat the oil in a heavy skillet until very hot. Drop heaping tablespoons of the batter into it and fry until crisp on both sides. Drain on paper towels in a hot oven. Continue making the fritters until all the batter has been used.

6 Serve promptly and hot, sprinkled with confectioners' sugar or with a sweet fruit sauce, such as Guava Sauce (page 329).

Variations

Excellent fritters can be made with any of the Caribbean fruits in season. We need only mention bananas, Barbados cherries (*Malpighia glabra*), black and white sapote, canistel, carambola, papaya, pineapple, and plantain, among others. Guava fritters also can be made with guava jam in place of the fresh fruit. The more unusual fruits are beginning to appear in our markets. The fritters are made in the same way as the previous recipe. The only important difference is in the amount of sugar to be added, and that can be adjusted to taste.

MANGO FRITTERS

◆

¾ cup all-purpose flour
2 teaspoons baking powder (optional)
½ cup milk
2 eggs
2 tablespoons granulated sugar
1 tablespoon lemon juice
1 teaspoon vanilla extract
½ teaspoon freshly grated nutmeg
Pinch of salt
1 tablespoon vegetable oil, plus additional oil for frying the fritters
1½ cups ripe mango (peeled and cut from the seed)

MAKES 12 FRITTERS

FLAKY PIE CRUST

◆

1 cup all-purpose flour
¼ teaspoon salt
½ teaspoon baking powder
2 teaspoons sugar
⅛ teaspoon freshly grated
   nutmeg
4 tablespoons butter
1 tablespoon solid shortening
½ teaspoon vanilla extract
1½ tablespoons cold wa-
   ter, plus 1 or 2 teaspoons
   additional cold water

**MAKES 1 9-INCH
PIE CRUST OR,
RECIPE
DOUBLED, 2 9-INCH
PIE CRUSTS**

1 Sift the dry ingredients into a large bowl, or mix in a processor with the steel blade.

2 Cut in the butter and shortening with two knives (see Note).

3 Mix the vanilla extract with the water and slowly add to the flour mixture, stirring with a fork. Add the additional water, if needed, to hold the dough together.

4 Roll out the dough between sheets of floured wax paper. Line a 9-inch pie pan with the dough. Flute the edge of the shell with your fingers to form an upstanding ridge.

5 Bake in a preheated oven following the instructions of the particular pie or tart recipe. The length of baking time depends on whether the crust is to be partially baked before adding an unbaked filling, or fully baked, to which is added an already cooked filling.

Variation

Other extract flavors can be added to the dough in place of the vanilla extract.

Notes

For dough mixed in the processor, add the butter and shortening cut into ½-inch dice to the dry ingredients in the processor. Add a third of the water and vanilla mixture (step 3) to the processor. Spin for a count of 6 and turn the ingredients over with a plastic spatula. Add another third of the water and vanilla mixture and spin for a count of 6. Add the remaining liquid and spin for a count of 8. If more water is needed, add no more than 2 teaspoons. The dough will be crumbly but will hold together when pressed into a ball.

As an alternative crust for baked *empanadas*, *pastechis*, and patties, (pages 190–197), use this recipe, eliminating the sugar and nutmeg, and adding ½ to 1 teaspoon of achiote oil (page 110) to the water. In place of the achiote oil, you can add ½ to 1 teaspoon turmeric powder to the flour. Use your own judgment as to the intensity of color for the dough.

At the very end of Philipsburg's traffic-jammed Front Street, overflowing with tourists and shops, is an unexpected quiet haven. Across a brick-paved courtyard, climb the steps and cross a porch to enter the old Dutch government's Guest House, Pasanggrahan, now an inn and restaurant. Quiet and softly lighted, the entrance room is dominated by a portrait of Queen Wilhelmina. Just beyond is the very wide, brilliantly white-painted porch-dining room, which overlooks a lush garden and the bay—a view seen through the tall trees that line the edge of the beach. This was a haven indeed, where we enjoyed wonderful, leisurely meals, one of which ended with this pie. Based on island brown sugar, this rich tart was served in small wedges. Its crisp, flaky crust and soft sweet filling form a satisfying contrast in textures and flavors.

Sint Maarten

BROWN SUGAR PIE

◆

1 recipe Flaky Pie Crust (page 298)
1 egg, beaten
⅔ cup light-brown *granulated* sugar
½ cup dark-brown sugar
1½ teaspoons all-purpose flour
Pinch of salt
1 tablespoon butter, softened to room temperature
1 teaspoon vanilla extract
¾ cup heavy cream

SERVES 6 TO 8

1 Preheat the oven to 350 degrees and butter a 7-inch metal pie pan.
2 Roll out the dough and line the pie pan, fluting the edge into an upstanding ridge. Brush the dough with half of the beaten egg; reserve the other half for the filling. Prick the bottom and sides of the dough with a fork. Place the pan in the preheated oven for 10 to 12 minutes to partially bake the crust, checking it after 5 minutes and pricking any bubbles that may have formed. Remove the pan from the oven to cool while making the filling.
3 Raise the oven temperature to 400 degrees.
4 Mix the sugars in a bowl, adding the flour and salt to blend. Add the butter and cream the mixture until it is smooth.
5 Stir in the reserved beaten egg and the vanilla, beating vigorously. Stir in the heavy cream with a large metal spoon, lifting up the sugar so it blends in with the cream.
6 Ladle the mixture into the pie crust, evenly distributing the sugar that sinks to the bottom of the bowl.
7 Place the pie on the center shelf of the oven and bake for 55 to 60 minutes or until the center is just cooked. Test with the blade of a table knife.
8 Remove the pie from the oven and cool on a cake rack. The pie can be reheated slightly just before serving, as it is best warm. The pie can also be made the day before, cooled, covered with aluminum foil, and stored in the fridge. Warm before serving.

Guadeloupe

COCONUT CUSTARD PASTRY STRIP

◆

1 9-x-9-inch sheet frozen commercial puff pastry
2⅔ tablespoons vanilla pudding mix, firmly packed
¾ cup half-and-half
½ cup sweetened, flaked or shredded coconut, lightly packed
1 teaspoon coconut extract
1 egg yolk
1½ teaspoons plus 4 tablespoons water
3 tablespoons sugar

SERVES 4 TO 6

There is a magical touch to the pastry confections on Guadeloupe, a mixture of down-island flavors and ingredients controlled by the know-how of French pastry traditions. We splurged every time we stopped at A. Kancel's Pastry Shop in Gosier on our way to the beach at Ste. Anne. A local cake called *tourmant d'amour* takes many forms, and the combinations played on the theme of vanilla custard, coconut, pastry, and plain cake are infinite.

This is a puff pastry strip with a custard and flaked coconut filling, covered with broad, crisscrossed, strips of pastry. After baking, the top strips are brushed with thick caramel syrup. Use either a narrow, shallow pan with fluted sides and removable bottom or a baking sheet, forming the free-standing strip in the center of the sheet.

1   Thaw the puff pastry, following the manufacturer's instructions, while you are making the custard.

2   Measure the pudding mix into a small saucepan and add the half-and-half, stirring until the mixture is smooth. Place over medium heat and stir with a wooden spoon until the custard comes to a boil. Take off the heat and add the coconut and coconut extract. Pour the custard into a small bowl, cover the top with a circle of clear plastic wrap so a skin will not form, and place the bowl in the fridge to cool.

3   Preheat the oven to 400 degrees.

4   Beat the egg yolk in a small bowl with 1 teaspoon of the water and set aside.

5   Spread the puff pastry on a lightly floured pastry board. Cut the sheet into 3 3-inch-wide strips. Roll out the first strip into a 4-x-13¾-inch strip. (It will shrink a bit during baking.) Place on the bottom of an ungreased 14-x-13¾-1-inch pan or in the center of an ungreased 10-x-15-x-¾-inch baking pan. Roll the second strip into a 3¾-x-13¾-inch strip and cut lengthwise into 5 ¾-inch-wide pieces, using either a sharp, pointed knife or a notched wheel cutter.

6   Brush a ¾-inch-width of the beaten egg around the outer margin of the bottom sheet of pastry. Place 1 13¾-inch strip on one long side margin of the bottom sheet of pastry, pressing it lightly into the egg. Then put a second strip on the opposite long side. From the third strip cut 4 2½-inch pieces, placing 2 of the pieces at each end of the strip. Brush all the tops of the strips with the beaten egg and cover them with the remaining 4 strips, pressing them down lightly. Be careful that the egg does not run down the sides of the strips, as this will prevent the pastry from rising.

7   Roll out the remainder of the third strip of pastry to 5½ x 16 inches and cut crosswise into 8 2-inch-wide strips.

8   Spoon the cooled custard over the bottom sheet of pastry up to the inside edges of the narrow sides, rounding it up in the center.

9   Brush the tops of the side strips with the beaten egg. Cover the custard with 4 of the 2-inch-wide strips, placed on an angle so the custard is showing in between the strips. Trim off any extra pieces of pastry on each side, pressing the 2-inch-wide strips lightly into the side strips. Brush the tops of the 2-inch strips with the beaten egg, then crisscross the first set of strips with the remaining 4 strips, placing them on a crossing angle so the covering is a set of X's with a little custard showing in between. Brush all the tops of pastry with the remaining beaten egg.

10   Put the pan in the oven on the lowest shelf. Bake for 30 to 35 minutes until the top is *very* brown.

11   While the pastry is baking, mix the sugar and ½ teaspoon of the water in a small pan. Place over medium heat until the sugar has melted and is a medium brown in color.

12   In a separate pot, boil the remaining 4 tablespoons of water. Add the water to the sugar in the pan and stir with a fork until blended. This should make a thick caramel syrup. (You may have to add another teaspoon of boiling water so the syrup will stay glossy and not turn to sugar when brushed on the hot pastry.)

13   When cooked, remove the pastry from the oven and brush the top strips with the caramel syrup while they are still hot. Let the strip cool in the pan.

Jamaica

GREEN MANGO TART

◆

Flaky Pie Crust (page 298)
2 tablespoons butter
2 tablespoons cornstarch
3 tablespoons dark rum
2 5½-x-3-inch green mangoes
1½ cups light-brown *granulated* sugar
2 ¾-inch-square chunks candied ginger
1 teaspoon lime or lemon zest
2 tablespoons lime or lemon juice
½ teaspoon freshly grated nutmeg
¼ teaspoon lemon extract

SERVES 6

As we discussed in the introduction, the Africans coming to the islands brought their foods and ways of cooking them, as did the natives of other countries. The northern European wives coming from a colder climate adapted their recipes to the tropical ingredients. This recipe may have begun when a sugar planter's wife substituted green mangoes for tart green apples in a tart. Her early recipe would have had unrefined sugar and the local allspice for flavoring. Gradually local cooks gave the recipe a life of its own, as it became a mango tart, not an imitation apple tart.

Here, green mangoes do not have an "unripe" flavor or texture, because they belong either to a variety that is ripe when green or yellow-and-red skinned just before the change from green. In both cases, the fruit is well flavored and sweet. The flesh is firm and not stringy, as is often the case when the fruit is soft and ripe.

We had settled into an apartment high over Ocho Ríos beach on the north shore of Jamaica. One evening we joined a group for an island buffet dinner at a local home. It was a magnificent spread, and we succumbed to trying everything—a bit of this and a bit of that. Among the desserts was an exotic-looking Green Mango Tart, and, as luck would have it, our hostess described in detail how to make it.

1 Bake the pie crust in an 8-inch buttered quiche pan with a removable bottom. Follow the recipe directions for a precooked filling approximately 30 to 35 minutes. When the crust is baked, cool the shell in its pan on a cake rack.

2 While the crust is baking, melt the butter in a small pan, let cool slightly, and stir in the cornstarch. When smooth, add the rum and stir and set aside.

3 Remove the skin from the mangoes. Slice the flesh from the large pit and cut the slices into 1-inch pieces. Place the mango chunks in a bowl and lightly stir in the sugar. Let stand to draw out the juice.

4 Cut the ginger into ¼-inch pieces and set aside.

5 When there is sufficient juice in the bowl to allow the mangoes to be cooked, pour the mango slices and their juice into a nonreactive saucepan. Add the lime zest, lime juice, the chopped ginger, and the grated nutmeg. Bring to a boil, then lower the heat and cook for 5 minutes. Stir in the butter and cornstarch mixture and cook another 5 to 10 minutes or until the mango chunks are soft but intact.

6 Remove the mango mixture from the heat and add the lemon extract. Let cool before spooning into the cooked pastry shell.

7 The tart can be served plain or with a bowl of sweetened whipped cream or Whipped Evaporated Milk (page 285) on the side.

The "dessert of record" from restaurant to restaurant on St. Thomas is Key Lime Pie. Not surprisingly, its ingredients are very much a part of the island. Limes in the Caribbean are small, almost round, with a beige-tone skin, the type we associate with Key limes of Florida. Condensed milk, as well as evaporated milk, were the only forms of milk in the prerefrigerator days of the islands, and they appear in some dishes right up to the present day. So a pie, using local ingredients, was a natural development in the islands, but "Key Lime Pie" is a name easily recognized by Stateside visitors.

1   Preheat the oven to 350 degrees and butter an 8-inch pie pan.

2   Fully bake the pie crust, following the recipe directions.

3   While the pie crust is baking, prepare the filling. Use 1 large and 1 medium-size mixing bowl to hold the eggs. In the large bowl, place 1 whole egg and 3 egg yolks. In the medium-size bowl, place 2 egg whites. (Freeze the remaining egg white for future use.)

4   Beat the whole egg and the egg yolks with a wire whisk until thick and fluffy.

5   Beat the egg whites until stiff and dry with an electric beater or mechanical hand beater.

6   Add the condensed milk to the beaten yolks, beating until well mixed.

7   Slowly add the lime juice in a thin stream, beating until the mixture thickens. Fold in 2 tablespoons of the beaten egg whites. Set aside the remainder of the egg whites.

8   Reduce the oven heat to 325 degrees.

9   Spoon the custard into the baked pie crust. Place in the oven for 5 minutes to form a slight skin on top of the filling.

10   While the pie is in the oven, add the sugar to the remaining egg whites and beat well. Remove the pie from the oven and swirl the meringue over the custard surface, anchoring it to the crust along the edge to prevent shrinkage. Return the pie to the oven, and bake for another 15 minutes or until the surface of the meringue is a light tan. Remove the pie from the oven and place on a cake rack. Cool to room temperature before serving.

St. Thomas

KEY LIME PIE

◆

1 recipe Flaky Pie Crust (page 298)
4 eggs, at room temperature
1 14-ounce can sweetened condensed milk
½ cup fresh or bottled lime juice
4 tablespoons sugar

SERVES 6

PINEAPPLE-MANGO TART

◆

ROUND TART SHELL

1 recipe Flaky Pie Crust
(page 298)

SERVES 6

Often we have made the two versions of this subtly flavored tart, following the two sets of directions given to us by a friend when we visited her one year. One is the version she served us—a round tart crisscrossed with strips of dough, still slightly warm from the oven. The other she described as an eighteen-inch-long strip made a day or two ahead, to save time on the day of entertaining. We have found that two nine-inch strips are easier to handle. Both the round tart and the long strip use the same amount of filling. Whichever style you pick, make and bake the crust according to directions—*then* make the filling.

1   Preheat the oven to 350 degrees. Butter an 8½-x-1-inch quiche pan with a removable bottom.

2   Follow the recipe for mixing the dough. Roll out the dough between 2 sheets of floured wax paper to a 13-x-13-inch square. Cut out a 10-inch circle and line the quiche pan, turning over the extra ½ inch to form a rim ¼ inch above the metal rim of the pan. Flute the dough rim, pulling it slightly over the pan's top edge to anchor the dough. This will prevent the dough from slipping down during the baking. Set aside the rest of the dough in the refrigerator.

3   Prick the bottom and sides of the dough with a fork and put the pan into the oven for 12 to 13 minutes for a partially baked shell. Check every 5 minutes, and prick with a fork any bubbles that develop.

4   Remove the pan from the oven and let the crust cool slightly before adding the filling. Roll and cut the latticework strips from the reserved dough and arrange them on top.

PUFF PASTRY

STRIPS

1 9-x-9-inch sheet frozen
   puff pastry
1 egg beaten with 1 tea-
   spoon water

SERVES 8

1   Preheat the oven to 375 degrees.

2   Thaw the puff pastry sheet according to the manufacturer's directions.

3   Roll out the sheet of pastry on a lightly floured board to a 10½-x-13½-inch rectangle.

4   With a notched wheel cutter or sharp knife, cut the rectangle into 3 10½-inch-long sections; 2 are 5¼ inches wide, the third is 3 inches wide. Cut 2 ¾-inch-wide strips from the narrow side of each 5¼-inch strip. Set aside. Place the 5¼-x-9-inch strips on an unbuttered 11-x-17-inch baking pan.

5   Cut the remaining 3-x-10½-inch piece into 4 ¾-inch-wide strips, 10½ inches long. Set aside.

6 Prick the rectangles on the baking sheet all over with a fork. Brush with the beaten egg. Place the ¾-inch pastry strips on each edge of the pastry rectangles, matching the outside edges and trimming the strips to fit. Brush the top of the strips with the beaten egg.

7 Bake for 25 minutes, checking after 5 minutes and pricking any bubbles that may have formed. When the crust is golden brown and crisp, remove the strips from the oven and transfer them to a cake rack to cool. The baked strips can be refrigerated for 1 to 2 days if necessary.

1 Peel, core, and cut the pineapple into ½-inch dice to fill 1 cup.

2 Peel, slice, and cut the mango into ½-inch dice to fill 1½ cups.

3 Combine the water and sugar in a stainless steel saucepan and bring to a boil. Add the diced pineapple and mango and bring the mixture to a boil. Lower the heat, add the beaten egg yolks (see Notes), and simmer for 15 minutes, stirring from time to time. Remove from the heat and add the almond extract, lemon extract, and rum. Let cool a bit.

4 To prepare the partially baked round shell, preheat the oven to 350 degrees. Ladle the filling into the pastry shell. Remove the reserved rolled-out dough from the fridge. With a notched wheel cutter or sharp knife, cut into ½-inch strips. Crisscross the strips over the top of the filling and brush them with half-and-half or cream. Bake the tart for 40 minutes. Remove from the oven and cool on a cake rack. Remove the tart from its pan for serving, leaving the bottom disk of metal in place, if you'd like.

5 To prepare the puff pastry strips, chill the filling in a covered bowl, in this way the crust will stay crisp when it is filled. Just before serving, spread the filling over the center area of the 2 pastry strips. Cut each strip into 4 slices for serving. Serve with a bowl of sweetened whipped cream or Whipped Evaporated Milk (page 285).

Notes

If you are using canned pineapple chunks, drain the cubes (saving the juice) and measure 1 cup of fruit. Use the juice as part of the liquid in the recipe.

If mangoes are unavailable, use peaches or nectarines.

If the filling is to be used with the puff pastry strips, add the cornstarch, mixed with 1 or 2 teaspoons of water, at the same time as the beaten egg is added.

PINEAPPLE-MANGO FILLING

1 small, ripe pineapple (see Notes)
1 large, semiripe mango (see Notes)
1½ cups water
¾ cup sugar
2 egg yolks
½ teaspoon almond extract
1 teaspoon lemon extract
3 tablespoons dark rum
Half-and-half or cream (for coating latticework on round tart)
2 teaspoons cornstarch (for filling for pastry strips)

MAKES ENOUGH FILLING FOR 1 ROUND TART OR 2 PASTRY STRIPS

Martinique

PINEAPPLE PASTRY STRIP

◆

1 9-x-10-inch sheet frozen puff pastry

2½ tablespoons vanilla pudding mix

¾ cup half-and-half

½ teaspoon almond extract, plus additional to taste

1 egg beaten with 1 teaspoon water

1 fresh pineapple, approximately 6 inches long

Sugar to taste

Demerara cane sugar crystals (optional)

SERVES 6

Surprisingly enough, the supermarkets on Martinique have frozen sheets of puff pastry and *pâte sucre* in the freezer, as do their counterparts in France. Gelatin, French fashion, is sold in sheets and not in the powdered form we are used to. Also available are packaged, quick-cooking custard puddings, of the same type found in France and the States.

We were served slices from a long Pineapple Pastry Strip one night at dinner at Le Matador in Anse Mitan, inland from the beach and ferry dock, and one of the best restaurants for island cooking with the proud down-island touch of service.

Being on vacation, we wanted to "cut down on kitchen time," so we bought the quick components of frozen puff pastry and vanilla pudding at the supermarket, plus a sweet, ripe pineapple from up-island. Once back in the States we've continued the simplified method, as it is a way to serve a spectacular dessert on short notice. Though, here, we buy a semiripe pineapple if it is fragrant, because the yellow, dead-ripe pineapples we get in the States have usually started to rot in the center, while the semiripe ones are firm. We add sugar for sweetness. A squiggle of whipped cream down the center of each portion is "gilding the lily," but . . .

1   Preheat the oven to 400 degrees.

2   Remove 1 sheet of puff pastry from the freezer and defrost according to the manufacturer's instructions.

3   While the pastry is defrosting, make the custard. Measure the pudding mix into a small saucepan, add ¼ cup of the half-and-half, and stir until all lumps have been smoothed. Add the remainder of the half-and-half and stir. Place the pan over medium heat. Stir until the custard comes to a boil, remove from the heat, and add the almond extract. Put the pan in the fridge to cool the custard quickly, covering the top of the custard with a circle of plastic wrap.

4   Dust the pastry board with flour and carefully unfold the sheet of puff pastry onto the pastry board. Lightly dust the pastry's top surface with flour. With a notched wheel cutter, cut off a 3-inch-wide strip from the 9-inch side, leaving a rectangle 6 x 10 inches. Cut off a 6-inch length from this 3-inch-wide strip of pastry. Turn the 6-inch length sidewise, matching it to the end of the 6-x-10-inch section. Brush the ¼-inch overlap of the 2 pieces with the beaten egg and press the edges of the dough together. You will have a rectangle measuring 6 x 12½ inches.

5 Roll out the rectangle until it measures 8 x 19 inches. Now, with the notched wheel cutter, cut 2 1-inch strips from the 4 sides of the rectangle of pastry. These will form the sides of the pastry shell. Place the remaining 4-x-15-inch rectangle of pastry in the middle of an ungreased 11-x-17-inch baking pan.

6 Brush a 1-inch-wide border of the beaten egg around the top outside edges of the pastry rectangle, and put four of the 1-inch strips in place around the edges. Brush the top of the strips with the beaten egg and cover with the second set of 1-inch strips, in both cases trimming away excess pastry. Brush their top surfaces with the beaten egg and put the baking sheet and pastry shell into the refrigerator until the pineapple has been sliced.

7 With a large, sharp knife, slice the pineapple in half lengthwise, removing the leaves. Cover half with a plastic bag and place in the refrigerator for a later use. Cut the remaining section in half lengthwise and remove the center core. With the knife remove the skin. Turn each section over, and cut out any "eyes" with the point of a paring knife. From the "core" area, slice downward, cutting each section into ¼-inch-thick slices, keeping the 2 sections separate.

8 Remove the baking pan and pastry shell from the refrigerator. Spread the custard over the bottom of the pastry shell in an even layer. On top, arrange a layer of overlapping slices from 1 section of the pineapple. Sprinkle with sugar. Add a second layer of pineapple, reversing the direction of the slices, and sprinkle with sugar. This layer will be higher than the sides, but in baking, the sides will rise well above the fruit filling. If there is any beaten egg left, brush the top edges of the pastry again, and sprinkle them with the sugar crystals, slightly pressing them into the dough. The fruit also can be sprinkled with the sugar crystals.

9 Place the baking pan in the preheated oven for 35 to 45 minutes or until the dough is cooked and brown. Lift up one corner of the strip to check the bottom crust, it should be cooked and light brown. If the top crust needs more browning, place the baking pan under the broiler, but watch carefully as the crust will brown rapidly.

10 Remove the baking pan from the oven and allow the strip to cool for 10 minutes. Transfer with 2 wide spatulas to a cake rack to cool. To serve, cut crosswise into 6 slices. Sweetened whipped cream or Whipped Evaporated Milk (page 285) flavored with almond extract to taste can be served on the side.

Guadeloupe

TOURMENT D'AMOUR TART

◆

THE CUSTARD

½ cup half-and-half
2 tablespoons plus 2 tea-
  spoons vanilla pudding
  mix (see Notes)
1 teaspoon vanilla extract

THE *PÂTE BRISÉE*

¾ cup plus 1½ table-
  spoons all-purpose flour
1 tablespoon sugar
¼ teaspoon baking powder
Pinch of salt
⅛ teaspoon grated nutmeg
5 tablespoons butter
1 teaspoon vanilla extract
2 tablespoons cold water

One is told that a local sweet, *tourment d'amour*, is made only on the Isle des Saintes off Guadeloupe's southern coast of Basse Terre, but we've had several versions of this tour de force cake in other parts of the island, each one containing all or some of the components of this Guadeloupian specialty—custard, coconut, crisp crust, and cake.

From Kancel's Bakery in Gosier we had a round tart version, consisting of four layers: a flavorful short, pastry crust, a syrupy coconut layer, and a pastry-cream layer, all topped by a ladyfinger-like cake known in the French islands as *pâte à biscuit*, and in France as *biscuit à la cuiller*. All this in a half-inch depth! The syrupy coconut, a local confection called *confiture de coconut* is a three-hour affair in which grated coconut is cooked in a sugar syrup. But be of good cheer because this delightful confection is available in eighteen-ounce cans in the States, as grated coconut in extra heavy syrup or *coco rallado en almibar*, at island grocery shops or in the Hispanic grocery section of a supermarket.

1   Mix the half-and-half and the vanilla pudding powder together in a small saucepan. Place the pan over medium heat and bring the contents to a boil, stirring to prevent the custard from burning. Remove from the heat and stir in the vanilla extract. Pour the custard into a small bowl and cover the surface with a circle of clear plastic wrap to prevent a skin from forming. Set aside until the custard cools.

2   Preheat the oven to 350 degrees and butter a 6-inch fluted quiche pan with a removable bottom.

3   Sift the dry ingredients together into a bowl. Cut in the butter with 2 knives, then crumble the larger pieces with your fingertips to make a coarse meal. Mix the vanilla extract with the water and stir into the flour mixture. Add a little more water if needed to form a dough that holds together without being soggy. (If using a processor, sift the dry ingredients into the processor container, add the butter cut into ½-inch chunks, and with the metal blade spin for a count of 6. Add the water and vanilla mixture and spin again for a count of 6. Add another teaspoon of water if needed and spin again for a count of 6.)

4   Press the dough into the quiche pan, making the sides thicker than the bottom. Extend the dough almost ½ inch above the rim of the pan, and flute the edge. Prick the shell all over with a fork to prevent bubbles.

5   Put the pan in the preheated oven. After 5 minutes check the crust, and prick any bubbles that may have formed. Bake for 5 minutes more, and again check the crust for bubbles. Bake for 2 to 3 minutes more, then remove the partially baked shell from the oven. Set aside.

6 Separate the eggs, placing the egg yolks in a mixing bowl and 1 egg white in a separate bowl. Freeze the remaining egg white for another use.

7 Beat the egg yolks. Add the sugar and beat with a wire whisk, adding the lemon extract and vanilla. Add the flour and mix well. Stop at this point and set the bowl aside.

8 To assemble the tart, spread the coconut over the bottom of the partially baked pastry shell.

9 Beat the custard with a spoon and spread it over the coconut layer.

10 Finish putting together the *pâte à biscuit*, by beating the egg white with the cream of tartar. When stiff, fold a fourth of the amount into the egg mixture, then add the rest of the egg white, folding it in lightly until well mixed. Quickly spread the batter over the custard, starting around the outside edge and increasing the depth at the center. Dust with the vanilla confectioners' sugar

11 Place the pan in the center of the 350-degree oven and bake for 45 minutes or until the cake tests dry with a thin skewer inserted into its center, and the top is a pale brown and the edges of the crust are light brown. Remove the tart from the oven to a cake rack, and cool it in its pan. To serve, remove the outer rim of the quiche pan, leaving the bottom metal disk in place, then center the tart on a serving platter.

Notes
You can substitute a made-from-scratch egg custard.

To make vanilla confectioners' sugar, put sugar in a metal sugar shaker with a section of vanilla bean thrust into the center of the sugar.

THE *PÂTE À BISCUIT*
2 eggs
6 tablespoons sugar
1½ teaspoons lemon extract (or grated zest of ½ lemon)
¼ teaspoon vanilla extract
4 tablespoons all-purpose flour
⅛ teaspoon cream of tartar

THE COCONUT
6 tablespoons grated coconut in extra heavy syrup (see Note, page 310)
Vanilla confectioners' sugar (see Notes)

SERVES 4

Sint Maarten

COCONUT ICE CREAM

◆

6 tablespoons plus 2 cups half-and-half

2 tablespoons unflavored gelatin

2 cups heavy whipping cream

¾ cup grated coconut in heavy syrup (see Note)

Pinch of salt

4 teaspoons coconut extract

¼ teaspoon almond extract

2 tablespoons dark rum

MAKES 6 CUPS

Coconut ice cream is a favorite dessert in Dutch Sint Maarten, and we became connoisseurs of this delectable, richly satisfying sweet. The best of all was sold at the ice cream stand at the ferry pier. On warm nights we would buy a double cone and stroll out onto the pier, watching the activity in the restaurants facing the bay, their soft lights reflected in the still water, hearing at a distance the hum of the never-ceasing traffic on Front Street.

1   Measure the 6 tablespoons of half-and-half into a small bowl and sprinkle the gelatin on the surface. Set aside until the gelatin is soft.

2   In the top of a double boiler placed over gently boiling water, scald the remaining half-and-half and ½ cup of the heavy cream. Add the grated coconut and salt to the scalded liquids, stirring well.

3   Mix the softened gelatin and half-and-half with a fork and scrape it into the hot liquid. Stir and cook for 1 minute or until the gelatin is dissolved.

4   Remove the pan from the heat and place it in a larger pot filled with cold water and ice cubes to chill the custard.

5   While the custard is chilling, beat the remaining heavy cream to the consistency of mayonnaise.

6   Add the coconut extract, almond extract, and rum to the cooled custard. Mix a quarter of the whipped cream into the custard with a wire whisk, breaking up the lumps of cream. Fold in the rest of the whipped cream.

7   Freeze the mixture in an ice-cream maker according to the manufacturer's instructions. For those without an ice-cream maker, see step 11 on page 316. When frozen, transfer to 3 2-cup plastic containers with snap-on lids and place in the freezer.

Note

Grated coconut in heavy syrup is sold in cans in island shops. If unobtainable, use dry, sweetened, flaked, or shredded coconut, plus ¼ cup sugar and ¼ cup light corn syrup added to the half-and-half and heavy cream in the top of the double boiler. Taste for sweetness, adding more sugar if needed.

If you think you know Baked Alaska, you are still unprepared for the elegantly presented *Glace Norvégienne*—which in France is often called *omelette à la norvégienne*. As it is served at *Au Régal de la Mer*, Anse Mitan, Trois-Ilots, it is a voluptuous, flat-topped oval of meringue enclosing a layer of genoise or *pain doux* topped with a layer of rum-raisin ice cream. The top and sides of the oval case are decorated by an inspired pastry chef with swirls of meringue. Nestled in the center of a circle of meringue on the top is half of a white eggshell, which, on serving, is filled with warmed rum. Upon setting the *glace* down on the table, the rum is ignited and the dancing blue flames are spooned over the surface before the confection is sliced into portions.

We've always enjoyed this when served in a restaurant. But it is impractical at home, either for family or guests as there is, of necessity, a long wait for dessert, unless there is a cook in the kitchen. Through sheer frustration with the classic process, we worked out a prepare-ahead-and-serve-quickly method—and here it is.

The three components of this spectacular dessert can be made two or three days before, assembling them quickly just before serving. We prefer to make the meringue cases in a size to serve two, and to make multiple cases, depending on how many people we are serving, as one large one can get very messy when slicing it into several portions!

1 Bake the *Pain Doux* according to directions in a 7½-inch square pan. This is enough for 2 cases, serving 4. (Increase the recipe for a larger, shallower pan, depending on how many cases you are making.)

2 After baking, store the shallow cake, wrapped tightly in clear plastic, in either the refrigerator or freezer.

3 Preheat the oven to 225 degrees.

4 Lightly oil 1 or more 11-x-17-inch baking pans and smooth a sheet of wax paper on each pan. Do not oil the wax paper. Place a pointed, oval cutter, 3¼ x 6¼ inches, at one end of the wax paper. With the point of a knife, draw a line on the wax paper, around the outside edge of the cutter as a pattern for the side of the case. Draw a second oval on the wax paper, ⅝ inches wider all around than the first oval for the cover. If you lack a metal cutter, make a pattern from a piece of light cardboard. Make as many ovals as needed for the number of servings you need. Set aside.

5 Measure 6 tablespoons of the sugar into a small bowl. Sift the cornstarch over the sugar and mix well. Set aside.

6 Beat the egg whites with the cream of tartar and the salt until soft peaks form. Gradually add the remaining 4 tablespoons of sugar, beating after each

Martinique

GLACE NORVÉGIENNE

◆

1 recipe unbaked *Pain Doux* (page 288)
10 tablespoons sugar
2½ teaspoons cornstarch
2 egg whites
¼ teaspoon cream of tartar
Pinch of salt
1 teaspoon vanilla extract
Rum
1 recipe Rum-Raisin Ice Cream (page 316)
½ clean, white eggshell

MAKES 1 CASE TO SERVE 2

addition. Add the vanilla and beat until mixed in. Now add the sugar and cornstarch mixture, 2 tablespoons at a time, beating after each addition. The meringue will be very stiff, but continue beating until all the sugar and cornstarch mixture has been absorbed. Scrape the bottom of the bowl with a spoon to make sure all the sugar has been incorporated.

7 Insert a number 6 pastry tube (½-inch-wide opening with jagged edges) in a pastry bag. Spoon a little more than half the meringue into the pastry bag. For the sides of the meringue case, squeeze out a ½-inch-deep by ¾-inch-wide line of meringue on the *outside* of the first oval's shape. Carefully add a second layer on top of the first, then top with a third level, adding more meringue to the pastry bag as needed. Do not smooth the outside.

8 For the top of the meringue case, fill in the larger oval starting *inside* the outer line and covering the full oval with a ½-inch-deep spiraled layer. Smooth the spirals with a broad spatula, then add a few swirls on top for decoration, including a raised-edge circle in the middle to hold half an eggshell.

9 Bake the meringue in the preheated oven for 50 minutes. Turn off the oven and allow the meringue to cool and dry in the oven for 20 to 30 minutes. Remove the pan from the oven, and carefully slip the wax paper onto a cake rack. Delicately remove the meringue case and top from the wax paper, and cool on the cake rack.

10 If not using the meringue case immediately, store the pieces in an airtight metal container. If using within a couple of days the meringue does not need to be refrigerated.

11 To assemble, make a pattern for the cake size and shape by placing the side of each meringue case upright on a sheet of typewriter paper. With a pencil, draw an outline of the *inside* of each case. (Each one may be different.) Place the meringue cases on a large, flameproof serving plate. Cut out the paper patterns, lay them on the top of the cake, and cut out around the edge with the point of a sharp knife. Sprinkle the surface of the oval piece of cake with rum, and fit it inside the meringue case. These steps can be done ahead of time, well before serving.

12 Just before serving fill the rest of the interior of the meringue case with the rum-raisin ice cream. Place the meringue cover on top. Put the eggshell half in place. In a metal ladle heat enough rum to fill the eggshell. Pour the rum into the eggshell and ignite. You may want to spoon the flaming rum around the bottom of the meringue case.

13 To serve once the flames have died down, remove the eggshell and cut the *Glace Norvégienne* in half across the width, using a sharp knife. Transfer each half to dessert plates.

Large mango trees are everywhere on the island, shading the houses and looming up over the steep mountainside roads, their wealth of fruit waiting to be turned into every conceivable dessert or just eaten out-of-hand, the tantalizing, juicy flavor matching the mainlander's dream of an exotic island experience. We had ice-cream cones in the heat of the day, mango melba late at night, fresh mangoes ripening in a basket on our terrace, their fragrance blown into the rooms through the open door. Glorious!

Jamaica

MANGO ICE CREAM

◆

½ cup half-and-half
2 cups heavy cream
½ cup cold water
2 packets unflavored gelatin
1 cup sugar
1 large, ripe mango
1 teaspoon lime juice
4 tablespoons dark rum
½ teaspoon vanilla extract
⅛ teaspoon salt

MAKES 6 CUPS

1 Pour the half-and-half and ½ cup of the heavy cream into the top of a double boiler. Place over simmering water to heat.

2 Measure the cold water into a small bowl and sprinkle the gelatin on the surface. Set aside.

3 When the half-and-half and heavy cream are hot but not boiling, add the sugar and stir until dissolved. Add the softened gelatin and stir for 1 or 2 minutes until dissolved. Remove from the heat and place the double boiler top inside a larger pan filled with cold water and ice cubes to cool the custard.

4 While the custard is cooling, peel the mango and slice the fruit from the pit. Cube the slices and puree them in a food processor to fill 1¼ to 2 cups. (Do not make the puree too smooth.) Stir in the lime juice.

5 Whip the remaining heavy cream until thick but not too stiff.

6 Stir the pureed mango into the cooled custard. Add the dark rum, vanilla extract, and salt.

7 Fold in the whipped cream until evenly blended.

8 Freeze the mixture in an ice-cream maker according to the manufacturer's instructions. For those without an ice-cream maker, see step 11 on page 316. When frozen, transfer to 2-cup containers with snap-on lids and store in the freezer until ready to serve.

St. Lucia

PIÑA COLADA ICE CREAM

◆

1 15-ounce can sweetened cream of coconut
¾ cup half-and-half
½ cup cold water
2 packets unflavored gelatin
¼ teaspoon salt
1 8-ounce can crushed, unsweetened pineapple (see Note)
1½ cups heavy whipping cream
½ teaspoon coconut extract
4 to 6 tablespoons dark rum
1 teaspoon fresh lime juice

MAKES 6 CUPS

At Albert Haman's Rain Restaurant in Castries, we relaxed over tantalizing piña coladas, called by the owner the "Reverend's Downfall," in keeping with the restaurant's name. We had spent the morning shopping for tropical vegetables and fruits inside and outside the large covered market. After lunch, on our way home to our cottage, we picked up cans of pineapple juice and coconut cream at the small supermarket, to re-create this joyful experience. After mixing up a batch, inspiration struck, and we put half of it into the freezer to be eaten later by small spoonfuls to the sound of the tree frogs in the palm trees overhead.

We have gradually refined the recipe and here it is with the addition of other ingredients which add to the smoothness of the ice cream. But we can't provide the tree frogs!

1 Beat the cream of coconut in the opened can with a fork to mix it. Pour the liquid into the top of a double boiler and add the half-and-half. Place over simmering water.

2 Measure the cold water into a small bowl and sprinkle the gelatin on top.

3 When the cream of coconut mixture is hot, stir in the softened gelatin. Add the salt and stir until the gelatin has melted, approximately 1 to 2 minutes. Remove from the heat and place the top of the double boiler inside a larger pan filled with cold water and ice cubes to cool the custard.

4 Pour the crushed pineapple into a food processor and spin until pureed.

5 Whip the heavy cream until it is thick but not too stiff.

6 Stir the pureed pineapple into the cooled coconut cream custard, mix well, then add the coconut extract, rum, and lime juice and stir until mixed.

7 Stir 4 tablespoons of the whipped cream into the custard mixture and stir lightly with a wire whisk breaking up any lumps. Fold in the rest of the whipped cream.

8 Freeze the mixture in an ice-cream maker according to manufacturer's instructions. For those without an ice-cream maker, see step 11 on page 316. When frozen, transfer to 2-cup plastic containers with snap-on lids and store in the freezer until ready to serve.

Note

Use only canned pineapple, as fresh pineapple will chemically react with the gelatin, preventing it from thickening and smoothing the ice cream. If you use an 8-ounce can of sweetened pineapple chunks, put the fruit through the processor and add 2 to 3 teaspoons of fresh lime juice to balance the sweetness of the ice cream.

One night we walked down the beach from our apartment in Ocho Ríos to listen to our favorite steel band at one of the hotels—and to have a late dessert. After relaxing at a beachside table, we chose an eclectic blend of "cultures"—a Mango Melba made with Mango Ice Cream, slices of fresh mango sprinkled with dark rum, and guava syrup poured over all. A voluptuous accompaniment to the balmy air and the purring music of the steel band.

Jamaica

MANGO MELBA

◆

4 ounces canned guava paste, cut into ½-inch dice (see Note)

3 tablespoons water or guava nectar

1 teaspoon rum, plus additional rum for fruit slices

1 large mango, 14 to 16 ounces

1 pint Mango Ice Cream (page 313) or vanilla ice cream

SERVES 4

1 Place the guava paste and water in a small saucepan over moderate heat. Stir until the guava paste has melted. Remove from the heat and add the rum. Pour the sauce into a small pitcher and cool to room temperature.

2 About an hour before serving, peel the mango and slice into 4 ¼-inch-thick slices. There will be additional slices and pieces as you work around the large, flat pit. Place all in a small bowl, cover with clear plastic wrap, and refrigerate.

3 To serve, divide the slices among 4 shallow dessert dishes. Sprinkle the fruit with the additional rum. Place 2 scoops of the mango ice cream on top of the fruit. Generously drizzle the guava sauce over the top of the ice cream and serve promptly.

Note

You can substitute 4 ounces of guava jelly for the paste in making the sauce.

Martinique

RUM-RAISIN
ICE CREAM

◆

1 cup dark raisins
10 tablespoons dark rum
2½ cups plus 6 table-
  spoons half-and-half
2 tablespoons unflavored
  gelatin
2 cups heavy whipping
  cream
¾ cup minus 2 table-
  spoons sugar
2 tablespoons dark-brown
  sugar
1 egg yolk
3 tablespoons vanilla ex-
  tract
⅛ teaspoon freshly grated
  nutmeg
Pinch of salt

MAKES 8 CUPS

One night at *Au Régal de la Mer*, when we ordered their spectacular *Glace Norvégienne* (page 311), we were surprised to find that the ice cream was rum-raisin, rather than one of the island's fruited ice creams. Our stylish waitress explained that while it was locally made, it was an *imported* recipe along with the raisins, *but* the rum was local.

1 Soak the raisins for 10 minutes in hot water just to cover in a small bowl. Drain and add 4 tablespoons dark rum and set aside to marinate for 2 hours.

2 After the raisins have marinated, start preparations for the ice cream.

3 Measure the 6 tablespoons of half-and-half into a small bowl and sprinkle the gelatin over the surface. Let stand until the gelatin has softened.

4 Pour the remaining half-and-half and ½ cup of the heavy cream into the top of a double boiler and place over gently simmering water. While the liquid is heating, mix the sugars together in a small bowl. When the milk reaches scalding temperature, stir in the sugar.

5 Slightly beat the egg yolk in a small bowl. Stir 3 or 4 tablespoons of the hot milk into the egg, then scrape the egg into the saucepan. Stir until the milk is slightly thickened.

6 Break up the softened gelatin with a fork, then spoon it into the hot custard. Stir for approximately 1 minute or until the gelatin has melted.

7 Remove the top of the double boiler from the heat and place it in a larger pan of cold water and ice cubes to cool the custard. Stir in the vanilla extract, 6 tablespoons dark rum, grated nutmeg, and salt.

8 Place the raisins in the refrigerator to chill.

9 When the custard has cooled, whip the 1½ cups of cream to the consistency of mayonnaise. Mix a quarter of the whipped cream into the cooled custard with a wire whisk, then fold in the rest of the whipped cream. For freezing, follow the manufacturer's directions for your ice-cream maker, adding the raisins and their marinade at the proper time.

10 When the ice cream is frozen, pack it into 4 2-cup plastic containers with snap-on lids, and place in the freezer compartment of your refrigerator.

11 If you do not have an ice-cream maker, pour the custard into a metal bowl and place in the freezer, set at the coldest temperature. Leave the bowl in for approximately 1½ hours; the custard should be lightly frozen around the edges but soft in the middle. Remove from the freezer and break up the mixture with a large spoon, turning it over, as the custard and whipped cream will have partially separated. Beat with a wire whisk or hand-held electric beater until smooth. Return the bowl to the freezer for 20 to 25 minutes. Take out and beat again.

12 Fold in the raisins and the marinade until the raisins are well distributed. Spoon the ice cream into 4 2-cup plastic containers with snap-on lids and store in the freezer.

◆ Sorbets ◆

One of the unforgettable food experiences in Martinique and Guadeloupe was the tropical fruit sorbets—a smoothness of texture combined with the intense essence of fruit flavor made the guava, passion fruit, and mango a heavenly treat. We finally decided that a member of the M. Berthillon family must have fled the Île St. Louis in Paris for the southern warmth of Martinique and had then set up shop—for it was only at a Berthillon stand on *that* île that we had experienced the same strong flavor in tropical fruit sorbets.

These sorbets became a necessary part of many dinners at the cluster of restaurants at Anse Mitan/Pointe du Bout on Martinique, as well as a beach treat at Saline Beach. This long stretch of white sand is overhung with palm trees on one side and matched with turquoise blue water on the other. Because it is a state preserve there are no hotels, restaurants, or houses anywhere near—only a few small food stands to satisfy midday hunger. One settles here for the day to eat barbecued chicken from Madame's small grill under the trees or pizza cooked over a wood fire inside a panel truck—and cooling, refreshing sorbets—to read, people watch, swim, surf-sail, or buy unique beach wear from the girls who stroll the beach, their baskets piled with brilliantly colored fabrics—a return to the uncluttered world of childhood summers.

With all the flavors to choose from, we mostly picked the refreshing Guava Sorbet when we wandered over to the sorbet stand at Saline Beach. The flavor seemed to fit the time and the place of this southernmost beach on Martinique, where we could look across the wide channel to St. Lucia's peaks showing above the horizon and remember friends' houses over there, and the remains of Rodney's Fort on Pigeon Island that guarded that channel so long ago, as did Diamond Rock looming starkly black out of the blue sea just up the Martinique coast from Saline Beach.

1   Shake the cans of guava nectar and pour the contents into a stainless steel bowl.

2   Weigh the guava shells, puree them in a processor or beat with a wire whisk, and add to the nectar in the bowl.

3   Measure the cold water into a small bowl and sprinkle the gelatin over the surface. When the gelatin is soft, place the bowl in a pan of just-boiled water (heat turned off) until the liquid is clear. Remove the bowl from the hot water and let the gelatin cool slightly.

4   Pour the cooled gelatin into the nectar mixture and add the corn syrup, stirring well.

5   Beat the egg whites with the salt until stiff. Add the sugar, 1 tablespoon at a time, beating between each addition.

6   Lightly add half the beaten egg whites to the guava mixture using a wire whisk. Fold in the remaining egg whites with a plastic spatula. Add lemon juice if needed to sharpen the flavor.

7   At this point follow the manufacturer's instructions for your ice-cream maker. Or pour the mixture into a clean stainless steel bowl and place the bowl, uncovered, in the freezer. After 1 hour, remove the bowl from the freezer and turn the contents over with a large spoon, as the liquid and whites will have partially separated. Return to the freezer for another hour or until the sorbet is almost hard. Remove from the freezer, turn over with a spoon, and beat with a mechanical hand beater until well mixed and smooth. Spoon into 2-cup plastic containers with snap-on lids and return to the freezer until firm.

8   To serve, spoon into chilled glass or china serving dishes.

Notes

All timing is approximate since all freezer temperatures vary. It is only after making the sorbet once that you can set your own time schedule.

If using fresh guavas, peel the fruit, cut it in half, remove the pulp, and weigh the shells. Cook in sugared water until soft. Drain and cool.

Sorbet can be made with nectar only. Makes 6 cups.

Martinique

GUAVA SORBET

◆

2 12-ounce cans guava nectar
14 to 16 ounces bottled, canned, or fresh guava shells (see Notes)
½ cup cold water or liquid from canned guava shells
2 tablespoons unflavored gelatin
½ cup light corn syrup
2 egg whites
Pinch of salt
4 tablespoons sugar
Lemon juice (optional)

MAKES 8 CUPS

Martinique

MANGO SORBET

◆

2 12-ounce cans mango
nectar
½ cup cold water
2 tablespoons unflavored
gelatin
1 14-to-16-ounce semiripe
mango (see Notes)
½ cup light corn syrup
4 teaspoons dark rum
2 egg whites
Pinch of salt
4 tablespoons sugar

MAKES 8 CUPS

On two different visits to Martinique, our favorite grilled-fish restaurant was the Langouste, perched over the waters of the bay, across from Fort de France and beside the ferry pier. It was the essence of the sprawling, wooden seashore shack, dimly lit with wooden tables lining the balustrade of the long, porchlike dining area, the water of the bay lazily advancing and retreating below. Inside, in the visible kitchen, the wood fire glowed red as our fish was quickly grilled, arriving piping hot with fried plantains on the side. And, inevitably, we topped off our meal with their glorious Mango Sorbet—pure mango flavor and not too sweet. Alas, on our most recent visit, the Langouste was no longer—Gilbert, the hurricane that roared up the islands, tore off the roof and demolished part of that long porch—but maybe it will be rebuilt.

1 Shake the cans of mango nectar and pour the contents into a stainless steel bowl.

2 Measure the cold water into a small bowl and sprinkle the gelatin over the surface. When the gelatin is soft, place the bowl into a pan of just-boiled water (heat turned off) until the liquid is clear. Remove the bowl from the hot water and let the gelatin cool slightly.

3 Peel the mango, cut into chunks, and put in the food processor. Reduce the fruit to a puree. If the mango has not been reduced to a smooth puree, transfer the pulp to a stainless steel sieve and press the pulp through the sieve into the bowl of nectar, using a wooden spoon. Discard the pulp left in the sieve.

4 Stir the corn syrup and the gelatin into the nectar mixture, then add the rum.

5 Beat the egg whites with the salt. When soft peaks form, add the sugar, 1 tablespoon at a time, beating after each addition.

6 Add about a quarter of the egg whites to the nectar mixture and gently beat in with a wire whisk to break up any lumps. Fold in the rest of the egg whites with a plastic spatula.

7 To freeze, check the manufacturer's directions for your ice-cream maker or put the uncovered stainless steel bowl and contents into the freezer, set at its coldest temperature. After 1 hour remove the bowl from the freezer and stir the semifrozen sorbet with a large spoon, turning it over and over to blend the slight separation of the liquid and egg white. Return to the freezer until the sorbet is almost hard, about 1 hour. Again remove the bowl from the freezer, turn the contents over with a large spoon, then beat with a mechanical beater until well mixed and smooth. Spoon the sorbet into 2-cup plastic containers with snap-on lids and return to the freezer until firm.

8 To serve, spoon into chilled glass or china dessert dishes—the sorbet can be especially impressive in wide, shallow champagne glasses.

Notes

If fresh mangoes are unobtainable, use canned mango slices, draining them well, and weighing out approximately 10 to 11 ounces of fruit.

All freezing times are approximate, since all freezer temperatures vary. It is only after making the sorbet once that you can set your own timing.

Guadeloupe

ORANGE
SORBET

◆

2 large, thick-skinned oranges, 9 ounces each
1 small lemon
¼ cup cold water
2 tablespoons unflavored gelatin
1 cup plus 1 tablespoon sugar
¾ cup light corn syrup
2½ cups water
2½ teaspoons orange extract
1 egg white

MAKES 6 CUPS

On Guadeloupe, the motorized kitchen wagons at Ste. Anne's beach serve a fresh orange ice, sharpened with the flavor of orange zest. Their crepes are the thinnest imaginable with up to twenty choices of savory fillings. All this to be consumed at tiny tables set on the sand nearby or carried back to one's beach towel "encampment" at the water's edge or under the shade of the trees.

Then one evening we encountered the special Orange Sorbet at *Chez Rosette* in Gosier, as part of an impressive dessert well named *Givre* (Hoarfrost) (below). Frozen orange or lemon skins containing orange or lemon sorbet develop a thin coat of frost on the outside as they are removed from the freezer into the balmy air at garden tables sheltered by large umbrellas and Norfolk pines.

1 Grate the zest from the oranges and set aside in a small bowl covered tightly with plastic wrap. Squeeze the juice from the oranges to fill 1¼ cups and the juice from the lemon. Set the combined juices aside in a small bowl.

2 Pour the cold water into a small bowl and sprinkle the unflavored gelatin over its surface. Let stand until softened.

3 Set the freezer at its coldest temperature.

4 Put 1 cup of the sugar, the corn syrup, and 2½ cups of the water into a stainless steel saucepan and bring to a boil, stirring continuously until the sugar has melted. Boil for 2 minutes.

5 Lower the heat and bring to a simmer. Add 3 or 4 tablespoons of the hot liquid to the softened gelatin and pour the gelatin into the rest of the liquid in the saucepan, stirring until the gelatin has melted, about 1 minute.

6 Take the saucepan off the heat and stir in the orange zest. Cover the pan and set aside for 45 to 50 minutes to steep and cool to lukewarm.

7 Strain the mixture through a fine plastic or stainless steel (not aluminum) sieve into a stainless steel bowl, pressing all the juice from the orange zest. Stir in the reserved orange and lemon juice and the orange extract.

8 If you are using an ice-cream maker, follow the manufacturer's directions for freezing. Otherwise, place the uncovered bowl containing the liquid in the freezer until a *heavy* slush forms throughout the mixture (see Note).

9 Beat the egg white until stiff, then beat in the remaining tablespoon of sugar. Remove the slushy orange sorbet from the freezer and beat vigorously with a wooden spoon or wire whisk until the mixture is of uniform consistency. Fold in the beaten egg white and return the bowl to the freezer.

10   When the sorbet is almost hard, remove the bowl from the freezer and beat the sorbet with a wooden spoon until well blended and smooth. Spoon the sorbet into 3 2-cup plastic containers with snap-on lids and return to the freezer until the sorbet is firm enough to serve or overnight.

11   To serve, spoon the sorbet into wide-mouth champagne glasses that have been chilled in the refrigerator or into frozen orange shells for *Givre* below.

Variation

***Givre* (Hoarfrost)**   Use 1 scooped-out shell of a whole orange or lemon per serving.

1   Cut off the top of each large, thick-skinned fruit so that there is approximately a 2-inch opening. Scoop out the fruit and membrane and use the juice for long, cool drinks. When the shells are clean, freeze the shells and top pieces until very hard and frosty.

2   An hour or so before serving, fill the shells with the frozen orange or lemon sorbet and smooth the tops. Return them to the freezer. Place the shells in narrow, glass serving dishes or in wine glasses and angle an edge of a top piece into the sorbet for a jaunty finish.

Note

An exact length of time for freezing the sorbet cannot be given as the temperature in freezers varies. It could range from as little as 1 hour to as long as 3 hours. It is only after making the sorbet once that you can set your own time.

Martinique

PINEAPPLE SORBET

◆

½ very ripe pineapple
2 tablespoons plus ½ tea-
spoon lemon juice (about
½ lemon)
5 teaspoons kirsch or dry
French vermouth
¼ teaspoon salt
¾ cup plus 1 tablespoon
sugar
6 tablespoons light corn
syrup
1½ cups water
1 egg white
Pinch of cream of tartar

MAKES 6 CUPS

In the northern part of Martinique we drove through lush greenery pressing in on the road. Fields and villages are tucked in amongst sharply silhouetted mountains with the long, rounded slope of Mt. Pelée dominating the sky. Here one sees the spiky fields of pineapple plants and the broad light-green leaves of banana plants, their long clusters of fruit enclosed in clear blue plastic bags, on the way through the working part of Leyritz Plantation. The inn at the end of the road has its dining rooms set into the buildings of the old stone sugar mill and distillery, surrounded by small "bedroom" cottages with porches that long ago housed the plantation workers. The former manor house has also been turned into a guest house.

Here, field-ripened pineapples become a tantalizing Pineapple Sorbet, served in tall glasses at the end of a Creole meal. The whole secret is a ripe, ripe pineapple for flavor and softness of fibers.

1   Set the freezer at the coldest temperature.

2   Remove the skin, green top, center core, and "eyes" from the pineapple. Cut the fruit into small pieces. Place the pieces in a food processor and spin until pureed; check for "spines" and remove them. Ladle 1¾ cups of the puree into a mixing bowl (see Notes).

3   Add the lemon juice, kirsch, and salt to the puree. Place the bowl in the fridge to keep cool.

4   Measure ¾ cup of the sugar, the corn syrup, and water into a stainless steel saucepan and bring to a boil, stirring while the sugar is melting. Boil the mixture for 10 minutes, then remove from the heat. Place the pan inside a larger pan filled with cold water and ice cubes to cool the syrup.

5   While the syrup is chilling, beat the egg white with the cream of tartar until it holds soft peaks. Add the remaining sugar and beat until the egg white is stiff.

6   Remove the chilled pineapple from the fridge and the saucepan with the cooled sugar syrup from its chilling water. Slowly pour the sugar syrup into the pineapple, beating it in with a wire whisk. Add 4 tablespoons of this mixture to the beaten egg white and stir lightly until mixed, then scrape all the egg white into the pineapple mixture and fold lightly until mixed together.

7   If you are using an ice-cream maker, follow the manufacturer's directions for freezing. Otherwise, pour the mixture into a stainless steel bowl and put into the freezer until a *heavy* slush forms (see Notes).

8 Remove the bowl from the freezer and beat the sorbet with a wooden spoon, turning and mixing, as the egg white will have risen to the top. Return the bowl and contents to the freezer.

9 When the mixture is almost hard, again remove the bowl from the freezer and beat the pineapple sorbet with a wooden spoon until well blended and smooth. Spoon into 2-cup plastic containers with snap-on lids. Return to the freezer until firm enough to serve or overnight.

10 Slightly soften the pineapple sorbet before serving if it is too hard. Spoon into prechilled glass dishes or parfait glasses.

Notes

If fresh pineapple is unavailable, substitute canned, crushed, unsweetened pineapple.

Freezing time depends on the temperature of your freezer and could range from 1 to 3 hours.

Tobago

COCONUT FLAN

◆

THE CARAMEL SYRUP

1 cup sugar
1 tablespoon water, plus
   additional ¼ cup boiling
   water
6 teaspoons sweetened
   coconut flakes
2 tablespoons strained
   lime juice (½ lime)

THE CUSTARD

2 eggs
4 tablespoons sugar (see
   Note)
¼ teaspoon salt
1 teaspoon coconut extract
2 tablespoons caramel
   syrup
6 tablespoons sweetened
   coconut flakes
1½ cups half-and-half
Grated nutmeg

SERVES 6

Grated coconut, as garnish, from the fruit of one of the trees lining the beach in front of our cottage and limes, to make lime-flavored caramel syrup, from the nearby lime tree did wonders for the ubiquitous custard flan, the simplest dessert to make.

1   For the Caramel Syrup, mix the sugar and the 1 tablespoon water together in a small saucepan and place over medium heat. As the sugar melts, tip the pan from side to side to mix the liquiefied and unmelted sugar together. Break up any lumps with a table fork and stir to mix. When the syrup is clear and a good brown without being burnt, remove from the heat to stop the boiling. Add the ¼ cup of boiling water, stirring the mixture vigorously. Return to the heat until the water and syrup are blended.

2   Pour the syrup into a heatproof glass measuring cup. There should be no more then ¾ cup of syrup; if less add hot water. Spoon 1 tablespoon of the syrup into the bottom of each of 6 2¾-x-1⅛-inch soufflé ramekins. Sprinkle 1 teaspoon each of the coconut flakes over the syrup in the bottom of each soufflé ramekin. Set aside.

3   Pour the remaining syrup into a small pitcher to cool, reserving 2 tablespoons for the custard mixture. When cold, mix the strained lime juice into the syrup in the pitcher.

4   For the Custard, preheat the oven to 300 degrees. On the center rack in the oven, place a shallow pan large enough to hold the 6 soufflé ramekins and add ½ inch of hot water.

5   Beat the eggs in a bowl and add the sugar. Beat together and add the salt, coconut extract, and the reserved 2 tablespoons of caramel syrup. Mix well, then stir in 3 tablespoons of the sweetened coconut flakes.

6   Scald the half-and-half in a small saucepan. When heated, pour it in a thin stream over the egg mixture, stirring with a wooden spoon. Be sure all the sugar is dissolved.

7   Ladle the liquid into the 6 soufflé ramekins and sprinkle the nutmeg over the tops. Place the ramekins in the prepared pan in the oven and bake for approximately 1 hour or until a thin table knife comes out clean when thrust into the center of the custard.

8   While the custards are baking, sprinkle the remaining 3 tablespoons of the coconut flakes on a baking pan large enough to hold the coconut in 1 layer. Put into the oven on the lowest shelf and let brown, but watch it carefully so it doesn't burn. Turn the coconut over with a cake turner when it begins to color. When done, remove from the oven and transfer to a small bowl to cool.

9 When the custards are done, remove from the oven and pan. Set aside to cool on a cake rack.

10 To serve, choose dessert plates that have a rim and a slightly sunken center. Unmold the custards by running a thin knife blade around the side of each ramekin, placing the plate upside down over the centered ramekin, and turning the dish and plate over together. You may have to lift one side of the soufflé ramekin and touch the side of the custard with the point of the knife to make it fall onto the plate. When all the custards are on the plates, spoon 3 tablespoons of the lime-flavored caramel syrup over each custard— the syrup will form a lake around the custards. Sprinkle the tops of the custards with the toasted coconut and serve.

N o t e s

Custards and syrup can be made the day before serving and kept in the refrigerator covered with plastic wrap. Take them out an hour before serving so they come to room temperature.

Light-brown *granulated* sugar can be substituted for white sugar in the custards.

Puerto Rico

COCONUT
TEMBLEQUE

◆

½ cup cornstarch
3 tablespoons sugar
Pinch of salt
2 cups half-and-half
1 15-ounce can cream of
  coconut
1 teaspoon vanilla extract
1 teaspoon coconut extract
3 heaping tablespoons
  sweetened, flaked or
  shredded coconut

SERVES 6

An exquisite, pure white, molded custard pudding fragrant with coconut, and set off by a tangy, fruity guava sauce, it is the classic pudding of Puerto Rico.

Driving eastward along the north coast of the island, well beyond Luquillo Beach, we stopped at a sheltered cove with a small curving beach. Lunch was at a rambling outdoor dining room near the beach, casually roofed over with palm fronds, the sides open to the beach and garden. We relaxed with piña coladas, shrimps, and Coconut *Tembleque* for dessert. After describing this dessert later to our hostess at the guest house where we were staying, she gave us her recipe, which we have used ever since.

1 Mix the cornstarch, sugar, and salt together in a bowl and set aside.
2 Measure the half-and-half and cream of coconut into a saucepan and stir together. Add ½ cup of this mixture to the cornstarch mixture and smooth out all the lumps. Scrape this slurry into the coconut cream in the saucepan, stirring all the while.
3 Put the saucepan over medium heat, stirring the custard with a fla bottomed wooden spoon or wooden spatula until the mixture begins to thicken. Keep stirring until the custard boils, being careful to scrape the bottom and sides of the pan, lowering the heat a little if necessary. Once the custard has boiled, cook for 3 minutes.
4 Remove the saucepan from the heat, add the vanilla and coconut extracts, and beat them in with a wire whisk for a smooth custard. Fold in the coconut flakes. Rinse a 3- to 4-cup mold with cold water and pour in the custard. Cool the custard to room temperature, then cover and place in the refrigerator for several hours.
5 To serve, unmold the custard onto a round serving dish. Cut into wedges with a knife that has been dipped in cold water. Serve with Guava Sauce (below).

1 In a small saucepan over medium heat, melt the guava paste or jelly, adding ¼ cup of water. Stir until all the paste or jelly has melted.

2 Remove the saucepan from the heat and add the lime juice, ½ teaspoon at a time, to add a tang to the guava sauce but not to overpower it. The same applies to the rum.

3 Pour the sauce into a decorative pitcher or bowl to cool to room temperature.

Variation

Mango or pineapple jam can be substituted. In the case of jam, the heated jam will have to be pressed through a stainless steel sieve to achieve a smooth sauce.

GUAVA SAUCE

◆

1 11-ounce can guava
   paste *or* 12-ounce jar
   guava jelly
Lime juice to taste
Dark rum to taste (op-
   tional)

**MAKES 1 ½ TO 2
CUPS**

Puerto Rico

ORANGE-COCONUT BAKED CUSTARD

◆

THE CARAMEL SAUCE

¾ cup sugar
2 tablespoons cold water
6 tablespoons boiling water

THE CUSTARD

3 tablespoons frozen concentrated orange juice
2 eggs
4 tablespoons sugar
⅛ teaspoon salt
1 teaspoon orange extract
1½ cups plus 1 tablespoon half-and-half
3 tablespoons flaked coconut in heavy syrup
Freshly grated nutmeg

SERVES 4

Up in the hills of Puerto Rico, we have picked intensely flavored oranges from abandoned trees. Because many people have similar trees in their backyards, it is no wonder that this unforgettable orange custard is a favorite dessert.

On that trip we stayed for several days at a sprawling guest house, nestled into the hillside of the coffee plantation high in the *cordillera* of western Puerto Rico. The meals, served at a long, polished-wood, colonial Spanish table lined with carved high-backed chairs, were as memorable as the dining room at ground level, open at each end to the night's breezes. For dessert one night, we were served an elegantly presented flan, lavish with orange and coconut flavors, surrounded by a pool of caramel syrup—a delicate ending to the taste-laden meal that had preceded it.

The flan should be baked in individual ramekins, as this is too soft a custard to bake in a large dish, turn out, and serve cut into sections.

1 For the Caramel Sauce, combine the sugar and cold water in a small saucepan, mixing them together with a table fork. Set the pan over moderate heat and let the contents boil and bubble undisturbed. When the sugar begins to color, tip the pan back and forth to swirl and mix the syrup. Use a fork to stir the syrup. Heat until the syrup is a golden brown.

2 Remove the pan from the heat and drizzle some of the syrup down the sides of each custard cup in an art nouveau fretwork. Set the cups aside.

3 There will be about half the syrup left. Add the boiling water to the syrup and put the pan over heat to blend the syrup and water, stirring all the time with a tablespoon. When blended, take the pan off the heat and set aside until the syrup cools. If when cool the syrup is the right pouring consistency, fill a small serving pitcher. If too thin or too thick, boil down to thicken or add enough boiling water to thin.

4 For the custard, defrost the orange juice in a small bowl.

5 Turn on the oven to 300 degrees. On the middle shelf of the oven, set a shallow pan large enough to hold 4 custard cups, each with a ⅔-cup capacity. Fill the pan with hot water to a depth of ¾ inch.

6 Beat the eggs in a mixing bowl and add the sugar, salt, and orange extract, beating with a wire whisk after each addition. Stir in the defrosted orange juice.

7 Scald the half-and-half and pour it over the egg mixture, beating all the while. Stir in the coconut in its syrup.

8 Ladle the liquid into the prepared custard cups, stirring the liquid in the bowl to prevent the coconut flakes from sinking to the bottom. Sprinkle the nutmeg evenly over the top surface of the liquid, and place the filled cups in the pan of hot water in the oven. Bake until a thin table knife inserted into the center of the custard comes out clean—approximately 1¼ hours.

9 Remove the cups from the oven and cool on a cake rack. To serve, run a thin knife blade between the custard and the inside of the cup. Place a small dessert bowl over the top of the custard cup and upend both together. The custard will fall into the bowl. Scrape out any remaining caramel. Serve with the pitcher of caramel syrup.

Tortola

ORANGE CREAM CUSTARD

◆

From island to island in the Caribbean, there are almost as many recipes for orange custards as there are islands, as oranges and eggs have been standard, island ingredients for generations. We have chosen two quite different concoctions from two of the islands—one a baked custard and, this one, a boiled custard. Orange Cream Custard is all its name implies—an unusual smooth texture with a flavor that is a triumph of intense orange.

4 oranges (2¾ inches in diameter)
4 eggs, at room temperature
½ cup plus 2 tablespoons sugar
Pinch of salt
2 teaspoons cornstarch
2 teaspoons cold water
4 tablespoons butter, cut into ½-inch dice

SERVES 4

1 Grate the zest from 2 of the oranges and set aside. Squeeze the juice from all of the oranges and set aside.

2 Separate the eggs, putting the egg yolks into the top of a double boiler and the egg whites into a mixing bowl. Set the egg whites aside. Lightly beat the egg yolks with a wire whisk, then beat in ½ cup of the sugar and the salt. When light and fluffy, slowly add the reserved orange juice, beating all the while.

3 Mix the cornstarch with the water and stir into the egg-juice mixture. Blend in the reserved orange zest.

4 Place the top of the double boiler over simmering water and stir the custard until it thickens, approximately 5 minutes. Add the butter, piece by piece—waiting as each one melts before adding the next—stirring all the while.

5 Remove the custard from the heat. Beat the egg whites to soft peaks, then add the remaining sugar. Beat the egg whites until stiff. Fold a quarter of the beaten whites into the custard until well blended, then fold in the rest of the whites until no white shows.

6 Return the pan to the simmering water and stir the custard with a large metal spoon, lightly turning the custard over and over. Cook for 5 minutes. Remove the pan from the heat, and spoon the custard into glass sherbet glasses. Cool a little, then place in the fridge to chill until serving time.

Variation

Spoon the custard into 6 small, shallow ramekins, inside measurements 2⅝ x 1⅛ inches. When chilled and ready to serve, turn the custards out onto flat dessert dishes. Surround the custards with orange sections marinated in curaçao or Grand Marnier, with a dollop of whipped cream on top of each custard. This will serve 6 persons.

Note

This recipe can be multiplied for more servings.

Trinidad

PAPAYA, COCONUT, AND SWEET YAM PUDDING

◆

We flew over to Trinidad from Tobago where we were living for two winter months, to visit the Mas' (Masquerade) Camps before Carnival. We wanted to see and photograph the costumes in the making, to learn just how each Camp organized its theme and went about buying the fabrics, cutting and sewing the costumes, and selling them for its presentation on Carnival day. We stayed at a guest house at Maraval, eating our dinners there or in the neighborhood; lunch was usually a quick roti or meat turnover in Port of Spain.

Dinner was restful in the quiet haven of private homes and one or two small hotels, away from the narrow, crowded, noisy streets of the city. Our hostess treated us to a soothing, tasty pudding at the end of one dinner, shared with her family and one other couple. Our interested questioning produced the recipe, and once back at our kitchen on Tobago, we tried it out while the memory of the taste was still fresh. Needless to say, on Tobago and Trinidad—and on other islands—half-and-half translates into canned evaporated milk thinned with water, and vanilla often becomes the ubiquitous essence.

The Caribbean sweet yam has yellow flesh, rather than the white flesh of the starchy yam. You can substitute the northern sweet potato.

1　Preheat the oven to 300 degrees and butter a 6-inch soufflé dish.

2　Heat the half-and-half and butter in a stainless steel saucepan and add the grated yam. Cook until the yam is heated through. Add the mashed papaya and stir the mixture. Remove from the heat and set aside.

3　Beat the egg in a small bowl. Beat in the sugar, salt, nutmeg, cinnamon, vanilla extract, lemon zest, and coconut extract. Stir into the half-and-half mixture, then add the grated coconut in its syrup.

4　Pour the pudding mixture into the buttered soufflé dish and put the dish into the preheated oven on the center shelf. Bake for 1¾ to 2 hours or until a knife blade inserted in the center of the pudding comes out clean.

5　Remove the dish from the oven to a baking rack to cool. Serve the pudding warm; it can be reheated if it has cooled too much before serving time. Serve with or without whipped cream or Whipped Evaporated Milk (page 285).

Note

Make the essence with ½ teaspoon vanilla extract, ¼ teaspoon almond extract, and ¼ teaspoon anise extract, if bottled essence is unavailable.

¾ cup half-and-half

3 tablespoons butter

¾ cup grated, raw sweet yam (slightly under ½ pound)

¼ cup mashed ripe papaya (approximately ¼ of a 6-inch papaya)

1 egg

4 to 5 tablespoons light-brown *granulated* sugar

¼ teaspoon salt

¼ teaspoon ground nutmeg

¼ teaspoon ground cinnamon

1 teaspoon vanilla extract or essence (see Note)

1 teaspoon grated lemon zest

½ teaspoon coconut extract

4 tablespoons grated coconut in heavy syrup

Whipped cream (optional)

SERVES 4

Guadeloupe

SOURSOP MOUSSE

◆

1 tablespoon unflavored gelatin
¼ cup cold water
1 12-ounce can soursop (*guanabana* or custard apple nectar)
3 tablespoons superfine sugar
2 egg whites
1 recipe Guava Sauce (page 329)

SERVES 6

We spent our first morning in Gosier, on Guadeloupe, exploring the small village, going to the post office and bank, looking at the shops, and scouting the shelves of a small grocery store. Our studio room overlooking the wide bay toward Basse Terre had a kitchenette. A quick swim and suddenly it was noontime. Wanting to see more of the island, we drove out of town. On the outskirts we passed *Chez Violette*, set back from the road with wide-open large windows and a welcoming porch. We drove in and settled at a window table, and, after a sea urchin appetizer and a blaff of seafood, we ordered Soursop Mousse, a new dessert for us. We knew the delicately flavored soursop from other islands, notably the ice cream from Tobago and the rum drink from Jamaica, but this dessert was an unforgettable blending of flavors and textures, a fitting welcome to Guadeloupe.

We were served half-inch-thick slices of pure white, light-as-snow mousse, surrounded by a clear guava sauce.

The soursop (*guanabana*) is a spectacular fruit covered with a thin, bright-green skin studded with soft, fleshy spines and vaguely heart-shaped averaging eight inches in length. Its flesh is pure white (sometimes slightly cottony), studded with shiny black-brown seeds. The fruit is peeled and the soft flesh is pressed through a sieve to remove the seeds and fibers. The juice is made into cooling drinks, ice creams, or, in this case, a chilled mousse. Although soursops are not easily available in the States, the nectar is an excellent substitute.

1 In a small ramekin, soften the gelatin in the water. In a small saucepan, heat enough water to the boiling point to come halfway up the ramekin. When the gelatin is soft, remove the saucepan from the heat and place the ramekin in the hot water. When the gelatin is clear, remove the ramekin from the hot water and cool the liquid at room temperature.

2 While the gelatin is cooling, pour the soursop nectar into an 8-cup mixing bowl. Stir in the sugar until it is dissolved. Add 3 or 4 tablespoons of the soursop nectar to the cooled gelatin and stir. Pour the gelatin into the bowl of soursop nectar, stirring and thoroughly blending the liquids. Place the bowl in the fridge until the mixture is the same consistency as the unbeaten egg whites, about 45 minutes.

3 Remove the bowl from the fridge and add the egg whites to the soursop mixture. Beat with an electric beater or mechanical hand beater until the mixture fills the bowl and is light and fluffy

4 Rinse a 9-x-3½-x-2¾-inch (6-cup capacity) loaf pan in cold water and ladle the mousse into it. Cover the top with clear plastic wrap and place in the fridge for 3 hours to stiffen, then put in the freezer for 2½ hours or overnight.

5 Remove the mousse from the freezer 20 to 30 minutes before serving. When serving, the mousse should not be frozen all the way through, just the center. Dip the pan briefly into hot water to loosen the sides, and turn out the mousse onto a chilled, oblong platter. Spoon 3 tablespoons of the guava sauce onto each dessert plate. Cut the soursop mousse into ½-inch slices and lay 3 slices in an overlapping fan shape on each plate on top of the guava sauce.

Variation

Any tropical fruit nectars—mango, pineapple, guava—or northern fruit nectars—such as apricot, peach, or pear—can be substituted for soursop nectar.

✦ ✦ ✦ ✦ ✦ ✦ ✦ ✦ ✦

◆ *Thirteen* ◆

BEVERAGES

✦ ✦ ✦ ✦ ✦ ✦ ✦ ✦ ✦

◆ Fruity Drinks of the Islands ◆

A first visit to grocery stores on most of the islands reveals an astonishing number of shelves devoted to canned fruit juices and bottled fruit syrups. We should note that, whereas most recipes for island drinks make a point of listing potent amounts of rum, the truth is, for most down-islanders, fruit juices—fresh, canned, or bottled and without alcoholic additions—are a daily accompaniment to meals.

We should expect that. People there are surrounded by fruit trees of many kinds that offer their juice for the picking, either from the flesh or pressed, and these juices can be combined in endless satisfying ways. They are not only one of the pleasures of tropical life but a main source of vitamins in the diet. Since we started spending more time among the islands in winter, we acquired the habit of stocking canned and bottled juices and syrups in summer and buying exotic fresh fruits whenever they appeared in the shops. And, on the mainland, we also happen to live near a community of Hispanic and island people whose local stores are a source of standard Caribbean fruits and of occasional fascinating rarities.

The repertory of canned fruit juices in the stores is constantly expanding. Guava, passion fruit, *guanabana* (soursop), apricot (tops for mixes with island fruits), and banana nectars are always available. Mango and papaya juices are beginning to appear. Coconut milk and cream are standard. Orange, lime, and lemon juices are canned and bottled. Quantities of raw gingerroot are sold. Island shops carry mauby and ginger beer concentrates, sorrel, orange squash, tamarind paste or liquid concentrate, and other specialties. There is enough here for a much greater variety of drinks than most American families ever encounter.

With the available ingredients anyone can concoct drinks that are to their taste. The piña colada is one of the few truly original Caribbean creations. Islanders are partial to very sweet drinks. We make a very pleasant, tangy mauby drink but in the islands it is usually sweet to insipidity . . . more sugar than fruit flavor. All the more reason to mix your own.

In the islands the diversity of fruits that yield palatable juices, either plain or mixed with a sweetener, is probably greater than anywhere else. One has, therefore, the choice of zestful, thirst-quenching, plain fruit drinks in every conceivable combination or these same drinks laced with rum to make drinks for convivial occasions.

This is not to deny the charm of good Caribbean rum as an ideal liquor for combination with the fruit juices. We'll get to that later in the chapter.

If you love ginger, ginger ale, and Ginger Beer, you may wish to make it fresh and enjoy the sharper bite and more distinctive flavor.

1 Soak the gingerroot for 10 minutes in lukewarm water. Peel the skin with a flexible peeler. Process the gingerroot, sliced thin, for 10 seconds.

2 Place in at least a 2½-quart bowl, jug, or other enamel, ceramic, or glass container.

3 Peel the lime and slice it. Add to the ginger along with the cream of tartar. Bring the water to a boil and pour it into the bowl. Allow to stand for a day, covered, at room temperature.

4 Add the yeast to the liquid and allow to stand for 15 minutes.

5 Strain the liquid into another similar container. Add the sugar. Stir well and let stand at room temperature for 3 to 4 hours, then store in the fridge overnight. The mixture will be ready to drink or to mix with other drinks the following day.

Variation

Ginger Ale   At step 3, double the amount of boiling water. The container will have to be large enough to hold the bigger quantity. Naturally, more sugar to taste will be needed.

GINGER BEER

◆

½ pound fresh gingerroot
1 large lime
1½ teaspoons cream of
    tartar
8 cups water
1 teaspoon dry yeast
Sugar to taste

MAKES 8 CUPS

*Jamaica and
Trinidad*

SORREL DRINK

◆

½ generous cup dried sor-
rel calyxes
2 1-inch pieces candied
ginger
3 whole cloves
2¼ cups water
½ cup plus 2 tablespoons
light-brown *granulated*
sugar

**MAKES 2 TO 2½
CUPS**

I n many of the Caribbean islands, the popular Sorrel Drink is made from the red, fleshy calyx of the *Roselle* shrub which is related to the *Hibiscus* plant. The red sorrel drink has always been served at Christmas time, as the calyxes are ready for picking in November and December, but now, dried sorrel calyxes are available all year round in island and Stateside stores, as well as in health food stores under the name Malva, a well-known European herb tea. The fresh calyxes are cooked with sugar as a sauce similar to our cranberry relish, for tart fillings, and as a jam.

1   Put the dried sorrel, candied ginger cut into ¼-inch dice, and the cloves into a large bowl.
2   Bring the water to a boil and pour over the bowl's contents. Cover the bowl with a plate and let the mixture steep at room temperature for 4 hours.
3   Strain the liquid into another bowl and stir in the sugar until dissolved. (If this seems like too much sugar, add the sugar gradually to taste.)
4   Pour the liquid into a glass jar with a tight-fitting cover and place the jar in the fridge until ready to use.
5   As the sorrel liquid is concentrated, it can be thinned out to taste with water or club soda and ice. Often a slice of lemon or lime is added to each glass. Sorrel drink is served in tall glasses with meals or on a hot afternoon.

Variations
A   Add ginger beer concentrate to taste or half ginger ale and half club soda.
B   Rum can be added for a preluncheon or dinner drink or cocktail cooler.

◆ Mauby ◆

Mauby or mabi is a popular drink in most of the islands. The basis is an extract from the bark of a shrub or small tree, *Colubrina reclinata*, which has a bitter taste. A concentrate—containing some citric acid, sugar cane syrup, mild spices, and coloring matter—is sold in bottles. Matouk's is a well-known brand. We buy it in the States from Hispanic and Creole shops. The concentrate mixes with water in the ratio of one part concentrate to four parts water. In the island bars it is served very sweet and laced with rum. We always stock a bottle and find it very versatile as a mix with various fruit juices and with concentrated ginger beer.

◆ Mixed Fruit Drinks with or without Rum ◆

The following set of fruit drinks are examples of the endless number of combinations that are possible. We have enjoyed all of these and many more. They are not specific to any particular island but are simply typical of what happens when fruits come into season and are combined on the spur of the moment. Lemon, lime, and tamarind are the principal souring agents. Without them many of the mixes become insipid. They are all good with or without rum. All recipes are for a single long drink. Both fresh and canned juices can be used.

Our glasses are tall, with a twelve-fluid-ounce capacity. Most of the quantities are measured in ounces or shot glasses. All the drinks are made with ice cubes and water, club soda, or tonic. The last is a matter of choice for it does not appeal to every taste. Rum is optional and the quantity is left to the discretion of the mixer. The mixtures are merely swirled with a long-handled spoon or swizzle stick. The amounts of ice and water are not given as the custom is simply to fill the glass. If the formula turns out too weak, it is easy to add rum or fruit syrup or juice and stir again.

Follow the procedure for all drinks:

1 Fill the glass with ice cubes.
2 Add the main ingredients to the glass in the order listed.
3 Top off with water, club soda, seltzer, or tonic, and stir.

MAUBY AND LIME OR LEMON

1½ ounces mauby concen-
trate
Juice of ½ lime or lemon
Ice and water or club soda
Rum to taste (optional)

MAUBY AND GINGER BEER

1½ ounces mauby concen-
trate
1 ounce ginger beer con-
centrate
Juice of ½ lemon or lime
Ice and water or club soda
Rum to taste (optional)

MAUBY AND COFFEE

1 ounce mauby concen-
trate
1 teaspoon instant coffee
Juice of ½ lime
1 tablespoon Cane Sugar
Syrup (page 347)
Ice and water or club soda
Rum to taste (optional)

COFFEE AND COCONUT DRINK

1 tablespoon instant coffee
3 ounces coconut cream
Ice and water or club soda
Rum to taste (optional)

MANGO AND PINEAPPLE DRINK 1

3 ounces mango juice
3 ounces pineapple juice
Ice and water or club soda
Rum to taste (optional)

MANGO AND PINEAPPLE DRINK 2

2 ounces mango juice
2 ounces pineapple juice
1 ounce ginger beer concentrate
1 ounce lime or lemon juice
Ice and water or club soda
Rum to taste (optional)

MANGO AND PINEAPPLE DRINK 3

3 ounces mango juice
3 ounces pineapple juice
1 ounce tamarind syrup
Ice and water or club soda
Rum to taste (optional)

GINGER BEER AND RUM

3 ounces ginger beer con-
  centrate
Ice and water or club soda
Rum to taste

GINGER BEER AND BANANA NECTAR

2 ounces ginger beer con-
  centrate
3 ounces banana nectar
Ice and water or club soda
Rum to taste (optional)
Garnish of grated nutmeg
  (optional)

Variation

Add 1 ounce lime or lemon juice.

GUAVA JUICE AND GINGER BEER

3 ounces guava juice (or
nectar)
2 ounces ginger beer con-
  centrate
2 tablespoons lime juice
Ice and water or club soda
Rum to taste (optional)

GUANABANA AND PINEAPPLE JUICE

3 ounces *guanabana* (soursop) juice
2 ounces pineapple juice
1 tablespoon lemon juice
Ice and water or club soda
Rum to taste (optional)

TAMARIND AND ORANGE JUICE

2 ounces tamarind syrup
3 ounces orange juice
1 ounce Cane Sugar Syrup (page 347)
Ice and water or club soda
Rum to taste

TAMARIND AND LEMON OR LIME

2 ounces tamarind syrup
Juice of ½ lemon or lime
1½ ounces Cane Sugar Syrup (page 347)
Ice and water or club soda
Rum to taste (optional)

BANANA AND APRICOT NECTAR

Enough for 4 highball
glasses
1 can banana nectar
1 can apricot nectar
Juice of 1 lime
Ice and water or club soda
Rum to taste (optional)

PASSION FRUIT AND MANGO JUICE

3 ounces passion fruit
juice
3 ounces mango juice
2 tablespoons Cane Sugar
Syrup (page 347)
Ice and water or club soda
Rum to taste (optional)

PASSION FRUIT AND BANANA NECTAR

3 ounces passion fruit
 juice
2 ounces banana nectar
1 teaspoon lemon juice
1 teaspoon Cane Sugar
 Syrup (page 347)
Ice and water or club soda
Rum to taste (optional)

TAMARIND AND RUM

3 ounces tamarind syrup
or 1 teaspoon tamarind
concentrate dissolved in
sugar and a little water
Ice and water or club soda
Rum to taste

TAMARIND AND GINGER CONCENTRATE

2 ounces tamarind syrup
3 ounces ginger beer concentrate
Ice and water or club soda
Rum to taste (optional)

◆ Rum ◆

Rum is the drink of the Caribbean people. As sugar cane—the source of molasses from which the liquor is distilled—is grown on all the larger islands, there are numerous large and small distilleries. The most famous of these have been in Cuba, Puerto Rico, Jamaica, Barbados, and Martinique.

Bottled directly from the still, rum is colorless and may run as high as 200 proof! Some local distilleries still make "white rum" for down-island drinks but its sale is mainly to tourists. Light colored rums such as those of Jamaica and Martinique, which are carefully refined, run 80 proof and have ample kick for enjoyable drinking. The trouble is that the islands are awash in cheap, badly distilled rums. But a superior distilled product, such as Jamaican Appleton, Mount Gay of Barbados, or the Martinique rums, is smooth, clean tasting, and superb for mixed drinks.

The reader will note that we stick exclusively to rum. The choice of hard liquor is a matter of fads and they do not last long. But even on the islands Scotch whisky, which was formerly the liquor used for the island "punches," has virtually disappeared in favor of local rum, and the amount of liquor in the drinks has been cut. The change only restored the normal situation because the staple liquor of the islands is rum all the way. They serve wines in the tourist restaurants, but even on the French islands they are usually almost undrinkable. So it's rum or nothing until something better comes along.

Please note that in our recipes, one shot glass is equal to one liquid ounce and one fruit juice glass is equal to three-quarters cup liquid. We use teaspoons and tablespoons for measures as usual.

◆ Guavaberry Rum ◆

Although down-islanders make spirits with various fruits, the only indigenous one we know of that is sold commercially other than rum is guavaberry liqueur or rum. Sint Maarten-St. Martin lays claim to be the "guavaberry capital of the world." There is some production in the Virgin Islands, but the quantities are never large.

Finding the tree *(Myrciaria floribunda)*, especially in fruit, it not a simple matter unless a down-islander leads you to it. They are not cultivated but are numerous on some of the islands and are not molested. It is in fact a substantial tree up to fifty feet high with long narrow leaves. The little berries are clustered at the base of the leaves. They are tart and flavorsome, making also an excellent jam. The rum is a pleasant memento to bring back from the islands. The following are a few of the more palatable recommended blends.

Cream of coconut, pineapple juice, and guavaberry. Pour over crushed ice and shake.

This might be called a Creole Kir. Add half a shot glass of guavaberry liqueur to a glass of dry white wine.

Called the Philipsburg Screwdriver. Guavaberry and orange juice with or without a shot glass of rum, as a short or long (12-ounce glass) drink.

Blend coconut cream with banana nectar and pineapple juice. Add a shot of guavaberry. Blend with chopped ice. Additional rum optional.

SHRUB

◆

A long-time favorite island liqueur. The recipe makes a little less than a quart, but it comes out just about to that if you use a liter of rum.

1 quart (or liter) light rum
1 cup grated orange zest
1 vanilla bean
1 2-inch piece cinnamon
  bark
Sugar or Cane Sugar Syrup
  (page 347) to taste

1 Into a wide-mouth container or bowl, pour the rum, orange zest, vanilla bean, and cinnamon.

2 Expose to the sun for 3 days.

3 Decant the liquor and filter through paper into another vessel.

4 Add the sugar. Fill a bottle adding a tight-fitting cork or stopper. Drink at any time.

◆ Rum Drinks ◆

In making rum drinks, down-islanders employ the method traditional in our own country, namely combining plain cane sugar syrup with fresh fruit juices or making a syrup that combines the fruit juices and the cane syrup. Liquor can be added; in the islands it is rum. One serves the drinks at room temperature or very cold.

This sugar syrup is used as an additive to offset bitter or acid juices.

1 Mix the sugar and water and bring just to a boil.
2 Simmer for 5 minutes. Cool and bottle.

CANE SUGAR SYRUP

◆

1 pound granulated sugar
1½ cups water

**MAKES
APPROXIMATELY 3
CUPS**

Peeled and seeded fruits, such as limes, star fruit, mangos, papayas, soursops, pineapple, bananas, sorrel (roselle) calyxes, cashew fruit, various local barks and berries, oranges, and lemons are frequently cooked up or steeped with their zests but seeds are removed.

1 Cook the fruit in a minimum of water with vanilla extract or vanilla bean, bark cinnamon, and grated nutmeg.
2 When thoroughly cooked, force the fruit through a sieve (using pressure) and filter the juice.

FRUIT SYRUP

◆

FRUIT PUNCHES WITH RUM

◆

We were astonished on our first visit to the islands to be served one of these "punches" in a fruit-juice glass (three-quarters cup of liquid when full) instead of either the American punch glass (plump and with a handle for such drinks as New Year's punch) or a taller glass, as for Planter's Punch and other exotic drinks bearing fancy names and frequently embellished with fancy colors served to tourists.

Fruit punch can be a very potent drink. The recipe is of the simplest and is the same for all except the Planter's *(Planteur)*.

Place a teaspoon of Fruit Syrup (page 347) in a fruit-juice glass (or equivalent), add cold light rum, perhaps also a little crushed ice, and stir.

This formula can be more or less an excuse for not drinking rum straight. Incidentally, a feature of island life is the delight in touting the virtues of the worst (least-refined) rums. It is the badge of the true, as opposed to the imitation, down-islander.

The drink may be served at room temperature or cold or diluted with ice or ice and water in taller glasses. These drinks are very versatile, and the juices make these drinks very tasty if properly mixed.

RUM SOUR

◆

1 shot glass rum
2 tablespoons lime juice
1 teaspoon Cane Sugar
  Syrup (page 347)
1 tablespoon orange juice
  (optional)
Crushed ice

SERVES 1

Shake, strain, and serve.

1 Combine and shake well.

2 Serve in a fruit-juice glass. Or, serve in a 12-ounce highball glass with more ice and water. Garnish with a slice of lime.

PLANTER'S PUNCH 1

◆

3 ounces rum
2 tablespoons lime juice
2 tablespoons Cane Sugar Syrup (page 347) *or* 1½ tablespoons sugar
3 tablespoons orange juice
A few drops Angostura bitters (optional)
Crushed ice

SERVES 1

In a tall glass mix together all the ingredients. Add ice cubes and water and stir with a long-handled spoon. Serve garnished with an orange slice, a wedge of pineapple, and 3 maraschino cherries.

PLANTER'S PUNCH 2

◆

2 ounces orange juice
2 ounces pineapple juice
2 ounces grapefruit juice
Light rum to taste
Cane Sugar Syrup to taste (page 347)
A few drops Angostura bitters

SERVES 1

RUM PUNCH

◆

1 part lime juice
2 parts Cane Sugar Syrup
  (page 347)
3 parts rum
4 parts water
Crushed ice
Angostura bitters (op-
  tional)
Grated nutmeg (optional)

SERVES 1

This recipe lists the proportions of ingredients. Use a shot glass to mea-sure.

Combine and shake all the ingredients except the nutmeg. Pour into a tall glass and sprinkle the surface with the nutmeg.

Puerto Rico

PIÑA COLADA

◆

8 shot glasses pineapple
  juice
4 shot glasses coconut
  cream
4 shot glasses light rum
2 tablespoons Cane Sugar
  Syrup (page 347) *or* 1½
  teaspoons sugar
Ice cubes

SERVES 2

1 Blend all except the ice at high speed to produce a smooth mix.
2 Pour into old-fashioned glasses or small highballs with ice cubes. Gar-nish with a wedge of pineapple.

Note
This drink is equally good and refreshing without the rum, which is replaced with 4 extra ounces of pineapple juice.

These famous cocktails, named after a Cuban town, are all made with rum. The basic Daiquiri of lime juice and rum spread through the islands and around the world. Now there exist various versions to suit various tastes. All are made in the same way; only the flavorants change.

Depending on whether ice cubes are shaken or crushed, and just how much rum is actually used, the yield of each of the recipes is one to three cocktail glasses.

DAIQUIRI COCKTAILS

◆

MAKES 1 TO 3 COCKTAILS

Place in a cocktail shaker, shake well, and decant.

DAIQUIRI 1

1 tablespoon lime juice
2 tablespoons rum
Ice cubes

DAIQUIRI 2

1 fruit-juice glass old rum
1 teaspoon pineapple juice
1 teaspoon guava juice
1 teaspoon grapefruit juice
1 teaspoon lime juice
1 teaspoon lemon juice
Ice cubes

DAIQUIRI 3

1 fruit-juice glass light
rum
1 tablespoon lime juice
1 teaspoon almond syrup
or Amaretto liqueur
Ice cubes

DAIQUIRI 4

2 tablespoons old rum
1 tablespoon lime juice
1 tablespoon pineapple juice
1 tablespoon grapefruit juice
1 tablespoon honey
Ice cubes

DAIQUIRI 5

1 fruit-juice glass old rum
1 tablespoon lemon juice
1 teaspoon grenadine
Ice cubes
Grated nutmeg and pinch
  of black pepper, as garnish

INDEX